"Can we stand firm as trustworthy witness̲ ̲ ̲ oring the vast diversity of cultures and religions that shape people? Benno van den Toren and Kang-San Tan emphatically respond with a yes, if we first explore how culture has shaped our core theological beliefs and assumptions about what it means to engage in Christian apologetics. Drawing on their rich epistemological, intercultural, and interreligious knowledge and experience, Van den Toren and Tan guide us to greater awareness of God, self, and others that, true to the title, equips us with humble confidence to participate persuasively in an apologetic dialogue with people from any and every background."

Mark R. Teasdale, E. Stanley Jones Professor of Evangelism at Garrett-Evangelical Theological Seminary

"In this refreshingly original approach to an issue of burning relevance to our world today, the authors present a convincing alternative to existing models of engagement that takes seriously the religious experiences and traditions of people of other faiths even while holding firmly to the essential truth claims of the Christian faith. Ambitious and courageous in its breadth of treatment, *Humble Confidence* is a worthwhile read for any serious Christ-follower—not just the specialist!"

Ivan Satyavrata, pastor emeritus of The Assembly of God Church in Kolkata, India

"This is a fine and sensitive study of the dynamics of engaging in faithful Christian witness to different religious traditions—and the complex tasks and demands in each new situation. It is written with deep learning and wide experience. It is an eloquent and much-needed apology for the importance of humble apologetics."

Gavin D'Costa, emeritus professor of Catholic theology, University of Bristol, and visiting professor in interreligious dialogue at the Pontifical University of St. Thomas in Rome

"Can apologetics play a positive role in Christian witness today in our cosmopolitan, multireligious, and multicultural societies? In this thoughtful and nuanced discussion, Benno van den Toren and Kang-San Tan persuasively argue that, properly understood, interfaith apologetics actually is indispensable in Christian witness in highly diverse contexts. They provide a relevant and wise guide for all concerned with effective ministry in our globalizing and fragmenting world."

Harold Netland, professor of philosophy of religion and intercultural studies at Trinity Evangelical Divinity School

"Remarkable, deep, stimulating, convincing, and compelling reading. This timely, transformative book helps the reader to discover the richness, the effectiveness, and the need for Christian apologetics as holistic, conversational, crosscultural, and contextual dialogue. It informs, educates, and guides humble witnesses of Jesus Christ to be confident as they effectively embrace and practice a Christian apologetics that is healthy and builds trust with people and communities living and rooted in diverse traditions, multireligious contexts, and a multicultural and secularized world."

Daniel Bourdanné, former general secretary of the International Fellowship of Evangelical Students

"A book like this is long overdue. As a way of giving account of the hope within us, apologetics ought to be closely related to missiology, but it is rarely included. Here it is made relevant again. Both apologetics and mission are changed in the dialogue: apologetics becomes contextual and mission becomes apologetic. The arguments are lucid and substantial. The illuminating case studies show what apologetics contributes to Christian witness in various religious contexts."

Paul E. Pierson, professor of world Christianity at Fuller Theological Seminary

"*Humble Confidence* occupies a perfect middle space, balancing patient listening with honest speaking, intellectual acumen with relational health, modern insights with postmodern themes, and as the title says, personal humility with reasoned confidence. A dialogical and embodied model for apologetics is all the more relevant today, since global Christianity encounters not only Western secularism but multiple non-Western religions and cultures as well. Tan and Van den Toren hit just the right notes for faithful apologetic dialogue in our time."

David Clark, professor of theology at Bethel Seminary

BENNO van den TOREN
& KANG-SAN TAN

HUMBLE
CONFIDENCE

A Model for Interfaith Apologetics

Academic
An imprint of InterVarsity Press
Downers Grove, Illinois

InterVarsity Press
P.O. Box 1400 | Downers Grove, IL 60515-1426
ivpress.com | email@ivpress.com

©2022 by Benno van den Toren and Kang-San Tan

All rights reserved. No part of this book may be reproduced in any form without written permission from InterVarsity Press.

InterVarsity Press® is the publishing division of InterVarsity Christian Fellowship/USA®. For more information, visit intervarsity.org.

Scripture quotations, unless otherwise noted, are from the New Revised Standard Version Bible, copyright © 1989 National Council of the Churches of Christ in the United States of America. Used by permission. All rights reserved worldwide.

While any stories in this book are true, some names and identifying information may have been changed to protect the privacy of individuals.

The publisher cannot verify the accuracy or functionality of website URLs used in this book beyond the date of publication.

Cover design and image composite: David Fassett
Interior design: Daniel van Loon

ISBN 978-0-8308-5294-9 (print) | ISBN 978-0-8308-5295-6 (digital)

Printed in the United States of America ♾

Library of Congress Cataloging-in-Publication Data
A catalog record for this book is available from the Library of Congress.

29   28   27   26   25   24   23   22 | 13   12   11   10   9   8   7   6   5   4   3   2   1

To our children

Chara, Wiger, Derk Anne, and Marten

CONTENTS

ACKNOWLEDGMENTS

A CENTRAL TRAIT OF THE MODEL OF APOLOGETIC WITNESS and dialogue we propose and develop in this book, is that it is a communal enterprise. It is not the work of the brilliant apologist by themselves or the analytic philosopher in their study. Apologetic witness needs to be embodied in communities and traditions. It needs people with a deep interest in the religious people, communities, and traditions among whom they live. It needs to relate to ever-changing contexts and encounters. We are therefore indebted to the Christian communities and friends in varied multireligious contexts who have welcomed us, and for the many fellow pilgrims on this journey who have shared their hospitality and wisdom. We are also grateful to the many representatives of different religious traditions whom we encountered and were willing to share their lives, experiences, and thoughts with us, sometimes in one-off encounters, sometimes in prolonged conversations that continued for months. These encounters were not part of a preconceived academic project, but it is such real-life experiences that motivated and shaped these academic explorations.

We are particularly aware of the communal nature of this project because of the wide-ranging themes and traditions that are covered in this study. We are therefore grateful that we could discuss the material we were developing with different multicultural groups of students in Malaysia, India, and the Netherlands. We have also shared all the chapters in the second part of this book with specialists who know these particular communities much better than we do. They have provided us with relevant sources and stories, but also commented on drafts of these texts. We particularly want to mention Thandi Soko-de Jong, Varughese John, David Singh, Charles Christian, Klaas Bom, Rory MacKenzie, Bernhard Reitsma, Max Baker-Hytch, Andrea Campanale, and John Drane. We also want to mention the expertise of Jon Boyd, our editor at IVP Academic, and the anonymous reviewer whose comments we received through IVP. In all these exchanges, we were encouraged by the convergence of the directions we were traveling, yet in such multidimensional questions as the nature of interfaith witness, we at times of course make different judgments and the final responsibility for the particular course we steer in this book and for the mistakes we make are ours.

We also want to recognize the support we have received at the institutions where we work, for study-leave, for the permission to teach abroad, and for the support of the PThU librarians who were able to track down some rare texts.

We want to give a special thanks to our spouses, Loun Ling and Berdine. They have shared with us the joys and challenges of international moves, travels, and encounters that nurtured this project and helped us to be sensitive to dimensions of the contexts and conversations that we would otherwise have easily missed. We dedicate this book to our children, Chara, Wiger, Derk Anne, and Marten, who now pursue their own journeys of pilgrimage and discipleship in a world where the experience of religious pluralism is more acute, intense, and colorful than when we were their age.

We are above all thankful to our Creator, Redeemer, and Inspirer who sustained us through these challenging years marked by a global pandemic. In this challenging quest, we discovered again and again that "he is not far from each one of us" (Acts 17:26) and how grateful we are that "he has given assurance to all by raising him [Jesus] from the dead" (v. 31).

Introduction

CONTEXTUAL APOLOGETICS
AS HOLISTIC DIALOGUE
AND ACCOUNTABLE WITNESS

THE NEED FOR CONTEXTUAL INTERFAITH APOLOGETICS

We wrote a significant part of this book on the fourteenth floor of a modern office building in a booming cosmopolitan city in Southeast Asia. In the same office building, there is a worship space of an international Pentecostal church reaching out to various groups of immigrants. Below us, in a radius of a few hundred meters, there are Hindu, Buddhist, and Chinese temples, a Lutheran and Methodist church, and a mosque. In the nearby luxury shopping mall, an advertisement invites us to "believe in God, invest in gold," so the worship of the Mammon of modern free-market capitalism is equally well represented.

These couple of streets surrounding us represent a microcosm of the globalizing world in which the community of followers of Christ are today called to give "a reasoned defense (*apologia*) to anyone who asks for an account of the hope that is in us, yet with gentleness and reverence" (1 Pet 3:15, translation by the authors). This is a world in which multiple religions present themselves to everyone willing to listen, a world in which both secularizing dynamics and religious resurgence can go hand in hand, a world in which religious encounters lead, on the one hand, to deep encounters, but on the other hand to conflict and even interreligious violence, and a world that is still desperately in need of the good news of the crucified and risen Christ.

Though much excellent work has already been done, we have written this book because we believe that many of the dominant approaches to apologetics are ill-equipped for the cosmopolitan, multireligious, and multicultural environments in which we find ourselves today. Western Christian apologetics is too often insufficiently contextual, because it focuses on questions Westerners (or a rather specific group of Westerners) might ask, objections they might raise, and points of contact in their specific beliefs and experiences. Christian apologetics are at the same time too often insufficiently Christian, because they are—in ways that we will explore—further indebted to particular Western ways of reasoning rather than focusing on ways of reasoning that are determined by the specific content of the Christian message: the foolish wisdom of the crucified and risen Christ. This book wants to contribute to finding a remedy for the Western captivity of much Christian apologetics. It does so by, on the one hand, binding it closer to Christ and the proper nature of the good news, while on the other hand, giving sustained attention to the great variety of both religious and secular audiences that we encounter today. Contexts are not just different, but differently different. They may not only raise different questions, but they raise different types of questions and do so in different ways. We believe that precisely such sustained attention to what Christian apologetics in interfaith dialogue should look like will also help us to become aware of the Western captivity of apologetic models developed in the context of Western modernity and postmodernity. We will interchangeably refer to such dialogues as *interfaith* or *interreligious*. Interreligious places a greater stress on religions as complex social constellations. Interfaith points to the fact that such human constructs are also responses, however limited, imperfect, or even distorted, to what people perceive of God through their traditions and experiences.

This book is thus intended as a travel guide rather than a manual. A number of writers on Christian apologetics have rightly argued that apologetics is an art rather than a science or a technique. Becoming a truthful and winsome advocate for the gospel is a long process that requires stretches of slow personal growth and leaps into unexpected discoveries. It is an individual and communal journey in deepening our understanding of the radically different perspectives on the world of our neighbors and in growing in confidence in the multifaceted relevance and truth of Christ for ourselves and others. It is a journey toward an increasing sensitivity to the particular needs and barriers of the people we meet, and in finding attractive ways to present Christ in the marketplace of ideas, ideals, and idols. This book is meant to support such journeys of personal discovery and encounter—possibly to jump-start such journeys, but not to replace them.

Apologetics receives bad press for being narrowly intellectualist, insensitive to where people truly are, and for trying to build faith on human reasoning rather than on the power of the gospel. In developing this proposal for a holistic and contextually embedded interreligious apologetic encounter, we will constantly face two opposite, critical attitudes. On the one hand, there is the criticism of Raimon Panikkar and similar thinkers who argue that "we must eliminate any apologetics if we really want to meet a person from another religious tradition."[1] On the other hand, there will be those who defend more evidentialist, rationalist, or other classical Western style approaches to apologetics, who may feel that we give in to cultural relativism. For some readers we will be too open and for others too committed, for some too intellectual and for others too focused on dispositions. We hope that readers who come with such critical questions—from different angles—will bear with us and critically ask whether this proposal may indeed present a constructive and faithful way forward.

Precisely because of the strong intellectualist and foundationalist associations with the term *apologetics*, we prefer compound expressions like apologetic witness, apologetic dialogue, and holistic apologetics. As witness, apologetics points to what God has done in Christ as the only ground for our faith, all the while arguing that this is the only truly reasonable response to this Christ. It is warranted or accountable witness, always ready to give an account of the confidence we have—the testimony we have also received ourselves has warrant and can be justified. As apologetic dialogue, apologetics demands attentive listening and mutual learning, all the while recognizing that true dialogue also requires critical consideration of questions of truth on which we differ. As holistic apologetics, it should address the entire person with their emotions, commitments, and attachments, all the while recognizing that persuasion which only appeals to the emotional level of our existence easily becomes manipulative. We take others and the gospel much more seriously if we ask them to consider not only its attractiveness and relevance, but also its truthfulness. Though apologetics can derail, we believe for reasons that we will further develop in the first chapter, that such holistic and dialogical apologetic witness is an essential aspect of the missionary and evangelistic calling of the Christian community. Without the willingness to given account of the hope to which we witness, evangelism risks becoming manipulative, a form of advertising or propaganda.

Apologetic witness is the task of the entire Christian community. The church in our era does need a new generation of trained apologists, but may God forbid that apologetics becomes the work of those who master the clever arguments and philosophical minutiae of their trade. Such skills and knowledge may be important for specific groups of interlocutors, but we are more in need of ordinary Christians who can meet their neighbors with a confidence in Christ that allows them to be deeply attentive to their beliefs, needs, criticisms, and experiences. We are particularly thinking of

---

[1] Raimon Panikkar, *The Intra-Religious Dialogue* (New York: Paulist Press, 1999), 62.

Christians in many parts of our global village who are confronted with both alternative religious perspectives and the gifts and pressures of moderniza-tion and globalization, whether students or professionals in Jakarta, Banga-lore, Cairo, or Chicago.

Jointly, we as authors have a range of experiences that help shape this book. Kang-San is a Malaysian Chinese Christian with an upbringing that combined Buddhism, Confucianism, and ancestor veneration. He worked extensively in Southeast Asia, but also lived and worked in North America and the United Kingdom. As a mission leader, he is in touch with new forms of Christian wit-ness in a great variety of contexts across the globe. Benno is from the Nether-lands, but taught for eight years in a theological school in French-speaking Africa, where the witness to Muslims and people deeply influenced by primal religions were a continuous aspect of Christian life and ministry. Born in a strong Christian family, he grew up in the Netherlands as one of the most secular countries in Europe. As many European Christians, he therefore effec-tively grew up as one with dual belonging. He also later lived and worked in North America and the UK. Together, we have a reasonably wide range of experience in different religious and secular contexts. Yet, we realize that there are many other relevant contexts and have wondered whether this book should not have been written by a range of authors rather than just by the two of us. We have come to the conclusion, however, that the need for developing an integrated approach to interreligious apologetic witness outweighed the advantages of a multiauthor approach. We have partially compensated for the limitations of our own experiences by seeking comments—from specialists in the field—on all chapters considering specific audiences.

This project originated at the launch of Benno's *Christian Apologetics as Cross-Cultural Dialogue* (2011), at which Kang-San spoke. This earlier book provides more of the theological and epistemological underpinnings for this new study, developing this earlier thesis in the field of interreligious dialogue and witness. It also draws on further studies we have written in the theology of religions that can be found in the bibliography.

Both of us are active as academics and as practitioners. It is our desire that this book will be of help to both groups. At the practical level, we present a new model for Christian witness in interfaith relations that combines humble listening and bold sharing, open, attentive dialogue, and confident witness.

A New Model for Apologetic Dialogue and Witness

This book is also intended as a contribution to an academic debate. It pro-poses a new practical and theoretical model for interreligious apologetic witness and dialogue. We propose this framework on the basis of a broad range of relevant experiences and insights. These include fundamental Christian beliefs concerning the way the triune God relates to humanity and the world, and more philosophical insights in epistemology, in the way cultures shapes us as we shape culture. We have further built on recent developments in mission practice and missiology and engaged with debates concerning the challenges of and calling to interreligious dialogue and witness. We also considered the multifaceted nature of what we often label religion, taking into account differences among the religions, within religions, and in how individuals relate to their religious traditions. We particularly included a specific type of experience: the stories of those who converted to the Christian faith from other religious backgrounds, stories that we believe are generally given insufficient weight in this discussion. Our proposal can be read as a creative synthesis of these insights coming from different disciplines and contexts. It is also a synthesis in a more Hegelian sense: it moves beyond the thesis of foundationalist models of an apologetics (a term to be explained later in §1.2) and the antithesis of postmodern religious relativism to a new understanding of interfaith apologetics. This new understanding is embedded in cultural contexts and communal traditions and yet witnesses with confidence to the truth received and discovered—a truth that it believes to be relevant for all.

In light of this range of experiences, insights, developments, and building on others who have worked in this field, we propose this model of contextual apologetics as an accountable witness and critical dialogue that is embodied, contextual, and holistic. We hope that it contributes to the development of an interreligious apologetic witness in which questions of truth are addressed, yet in the awareness that our knowledge is always culturally embedded, that our message should be embodied in the life of the Christian community and contextually relevant, that it should holistically address the entire person in the context of the community to which that person belongs. Given the wide range of material we use, this framework cannot be neatly deduced from a number of clear premises nor be presented as a simple generalization of a range of data. The proposal will demand an imaginative leap, looking at the same world from a different perspective. It will therefore inevitably depend on the selection of what we consider the most relevant data. It will be shaped by insights on how these data should be interpreted and weighed in relation to each other. This is of course a matter of debate and we present this proposal in the hope that it will lead to further constructive exchange and exploration.

THE FLOW OF THE ARGUMENT

Let us give a short overview of the characteristics of the approach to and style of apologetic witness and dialogue which we recommend in this book. This will also give an indication of what can be expected in the following chapters. From the very beginning, we want to ground our understanding of apologetic witness and dialogue not in abstract and general epistemological considerations, but rather in lived experience of interfaith encounters on the one hand, and in the particular nature of the Christian faith on the other. That is why we begin with a consideration of the place for truth in stories of interreligious conversion, and in the challenges for apologetic witness in our religiously pluralist world. In order to do justice to the particularity of the Christian faith, we develop a theological argument for the need, possibility, and relevance of apologetic witness based on the Christian understanding of God's salvific plans for humanity (chap. 1).

We are aware that Christian apologetic witness is too often reduced to finding and using abstract arguments. We are convinced that truthful and effective witness always needs to be embodied in the life of the Christian community, in the life of the witness, and in the reality of concrete encounters. Questions concerning this embodiment of apologetic witness should not be a practical afterthought, after long theoretical elaborations, but should shape apologetic witness from the beginning (chap. 2).

In the second place, this book takes seriously the profound influence of culture on everything we do and believe, yet without succumbing to cultural relativism. Everything is cultural, but culture is not everything. In chapter three, we will explore how we know as human beings, how our human search for truth is deeply embedded in particular cultural contexts, yet how we are not necessarily imprisoned by them.

Witnessing to Christ in our pluralist, planetary village also requires a reflection on how as Christians we should theologically understand non-Christian religious traditions and other religionists. Should we see them as idolaters who live in enmity with the true God? Or should we embrace them as fellow pilgrims to God's future? Can we expect to find truths, errors, or lies? We will conclude that multiple perspectives are needed to do justice to the complex ways in which such traditions and believers relate to God as Creator, incarnate Redeemer, and Spirit (chap. 4).

The cultural embeddedness of all human understanding has two main consequences for apologetic dialogue. First, it applies to the Christian understanding of the world, which has been opened to us by God's action in the history of Christ. This revelation was both shaped by the culture of Israel, which God prepared to receive the Messiah and subsequently became a culture-shaping force. Chapter five explores how this Christian apologetic witness is precisely the character of witness: a *witness* to God who came to us in Christ and lives among us as Spirit.

Alternative religions and worldviews are of course equally culturally embedded, and Christian apologetic witness therefore is always *dialogical*. Apologetic witness begins with and keeps listening to where others come from, avoiding as much as possible the a priori judgments that cloud our view. We are called to explore and discern how the trinitarian God is already present among our dialogue partners and how we ourselves can also be enriched through this encounter. This will be a proper starting point to also explore how Christ can be commended in such specific situations and how bridges can be built to these particular conversation partners (chap. 6).

In chapter seven, we enter in-depth into the question: What entails an apologetic witness to be holistic? Where chapter two focuses particularly on the Christian community, this chapter focuses on our conversation partners and how we address them as persons in their entirety, taking their desires and their will into account even when exploring questions of truth.

In the course of these chapters, we will also touch on many particular apologetic questions and themes that provide both barriers that need to be overcome and opportunities to show the truth and relevance of Christ. As such, we will touch on issues such as the finality of Christ (§4.4), cultural relativism (§3.2), the trustworthiness of the biblical witness to Christ (§5.4), the reproach that Christian mission is imperialistic (§7.3), and—throughout this volume—religious pluralism. In this way, our methodological explorations will not remain abstract, but remain earthed in real issues that come up in apologetic conversations.

In the second part of this book, we will attend to specific audiences from various religious backgrounds. Every major religious tradition presents itself in many varieties. Within the religious traditions discussed we had to choose our conversation partners, focusing for example on Theravada rather than Mahayana Buddhism. Because of their varying contexts, experiences, and their own journeys and quests, individual believers will each relate to these traditions in unique ways. Hinduism will mean something very different to a woman in a remote village in Nepal than to an IT specialist in Bangalore. Yet, we hope that the examples we give in the second half of this book—namely, particular ways to engage a number of specific audiences—will together present a mosaic that helps readers engage in new ways with their own contexts.

These chapters can also be read as case studies that, as such, provide further support for the new model of contextual apologetic witness developed here.

We sadly had to limit the range of contexts to which we give particular attention. Judaism has been left out because of the special relationship between it and Christianity, and because of the unique theological and practical issues it raises. Sikhism has not been addressed and neither has the complex conglomerate of Chinese religions. Other examples can be given.

This introduction to apologetics differs from similar introductions in that it takes the multiplicity of audiences from different religious traditions with utter seriousness, rather than supposing that we can develop one form of apologetic argumentation that would be universally applicable. In view of the religiously pluralistic context in which we live, we therefore propose a model of contextual apologetics as holistic dialogue and accountable witness. This model is equally promising for Christian witness to Western (and other) secular audiences. Rather than supposing that our conversation partners in the West share universal rational beliefs, values, and experiences on which we can build, it is much more helpful to presuppose that they have cultural outlooks and embrace a pseudoreligious worldview that differs fundamentally from the Christian view of life and the world. Apologetic witness to Western audiences demands the same forms of crosscultural and interreligious dialogue, witness, and persuasion to which Christians in other parts of the world are much more accustomed than Christians in the North Atlantic.

We have structured the book so that it is also useful as a textbook for courses in apologetics at the upper BA- or MA-level. We have tested the material with different groups of international students in western Europe, and South and Southeast Asia. The book is premised on the conviction that apologetic challenges vary widely from one context to another. We are therefore well aware that a study like this can never cater equally well to every context. We hope, however, that this book will help to both grow confidence in the uniqueness and universal relevance of our faith in the triune God and will help develop a sensitivity to the variety of contexts in which this faith is shared.

PART 1

REIMAGINING INTERFAITH APOLOGETICS

1

APOLOGETIC DIALOGUE
IN A MULTICULTURAL WORLD

CHRISTIANS ENGAGE IN DIALOGUE with their religious and nonreligious neighbors for a variety of reasons: simply in order to get to know them better; in order to draw from their wisdom, which they have acquired in the course of their lives; sometimes in order to work out how to live together in a time of tensions between ethnic and religious communities; or in order to discuss projects of joint interest for the common good.[1] One of the principal reasons for engaging in such attentive dialogue is the desire to share our faith in Jesus Christ as Savior and Lord, in whom we find the fullness of life, in the hope they will discover this precious gift for themselves. In this first chapter, we will consider the place of apologetic witness in this dialogue and why this is the case. This will also provide us with the central elements for a definition of apologetics. Such a definition will need to be open enough to allow us to develop forms of apologetic witness and dialogue that do justice to the nature of the message of Christ crucified, a message that is both foolishness and wisdom. These forms are holistic in that they address the entire person, and are sensitive to the great variety of people and con-texts we encounter.

1.1 THE MULTIFACETED NATURE OF CONVERSION AND WITNESS

When we reflect on the role of apologetic witness in sharing the good news of Jesus Christ, we need to take into account that a broad range of factors play a role when people from different religious or ideological backgrounds come to faith—not just in how we imagine that they should come to faith, but in how

---

[1]Parts of this chapter have been published before in Benno van den Toren, "Why Inter-religious Dialogue Needs Apologetics: Intrinsic to Bearing Witness to Christ Is Making Truth Claims," *IFES Word & World*, 33, no. 4 (2017): 19-26, https://ifesworld.org/wp-content/uploads/2019/08/IFES -Word-World-Issue-4-You-will-be-my-witnesses.pdf.

people actually do come to faith.[2] Rahil Patel, for example, born in a Hindu family in East Africa, became a leading figure in the European branch of a worldwide Gujarati Hindu movement. He tells his story about how he left all to become a swami, how he was gradually dissatisfied with the movement, particularly with the lack of room to ask critical questions and with the impossibility to find the spiritual freedom and fulfillment their guru promises. The decisive event that brought him to faith in Christ after having left and being cut off from his former spiritual home was an overwhelming experience of the presence and love of God in Christian worship.[3] In other conversion stories, other factors take the lead. Sometimes, the welcome and care provided by the Christian community played a major role, as in the case of the Ahmadiyya Muslim Steven Masood.[4] The Chinese Christian artist He Qi shared in a personal testimony to us that a major factor contributing to his conversion was him secretly copying a picture of a mother and child by the Italian Renaissance painter Raphael during the Cultural Revolution. Only much later, he discovered that it was a picture of Mary and Jesus. This painting really was an icon to him in the sense that it mediated a peace and divine presence that guided him on his way to faith.

These stories should not merely be read on a human level, but point to the importance of bringing God into the picture, to better understand such conversion stories. Sometimes this is very explicit, as when Muslims testify to appearances of Christ. There are other stories of conversion instigated by the experience of healing and deliverance through the power of the Holy Spirit, as testified in Buddhist communities in Sri Lanka. God can equally show God's presence in the ordinary, as witnessed in the conversion story of the Oxford zoologist Andy Gosler. Andy came to Christ from a secular background and met God through apparently "coincidental" encounters, events, and receiving the right messages at the right time.[5] God often works indirectly, through events, experiences, people, and communities. This is why the recognition of the decisive role of the Holy Spirit in the conversion process does not make consideration of other more human factors redundant.

---

[2]Cf. Hendrik Kraemer, *Why Christianity of All Religions?*, trans. Hubert Hoskins (London: Lutterworth, 1962), 100.
[3]Rahil Patel, *Found by Love: A Hindu Priest Encounters Jesus Christ* (Watford, UK: Instant Apostle, 2016), 194-95.
[4]Steven Masood, *Into the Light: A Young Muslim's Search for Truth* (Carlisle, UK: OM, 1986), 58.
[5]Andrew G. Gosler, "Surprise and the Value of Life," in *Real Scientists, Real Faith*, ed. R. J. Berry (Oxford: Monarch, 2009), 173-89.

Among these different factors, an intellectual search for truth may also play a crucial role. Masood tells the story of how the Qur'an itself motivates him to search for the truth, but how deeply dissatisfied he becomes when his own religious community repeatedly asks him to blindly accept the traditions of the community and discourages an open quest for truth.[6] The study by Jean-Marie Gaudeul—stories of Muslims converting to Christ—points out that this is not a one-off, but that the discovery of the reasonableness and truthfulness of the Christian faith is one of the five recurring motives Gaudeul detects in such stories.[7] Philosopher of religion Anthony Flew was a major atheist voice in his field but reviewed his position well after his retirement, because the intricacy of the DNA molecule since discovered and the fine-tuning of the universe convinced him that belief in God is more rational than atheism.[8]

Conversion processes are, of course, often multilayered. Different factors and processes are intertwined. It may be sudden or gradual, but always concerns a change of worldview, of our will, of our values, and of what we desire most. It may be both triggered and hampered by social relationships. In many stories, the search for truth may not be the prime trigger of conversion but still plays an important role. As the conversion stories of Patel, Masood, Gosler, and others show, experiences of divine encounter, of healing, and of a welcoming community gain importance because of growing doubts about existing convictions and inklings that Christ may carry a deep truth and realism not found elsewhere. Witness to other religious communities should therefore be as holistic and multilayered as conversion is. In the remainder of this chapter, we will explore the place of apologetic witness in this multifaceted missional outreach by the Christian community.

1.2 Challenges to Christian Apologetic Witness in a Globalizing World

For Christians in many parts of the world, such as South Asia, the Middle East, and Africa, religious pluralism has always been a fact of life. Yet, Christians in Europe and North America lived for many centuries in relatively homogenous Christian societies. With the rise of modernity, the main challenges to their faith did not come from other religions, but from Enlightenment rationalism,

---

[6]Masood, *Into the Light*, 60, 152; cf. Mark A. Gabriel, *Jesus and Muhammad: Profound Differences and Surprising Similarities* (Lake Mary, FL: Frontline, 2004).

[7]Jean-Marie Gaudeul, *Called from Islam to Christ: Why Muslims Become Christian* (Crowborough, UK: Monarch, 1999), 57-86.

[8]Antony Flew, *There Is a God: How the World's Most Notorious Atheist Changed His Mind* (New York: HarperOne 2007).

secularism, and later from postmodern relativism. Western Christian apologetics has therefore been ill-equipped to deal with the apologetic challenges presented by other religions and by radically different cultural outlooks on life.

Because of the global dominance of Western theology, this limitation has influenced Christian apologetics more widely. This is one of the reasons that apologetics is often experienced as irrelevant, because it is too Western and intellectualist. Local intellectual challenges were often addressed without reference to apologetics. John Mbiti and other representatives of the first generation of modern African theologians, for example, gave significant attention to the question of whether the God of the Bible was already known in Sub-Saharan Africa before the missionaries arrived.[9] This was in fact an apologetic question, because one of the greatest challenges to Christianity in Africa was precisely that Christianity was the White man's religion and therefore not for Africans.[10] Mbiti was addressing this challenge by showing that this God was already in Africa before the missionaries came, but did so under what we would call "African contextual theology" rather than apologetics.

Religious pluralism presents one of the main apologetic challenges in today's world. This is now also true for the Western world which through the media and international migration is confronted with the depth, existential relevance, and vitality of other religious traditions at a time when the Christian faith is waning and often suspect. At one level, the experience of religious pluralism in general can easily undermine the credibility of any particular religion. At another level, each religious tradition presents its own particular apologetic challenges for Christian witness. The more general challenge of religious pluralism will also present itself differently depending on which cultural and religious traditions shape the cultural environment. In a secular environment, it may lead to the idea that all religions are mere human constructs. In a Hindu context, it may lead to a belief that there exists an unknown divine mystery beyond every particular religion and that each one should simply adhere to the tradition in which they are born.

Religious pluralism is closely related to cultural pluralism, because religious outlooks deeply shape cultures. They are not the same, however, for particular religious traditions can be expressed in different cultural forms. Southeast Asian Islam looks different from the Islam of the Arabic heartlands. In a different manner, the Christian faith can also be embodied or incarnated

---

[9]John S. Mbiti, *Concepts of God in Africa* (London: SPCK, 1975).
[10]Jesse N. K. Mugambi, *Critiques of Christianity in African Literature: With Particular Reference to the East African Context* (Nairobi, KE: East African Educational Publishers, 1992).

in many cultural forms. We will keep returning to the relationship between religion and culture. Just as religious pluralism has led to religious relativism (the idea that no one can make a universal religious claim), cultural pluralism has led to cultural relativism (the idea that what we believe to be true is determined by our cultural location).

The problems of religious and cultural pluralism are not merely intellectual problems, but have existential ramifications. They shape how we experience ourselves in this world. In terms of the "sociology of knowledge," they lead to the "vertigo of relativity"[11]: the moment we start realizing that there are so many options of understanding this world, it becomes much harder to choose at all. This results in an experience like the vertigo of someone spinning at high speed and being unable to find one's balance and orientate oneself in the world. As a reaction to that vertigo, Berger says, people may also look for new certainties by simply avoiding all difficult questions, resulting in different sorts of fundamentalisms.[12] Some people would call everyone with a sturdy religious conviction a fundamentalist, yet the term is better used for people who are unable or unwilling to reflect on critical questions with regard to their religious or ideological positions. In this sense, there are not only religious but also secular fundamentalisms.[13] Both relativism and fundamentalism are inimical to apologetic dialogue: religious and cultural relativism because it does not make sense to argue for the universal validity of a culturally relative standpoint, and fundamentalisms because they are unable or unwilling to engage in an open conversation with alternative points of view.

Cultural pluralism raises particular issues for a number of dominant forms of Christian apologetics. As argued elsewhere, Western apologetics in the modern era has most often followed a particular structure characterized by what we might call "universalist foundationalism."[14] *Foundationalism* is an epistemology (a theory of knowledge) that understands human knowledge after the analogy of a building. A building is solid and trustworthy if it has a solid foundation and if the entire building is constructed well on that foundation. In the same way, human knowledge should start from a good foundation and should use appropriate forms of construction so that everything we

---

[11]Peter L. Berger, *The Heretical Imperative: Contemporary Possibilities of Religious Affirmation* (Garden City, NY: Doubleday, 1980), 9.

[12]Peter Berger, ed., *The Desecularization of the World: Resurgent Religion and World Politics* (Grand Rapids, MI: Eerdmans, 1999), 7.

[13]Vinoth Ramachandra, *Subverting Global Myths* (London: SPCK, 2008), 154-56.

[14]Benno van den Toren, *Christian Apologetics as Cross-Cultural Dialogue* (London: T&T Clark, 2011), 35-92.

believe can be grounded on that foundation. *Universalist* foundationalism is the form of foundationalism that says that only those beliefs can be the foundation of a sound knowledge structure that are universally accessible or acceptable. All ideas that cannot be argued for on the basis of such universally acceptable foundational ideas must be rejected. This universalist foundationalism characterized most of the modern Western philosophy that started in the Enlightenment. In response to the religious wars that devastated Europe in the seventeenth century, intellectuals started looking for a universal starting point for knowledge, culture, and values.[15] Values and beliefs should therefore no longer be based on any religious revelation or other inherited beliefs that could be contested. Such a universalist foundation could, for example, be found in the universal truths of reason, thus leading to rationalism. Or one could look for such a foundation in neutral empirical observations, thus leading to empiricism. Beliefs and values could only ask for universal acclaim if they could be based on such a universally acceptable foundation.

Most modern Western forms of Christian apologetics accepted the basic structure of this universalist foundationalism and argued for the universal value and truth of the Christian faith precisely on the basis that it had a universally valid foundation. This basis could be universal truths of reason,[16] neutral empirical observations of the universe,[17] or a universally recognizable religious experience.[18] Other apologists looked for hybrid forms of apologetics that tried to respect the unique structure of the Christian faith but still intended to formulate universally valid apologetic arguments. One form would be an apologetic based on supposedly neutral and accessible historical facts about Jesus Christ, proving his resurrection and divinity.[19] Others might be looking for universally valid criteria by which competing worldviews can be judged, such as criteria for consistency and empirical fit.[20]

---

[15]Brad S. Gregory, *The Unintended Reformation: How a Religious Revolution Secularized Society* (Cambridge, MA: Belknap Press, 2012), 112-15.

[16]Norman L. Geisler, *Christian Apologetics* (Grand Rapids, MI: Baker Book House, 1976); Stuart C. Hackett, *The Resurrection of Theism: Prolegomena to Christian Apology* (Grand Rapids, MI: Baker Book House, 1982).

[17]William Paley, *Natural Theology: Or, Evidences of the Existence and Attributes of the Deity, Collected from the Appearances of Nature* (Farnborough, UK: Gregg, 1970).

[18]Friedrich Daniel Ernst Schleiermacher, *On Religion: Speeches to Its Cultured Despisers*, ed. and trans. Richard Crouter (Cambridge: Cambridge University Press, 1996 [1799]).

[19]Wolfhart Pannenberg, *Jesus, God and Man*, trans. Lewis L. Wilkins and Duane A. Priebe (Philadelphia, PA: Westminster Press, 1968); John Warwick Montgomery, *Faith Founded on Fact: Essays in Evidential Apologetics* (Nashville, TN: Nelson, 1978).

[20]Harold A. Netland, *Dissonant Voices: Religious Pluralism and the Question of Truth* (Grand Rapids, MI: Eerdmans, 1991); Ronald H. Nash, *Worldviews in Conflict: Choosing Christianity in a World of Ideas* (Grand Rapids, MI: Zondervan, 1992).

These modern forms of apologetics have met with a lot of criticism, both theological and philosophical. Theologians such as Karl Barth argued that Christian faith is uniquely founded on God's self-revelation in Jesus Christ and can never be based on any rational truth or empirical observation that is universally accessible.[21] Furthermore, it is argued that such supposedly neutral apologetic arguments are not sufficiently serious about the fact that the cross of Christ is foolishness for unbelievers, who cannot but reject this because of their sin (1 Cor 1:23). Cultural pluralism raises further issues for this form of Christian apologetics following a universalist, foundationalist pattern. It has, after all, become apparent that far from being universally valued, empirical observations, rational truths, religious experiences, criteria for judging worldviews, or whatever was used as the basis for such supposedly universalist arguments, were themselves shaped by a particular historical-cultural development and not universally shared. Certain forms of Hinduism understand the world as *māyā* and would not consider empirical observations to be a trustworthy basis for coming to know the divine. Mahayana Buddhists believe the highest transcendent reality to be beyond our rational logical distinctions and an apologetic argument based on logical deductions would make little sense. Neither can religious experience be considered a universal starting point, because religious experiences are themselves shaped by the cultural and religious contexts in which they occur.[22] The religious experiences of a Baptist pastor in prayer, a Hindu *sadhu*, a Sufi mystic, and an African traditionalist will not be the same but are shaped by their expectations and spiritual practices.[23]

Next to religious and cultural pluralism, we need to consider a third characteristic of our planetary village that raises significant issues concerning the validity and nature of apologetics. Our current society is deeply worried about the relationship between religion and power. In the West, religious tensions are often seen to be at the origin of violent conflict and therefore religions need to be kept in check by a society dominated by secular values.[24] This link between religion and abuse of power seems to be substantiated by a range of political conflicts that are framed as religious conflicts, such as the

---

[21]Karl Barth, *Church Dogmatics,* ed. Geoffrey W. Bromiley and Thomas F. Torrance, trans. Geoffrey W. Bromiley et al. (Edinburgh: T&T Clark, 1956–1975), 25-36; cf. van den Toren, *Christian Apologetics,* 77-86.

[22]George Lindbeck, *The Nature of Doctrine: Religion and Theology in a Postliberal Age* (Philadelphia, PA: Westminster Press, 1984), 32-41.

[23]Van den Toren, *Christian Apologetics,* 42-43.

[24]Cf. Vinoth Ramachandra, *Faiths in Conflict? Christian Integrity in a Multicultural World* (Leicester, EN: Inter-Varsity Press, 2000), 141-65.

former civil war in Northern Ireland, the continuing conflict in Kashmir, and the tensions between the Burmese majority and ethnic minorities in Myanmar. In Western Europe, the suspicion concerning the relationship between religion and power is also linked to a feeling of guilt about its colonial past, which in the collective memory is closely linked with the expansion of Christianity through the modern mission movement.[25] Christian mission is therefore seen as an expression of Western imperialism. This colonial legacy is not only brought up by Western critics of Christian mission and apologetics but is also used in postcolonial societies such as India as one of the reasons for rejecting the Christian legacy, a colonial heritage that needs to be abandoned.[26] Historically, Christian missions have indeed colluded with colonial powers, and the church will need to repent of this. Yet, the relation between mission and colonialism is varied and in many other instances, missionaries have rather opted for the local populations against the colonial powers.[27] Furthermore, looking back, many churches established by Western missionaries are now able to embrace the gospel as a gift in itself—even if it originally arrived in the colonial era. It can even be used in the struggle for political freedom and the development of one's own cultural identity over against neocolonial powers.[28]

These close associations between religion and power will not only throw suspicion on mission and evangelism in general, but also on apologetics. Postmodern and postcolonial heirs to Michel Foucault will deconstruct all religious positions in terms of the power-plays that they supposedly reflect. Such an analysis understands apologetic witness not as concerned with truth but with power. Arguments that claim to search for and appraise truth are deconstructed as camouflaged bids for power. From a Christian perspective, we would not agree with this analysis. Though arguments and ideas can be and often are weapons in a power struggle (cf. Lk 22:25), they need not be. As we will explore below, the search for truth and goodness is the only real answer to the oppressive abuse of false truth claims. A faith in a crucified

---

[25]John Hick, "The Non-Absoluteness of Christianity," in *The Myth of Christian Uniqueness*, ed. John Hick and Paul Knitter (London: SCM Press, 1988), 17.

[26]Arun Shourie, *Missionaries in India: Continuities, Changes, Dilemmas* (New Delhi: ASA Publications, 1994).

[27]Ramachandra, *Faiths in Conflict?*, 168; Brian Stanley, *The Bible and the Flag: Protestant Missions and British Imperialism in the Nineteenth and Twentieth Centuries* (Leicester, UK: Apollos, 1990); Vishal Mangalwadi, *Missionary Conspiracy: Letters to a Postmodern Hindu* (Mussoorie, India: Nivedit Good Books, 1996).

[28]Benno van den Toren, "The Significance of Postcolonial Thinking for Mission Theology," in *Interkulturelle Theologie. Zeitschrift Für Missionswissenschaft* 45, nos. 2–3 (2019): 210-28.

Lord is particularly well placed to unmask such false claims to power and truth (see further §7.3).

Looking back over this section, we can conclude that the religious and cultural pluralism of our global village on the one hand, and the suspicion and abuse of power in our postcolonial world on the other, raise a number of crucial issues for apologetic witness. They relate to the content of such witness, methodology, style, and even legitimacy of the entire enterprise of apologetic witness. In terms of its *content*, we will need to develop an approach to apologetic witness which takes into account the great variety of audiences, rather than doing it as if only Western critical questions are worth serious attention.

That it has been so hard to develop such a contextually sensitive apologetic witness also raises questions concerning apologetic method. As we have seen, much of Western apologetics presupposes that a valid apologetic argument needs to start from a universally shared foundation. We need to develop new methods of apologetic witness that rather ask how the unique truth and relevance of Christ can be commended to a particular audience. We further need to look for an approach to apologetic witness that is not narrowly rationalist, but that takes the entire person with their history, culture, and communal ties into account. In terms of style, we need to look for forms of apologetic witness that testify to truth in humble and vulnerable manners, rejecting all cultural or political power games.

This leaves the question open concerning the *legitimacy* of the entire apologetic enterprise. Does it make sense to give an account of the Christian hope, or is this simply an expression of a camouflaged imperialistic power play? Can we argue for the universal relevance of the gospel or will all words about God evaporate in confrontation with the ineffable mystery that all religions can only partially grasp? Do we have an anchor beyond our particular cultural location or are all beliefs merely rafts on which we float past each other in the vast ocean of cultural relativity? Can we acclaim our faith universally or is faith in Christ just that: faith that has no other basis than our unique personal encounter with him? In the next two sections, we will give an initial defense of the importance of apologetic witness in Christian mission, both on theological and missiological grounds. The issues of power and of cultural and religious relativism, are, however, complex and will remain with us in a number of subsequent chapters.

1.3 A THEOLOGICAL APOLOGY FOR APOLOGETICS

The biblical exhortation in Peter's first letter—to give "an account for the hope that is in you"—is not an isolated occurrence in Scripture, which we might leave aside in different contexts. Neither is it required for merely pragmatic reasons for a church that wants to survive in a multireligious environment. We want to argue rather that apologetic witness is inherent to the Christian faith and given with the nature of the salvation we have received. In this section, we will first explore theological reasons behind the call to engage in apologetic dialogue, and in the following section we will further develop some of the missiological reasons that are particularly relevant in light of the processes of globalization we have sketched above.

The crucial role of apologetic witness is given with five interrelated characteristics of the Christian faith,[29] the first four of which make it a missionary religion. Christianity is a missionary religion because it believes that the God it serves is the one God, Creator of *the whole earth*. In this respect, it differs from ethnic religions that consider their religious practices only to be relevant for the members of their clan, tribe, or people group that have the same ancestors. Such ethnic religions will rarely engage in mission outside the boundaries of their group. If some religious practices that originated in such religions, such as voodoo, are now claiming a much wider following, it is because they are changing under the influence of global migration. A second characteristic that makes Christianity a missionary religion is that it believes that God can be *known*. Though God is infinitely greater than what our finite minds can ever grasp (1 Tim 6:16), the God of Jesus Christ has revealed Godself in God's history with the people of Israel and in living among us in Christ. We have come to know God's character—not exhaustively, but truly and adequately. This is different from religions which understand the divine mystery to be utterly ineffable, beyond all human words. If that is the case, there is no reason to suppose that the stories, words, and symbols a particular community uses to talk about the divine are any better than those of others.[30] We argue therefore that Christians are committed to a critical realist epistemology with respect to God,[31] a position that we will further develop in chapter three. The third characteristic is the fact that Christians believe that they have received knowledge concerning *salvation*. Christians believe that God has acted once and for all for the salvation of the world in Jesus Christ. This does not necessarily

---

[29]Van den Toren, *Christian Apologetics*, 15-25.

[30]Cf. Andrew Walls, "The Translation Principle in Christian History," in *The Missionary Movement in Christian History: Studies in the Transmission of Faith* (Edinburgh: T&T Clark, 1996), 26.

[31]Van den Toren, *Christian Apologetics*, 16-18; 120-38.

mean that all who have never heard consciously about Christ in their earthly lives will be eternally lost. That is a separate question that falls beyond the scope of this study. Yet, it does mean that redemption from death and fullness of life can only be found in Christ. Christians therefore desire to share this precious gift with others.

A fourth characteristic may be less obvious—or it may rather be so obvious that in certain contexts it is not even worth mentioning. Christian belief concerns *a divine reality beyond and before our human ideas*. In our postmodern world, it is increasingly common to think of religions as human constructs, as ways in which communities organize their lives and structure their worlds in order to make it livable and meaningful. This is sometimes argued for with the help of Ludwig Wittgenstein's notion of a language game, according to which religions are like cultures by which people structure their lives.[32] If all religions are human constructs, they may still be valuable, but living a religion does not compel someone to be evangelistic about it. It can be perfectly okay for different communities to organize their lives differently and to give a particular meaning to how they live, but this would only be valuable for this community, recognizing that other ways of providing structure and giving meaning may be equally worthwhile. It is of course possible that certain religions or aspects of religion are no more than human constructs, in some respects wise and beneficial, in others foolish or even destructive. Those who reject the Christian faith may consider it a social construct. For believers, however, the Christian faith cannot be understood as merely a human construct, for this religion is all about God's self-revelation. This self-revelation demands we critically deconstruct our human-made images of God, which are unmasked as idols. And it is about God saving us from sin and death, precisely because we cannot save ourselves. Because of these theological traits, the Christian faith demands a realist or, more precisely, a critical realist understanding of theological knowledge. In chapters three and five, we will develop a number of crucial building blocks needed for a critical realist epistemology in view of the interfaith apologetics project. This is of course particularly acute in light of the way religious and cultural pluralism makes us aware of the degree to which our understanding of reality in general—and of ultimate reality in particular—is shaped by our cultural and historical location.

These four characteristics make Christianity a missionary religion that desires to share what it has received in Jesus Christ with all nations to the ends

---

[32]James Kellenberger, "The Language-Game View of Religion and Religious Certainty," *Canadian Journal of Philosophy* 2, no. 2 (1972): 255-75.

of the earth. It does not yet necessarily give a place to apologetic witness. Some argue that faith in this message is only and entirely a gift of the Holy Spirit. Faith is therefore considered a unique form of knowledge. In evangelism, we therefore simply proclaim the truth of the gospel, praying that the Holy Spirit will allow the hearers to accept it. This position is called fideism because of the central role of faith (*fides*). Fideism is different from relativism. Fideism rather believes that there is a universal objective truth for all, but this truth can only be known through the supernatural gift of faith and can never be understood by unregenerate people.

This position may sound pious because it gives such a central place to the Holy Spirit. But it is not biblical. The work of the Holy Spirit is central in evangelism and in people coming to faith. Yet, the Holy Spirit also works through ordinary human means, including ordinary means by which we come to know and judge different truth claims.[33] The Bible itself not only exhorts us to give an account of our hope, but constantly gives such accounts itself. Both the prophets of the Old Testament and the evangelists of the New do not simply invite people to believe the otherwise unbelievable, but constantly plead and reason with their hearers and readers. However, they do not use the supposedly universally valid arguments that modern Western apologists might expect. They point to God's decisive actions in the history of Israel and Jesus Christ and address the specific issues of their particular audiences. The prophets explain why not all prophets are to be trusted equally and how to distinguish between false and true prophets (e.g., Jer 23:9-40).[34] The four evangelists all tried to persuade their particular audiences that their testimony was trustworthy (see further §5.3). This biblical practice is reflected in the long history of Christian apologetic witness that in each generation and context addresses new challenges.[35] Furthermore, God holds people accountable for their unbelief in Jesus. They will even be judged for it: "Woe to you, Chorazin! Woe to you, Bethsaida! For if the deeds of power done in you had been done in Tyre and Sidon, they would have repented long ago in sackcloth and ashes. But I will tell you, on the day of judgement it will be more tolerable for Tyre and Sidon than for you" (Mt 11:21). Faith is not a gift presented to some and denied to others. The gospel is presented to all, and people are

---

[33]Stephen C. Evans, *The Historical Christ and the Jesus of Faith: The Incarnational Narrative as History* (Oxford: Oxford University Press, 1996), 285-87.

[34]John Goldingay, *God's Prophet, God's Servant: A Study in Jeremiah and Isaiah 40–55* (Exeter, UK: Paternoster Press, 1984), 43-57.

[35]Cf. Avery Dulles, *A History of Apologetics*, Modern Apologetics Library (San Francisco, CA: Ignatius Press, 2005).

invited to make up their minds—and they will be judged if they will not embrace the truth in their unwillingness to come clean with this God. Yet, this biblical apologetic witness is far from narrowly rationalist. It addresses the entire person with its deepest desires; it calls for conversion of the will; it takes relational bonds seriously and is aware that the call to conversion also involves a spiritual battle in which we need to depend on the power of the Holy Spirit who is able to overcome strongholds.

The Roman Catholic philosopher Paul Griffiths argues that the above arguments do not just hold for the Christian faith, but for all religious and secular worldviews that claim to have an understanding of what true salvation means for all humanity. They have a moral obligation to share this salvation with others and to try to convince others that this salvation is available and where it can be found.[36] That is why interfaith dialogue that involves missionary religions will regularly and naturally lead to apologetic interchange. The "truth" question is inevitably on the table: Is what we believe to have received concerning salvation indeed the greatest conceivable gift, or is it rather something of limited value, or even a figment of the human imagination?[37]

1.4 MISSIOLOGICAL MOTIVATIONS FOR INTERRELIGIOUS APOLOGETIC DIALOGUE

Alongside these theological reasons, there are a number of broader missiological reasons why apologetic witness is a crucial part of the broader missional calling of the church in today's world. The first reason has to do with the ethics of mission. Christian mission is radically different from propaganda and averse to all forms of manipulation and "proselytization" in the negative sense.[38] If missions in the past have sometimes used power and manipulation, thus producing what can be called "rice Christians," the church should repent from it. We should repent from it because God never forces God's love on people but always offers Godself freely, allowing for rejection. Prophets could be rejected, as could the message and the gift of the Son himself who accepted rejection up to the point of going to the cross. God wants us to freely embrace this free gift of love. God might be able to force us to become subjects of a divine king or slaves of a divine master, but God rather wants us to be children

---

[36]Paul J. Griffiths, *An Apology for Apologetics: A Study in the Logic of Interreligious Dialogue* (Maryknoll, NY: Orbis Books, 1991).

[37]Cf. Mark S. Heim, *The Depth of the Riches: A Trinitarian Theology of Religious Ends* (Grand Rapids, MI: Eerdmans, 2001), 24.

[38]Ajith Fernando, *The Christian's Attitude Toward World Religions* (Wheaton, IL: Tyndale House Publishers, 1987), 152-55.

of the heavenly Father, friends and even bride of a heavenly lover. Such gifts can only be accepted freely. The father of the prodigal son was also a parable of God's character in that he did not force his son to stay with him, but allowed him to move to a far land, all the while waiting eagerly for his return. In the same way, the apostles and evangelist used nothing but an appeal to the truth and goodness of the message of Jesus to bring people to conversion, trusting in the power of the Spirit rather than on clever manipulation.

This appeal to a free acceptance of the truth and goodness and the gospel reflects the enduring nature of the relationship God intends with us. It also has a particular importance today. When, as pointed out above (§1.2), religions are so easily associated with the abuse of power, we need to stress that we invite others to believe this message because of its truth and goodness, not because we want to enlarge our community, feel threatened, or whatever interests people might suspect. We should avoid all manipulation. It needs to be clear first that our evangelistic efforts are not about growing the political influence of our community, but about God and salvation. It needs to be clear that conversion is not primarily a change of political or communal belonging (though it may result in such a change) but primarily a change of allegiance to Christ as Lord and Savior. It will also need to be underlined where religious communities use political power and other manipulative means to induce conversions that this doesn't do justice to what religion should be, at least not insofar as we have come to know God in Christ. Others may not be convinced because the power interests at stake are too great. But we have good reasons to keep challenging them and to do so with integrity.

Second, the apologetic aspect of Christian witness is crucial because otherwise we do not have a response to cultural relativism. People embrace cultural and religious relativism for a variety of reasons. It may be that like Pontius Pilate they have a profoundly pragmatist attitude to life and relationships and have pushed questions of truth to the margins of their lives (Jn 18:38).[39] This may be because it allows them to live comfortably in the present without considering any questions about the ultimate meaning of life. It may be because they have political interests to push religious convictions to the private sphere. It may be that they have given up on ever finding the truth about God, salvation, or ultimate meaning because of the "vertigo of relativity" induced by the many options. In all cases, a simple claim that Christianity is different will not provide an answer. We will need to argue what is at stake in

---

[39]Cf. Samuel Wells, *Speaking the Truth: Preaching in a Diverse Culture* (Norwich, UK: Canterbury Press, 2018), 169-74.

what religion or worldview we embrace. Religious beliefs and practices are not just a byproduct of other realities such as economics, politics, or social and psychological wellbeing. We will need to argue that the cultural and religious relativisms need themselves to be relativized as particular cultural and religious positions. And we will need to show that we can take our cultural location with utter seriousness without succumbing to relativism (see chaps. 3 and 5). In late-modern cultures, not explaining or showing a readiness to explain why we believe our convictions to be true and good for others will automatically mean that we have no answer to the paralyzing influence of relativism. This relativism tends to make any exchange of religious ideas a harmless game rather than a deeply serious affair addressing questions of ultimate truth, significance, and salvation.

A third missiological reason to give appropriate attention to apologetic witness in interreligious encounters is that we will otherwise have no message for those who are deeply invested in other religions.[40] Christian missional outreach too often invests most of its energy in the disenfranchised and marginalized of other religious communities. It is obvious that those who are well-rooted in their own religious traditions may be less open to consider alternatives. If, however, Jesus Christ is not only an answer to poverty and injustice—or a search for community or identity—but truly the answer to our deepest need for truth and salvation and to our longing for God, then we also (and particularly) have a message for those who are deeply embedded in their religious communities. We can only reach them if we start to dialogue with openness and integrity about their and our religious beliefs, asking whether beliefs are justified and what promises real salvation.

The issue of addressing those who are at the heart of other religious communities is compounded by the fourth missiological reason for taking apologetic dialogue seriously as an intrinsic aspect of interfaith encounter and witness: other religious traditions have their own apologetic discourse, both in favor of their own beliefs and against the Christian tradition. Many Muslims, for example, have a strong conviction that Islam is a more rational religion than Christianity, with its irrational beliefs in the Trinity, the atonement, and its corrupted scriptures and morals. Consider for example the widely available publications of Ahmed Deedat.[41] Our personal experience in interreligious encounter is that these views have such a strong warrant in these communities

---

[40]Harold Netland, *Encountering Religious Pluralism: The Challenge to Christian Faith and Mission* (Downers Grove, IL: InterVarsity Press, 2001), 247.

[41]David Westerlund, "Ahmad Deedat's Theology of Religion: Apologetics through Polemics," *Journal of Religion in Africa* 33, no. 3 (2003): 263-78.

that many of its members will rarely consider seriously the Christian faith as an alternative, even if they are on a spiritual quest and aware of the Christian message. Many Hindus would not consider conversion because their apologetic for their own religious tradition tells them that everyone should grow spiritually within the religious tradition in which they are born.[42] Some skeptical onlookers would argue that this is precisely why interreligious apologetics does not make sense: Does this not prove that the truth cannot be known? Yet, diversity of opinion, even between well thought-through opinions, does not show that truth can never be ascertained. Consider a parallel case. People come up with contrasting views concerning economic policies, concerning vaccination against Covid-19, and about how to best address the climate crisis. A critical debate about these issues is complex and multilayered, particularly if we also consider ideological biases, personal interests, and historical loyalties that may be at stake. Yet the complexity of the issue does in no way mean that the debate isn't worth having and that either side is equally justified in their beliefs.

1.5 DEFINING APOLOGETICS

In light of the foregoing theological reflections on the need for Christian apologetic witness and dialogue, we can define Christian apologetics as *the reflection on the dialogical witness to the truth and relevance of the Christian faith in order to recommend and present an accountable witness of the Christian faith to those who do not yet believe.* Let me point to a number of elements in this definition. First, this book is not itself an apology, but a study in *apologetics*, which is the study and critical reflection of how to engage in apologetic dialogue and witness. Concrete *apologies* (examples of apologetic witness and dialogue) should always be contextual and addressed to a particular audience. Furthermore, apologetic witness and dialogue most often do not happen in written form but in personal encounters, either one-to-one or while addressing larger audiences. This book is meant to help readers reflect on such ongoing dialogues in which they are probably already involved.

In the above definition, apologetic witness is directed to those outside the Christian community. We call this *external* apologetics as distinguished from *internal* apologetics, which is aimed at answering doubts and strengthening the faith within the Christian community. Though this study focuses on external apologetics, this cannot be neatly separated from internal apologetics, because the best way to grow in the ability to witness to outsiders is to grow

---

[42]Netland, *Encountering Religious Pluralism*, 256-59.

in one's personal confidence in the truth and all-surpassing relevance of Christ. We believe that many aspects of the argument in this study may also help to strengthen the faith of those who are wondering whether and how one can have confidence in Christ in a multireligious world.

In the above definition, apologetic witness intends to recommend and present an accountable witness of the faith. Apologetics is not about winning arguments but about winning people. People may still reject it even after they have heard the best possible exposition. This is evidenced when we look to people who encountered Jesus. Though no one represented the love of God more persuasively than he did, the clarity of the conviction it brought could also lead to rejection, precisely because people understood the power and implications of his message.

2

EMBODIED APOLOGETICS

IT IS OFTEN NOTED THAT JESUS did not leave a book or a doctrine, but a community.[1] His invitation to a new life had no meaning if it was not actually going to be lived. Conversely, this new life cannot be separated from the message of the first Christians and from the truth which they believed. The Christian life radiates hope precisely because of the joyous proclamation that death has been conquered and because of the experience of the first fruits of the new creation. The Christian community can even be said to have been "given . . . new birth into a living hope" (1 Pet 1:3), and it was precisely this "hope that is in you" which Peter supposed was going to lead to questions—people around the community that would invite them to give an "*apologia*" of their faith (1 Pet 3:15). This hope can never be separated from the message of "the resurrection of Jesus Christ from the dead," by which they are reborn into this hope (1 Pet 1:3). The life of the Christian community is of course in many other ways linked to the truth it has received: the knowledge of the love of the caring Father; the discovery of a treasure, which will determine where we will put our hearts; the acknowledgment that love is not an epiphenomenon of a blind evolutionary process or something to be left behind in the process of detachment, but the origin of the universe and goal of our lives.

Christian apologetic witness should be holistic, addressing not just free-floating minds, but dialoguing with real human beings as integrated personalities—body, mind, and soul, all embedded in their histories, relationships, communities, and societies. Apologetics cannot merely design the perfect argument to which we then add some practical considerations as an afterthought. The witness should be embodied witness from the very start, or it is not a fitting witness to the way, the truth, and the life found in Jesus Christ. Apologetic witness should therefore be embedded in the life of the Christian

---

[1]Lesslie Newbigin, *The Gospel in a Pluralist Society* (Grand Rapids, MI: Eerdmans, 1989), 227.

community (§2.1) and it needs to be incarnated in real-life encounters (§2.2). In a later chapter, we will also explore how it will also need to be embodied in the life and character of the witness (§7.3).

2.1 COMMUNITY

Religion as multidimensional. The scholar of religion Ninian Smart distinguished seven dimensions of religion: (1) the ritual dimension of ceremonies, (2) the narrative and mythic dimension that interprets the universe and humankind's place in it, (3) the experiential dimension in feelings such as awe, guilt, dread, joy, ecstasy, and so on, (4) the social and institutional dimension, (5) the ethical and legal dimensions in religion's rules concerning human behavior, (6) the doctrinal and philosophical dimension and (7) the material dimension in the objects and places used through which people relate to the divine.[2] All religious traditions manifest most of these dimensions, but that does not mean that all these dimensions are equally important for all religious traditions or for all of their adherents. There may also be different stresses among different streams within the world religions. In Christianity, certain traditions have a stronger focus on the doctrinal and philosophical dimension, others on the material, institutional, or experiential aspects of the Christian faith.

The place given to Christian apologetic witness within the broader mission of the church will, in part, depend on the place one gives to doctrine and truth claims within Christianity. Some would argue that a focus on doctrine is a particular Protestant or even post-Enlightenment Protestant feature. It is true that Protestantism and particularly modern Protestantism has tended to narrow the Christian faith to doctrinal aspects, though it would be a caricature to suggest that conversion became first and foremost a question of accepting certain doctrines or a change of worldview. Pietist and evangelical Protestantism has also had a strong experiential dimension, with its focus on a personal relationship with God and Pentecostalism on the experience of the power of the Spirit. In recent decades, many Protestants have rediscovered more ritual and sacramental (therefore material) aspects of the Christian faith: we encounter God in the breaking of the bread and the sharing of the wine.[3]

---

[2]Ninian Smart, *The World's Religions: Old Traditions and Modern Transformations* (Cambridge: Cambridge University Press, 1989).

[3]John Colwell, *Promise and Presence: An Exploration of Sacramental Theology* (Waynesboro, GA: Paternoster, 2005); Hans Boersma, *Heavenly Participation: The Weaving of a Sacramental Tapestry* (Grand Rapids, MI: Eerdmans, 2011); Gordon T. Smith, *Evangelical, Sacramental, and Pentecostal: Why the Church Should Be All Three* (Downers Grove, IL: IVP Academic, 2017).

The stress on doctrine in the Christian tradition is, however, not a Protestant phenomenon, but has deep roots in the early church.[4] It is a consequence of some fundamental characteristics of the Christian faith, some of which we already mentioned (§1.3): Christians believe that God can be known because of God's self-revelation; according to the Christian faith, salvation does not originate from a religious experience of an inexpressible reality, but from God's actions in the incarnation, death, and resurrection of Christ. It becomes therefore crucial to find words that do justice to this person and to these events. These words will need to guard their mystery, but will at the same time need to be adequate to convey what truly matters. This is why Christian theologians have been deeply concerned about questions of true doctrine.[5] This is why the Christian mission has a message at its center—even though it can never be reduced to proclaiming a message alone.

In apologetic encounters, we should be aware that this doctrinal aspect is not equally important in all religious traditions and not equally for all religious people. What this means for Christian witness becomes clear in a detailed study by Simon van der Lugt[6] of a prolonged missionary project among Hindustani in the Rotterdam area in the Netherlands. In this context, "Hindustani" refers to Indian Hindu immigrants who came to the Netherlands via Surinam where earlier generations had worked on plantations. The research shows that one of the reasons for significant miscommunication was the difference in understanding religion and religious encounter between the native Dutch and the Hindustani immigrants. The Dutch (Reformed) community mainly tried to share doctrine, inviting a change of worldview, while in the experience of the Hindustani, religion was first and foremost characterized by a number of rituals.

When we realize that the Christian message is embodied in the life of the Christian community, we will be able to witness to communities who may place a greater stress on different dimensions of religion, as listed by Smart. Some will, first of all, relate to other levels, such as the material, the experiential, or the ethical. Allowing for this does not undermine the crucial place of doctrinal convictions, but shows that the entry point may vary and that such doctrinal convictions are relevant because they work out in experience and in

---

[4]Frances M. Young, *The Making of the Creeds* (London: Trinity Press International, 1991).
[5]Benno van den Toren, *La doctrine chrétienne dans un monde multiculturel. Introduction à la tâche théologique* (Carlisle, UK: Langham Global Library, 2014), 10-18.
[6]Simon van der Lugt, "Gereformeerde christenen ontmoeten Surinaams-Hindostaanse hindoes in het Rijnmondgebied: een analyse van de ontmoeting vanuit de verschillen in cultuur en religie" (PhD Thesis, Kamoen, NL: Theological University Kampen, 2016).

life and are also communicated through ritual and matter. Sometimes witness may be first embodied in solidarity or in inviting others to join the Christian feasts as an entry point through which our guests may discover that what religion is may not be the same for all of us.

Plausibility. A community is, in the second place, necessary for a perspective on the world to become plausible. Plausibility is a term from the sociology of knowledge. This branch of sociology looks at how what humans believe is influenced by the social context in which they find themselves. Whether some belief is acceptable is not only—and often not even principally—determined by the strengths of arguments that could be brought in to support it, but also by its plausibility: Is it plausible in the social context in which I find myself?[7] "Only a genius or a madman can believe by himself or herself."[8]

Before we even start considering the truth and relevance of a certain belief, it needs to have a certain plausibility. I can look at a televised declaration of Shiite clerics in Iran, declaring that the Islamic state has been the greatest blessing to the country in modern times, but from my Western Christian or secular perspective, this is entirely implausible. I can read about Hindu ascetics walking on burning coals and explaining how beneficial the practice is, but I may look with a combination of amazement and abhorrence, without being able to relate to it in any meaningful way. For the majority of non-Christians, their experience of the Christian faith is similar. They may here and there note an idea they find attractive, beautiful, or impressive. Yet, from their secular perspective—or popular Hindu, Shiite, or Tibetan Buddhist perspective—the Christian faith as a whole is entirely implausible. From their perspective, it simply cannot be true, it seems to be irrelevant to where they are, or there are simply an overwhelming number of factors weighing against it.

The community plays a crucial role in providing plausibility both for believers and those who do not yet believe. The faith of believers is supported by their belonging to the community that makes it plausible: the community shows how it is relevant, how it makes sense of the world around us and how it can be lived. It also shows that it is not entirely idiosyncratic, but is shared by others who live it and find it sensible and meaningful. The community also helps individuals deal with the particular challenges they encounter: others who have gone before them can share their wisdom and insight. And even if

[7]Cf. Peter L. Berger and Thomas Luckmann, *The Social Construction of Reality: A Treatise in the Sociology of Knowledge* (Garden City, NY: Doubleday, 1966).

[8]Lars Johansson, "New Age—A Synthesis of the Premodern, Modern and Postmodern," in *Faith and Modernity*, ed. Philip Sampson, Vinay Kumar Samuel, and Chris Sugden (Oxford: Regnum Books, 1994), 344.

people do not know how others lived through such challenges, the simple fact of knowing that they did is of help. This also underlines the need for lively and supportive communities for the Christian education of children and young people within this community. The support of a strong Christian community does not make you a Christian and does not determine someone's personal convictions, as we all know. Yet, it plays a crucial role to make the Christian faith a "live option."

The Christian community cannot provide the same plausibility for someone who is an outsider and does not experience this life and this perspective on life and the world firsthand. Yet, such a community does at least provide an "initial plausibility." It is only when one encounters people who live the Christian faith in attractive and realistic ways that it becomes worth considering seriously. Otherwise it simply remains the life of a strange community in another part of the world or from other times, that I encounter in a television documentary or read about in a book, but that does not feel real to me. It lacks plausibility.

In 1978, I (Kang-San) was converted through a church planted by Southern Baptist missionaries. Conversion was such a radical event that we knew following Jesus meant a complete break from past Chinese ancestor worship and observing Chinese religious and cultural practices. There were aspects of those religious practices, such as giving red packets, celebration of the Chinese New Year, and ancestor venerations (in contrast to worshiping of ancestors) which over the centuries became a mixture of religious as well as cultural elements. In certain contexts, and for certain people, the foreignness of Christianity and its distance from local religious practices may be part of its attractiveness. Yet, as a result, many Chinese who were steeped in Confucian traditions rejected Christianity as a foreign religion which seeks to break up family ties. "One more Christian meant one less Chinese," and following Jesus meant losing one's Chinese identity. In recent times, there are second- and third-generation Christians among Chinese diaspora communities who began to recover the possibility for Christians to follow Jesus while maintaining a healthy perspective—that the Christian gospel both rejects as well as redeems Chinese cultures. Through the positive embrace of ancestor respect, valuing family, practicing Chinese traditional medicines, Tai Chi as praise exercises, worship songs which are based on Chinese opera as well as folk music, Christian celebrations of Chinese New Year, rituals and prayers of psalms during visits to ancestor graves, the overall fear that following Jesus required a complete rejection of Chinese belonging and culture had broken down. Therefore, among Chinese diaspora communities in Southeast Asia, following Jesus became a more plausible option, a loved response to the misunderstanding that Jesus is alien to Chinese Christianity.

Communities do not necessarily need to dominate a society before they can provide plausibility. They do so, of course, in fairly homogeneous societies such as medieval Christian Europe, the Muslim Middle East, and communist North Korea. Sociological factors will, however, only *influence* what we believe, but not *determine* our convictions. They leave space for other factors. There can be many reasons to doubt dominant convictions and if people see that power is abused to suppress dissenting voices, this will undermine the credibility of the dominant view—at least for some, such as Mark Gabriel whom we encountered in chapter one. This is why marginal communities can provide alternative plausibility structures, not only for their members, but also within broader society. In many parts of the contemporary world, in the secular West or in countries dominated by other religious communities, Christians will form such marginal communities. Such a marginal position can be precisely the right place to recommend the truth, where people are weary of political or economic powers manipulating religions and ideologies to their advantage.

Contextuality. The degree of plausibility a Christian community provides for nonbelievers will also depend on the contextuality of the community. It will depend on whether the community represents a form of the Christian faith that makes sense in this particular context. In this sense, the local church is, in an expression by Lesslie Newbigin, "the hermeneutic of the Gospel."[9] In his discussion, Newbigin points to a number of characteristics in the life of the church which show what the gospel means in real-life terms. The church is, for example, a community of praise: by praising God in its worship, the Christian community relativizes all other powers and ideals that claim our highest aspiration and our best efforts. It dethrones and unmasks all idols. In other societies or for other people who are disappointed in their former ideals, values, and hopes, it shows that this community lives in the confidence that there is one reality, or rather one person, truly worth our highest praise and utmost admiration.

We need to go one step beyond what Newbigin elaborates here. The local congregation is not only the hermeneutic of the gospel in that it embodies and lives out the truth of the gospel. It is also a living exposition or interpretation ("hermeneutic") of this message. The problem with noncontextualized churches is that they cannot show the context in which they are called to

---

[9]Newbigin, *Gospel in a Pluralist Society*, 222.

witness, what the freedom of the gospel can mean in this particular context. In many cities and villages, there may be churches around, but they do not necessarily represent a "hermeneutic of the Gospel" for significant parts of the population. They may feel like medieval, nineteenth-century, or colonial relics or represent ways of life that are appropriate only to certain ethnic groups. They may present a lifestyle for the middle classes or for an older generation to which one's age or professional group may not relate. Churches need to consciously invest in becoming a representation of the gospel to which a great variety of people can relate and that will also demand creating different sub-communities. There will probably never be a church for every small social niche or village. There need not be one, because the Christian congregation needs to be a place where people across social strata and ethnic groups can recognize the relevance of this faith for their lives and feel welcome. The church in Benno's university city north of the Netherlands discovered that with only one local expression of Christian community, they could not effectively attract both the student population and other socially marginalized groups, with less formal education and with a different attitude toward life. They needed to start a new meeting place and worship service to be able to extend a real welcome to the latter group that would otherwise be left out. Earlier, the local congregation was of course inviting them to their traditional service, but this was only a formal invitation, because people might simply not be able to feel at home in the existing congregation. Many historic churches in a Muslim majority environment have the same experience. They will only be able to present a recognizable witness if they encourage the growth of communities in which new believers from a Muslim background may worship in a way that is relevant to their experience and respects their cultural sensitivities.

What should a church look like if, like Victory Outreach, they feel particularly called to show the relevance and truth of Jesus Christ to drug addicts? What church would be needed to relate to slumdwellers in a Brazilian *favela*, or to show the relevance and truth of the gospel to young urban professionals in Bangalore? We can of course present multiple examples. The question of how a local congregation can be contextualized so that it becomes a locally embodied incarnation of the gospel message is extensively discussed in missiological literature.[10] One aspect that needs to be mentioned here is the necessary tension between cultural resonance and difference. On the one hand a community needs to be recognizable so that people can relate to the hope

---

[10]E.g., Michael Moynagh, *Church for Every Context: An Introduction to Theology and Practice* (London: SCM, 2012).

expressed in its message and lifestyle, as well as feel welcome. On the other hand, it needs to be sufficiently different to represent a real alternative and a real source of hope that is unlike what could be imagined before. Some churches represent the values of the surrounding world to such a degree that if they are attractive, it is only as a different social club that may attract some lonely people, or people who like this particular crowd, but may easily be exchanged for any other club or association. As a local hermeneutic of the gospel, the local congregation needs to be contextually recognizable in its difference, yet it needs to be radically different in its contextuality. We need to be realistic and accept that in many cases its message, and life of discipleship to which it invites, are so different from the surrounding world that it will take considerable time before outsiders can truly judge it for what it is worth. The Christian community will therefore need to allow for ways to get acquainted with its message and lifestyle, as we will further explore in the next section. Yet, the barriers should be limited to those intrinsically related to the foolishness of the gospel as much as possible, while lowering unnecessary cultural hurdles as much as possible.

A cloud of witnesses. A final reason that the Christian community is crucial to apologetic witness is precisely that Christian apologetics is *witness*. Witness is used here not in the general sense—referring to a community that has a message—but in the limited technical sense of a community that testifies to an event in history that it has seen and to which it bears witness. As we will explore in further detail in chapter five, this central place of witness is given with the nature of the Christian faith itself. This faith is not based on purely individual experiences that can never be captured in words. Neither is the Christian faith based on a belief in a benevolent creator that every keen observer of nature could discover wherever they might find themselves. The Christian faith may include such elements and they may provide additional apologetic entry points. Yet, such elements are not what characterized the Christian faith: we have come to know God because we have discovered that God acted decisively for the salvation of humanity and the entire creation in the cross and resurrection of Jesus Christ (see further §4.3). Apologetic witness is, furthermore, witness to the gift and redeeming presence of the Spirit within the Christian community. Therefore, these truths can only be shared through witness, and Christian apologetics cannot be other than testimony. In chapter five, we will argue that an apologetic that is fundamentally witness is not therefore less rational or objective. It is unavoidably witness, because only as such can it be truly objective, only then can it do justice to the nature of its object: God's salvific acts in Christ. This central place of witness will of course determine that certain apologetic issues become decisive, issues such as the trustworthiness of the testimony and of the witnesses.

This does mean that Christian apologetic witness is inextricably linked with the historic community that bears witness: today's witnesses are part of a chain of witnesses. They faithfully transmit what they received from the first disciples, which has been faithfully accounted in the New Testament and continuously retold. Through the ages this witness continues to be confirmed in the experience of new generations of believers that discover the truth, relevance, and power of this Christ in ever new contexts.

2.2 ENCOUNTER AND DIALOGUE

The dialogue of life. In the last section, we explored the importance of Christian witness in the embodied character of the Christian faith within a community: only if people can see the way the Christian faith is lived out in a certain context can it become plausible and relevant. This is even more relevant because of the postmodern and postcolonial skepticism toward all claims of truth that are deconstructed as culturally relative values of a community or as power play. This does therefore mean that a crucial prerequisite for apologetic witness—or rather the only context in which apologetic witness makes sense—is encounter. In certain contexts, with a serious threat of persecution, this may not be possible. Yet ordinarily, Christian communities should be thinking seriously about events, encounters, and places that allow outsiders to experience the life of the community. This is even more relevant because many people need time to explore the Christian life and outlook, as if from the inside, before fully committing themselves (see also §6.3).

This presents the church with major challenges in its witness in general, and apologetic witness in particular. In many contexts, Christians and non-Christians live their lives separately. They may meet others on the streets, at work, at the school-gate, or in the marketplace, but this will rarely lead to a deep sharing of lives. This is one of the reasons why recent converts are often among the most effective witnesses. This is not only because they are full of fervor or others around them perceive a change in their lives, but also because they still have many friendships and deep relationships of trust with family and other members of the community that do not share their faith. Apologetic witness will in most cases only be effective when relationships of trust are built, and lives are shared in meaningful encounters. This may be one of the main challenges if Christian communities see "mission" and "evangelism" primarily as isolated activities, happening in well-circumscribed environments such as vacation Bible clubs, mission trips, and soup-kitchens. Christian communities and individuals may need to explore both natural and new, creative social opportunities to share their lives in depth.

Theologians who reflect on interreligious dialogue and encounter distinguish among three types of dialogue: (1) The dialogue of *life* is the dialogue that happens, often without words, when people of different religions share their daily lives or when representatives of different communities come together to address practical issues of common concern; (2) The dialogue of the *mind* concerns the sharing of ideas. Küster refers to scholars interested in other scholars, but this will of course also happen when neighbors or members of the same family show a real interest in each other's deepest convictions, drives, hopes, and ideals; (3) The dialogue of the *heart* happens when people in different religions share different religious experiences and try to enter in the experiences of others—for example, when Christian retreat centers invite Zen-Buddhist masters or when Christians and Muslims enter into a joint prayer session.[11]

We believe that the dialogue of the heart as understood here is inappropriate for Christians because of the central Christian conviction that we can only come to the Father through Christ (John 14:6) and therefore only pray in the name of Christ. This is not only a question of spiritual purity, but also of consistent witness. This is, however, not to say that a Christian could never learn and borrow from certain religious practices or from other religious traditions. We will later encounter Sadhu Sundar Singh, who integrated certain Hindu practices in his life of discipleship, not merely for pragmatic reasons but because he felt they allowed him to grow in ways that the existing Western forms of Christian practice available to him could not (§9.3). Christians can also share in a dialogue of the heart at another level—when they want to listen to the deepest motivations and highest ideals of their conversation partners. They can also share the joys and sorrows of others when they extend or accept invitations to religious festivals such as Christmas, Wesak Day, or *Eid Ul-fitr,* or when they attend funerals. This can be done as joyful guests or as compassionate neighbors without joining in prayers or meditation.

If apologetic witness should always be embodied, the dialogue of the mind can never be separated from the dialogue of life. On the one hand the dialogue of the mind only has an appropriate context when it happens in the setting of shared lives. This is also true for the dialogue of the mind in academic settings, which is meaningful if it considers how religious beliefs are related to different

---

[11]E.g., Volker Küster, "Who, with Whom, about What? Exploring the Landscape of Inter-Religious Dialogue," *Exchange* 33, no. 1 (2004): 78-79.

ways of life. In the other direction, the dialogue of life invites one to a dialogue of the mind. Sometimes the dialogue of the mind can be so overshadowed by immediate needs that there is little space for a dialogue at other levels. This is the case when there is an immediate pressure to work out how to live together peacefully when different forces in society and religious community raise tensions or even result in violent conflict. Normally, however, Christians will desire to share the source of their hope, patience, and love. Christianity is not simply a lifestyle option to which they feel attracted. It is a hope to which they themselves are invited by the resurrection of Christ and it is the nature of this invitation that it extends to all people.

Styles of communication. When engaging in interreligious encounters, we need to be well aware of the cultural differences that come into play in our communication: What style of argumentation do we find persuasive? What type of people do we consider trustworthy? How do we feel that differences of viewpoint should be properly discussed? Attention to such cultural differences is not unique to the study of crosscultural mission. Helpful work has been done by business consultants who, because of globalization processes, are increasingly attentive to differences in cultural styles.[12]

The consultant and trainer Erin Meyer helpfully maps different cultures on a number of scales. One such scale, with regards to communication, is the one from "low context" to "high context." Certain cultures are located toward the high context end, where you need to be very aware of hidden and indirect messages that only insiders can understand. Other cultures are low context in the sense that much more of what needs to be communicated is made explicit.[13]

A further cultural difference concerns how different communities manage disagreement. In certain cultures, such as Benno's Dutch culture, disagreement is expressed fairly openly, while other cultures avoid confrontation. The United Kingdom is much more comfortable with open disagreement than for example Japan or Thailand, but much less than the Netherlands. How one properly disagrees is obviously crucial for apologetic dialogue: How does one address differences of opinion in a way that allows conversation partners to address these as comfortably as possible? To make it more complex, what

---

[12]E.g., Geert Hofstede and Gert Jan Hofstede, *Cultures and Organizations: Software of the Mind*, 2nd ed. (New York: McGraw-Hill, 2004); David A. Livermore, *The Cultural Intelligence Difference: Master the One Skill You Can't Do without in Today's Global Economy* (New York: AMACOM, American Management Association, 2011).

[13]Erin Meyer, *The Culture Map: Decoding How People Think, Lead, and Get Things Done Across Cultures* (New York: Public Affairs, 2015), 37-41.

degree of open disagreement is appropriate may also depend on the relative social status of the participants in relation to each other: in many cultures, you express disagreement with an equal differently from disagreement with a person with a higher status—if you can express it at all.[14]

The degree of confrontation intersects with another cultural feature: cultural expressiveness. Some cultures may be emotionally and relatively unexpressive, yet happy with open confrontation, while other cultures may be much more emotionally expressive in engaging in confrontation than others. These two intersecting scales lead to a quadrant which allows us to map different cultures along two axes: from confrontation-prone to confrontation-avoiding and from emotionally unexpressive to emotionally expressive.[15]

Different cultures also have different argumentation patterns. Western apologetics has often lacked awareness of this difference because of the desire to look for universally valid argumentation patterns that are therefore culturally neutral. Yet, even among North-Atlantic cultures, there are significant differences with respect to which argumentation patterns are considered persuasive. Consider the contrast between writers from the United States and from France. The United States is a very pragmatic culture that appreciates immediate results and looks for direct applicability of ideas. Books are therefore filled with elaborate practical examples and applications. Meyer's book is a case in point: every chapter starts with a case study about intercultural miscommunication or mismanagement, and from these case studies she moves on to discuss general principles. French authors tend to be on the other end of the spectrum with a focused attention on principles and abstract argumentation.[16]

Many Asian cultures do not fit within this scale, from principles first to application first. They are rather "holistic" in their thinking. They start from a holistic vision in which everything is related, moving from the whole to questions of detail. If you come from such a culture, you would find many Western ways of reasoning reductionist, because they isolate one part of the picture. On the other hand, if you come from a culture that studies the details before moving to the larger picture, holistic ways of reasoning feel muddled and imprecise.[17]

A form of reasoning that does justice to our full humanity, to the rich nature of the universe and to the nature of the Christian faith, needs to take

---

[14]Cf. Meyer, *The Culture Map*, 197-201.
[15]Cf. Meyer, *The Culture Map*, 201-3.
[16]Meyer, *The Culture Map*, 93-97.
[17]Cf. Meyer, *The Culture Map*, 105-12.

all three aspects into account, but the appropriate entry point can well vary from culture to culture. The Christian Scriptures draw us into a new world and are thus characterized by holistic persuasion. The personal testimonies of encounters with Christ allow, however, to start from concrete experiences of liberation, healing, and enlightenment, while there is also room for broad universal principles, for example when the entire law is summarized in two commandments (Mt 22:34-40) and when love is seen as the essence of the very being of God (1 Jn 4:8).

A final factor of cultural diversity that is crucial for apologetic dialogue is how you build trust across cultures. Meyer points to a fundamental cultural difference with regards to building trust between, on the one hand, cultures that grant trust based on someone's knowledgeability and skill or, on the other hand, cultures in which trust is built not on skill but rather on relationship.[18] In many cultures, both are important: some people may only be open to a relationship when you have proven knowledgeable, but the opposite could also be the case. This is again particularly tricky when you and your host culture don't share the same priorities in this respect.

When considering such cultural differences, we need to constantly ask three series of questions. The first series of questions is, Where do I—and where does the community in which I feel at home—fit in? What are my preferred ways of persuasion? What makes me trust someone? What do I find are appropriate and helpful ways to disagree? In this respect, am I a product of my community? Or do I have preferences that differ slightly? The second series of questions raises the same issues with regards to the community or communities and individuals with which we are currently engaged in dialogue: Are they in these respects similar to us or are they significantly different? Should I learn to adapt my communicative styles and the ways I am used to disagreeing and building trust? Such styles may also be related to the religious characteristic of the communities involved: Do basic religious attitudes, for example, focus on eternal truths of concrete experiences? Do they value religious insights because of the potential for concrete application or for the comprehensive perspective it provides? The third series of questions is what styles of communication are most faithful to the message of Christ and whether certain styles might implicitly undermine or even contradict the message. This last question will remain with us for the chapters to come.

---

[18]Meyer, *The Culture Map*, 170-74.

3

THE CULTURAL EMBEDDEDNESS
OF BELIEF

WHAT PEOPLE FIND CONVINCING and what people are even willing to consider seriously depends on their cultural and social location. For a secular social climber in Amsterdam, belief in God seems unreasonable and the idea that following Christ would mean giving up a significant part of one's personal autonomy and freedom would be deeply troubling. A Muslimah in Hyderabad would find belief in God much more rational than atheism (look at creation!) and accept that true freedom can be found in submission. Yet, she might find the Christian idea of unconditional forgiveness much more worrying: Can you build a stable society if people can sin as much as they want knowing that God is always ready to forgive?

Apologetic witness therefore needs to be contextual and dialogical, taking different contexts and the individual histories of our dialogue partners into account. We already noted that dominant strands of modern Western Christian apologetics are lacking in this respect. For practical reasons, they have of course focused on the issues that dominated their particular context. The content of these apologies is therefore less appropriate for other cultural contexts and audiences. What is more, these "foundationalist" Western apologetics often presuppose that the valid arguments can only start from presumably universally accepted or acceptable starting points (see §1.2). If this is the case, once a good apologetic argument is found, it should be equally attractive to all people. This means that modern Western apologists often supposed that the arguments they experienced as valid in their own context were supposed to be so everywhere. They were after all built on a universally valid foundation. This made them less sensitive toward cultural difference.

In this chapter, we will further explore what it means for apologetic witness that human beliefs are deeply embedded in the cultural contexts that shape them. In the first section (§3.1), we will show that this awareness of the importance of location is not imposed on Christians from the outside because of the pressures of cultural plurality and cultural relativism. The experience of religious and cultural pluralism may make us more aware of this reality, but it does in fact reflect the biblical understanding of what it means to be human.

In the following sections, we will show that this cultural location will not necessarily lead to cultural relativism, but that humans who indwell their cultural contexts can from that perspective still relate to the truth (§3.2) and evaluate the relative value of different cultural and religious perspectives on life, the world, and God (§3.3). This will help us sketch the first outlines of what contextual Christian apologetic witness and dialogue can look like: How can we discuss questions of truth across cultural and religious boundaries, while taking our cultural embeddedness with utter seriousness?

In this chapter, we will therefore be grappling with cultural relativism at different levels. Cultural relativism is a position that Christians encounter in dialogue with other religionists or with postmodern Westerners, whether they consider themselves as secular or spiritual. Yet, cultural relativism is not merely one of the themes that comes up in apologetic dialogue. If true, cultural relativism would undermine the validity of the entire project of Christian apologetic witness: if the Christian truth is only valid for those already sharing the Christian outlook on the world, there would be no basis for witnessing to the truth of Christ to people with radically different outlooks on life and the world.

This chapter should be read in tandem with §4.4 and chapter five, regarding the nature of Christian apologetics as witness to Christ. This is an essential element of the argument that our cultural embeddedness does not preclude us to find a truth that is worth sharing with all. In these later sections, we will consider why Christians believe what we have come to know about God and his plans for humanity in Christ as trustworthy and of transcultural value.

3.1 THE CULTURED NATURE OF HUMAN EXISTENCE

In biblical theology. The modern Western foundationalist theory of knowledge has long sought a universally acceptable or universally accessible—and therefore neutral—starting point for all knowledge. This theory of knowledge has been unduly accepted by many Christian apologists who started to look for universal experiences or principles which could ground or underpin the Christian faith. Christian apologetic witness should first of all be faithful to the content of the Christian faith. If these apologists would have realized who they are as human beings before God, they would have been less amazed and troubled that the search for a neutral foundation for human knowledge ran aground as modernity was succeeded by postmodernity. For this modern search presupposes that the human mind works like the divine mind—looking from an overarching perspective and neutral standpoint. This idea is rooted in Greek antiquity when the human mind was understood to correspond to the divine mind, and where the human mind was trustworthy in as far as it participated in or mirrored the divine mind.

According to the Jewish and Christian Scriptures, the human mind is not a spark of the divine mind, neither is the human spirit part of the divine Spirit. Human beings are rather created "in the image of God" (Gen 1:26-28) and as such they belong to the created order. That the human being is created in the image of God points to three relationships for which we are created: with the earth, with fellow human beings, and with God.[1] In the first place, the human being is called to represent the Creator within the creation. In the ancient world, an image of a god would represent the authority of this god. In the same way humankind is called to be God's regent or representative. Humankind is called to subdue the earth, develop, and care for it (Gen 1:26, 28; 2:15; Ps 8). This is sometimes called the "creational mandate" because this mandate refers to the role of humankind in relation to the wider creation. It is also called the "cultural mandate" because it refers to the task of humanity in the development of culture. This mandate played an important role in the development of modern science. In order to take care of creation and develop it, we need to seek to understand it, and we can therefore trust that it is open to our probing.[2] Yet, as the created image of God, humankind is still an integral part of creation. Humankind is created on the sixth day, together with the animals. Though the crown of creation, humankind is still part of creation. We can only know creation by "indwelling" it, by being part of it, by trusting our created senses and our created brain. We have no universal perspective from "nowhere" on creation—we can only look from where we are, as we are, trusting in what we are made and given as creatures in God's image.

Second, our creation in the image of God also means that we are created for community. Karl Barth famously linked this insight with the expression "in the image of God he created them; male and female he created them" (Gen 1:27).[3] In the wider context of the canon of the Scriptures, we can see

---

[1] Benno van den Toren, *Christian Apologetics as Cross-Cultural Dialogue* (London: T&T Clark, 2011), 94-113.

[2] Cf. Thomas F. Torrance, *Ground and Grammar of Theology: Consonance Between Theology and Science* (Edinburgh: T&T Clark, 2005), 52-60; Christopher B. Kaiser, *Creation and the History of Science* (Grand Rapids, MI: Eerdmans, 1991).

[3] Karl Barth, *Church Dogmatics*, ed. Geoffrey W. Bromiley and Thomas F. Torrance, trans. Geoffrey W. Bromiley et al. (Edinburgh: T&T Clark, 1956–1975) III/1, 195.

that this verse not only means that we are created for marriage, but for community in a wider sense. Humankind was called to multiply and spread out over the earth (Gen 1:29). This also means that they were called to spread out as peoples who would inhabit different parts of the world, as reflected in the *table of nations* in Genesis 10 and 11. God assigned all peoples their place (cf. Deut 32:28; Acts 17:26).

A theological reading of these texts suggests that God intended different communities would develop different languages and cultures. The diversification of humanity was not simply a punishment after the building of the tower of Babel, but according to God's original plan.[4] This is confirmed when we read these texts in the light of Pentecost and the book of Revelation. At Pentecost, the curse of the confusion of languages at Babel is not simply reversed. It is not the case that from Pentecost on everyone again speaks the same language. It is rather the case that these language and cultural differences no longer form a decisive barrier: the great deeds of God can be understood and proclaimed in all these languages. At the end of the book of Revelation, we see how at the end of history when creation attains its destination, cultural diversity is not overcome, but celebrated. We encounter "a great multitude . . . from every nation, from all tribes and peoples and languages" (Rev 7:9; cf. 5:9).

Our belonging to a community and culture means that as human beings we not only indwell a physical space and body, we also indwell a cultural framework. We only relate to the world with the help of the language and conceptual framework we have inherited from our parents and educators. Even before we start thinking for ourselves, our thinking is shaped by the cultures in which we are born.

The third relationship that is constitutional for being human—implied in the creation of humankind "in the image of God"—is the relationship with God. Within creation, humankind is created in and for a special relationship with God. Because our relationship with God is central to who we are, we can never relate to the question of who God is and what God is for us neutrally. We are always existentially involved (see further §5.2; §7.2). This relationship with God also means that though humans cannot be understood apart from the communities to which they belong, they cannot be reduced to these communities either. The Christian perspective therefore differs on the one hand from modern individualism, but, on the other hand, differs from forms of communalism in which the individual has no value apart from

---

[4]Bernhard Anderson, "The Babel Story: Paradigm of Human Unity and Diversity," *Concilium* 121 (1977): 63-70; Theodore Hiebert, "The Tower of Babel and the Origins of the World's Cultures," *Journal of Biblical Literature* 126, no. 1 (2007): 29-58.

the community. Precisely because people also exist before God, they are not simply an extension of their communities. As many biblical stories beginning with Abraham show, they can even be called out of their family and community on a new pilgrimage with God and to God's kingdom.[5]

Our biological, cultural, and spiritual constitution. Because of who we are as human beings we are all deeply embedded in the cultures in which we are born and raised. The philosopher and sociologist Arnold Gehlen pointed out that the human species is different from all other animal species in its radical "world-openness."[6] Animals can basically live only one lifestyle: they live either as eagles, rabbits, lions, or as wild donkeys and they therefore can only live in the environments that support their lifestyles. Their life in the wild is almost entirely determined by their instincts. In contrast, human beings are open to the world in that they can learn to live in radically different environments: human beings live as nomads in semi-deserts, as hunters in the arctic, as farmers in tropical rainforests, and in fishing villages on atolls in the Pacific. Human beings can even adapt to the lifestyle required in modern megacities.

This openness to the world is part of the greatness of being human. It means that we can develop ourselves and develop cultures. Yet, it also means that we are much more dependent on our parents than (other) animals: we can only survive in the arctic, in the semi-desert, and in the city if we are socialized in the highly adapted cultural lifestyles of our educators. This includes conceptual frameworks that determine how we look at the world. One needs a different linguistic toolset to function as an office worker than as a subsistence farmer. The culture which we inherit also includes tools, social structures, and ethical values that may be more appropriate to either a nomadic or sedentary lifestyle. It includes views about others outside our community: Who do we see as friends, as dangerous, and to whom may we be completely indifferent? It also includes a religious outlook on the world. We indwell our cultures, and it is only by indwelling our cultures that we can indwell the world.

Because cultures function like lenses which present an all-encompassing perspective through which we view the world and relate to it, no aspect of our life is free from its influence. And because this is the view of reality in which

---

[5]Cf. Emil Brunner, *Man in Revolt: A Christian Anthropology*, trans. Olive Wyon (London: Lutterworth Press, 1939), 183; 187-91; B. J. van der Walt, *Afrocentric or Eurocentric? Our Task in a Multicultural South Africa* (Potchefstroom, ZA: Potchefstroomse Universiteit vir Christelike Hoër Onderwys, 1997), 28-49.

[6]Arnold Gehlen, *Man, His Nature and Place in the World* (New York: Columbia University Press, 1988), 27; see how this idea was taken up in Clifford Geertz, *The Interpretation of Cultures: Selected Essays* (New York: Basic Books, 1973), 49-50; Wolfhart Pannenberg, *Anthropology in Theological Perspective*, trans. Matthew J. O'Connell (Philadelphia, PA: Westminster Press, 1985), 34.

we are educated, our own lenses feel most natural to us. Before people have seriously encountered alternative cultural outlooks, they will normally think that how their community sees the world is simply how it is. How they live life is simply how it ought to be. There are no questions asked because the questions do not even come up.

From a Christian point of view such differences about worldviews, life-styles, and values are not mere cultural differences. They are also moral and spiritual. If communities are socialized in outlooks on life, lifestyles, and value systems, they are inheriting a culture and worldview that contains many gifts but is, in other respects, defective or even sinful. The theological concept of original sin is used to express the belief in the hereditary character of the human disposition to sin. The concept is multifaceted, but it seems right to see culture as one of the channels through which sin is transmitted from one generation to another. Children can only grow up and develop themselves if they are first of all socialized in the patterns of life (e.g., parents and educators). It is only afterward that they can start thinking for themselves and develop their own lifestyles. What they have inherited will continue to shape their lives, for good and for evil.[7]

Cultures can be channels and expressions of the goodness of creation, of God's grace on the one hand and of sin on the other. A Christian understanding of culture should take seriously that cultures hold spiritual power over people and can be abused by spiritual powers to obscure the human mind. Christian witness is therefore also taking place in the context of a power encounter, the encounter between the power of the cross and the powers of this world, both social and spiritual.[8]

3.2 Discovering and Debating Truth

The cultural location of cultural relativism. The study of culture shows us that what we see when we look to the world and to others is deeply influenced by our cultural perspective. Yet, if our cultural perspective shapes all we see, this is of course equally true of our view of cultural relativism itself. This perspective is itself culturally located. It is first of all located in the cultural context of globalization in which we are confronted with the power of cultural perspectives and in which we look for ways to respect the value of cultural difference. Second, it is also located in the history of Western modernity.

---

[7]Benno van den Toren, "Human Evolution and a Cultural Understanding of Original Sin," in *Perspectives on Science and Christian Faith* 68, no. 1 (2016): 12-21.
[8]Lesslie Newbigin, *The Gospel in a Pluralist Society* (Grand Rapids, MI: Eerdmans, 1989), 204-8; David Naugle, *Worldview: The History of a Concept* (Grand Rapids, MI: Eerdmans, 2002), 274-84.

Western modernity promised a culture-independent, universally accessible, and acceptable starting point for human thought and culture. When it failed to provide such a universal foundation for society and thought, it opened the door for postmodern relativism.[9] Third, cultural relativism is located in the academic discipline of cultural anthropology, which studies the world in a certain way. It is therefore also strongly represented in other fields of study such as religious studies that borrow from cultural anthropology. This tendency to reduce the multifaceted nature of reality to what you look for is present in many—and possibly all—academic disciplines. If you study the world as a psychologist, it is easy to think that people's psychological state will be the principal factor for determining what people think, just as a sociologist might conclude that one's sociological location is what really matters, and a neuroscientist might come to the conclusion that what we come to believe is determined by impersonal neurological processes.

In this section, we will argue that cultural relativism itself needs to be relativized. Our cultural perspective does not entirely determine what we believe about reality. We will first argue that our cultural perspectives do not imprison us, but that through our cultural lenses we can still perceive a world beyond these lenses. We will then argue that different cultural perspectives can critically engage with each other and allow for a critical evaluation of their relative validity.

Cultural and religious perspectives are open to the world. The cultural and social embeddedness of our human beliefs does not exclude that we come in touch with a world beyond our language and culturally embedded perspectives. How this is the case becomes clear when we look to the natural sciences. Science has long been understood as based on purely empirical observations and neutral facts. The success of the natural sciences in explaining the world may be one of the reasons for the persuasiveness of what we call "universalist foundationalism" (§1.2), the idea that all valid knowledge should be based on a foundation of universally accessible and verifiable beliefs. Natural science seems to promise this type of knowledge. This scientific model is then subsequently taken as the only model for how one arrives at trustworthy beliefs.

The sociological study of the history of science by Thomas Kuhn (1996) has shown, however, that what scientists find acceptable is shaped by their social setting. When scientists present a new "paradigm," a radically new way of

---

[9] Alasdair MacIntyre, *Whose Justice? Which Rationality?* (Notre Dame, IN: University of Notre Dame Press, 1988), 334-35; van den Toren, *Christian Apologetics,* 42-43.

looking at the world, this will at first be resisted by most active scientists who are deeply invested in the older paradigm. The new paradigm will only be gradually accepted as individual scientists recognize its value and start developing an alternative scientific tradition until finally the old school dies off.

One could conclude from this that the whole idea that science is describing an objective reality is a myth, as some of the radical followers of Kuhn have done. That would, however, be another example of believing that your particular perspective on reality (in this case the sociological perspective on the history of science) tells the entire truth. The reality of the development of the natural sciences is much more complex. Though sociological factors profoundly influence what scientists find plausible, they cannot entirely determine what they see. In an expression from Kuhn himself, scientists cannot simply "beat nature into line" of their cultural expectations and of the conceptual frameworks with which they approach the reality they study.[10]

When scientists observe the world with their theories, they will primarily design experiments and collect findings that fit their existing paradigm. Yet, they will also encounter "anomalies," observations that do not fit their expectations and preconceived theories. They will, in the beginning, try to interpret these as much as possible within their existing paradigm and if possible only make minimal changes to do justice to these new observations and experiences. But at a certain moment, the build-up of anomalous data becomes too significant to ignore. In this way, it was an accumulation of observations that did not fit the older Newtonian understanding of the universe that invited scientists to look for alternative understandings and led to the development of the theory of general relativity (proposed by Albert Einstein) and quantum physics (developed by Max Planck and others).

The philosopher of science Michael Polanyi (1962) develops a fuller account of the natural sciences than, on the one hand, the empiricist foundationalist view and, on the other hand, the relativist view that sees science as no more than a human construct. Polanyi argues that all science is a personal endeavor and embedded in community. Science is not done from a neutral perspective, but from a personal one. The personal perspectives of scientists are furthermore a matter of faith: they approach the world believing that a certain scientific tradition represents an adequate approach to reality. Yet, while working within this tradition, they may have an intuitive grasp of reality as it is in itself, and they come up with proposals for new theories they experience as more

---

[10]Thomas S. Kuhn, *The Structure of Scientific Revolutions*, 3rd ed. (Chicago: University of Chicago Press, 1996), 135; cf. J. C. Polkinghorne, *Rochester Roundabout: The Story of High Energy Physics* (New York: W.H. Freeman, 1989), 167-70, 173; van den Toren, *Christian Apologetics*, 122-27.

adequate to the world they experience. This Polanyian notion of "indwelling" fits well with the biblical understanding of the human being as the image of God within creation used earlier in this chapter. We have the ability to know adequately, not from a divine perspective, but from within creation. We know also that, while indwelling the conceptual systems, we learn through our communities and research traditions.[11] These culturally shaped concepts are culturally located rather than universally shared or accessible, yet they also help us in relating to the world and in gaining an increasingly better grasp of what the world is in itself. We therefore always develop our beliefs from our particular cultural and historical location, but we make our truth claims "with universal intent."[12]

Religious traditions similarly look to the world through a certain lens, but that does not mean that they cannot at the same time be open to reality as it is in itself. The prime example for our exploration in apologetic witness is what happened when Jesus of Nazareth began his ministry and particularly when he died on the cross and rose from the dead. The people around him tried to make sense of him within the cultural frameworks they knew. That is why some took him for a political rebel, others for a rabbi, a prophet, or even the promised Messiah. Yet, in the end, he did not fit any of the available cultural and religious categories. Even when called *Messiah* or *Christ*, he appeared to be both greater than and different from the expected anointed king. In the end, all available images of Messiah, suffering servant, Son of God, high priest, and sacrifice needed to be combined and expanded in order to do justice to this unexpected reality.

Comparing cultural and religious perspectives. People can thus change their understanding of reality, because while looking at the world from their cultural and religious perspectives, they will have experiences and be confronted with aspects of reality and life that do not fit their preconceived ideas. It is also possible that we start looking differently at reality because, when we encounter an alternative view of life, we start comparing both views of reality and discover that this new understanding of reality makes more sense than our former understanding. A person may believe that illness has merely physical causes, but after studying the sociology of disease, that person comes to realize society may also make people ill. A person may have grown up in a tribal

---

[11]Michael Polanyi, *Personal Knowledge: Towards a Post-Critical Philosophy* (Chicago: University of Chicago Press, 1962), 60; cf. John Flett, "Alasdair MacIntyre's Tradition-Constituted Enquiry in Polanyian Perspective," *Tradition and Discovery: The Polanyi Society Periodical* 26, no. 2 (1999): 6-20.

[12]Polanyi, *Personal Knowledge*, 311.

society and believe that contributing to the flourishing and continuity of the clan is what makes life worth living, yet, after listening to Christian evangelists, starts considering whether an eternal loving relationship with a God who is love does not far surpass what was first believed to be the highest obtainable goal in life.

Alasdair MacIntyre's notion of "rationality of traditions" provides a good model for comprehending how different traditions can interact. He has developed this model for understanding the interaction of different traditions of ethical reflection,[13] but has equally seen the value of this model to understand the interaction between different scientific paradigms.[14] This model can also be helpful for gaining insight into important aspects of the interaction between religious traditions.

Religious traditions are multidimensional, and one dimension includes the forms of rationality embedded in traditions. Religions have developed from an original set of experiences—such as an experience of the Enlightenment or of a crucifixion and resurrection. They relate to the world through the lenses of these traditions but do not thereby throw reason out the window: many thinkers have embraced such perspectives precisely because they experienced them as rational. They have not stopped thinking because they were religious but have continued to develop the rationality they saw embedded in these traditions and through which they related to the world around them. This is one of the reasons that religious traditions are not static but change in relation to the contexts in which they are lived, and in response to the experiences that feed into them. In this respect, religious traditions evolve in ways that are similar to the development of scientific traditions in academic communities.

Religious traditions do not evolve in isolation from each other, because religious communities encounter each other and interact. In the process, religious and ideological traditions can, for better or for worse, incorporate elements from other traditions. Examples may be the incorporation of certain elements of Marxist thinking in Christian liberation theology[15] and the influence of Christianity on the development of Buddhist social ethics.[16]

---

[13]MacIntyre, *Whose Justice?*, 164-82, 349-69.

[14]Alasdair MacIntyre, "Epistemological Crises, Dramatic Narrative, and the Philosophy of Science," in *Paradigms and Revolutions: Appraisals and Applications of Thomas Kuhn's Philosophy of Science*, ed. Gary Gutting (Notre Dame, IN: University of Notre Dame Press, 1980), 54-74.

[15]David J. Bosch, *Transforming Mission: Paradigm Shifts in Theology of Mission* (Maryknoll, NY: Orbis Books, 1991), 440-42.

[16]Volker Küster, "Who, with Whom, about What? Exploring the Landscape of Inter-Religious Dialogue," *Exchange* 33, no. 1 (2004): 84.

Members of particular religious traditions will of course initially look at other traditions from within their own religious rationality. In most cases, when looked at from within a particular religiously and culturally embedded rationality, other traditions will most of the time not appear very rational. It is, however, possible to explore other traditions at much greater depth when one gets to know other traditions from the inside, as alternative rationalities with their own integrity. Then people can start looking at the same experience or event from different perspectives. If I know what my experience of grief feels like as a Christian, I may start considering how a Buddhist should relate to such an experience of grief—and vice versa. If I know how I should relate to an experience of illness or death from within an African Traditional Religion, I can also begin to imagine what it looks like from a Christian perspective. It may at a certain moment also be possible to compare two perspectives integrally: How does my current religious tradition make sense of the world and of my life as I currently experience it, and what would an alternative religious perspective on the same life and an alternative practice look like?

Such comparisons may also trigger conversion from one religious tradition to another, as exemplified in the conversion of Paul Williams from Tibetan Buddhism to Roman Catholic Christianity. In the language of MacIntyre, this may be a rational conversion—though many more dimensions are involved. It is rational, because when comparing these two perspectives, people may conclude that in the light of a new religious outlook, they can make more sense of the world and life than before. They may even come to see why their earlier understanding of life was shortsighted and wrong. MacIntyre provides, in this way, a good model for what happens in conversion from another religion to the Christian faith:

> When an epistemological crisis [we will return to this expression later] is resolved, it is by the construction of a new narrative which enables the agent to understand both how he or she could intelligibly have held his or her original beliefs and how he or she could have been so drastically misled by them. The narrative in terms of which he or she at first understood and ordered experiences is itself made into the subject of an enlarged narrative.[17]

On the (ir)rationality of (non)conversion. We have just argued that it is possible for people to evaluate the truthfulness of another religious tradition in comparison to their current religious tradition, a process which might lead

---

[17]MacIntyre, "Epistemological Crises," 56.

to a radical change of perspective and conversion. This does not imply, of course, that all conversions or even most conversions happen because people are convinced of the rationality of such a step. People can change religious adherence because of social pressures (political or cultural) or because they see social advantage in embracing another religion. People may in the same way remain in their religious tradition and not convert for a variety of reasons, many largely subconscious or only half conscious such as a general conservative attitude toward life or the desire to maintain good relationships with family and friends. Such reasons or motifs will often keep people far from even considering other religious traditions seriously.

The fact that so many factors can play a role in instigating or obstructing conversion reflect the multiple aspects of our human existence that come into play in conversion (cf. §1.1). It does mean that a proper call for conversion needs to address the entire person, including will, attitudes, and emotions as well as sociocultural realities and communal loyalties (see further chap. 7). Yet, religious commitment is also a question of rationality and truth, and people can and should be addressed accordingly. It means that the common self-understanding of converts—that they have embraced a new religion (at least in part) because it is true—can be respected and does not need to be deconstructed. This is precisely why holistic Christian mission should also encompass apologetic witness as one of its constitutive threads.

3.3 UNDERSTANDING OTHER RELIGIOUS TRADITIONS

Levels of understanding. In order to make adequate comparisons between the value and truthfulness of different and religious perspectives on the world, one will need to understand them well. This is much harder than it may look at first sight, because we initially interpret others and their beliefs always in terms of our own view on the world. This tendency to understand others from our own perspective is so ingrained that some people would even consider it impossible to truly understand others: we can never be in someone else's shoes. We would want to argue to the contrary, that understanding others is possible, never completely, but at least adequately enough to arrive at valid communication. Someone may, for example, believe at first instance that the Islamic practice of wearing the *niqab* is oppressive for women, but after getting to know Muslimahs and listening intently to their stories, that person discovers that some of them may experience it as liberating—liberating, for example, from the sexualization of the woman in many modern societies. The fact that we can point out misunderstandings and that our own culturally shaped preconceptions of others can be challenged in dialogue shows that a growth of mutual understanding is possible.[18]

Understanding others is of course a matter of degrees. Different degrees of understanding may suffice depending on the goal of the conversation. Do we, for example, want to simply collaborate on a certain project? Or do we want to express the views of others as adequately as possible, as cultural anthropologists and intercultural theologians might want to do? There is also no general answer to the question of how much understanding is needed for adequate Christian witness to other religious communities. In certain contexts, a relatively limited understanding may be sufficient, but, particularly when one starts witnessing to people more deeply rooted in their traditions, a more profound understanding is called for.

Witness to Christ therefore happens out of different levels of understanding of others. Our witness itself is, first of all, based on our confidence in Christ and not in our ability to understand and compare different cultural perspectives (see further chap. 5). We need not have passed a minimal threshold of understanding before we can begin witnessing. Witness may for example be a simple reference to my love for Christ to a Sikh taxi driver, even if I only have the faintest idea of what Sikhism is. Yet, if we believe that Christ can relate to their life, all our witness should express a real interest in others, even if it remains limited to what is appropriate for a single taxi journey.

If someone is particularly called to witness cross-culturally and interreligiously to a particular people group, they will want to understand this group, their culture, and their religion as much as possible. A systematic study of their beliefs and practices may well be part of preparation and ongoing learning. However, limited initial understanding need not hinder witness to Christ, not only because our confidence is first of all in Christ, but also because a truly dialogical witness to Christ may be one of the best ways to grow in our understanding of others. When witnessing to Christ, we should be fully attentive to how others understand and experience this message: What do they find attractive or unattractive? How does Christ relate to the lives they are currently living and how does he relate to their current views and values? How do they challenge me in my understanding of Christ, now that I am called to bring him in conversation with this new world? Where do I think they misunderstand what I am trying to share, and how might that be related to where

---

[18]Cf. Harold Netland, *Encountering Religious Pluralism: The Challenge to Christian Faith and Mission* (Downers Grove, IL: InterVarsity Press, 2001), 287-89.

they come from? Furthermore, their interest in Christ may grow when the Christian witness shows a genuine interest.

Learning a "second first language." The highest attainable level of understanding of another cultural perspective and religious tradition may well be understood with the analogy of speaking a second first language. We present this analogy for three reasons: (1) It contradicts the idea that one can never adequately understand another cultural perspective; (2) it shows why certain people can be particularly effective in crosscultural and interreligious witness; and (3) though most of us might never fully attain it, it gives us an ideal that is still worth striving for in prolonged interreligious encounter.

The image of a second first language was first introduced by MacIntyre[19] and later applied to interfaith dialogue and mission by Newbigin.[20] In the modern world, most of us learn a second language in a classroom setting. I (Benno) learned French by having its grammar explained in comparison to Dutch and by learning the vocabulary through the Dutch equivalents: *Maître* ("teacher" in French) means *meester* (in Dutch). The inevitable problem of this approach is, of course, that it understands French as analogous to Dutch. This may be adequate in view of rudimentary conversation, but does not take French seriously as a language of its own. The French language organizes the world and thought in its own way and gives aspects of reality its own meaning. This way of learning a foreign language is also how we often learn about other cultures and religions, we compare them with what we know: "The Koran is similar to the Bible and going to a Hindu temple is like going to a church." We therefore also misrepresent them, either more crudely or almost imperceptibly. The Qur'an does in fact have a different function in Islam than the Bible and may in certain respects be better compared with Jesus Christ in the Christian faith.

When our family went to the Central African Republic, our three boys aged three to eight went to the local French school. They learned French in a very different way. They learned it as they had learned Dutch, as their first language: by living in a certain environment in which the language is used and by gradually picking up how to use it themselves. They simply went to the French school or kindergarten, looked at how their classmates and teachers used French, and started using it accordingly. For them French was not a second language as for their parents, but a "second first language." They learned in the same way they had earlier learned Dutch as their first language. From the very

---

[19]MacIntyre, *Whose Justice?*, 374.
[20]Newbigin, *Gospel in a Pluralist Society*, 55-56, 65; cf. George A. Lindbeck, "The Gospel's Uniqueness: Election and Untranslatability," *Modern Theology* 13, no. 4 (1997): 428-29.

beginning they understood the language from an insider's perspective and not by comparing it to Dutch. They were from the very beginning aware that the French *maître* has a different meaning from the Dutch *meester*. After all, they learned to use the word in a classroom where they related to the *maître* in a very different way from how they would have related to the *meester* at home in the Netherlands.

Just as you can learn a second first language, you can also learn a "second first culture." You can learn another culture by being socialized in the community firsthand rather than having the culture explained to you in a book or classroom in relation to what you already know. This is how our boys were socialized in the French school culture. This is how many people are raised not only bilingually, but also biculturally, and increasingly so in our multicultural world. I myself am—to a certain level—raised biculturally, because I was raised in a strong Christian family in a secular country. I imbibed the values, ethos, and Christian worldview at home while I learned a secular outlook on life by being socialized in a secular (though nominally Christian) school among secular friends. This is why I can often move with relative ease from looking at certain realities from a Christian perspective to looking at them from a secular perspective. In certain areas of my life, the secular perspective is even more influential than I would like it to be, even though I see myself first and foremost as a Christian.

The possibility of learning a second first culture is one more sign that it is not true that we can never understand another cultural or religious perspective: certain people can actually look at reality from different cultural perspectives and always as relative insiders. They can therefore also compare the value and validity of these perspectives. Conversion from one cultural or religious perspective to another often follows a longer period in which the person concerned is engaged in an internal dialogue in which that person moves back and forth between different perspectives, unable to decide which is most convincing until a decision is made and a new identity is embraced.[21] This is one reason why those who have grown up in a particular culture after conversion make the best witnesses to Christ in that culture: they know what life and the world looks like for insiders and they know what difference Christ makes in terms insiders can understand.

Knowing another language or another culture as a second first language is relatively rare. It is often a gift you receive by growing up in a certain multicultural or multireligious context or family. Or it is an inheritance that will

---

[21]Renford Bambrough, "Fools and Heretics," *Royal Institute of Philosophy Supplement* 28 (1990): 244.

remain with a convert who has come to Christ from another religious background. Yet, even if you enter a culture as an outsider or a guest, you do not need to keep speaking the language simply as a second language, translating your own language continually in the language of your guest community. When you live in a host community for a longer period, you may start speaking the foreign language without thinking in terms of your mother tongue. You increasingly use the vocabulary on its own terms and become aware of the differences sometimes unconsciously, sometimes consciously: as parents, we became well aware that the French *maître* had a different role than the *meester* at home. We also came to understand the Central African culture in which we worked more and more from the inside. Behaviors and beliefs that were strange and even illogical or ridiculous at first gradually became insightful and significant when understood in relation to the inner structures of that culture and in relation to the social realities that needed addressing. By itself, this is an important rule when interpreting other cultures: as long as beliefs and practices appear ridiculous, you will not have understood them. Insiders believe these things and behave this way because it makes sense to them. This does not mean that you always need to agree with such ideas, but it does mean that you can only start to disagree legitimately after you have understood why these ideas and practices makes sense to those who hold them.

4

GOD'S PRESENCE AND TRUTH
IN THE WORLD OF RELIGIONS

4.1 THEOLOGY OF RELIGIONS AND INTERFAITH APOLOGETIC DIALOGUE

Is God present in other religious traditions and, if so, how? The answer to this question will significantly shape proposals for how to engage in interreligious dialogue, witness, and apologetics. On the one extreme we have the position of Karl Barth, who has a radically critical understanding of all human religion. Though his position is more complex than often presented, he is known for his thesis that all human religion is idolatry and a self-righteous effort to reconcile ourselves with God rather than depend on God's grace in Christ.[1] If this is the case, there is of course little to no scope to engage in a form of apologetic dialogue which tries to build bridges to religious truths that may be found in other religious traditions. At the other extreme, the Indian pluralist theologian Stanley Samartha argues that each religious tradition presents its own symbolic expression of the shared divine mystery beyond human grasp and that no religious tradition can claim superiority over others.[2] This position can be visualized with the well-known image of the blind men touching the elephant. Each of the blind men tells a different story about the elephant depending on the parts of the elephant they touch, but these perspectives are all equally true and equally partial. If this is the case, apologetic witness is no longer needed because there is no uniquely valuable truth in

---

[1]Karl Barth, *Church Dogmatics*, ed. Geoffrey W. Bromiley and Thomas F. Torrance, trans. Geoffrey W. Bromiley et al. (Edinburgh: T&T Clark, 1956–1975), I/2, 17.2; Sven Ensminger, *Karl Barth's Theology as a Resource for a Christian Theology of Religions*, T&T Clark Studies in Systematic Theology 28 (New York: T&T Clark, 2014); Benno van den Toren, "Christianity as 'True Religion' According to Karl Barth's Theologia Religionum: An Intercultural Conversation with Selected Asian Christian Theologians," in *Asia Journal Theology* 35 (2021): 155-70.
[2]Stanley J. Samartha, "The Cross and the Rainbow: Christ in a Multireligious Culture," in *The Myth of Christian Uniqueness*, ed. John Hick and Paul F. Knitter (London: SCM Press, 1988), 69-88.

the Christian faith that needs to be shared with those who belong to other religious communities.

The question concerning God's presence in the world of religions is central to the theology of religions. Religions can be studied from different perspectives, for example, with the help of historical investigation, sociological analysis, or ritual studies. Theological analysis asks how the world of religions relates to God. The theology of religions asks a range of questions, such as whether those who have never heard about Christ can be saved or whether Christians can and should invest themselves with other religionists for the common good. With respect to interfaith apologetic dialogue, the relevant questions concern how far God can be known through other religious traditions and how he works through these. Where is God? What is merely human? What might even be demonic?

The theology of religion speaks about the world of religions in general. In line with our conviction that human knowledge is always culturally embodied (chap. 3) we believe that it is not possible to develop a theology of religion from a neutral position apart from any religious commitment. All positions worth entertaining are committed and those that claim to be neutral have their own hidden theological presuppositions about the value of religions. Many secular academic approaches will, for example, presuppose that religious commitment is a private affair and cannot be critically judged. The pluralist position of Samartha is based on a metaphysical understanding of the divine which resembles Advaita Hinduism.[3] Contrary to his claim, it is not religiously neutral. In this chapter, we develop an explicitly Christian theology of religions, in the awareness that a theology of religions will itself be part of the apologetic exchange between the religions. Islam, Hinduism, Buddhism, and other religious traditions all have their own understandings of religious plurality. We need to understand how our conversation partners understand the reality of religious pluralism, which becomes of course a tangible and sometimes pressing theme for critical dialogue itself. The fact that this pluralism can be interpreted in radically different ways does not mean that it is not possible to critically discuss the value of such approaches: If they do claim to be based on some form of revelation or enlightenment, does this have sufficient warrant? Are they consistent? Can they do justice to the complex reality of religious plurality or does one need to close one's eyes to this reality in order to maintain the view one wants to impose?

In the next section, we will argue for a trinitarian theology of religion (§4.2), because a Christian understanding of religious pluralism should be shaped by

---

[3]Samartha, "Cross and the Rainbow," 75-76.

a Christian understanding of how God relates to this world as Father (§4.3), Son (§4.4), and Spirit (§4.5). We will subsequently explore how this understanding of God's threefold relationship with the world of religions allows for both commitment and openness—commitment to the central message of salvation in Christ and openness to learning from others and growing through our engagement with them (§4.6).

In the earlier chapters of this study, we have purposely used the term *religion* without a clear definition. The term religion is notoriously hard to define.[4] We will come back to this question in the chapter in which we explore how far secular worldviews can be understood as religions or quasi-religions (§13.1). For now, it is sufficient to work with an intuitive understanding of the notion of religion with which most of us operate. This intuitive understanding can be based on what the philosopher Ludwig Wittgenstein called the "family-resemblance" between what we call religions,[5] even if no single feature is decisive and present among all. It might equally be based on a normative understanding of religion which is used in a particular religious tradition (in our case Christianity) and under which we group different phenomena that sufficiently resemble the ideal.[6] Both approaches work for the purpose of the chapter and of this study.

If there is no such thing as a clearly defined "religion," this has implications for the enterprise of a theology of religions. All religions have unique characteristics. Different religions also raise different theological issues. We do therefore not only need a general theology of religions, as developed in this chapter. We also need a theological analysis of particular religions.[7] In the chapters on different religions and quasi-religions discussed in the second part of the book, we will also consider specific theological questions raised by, for example, primal religions, Islam, and secularism.

4.2 A TRINITARIAN THEOLOGY OF RELIGIONS

Christians believe that the God of the universe is revealed most clearly in Jesus Christ. Guided by the Holy Spirit, the church has taken centuries to work out what this meant for the understanding of God and concluded

---

[4]Christoph Auffarth and Hubert Moher, "Religion," in *The Brill Dictionary of Religion*, ed. Kocku von Stuckrad, trans. Robert R. Barr III (Leiden: Brill, 2006), 1607-19.

[5]Ludwig Wittgenstein, *Philosophical Investigations: The German Text with a Revised English Translation*, trans. G. E. M. Anscombe, 3rd ed. (Malden, MA: Blackwell Publishers, 2001), secs. 66, 67.

[6]Benno van den Toren, "Religion," in *Evangelical Dictionary of Theology*, ed. Daniel J. Treier and Walter A. Elwell, 3rd ed. (Grand Rapids, MI: Baker Academic, 2017), 736-37.

[7]Veli-Matti Kärkkäinen, *An Introduction to the Theology of Religions: Biblical, Historical, and Contemporary Perspectives* (Downers Grove, IL: InterVarsity Press, 2003), 21.

that this God can only be adequately spoken of as three-in-one, as Father, Son, and Spirit, yet one God. Though the theological concept of Trinity was only developed in the course of this debate, the reality was not new. This was the God the New Testament writers had encountered, even though they expressed this in language that was more appropriate to the context of the first generation of believers.[8] This central Christian under-standing of God that received particular attention in the early church will need to be expressed anew, in new language, every time it meets new thought worlds.[9]

According to the doctrine of the Trinity, God relates to humanity and the world in three different but related manners: as the Father who creates and cares, as the Son who redeems and reconciles, and as the Spirit who recreates and guides. This has implications for all central Christian doctrines and prac-tices that have a trinitarian structure, such as theological anthropology,[10] the nature of mission,[11] or the practice of prayer.[12]

Looking at the theology of religions from a trinitarian perspective, it becomes apparent that a number of theological approaches to religious diver-sity are mainly developed by focusing on the Son, on God's unique self-giving in Christ. As visible in the position of Karl Barth, this would normally lead to a negative appreciation of other religions.[13] Other approaches place a greater stress on the Creator who can be universally known through creation. According to the Nigerian theologian Bolaji Idowu, the creator is equally known by Africa's three great monotheisms of Christianity, Islam, and Afri-can Traditional Religions.[14] The growing attention to pneumatology in the second half of the twentieth century has also influenced the theology of reli-gions, where theologians from different backgrounds have argued that we

---

[8]See Richard Bauckham, *God Crucified: Monotheism and Christology in the New Testament* (Grand Rapids, MI: Eerdmans, 1999); Max Turner, *The Holy Spirit and Spiritual Gifts: Then and Now* (Carlisle, UK: Paternoster, 1996), 169-80.

[9]E.g., James Henry Owino Kombo, *The Doctrine of God in African Christian Thought: The Holy Trinity, Theological Hermeneutics, and the African Intellectual Culture* (Leiden: Brill, 2007).

[10]David H. Kelsey, *Eccentric Existence: A Theological Anthropology* (Louisville, KY: Westminster John Knox Press, 2009).

[11]Lesslie Newbigin, *The Open Secret: An Introduction to the Theology of Mission* (Grand Rapids, MI: Eerdmans, 1995).

[12]Sarah Coakley, *God, Sexuality and the Self: An Essay "on the Trinity"* (Cambridge: Cambridge University Press, 2013).

[13]Barth, *CD* I/2, 17; so also Hendrik Kraemer, *Why Christianity of All Religions?*, trans. Hubert Hoskins (London: Lutterworth, 1962).

[14]Bolaji E. Idowu, *Olódùmarè: God in Yoruba Belief* (London: Longmans, 1962); Idowu, "God," in *Biblical Revelation and African Beliefs*, ed. Kwesi A. Dickson and Paul Ellingworth (London: Lut-terworth Press, 1969), 17-29.

need to be open to the Spirit's activity outside the church and also in the world of religions.[15]

If God is a trinitarian God, then each of these three perspectives presents an important contribution to the theology of religion, but each would remain narrow and reductive. In line with the general revival of interest in trinitarian theology, a number of theologians have begun exploring trinitarian approaches to the theology of religions (and we join this exploration).[16] A trinitarian theology of religions allows for a nuanced approach that combines a focus on the uniqueness of God's revelatory and redemptive action in the history of Jesus of Nazareth with an openness to various ways in which God as Creator and Spirit may be present in the world of religions.

A trinitarian theology of religions will also have an apologetic value. Religious pluralists and secularists often see religious diversity as an argument for the idea that all religions must be equally right or equally wrong. It is, however, not the case that only the (theological) pluralist positions or agnostic positions make sense of (the social phenomenon of) religious pluralism. Relativism or pluralism is not a necessary consequence of a plurality of opinions. Whether this is the case will depend on the confidence one has in one's own position and with regards to Christianity it will depend on the reasons one has for confidence in the God we have come to know through Christ. Whether a plurality of views will necessarily lead to pluralism will furthermore depend on the question of whether there is an adequate explanation of such a plurality of opinions.[17] A Christian theology of religions has its own explanation of religious plurality. A trinitarian understanding of religions can make sense of the pervasive religiousness across many cultures, of the existence of both commonalities and differences across religious traditions, and of the fact that human religion can be a place of lofty aspirations and profound corruption, of truth and error, of beauty and ugliness, and of blessing and curse.

---

[15]George Khodr, "Christianity in a Pluralist World: The Economy of the Holy Spirit," in *Living Faiths and the Ecumenical Movement*, ed. Stanley J. Samartha (Geneva: World Council of Churches, 1971), 131-42; Clark H. Pinnock, *Flame of Love: A Theology of the Holy Spirit* (Downers Grove, IL: IVP Academic, 1996); Amos Yong, *Beyond the Impasse: Toward a Pneumatological Theology of Religions* (Carlisle, UK: Paternoster Press, 2003); cf. Benno van den Toren, "The Relationship between Christ and the Spirit in a Christian Theology of Religions," *Missiology: An International Review* 40, no. 3 (2012): 263-80.

[16]Veli-Matti Kärkkäinen, *Trinity and Religious Pluralism: The Doctrine of the Trinity in Christian Theology of Religions* (Aldershot, UK: Ashgate, 2004); Gerald R. McDermott and Harold A. Netland, *A Trinitarian Theology of Religions: An Evangelical Proposal* (Oxford: Oxford University Press, 2014).

[17]Paul J. Griffiths, *Problems of Religious Diversity* (Malden, MA: Blackwell Publishers, 2001), 79-80.

Following Jerome Gellman,[18] Mark Heim argues that a Christian theology of religions is in fact confirmed by a greater range of religious experience across the different traditions than the "pluralist hypothesis."[19] According to the pluralist, most religious opinions are mistaken. All religionists, who believe in order to experience the divine in more defined ways, are supposed to be wrong. A Christian theology of religions can make sense of a much wider range of religious experience. As we will see below, a trinitarian perspective on religious pluralism will not only be able to respect the experience of Christians who believe that in Christ they have decisively encountered the Creator of the universe. It will also be able to respect many experiences and beliefs in other traditions because of the expectation that many people have intimations of the Creator through creation, and the Spirit may also be leading different communities in particular ways. At the same time, the world of religions is such a mixed bag of both the sublime and the depraved that a theology of religions that sanctifies all religious beliefs, experiences, and practices is hardly credible. A Christian theology of religions also allows for a much-needed criticism of the aberrations of religions, including first of all religious aberrations in the Christian community itself.

4.3 CREATOR OF ALL

According to the Christian Scriptures, the God of Israel does speak through creation, as is clear from the nature psalms (e.g., Ps 19:1-6; cf. Job 38–41; Is 40:26). According to the apostle Paul, God's "eternal power and divine nature, invisible though they are, has been understood and seen through the things he has made" (Rom 1:20). This possibility of perceiving God in creation is presupposed in Paul's famous speech on the Areopagus in Acts 17, which in Luke's history of the Acts of the Apostles functions as a model of Christian witness to the intellectuals in the Hellenistic world at that time. Paul invests in building bridges to his audience when referring to an altar "to an unknown god" (v. 23) and when he quotes philosophers and poets who are aware that "in Him we live and move and have our being" and "for we too are his offspring" (v. 28).[20]

A number of characteristics in the way Paul addresses the Athenian intellectuals reflect broader traits of how the Christian Scriptures relate to the

---

[18]Jerome I. Gellman, *Experience of God and the Rationality of Theistic Belief* (Ithaca, NY: Cornell University Press, 1997).

[19]Mark S. Heim, *The Depth of the Riches: A Trinitarian Theology of Religious Ends* (Grand Rapids, MI: Eerdmans, 2001), 37-43.

[20]John Stott, *The Message of Acts: To the Ends of the Earth*, 2nd ed., Bible Speaks Today (Leicester, UK: Inter-Varsity Press, 1991), 286-87.

surrounding world. They are crucial for understanding the value of the human relationship to God as Creator. First, Paul presupposes that his audience has a certain understanding of God, to which he can relate his message, but that this is not a type of neutral and universally available knowledge of God that can be used as the basis of a supposedly, universally valid, foundationalist apologetic argument in the style of modern Western apologetics (cf. §1.2). The understanding of God at both sides is embedded in a tradition. Paul's own understanding is embedded in the Jewish-Christian tradition. The biblical language about God's revelation in nature is set within the wider knowledge of Israel's God. The biblical authors always speak about the God they have come to know in the history of Israel's liberation from Egypt and in the person of Jesus Christ. They confess that this God is also the Creator of heaven and earth whose care is visible in the seasons.[21] The Stoic experience of God to which Paul refers is also embedded in a cultural tradition, but in a pantheistic understanding of the divine: "For we too are his offspring." The cultural embeddedness of these beliefs reflects the postmodern understanding that all human knowledge is located in traditions. Yet it does not agree with postmodern interpretations that conclude that all human ideas are therefore human constructs. Paul presupposes that these Athenian ideas are a reflection or an inkling of the God of the Bible. That is why he can use these ideas as a seed of truth and therefore a positive bridge to the gospel, even while being aware that this understanding of the divine will, at the same time, needs to be critiqued and purified. They form an apologetic bridge, but no neutral basis for a universally acceptable natural theology (see further §6.5).

A second characteristic of Paul's apologetic use is that the reference to the recognition of God among his hearers can be combined with a profound criticism. In an appropriate desire to look for what is good in different religious traditions, it is easy to forget that religions also have darker sides. Religions can be used to oppress and manipulate[22]; religions are not only places that reveal how people have invested themselves in their quest for God, but they are also places of idolatry. Upon his arrival in Athens, Paul "was deeply distressed that the city was full of idols" (v. 16). In this respect it is important to note that a number of theologians most aware of the darker sides of human religions, such as Karl Barth and Hendrik Kraemer, have stressed that the Christian tradition as a human religious enterprise is not at all

---

[21]Gerrit C. Berkouwer, *General Revelation*, Studies in Dogmatics (Grand Rapids, MI: Eerdmans, 1955), 122-34, 318.

[22]Vinoth Ramachandra, *Faiths in Conflict? Christian Integrity in a Multicultural World* (Leicester, UK: Inter-Varsity Press, 2000), 116.

exempt from such distortions. It can equally be a place of idolatrous practices, of self-justification, and of the abuse of religion for one's own interests
and to justify oppression.[23]

Paul can partly relate to the internal criticism of religions often going on in
the religions themselves. Some Greek philosophers would agree that "the God
who made the world and everything in it, he who is Lord of heaven and earth,
does not live in shrines made by human hands, nor is he served by human
hands, as though he needed anything, since he himself gives to all mortals life
and breath and all things" (vv. 24-25). At the same time, the full critical perspective is only revealed in Jesus Christ, through whom God will judge the
world (v. 31). Erroneous and corrupt religious practices and misconceptions
about the divine are therefore the result of a complex combination of "ignorance" (v. 30) and of unrighteous suppression of the truth (Rom 1:18) of which
people will need to "repent" (Acts 17:30). In individual cases, we may not be
able to work out how much is ignorance and how much is a conscious or
unconscious evasion of the truth. The notion of "self-deception" may be an
appropriate way to describe the dynamics of religious experience that Paul
describes in Romans. Self-deception is a philosophical conundrum: How can
someone be both the deceiver and deceived? Yet, self-deception is a reality. In
the world of religion, the application of the notion of self-deception has an
extra complication—religious traditions are handed down in communities
in which people's role in the web of deceiving and being deceived can
vary significantly.

The refence to the resurrection of Christ at the end of Paul's speech points
out that a theology of religions focusing on a shared knowledge of the Creator
among the religions is not enough. It is unable to do justice to the varied ways
in which knowledge of the Creator is in fact distorted in all religious traditions.
It does not take seriously that religions and human religiosity itself are in need
of redemption and a Redeemer.

4.4 THE FINALITY OF CHRIST

Modern Western apologetics invested much energy in finding a universally
accessible or acceptable foundation on which the Christian faith could be
based. These apologists supposed that the Christian faith could only have
universal value and be acceptable to all rational human persons if such a universal foundation could be found (§1.2). However, the universality of the

---

[23]Barth, *CD* I/2, 300; Hendrik Kraemer, *Why Christianity of All Religions?*, trans. Hubert Hoskins.
(London: Lutterworth, 1962), 77, 89.

Christian faith is not based on the way we gain knowledge of this reality, but rather on the nature of the events at the origin of the Christian message and on the nature of the truth of the Christian faith: the God whom Christians have come to know in this particular history of Jesus of Nazareth is the God of the entire universe, and salvation in Christ is offered to all humanity.

Furthermore, God's revelation in Jesus Christ is not only universally valid; it is also *final* in the sense that it cannot be surpassed by any other revelation before the final judgment and the complete establishment of the new creation. As Christians, we do not expect that we can encounter a greater revelation elsewhere because of the finality of what we have received in Christ. As with the universality of the Christian faith, this finality is not related to a specific way we have come to know Christ—as if the quality of our religious experience is far superior to other religious experiences. Other religious traditions have ascetics and mystics who invest years of meditation in order to deepen their experience of the divine—practices that may well be more impressive than comparable Christian practices. The finality of what we have received in Christ is not based on the superiority of the human quality of our knowledge; it is based on the nature of what is revealed.

There are at least two reasons for this. First, Jesus of Nazareth is more than a prophet who could be surpassed by a more complete prophetic revelation. Jesus is the Son of God incarnate in whom we encounter Godself. He is therefore also much more than a religious genius or mystic who had a supreme experience of enlightenment or God. Such an experience could still be surpassed or at least be matched by other such experiences of human mystics who are equally well placed and well prepared. In Jesus, we encounter Godself. According to Lesslie Newbigin, it is as if we are discussing together what a person is like and amidst our contradictory views, this person himself enters the room.[24] From that moment on, the situation changes radically. We are no longer speculating about an absent person, but we will try to relate to this person to discover what he is like. In this respect, it is also important to recognize that Jesus Christ as God incarnate is much more than an *avatar* as we encounter in Hinduism.[25] An avatar is merely an appearance of a god. As such an avatar only shows what this god intends to do in this time and place, not necessarily what this god is like. Furthermore, there can be many avatars, even multiple avatars of the same god, such as Vishnu or Shiva. Yet in the

---

[24]Lesslie Newbigin, *Proper Confidence: Faith, Doubt, and Certainty in Christian Discipleship* (Grand Rapids, MI: Eerdmans, 1995), 11.

[25]Vinoth Ramachandra, *The Recovery of Mission: Beyond the Pluralist Paradigm* (Grand Rapids, MI: Eerdmans, 1997), 240-44.

incarnation, God did not merely appear in human form, as the God of Israel also did in the appearance to Abraham (Gen 18). In the incarnation, the Son of God took on human nature and completely identified with it. As such it is a one-off and nonrepeatable. It seems to us that it belongs to the essential characteristics of human existence (at least according to the Christian faith) that we only exist once and that we cannot redo our lives, as much as we sometimes would want to. If the Son of God as a human being could have repeated his human existence, he would not have *become* a human being like us, he would merely have appeared in the outward form of a human being.

The second reason this revelation of God in Christ is final is that it inaugurates the end times. The cross and resurrection of Christ are in technical terms *eschatological* events. Christ's resurrection is not merely a resuscitation of a dead person, coming back to life. The risen Christ enters a new form of existence; he is the firstborn of the new creation (Col 1:18; cf. 1 Cor 15:20-23). With his death and resurrection, he also acquired the gift of the Holy Spirit which according to the Old Testament, together with the resurrection (Ezek 37:1-14; Dan 12:1-4) and the new covenant (Jer 31:31-34), are the prime gifts of the end-time (Joel 2:28; cf. Ezek 37:1-14). Like the resurrection of Christ (1 Cor 15:20-23), the Holy Spirit can therefore also be called the first fruits of the new creation (*aparchē*, Rom 8:23). It is not just a promise, but a down payment (*arrabōn*, 2 Cor 1:22; 5:5; Eph 1:14) of the new creation and thereby inaugurates the kingdom of God.[26]

The finality of the Christian faith in a world of many religions is therefore not based on the quality of the Christian religious experience but on the unsurpassability of the Christ-event. This also means that our confidence in Christ is not based on our ability to compare the many different religious perspectives and then conclude that the Christian faith is superior. We can indeed compare different worldviews and ask which of these makes best sense of reality in the various ways it presents itself to us. An early example of this type of apologetics argument is from Theodore Abū Qurrah (c. 750–825) in his treatise "The Existence of God and the True Religion,"[27] and contemporary examples are given by Netland and Nash.[28] Such arguments can give an account of the relative validity of the Christian message. As such they

---

[26]Cf. Oscar Cullman, *Christ and Time: The Primitive Christian Conception of Time and History*, trans. Floyd V. Filson (Philadelphia, PA: Westminster, 1964).

[27]Thāwdhūrus Abū Qurrah, *Theodore Abū Qurrah*, trans. John C. Lamoreaux, Library of the Christian East 1 (Provo, UT: Brigham Young University Press, 2005).

[28]Harold A. Netland, *Dissonant Voices: Religious Pluralism and the Question of Truth* (Grand Rapids, MI: Eerdmans, 1991); Ronald H. Nash, *Worldviews in Conflict: Choosing Christianity in a World of Ideas* (Grand Rapids, MI: Zondervan, 1992).

do have apologetic value. But such comparative arguments can never show the finality of the Christian faith. We would after all always need to be open to the possibility of new religions or worldviews presenting themselves as superior. Or religious or philosophical traditions that have so far not been properly studied may appear to present superior insights. The idea that we would need to compare religious perspectives to choose the best option also implies that Christians who have never had the ability to do so or have never felt the need to make such a comparison would not be justified in their confidence in Christ. Confidence in Christ is, however, not based on such comparisons and not even on our grasp of this reality, but on the nature of Christ: it is because he is in himself unsurpassable that we can have confidence in him.

The fact that the Christian confidence primarily rests on who Christ is rather than in the quality of understanding or knowledge also has implications for the nature of Christian assurance. In the tradition of Western modernity, knowledge is closely linked with control. I can know what I can "grasp" or "comprehend." In that sense, we can of course never know God: God is beyond our grasp or grip. Our knowledge of God is always imperfect from our side. It is only secure in God. Consider the dialectic of Paul's understanding of the nature of his faith: "I want to know Christ and the power of his resurrection and the sharing of his sufferings. . . . Not that I have already obtained this or have reached the goal; but I press on to make it my own, *because Christ has made me his own*" (Phil 3:10-12; italics added). The relationship is certain because of who God is. It is therefore not a matter of mastery but of confidence. The same dialectic is expressed beautifully by the Swiss theologian Karl Barth:

> The dialectic [between certainty and uncertainty] still remains on our part: yet not in such a way that we are still in the grip of that dialectic; rather in such a way that the dialectic is directed and controlled from the side of the event which is God's part. For us the event of our knowledge of God shews itself to be a continual winning and losing, winning again and losing again. But through it all the will of God is there as the preponderant force, so that we are not lost in that ascending and descending movement, but held—held as by the mercy of God, but for that reason really held.[29]

From a modern epistemological perspective, this may seem unsatisfactory because it doesn't allow us control. From the perspective of certain South

---

[29]Barth, *CD* II/1, 75.

Asian religions, it may seem unsatisfactory because it doesn't promise us direct oneness with God. The Christian answer is that the nature of this knowledge as confidence reflects who we are as human beings and who God is: we cannot know from an absolute perspective, but only by indwelling the world, only by living in relationships. This is also true for our knowledge of God. Yet, in this particular relationship, we are truly held and truly known. Conversely, because this is what we are as finite created human beings, we can never know reality from an absolute divine perspective nor can we find the divine in our inner beings (cf. §.3.1). Neither these South Asian religions nor this version of Western modernity can therefore fulfill their promises.

We have argued that in the current era of salvation history, the event of the revelation of God in Christ should be considered final. Yet, this does not mean the Christian understanding of what this entails is final, as if this revelation were complete. Throughout history, Christians have continued to grow in their understanding of what this event entails and learning in dialogue with other religious traditions may well be one of the triggers for such growth. Also, we are still waiting for the full revelation of God at the second coming of Christ when his reign will be fully revealed. This is also the reason why this revelation, though final, is not undeniable. It doesn't overcome all human unbelief. It can be embraced with confidence, but it can also be denied. We live in this period between the "already" of the inauguration of the kingdom of God and the "not yet" of its complete arrival. It is precisely this intermediate period that allows for the proclamation of the gospel to the ends of the earth while people can embrace it without being forced to do so (cf. 2 Pet 3:9). Considered from another perspective, God has made Godself sufficiently known that we can embrace God's offer of love with confidence, yet God does not make Godself known so undeniably that people would be forced to accept this message. As French philosopher Blaise Pascal notes, "There is enough light for those who desire only to see, and enough darkness for those of a contrary disposition."[30] Our response in this intermediate time allows for a free response of love yet demands openness, conversion, and trust.

4.5 DISCERNING THE SPIRIT

As we indicated in the introduction, recent decades have seen—across a number of Christian theological traditions—a growing interest in the presence and

---

[30]Blaise Pascal, *Pensées*, trans. A. J. Krailsheimer (London: Penguin Books, 1995), no. 147; cf. Martin V. Nemoianu, "Pascal on Divine Hiddenness," *International Philosophical Quarterly* 55, no. 3 (2015): 325-44.

work of the Holy Spirit in the world of religions. One of the early indications of this interest is seen in the following statement of the Second Vatican Council: "For, since Christ died for all men, and since the ultimate vocation of man is in fact one and divine, we ought to believe that the Holy Spirit known in a way only to God offers to even man the possibility of being associated with the paschal mystery."[31]

The belief that the Spirit works more widely than the community of Christ believers is rooted in the universal role of the Spirit in creation (Gen 1:2, Ps 104:30). If the Holy Spirit is universally and creatively present, it seems to be arbitrary to exclude the human sphere of religion from this influence, because religion cannot be neatly separated from other areas of human culture, and because this is after all an area where the desire for God can be particularly kindled.[32]

Awareness of the Spirit will draw attention to a presence and activity of God in the world of religions that is different from the universal presence of God as Creator. As Creator, God is present as the one whose majesty, power (Rom 1: 20), and care (Acts 14:17) can be discerned in a more general way. In all areas of God's work—creation, salvation history, and in the church—God's presence as Spirit is more intimate, more particular, and more varied. The Spirit is the one who inspired each of the biblical authors in their particular way, who allows the message of the gospel to be understood in different languages and therefore in different cultural expressions (Acts 2:11), and who gives a great variety of gifts to the church (1 Cor 12). If this is so characteristic for the Spirit, we may be looking for a great variety of ways in which the third Person of the Trinity has been leading different people and different communities in their lives and search for God.[33] Those who describe their conversion to Christ from different religious backgrounds point virtually always to instances where God had been nudging them on and guiding them even before they encountered the Christian community or tradition. This presence of the Spirit may also be the best way to explain how missionaries in many cultures have found stories and symbols that, in particular ways, prepared the communities to which they were reaching for the message of Christ.[34]

---

[31]Paul VI, "Gaudium et Spes: Pastoral Constitution on the Church in the Modem World, Promulgated by His Holiness, Pope Paul VI on December 7, 1965," paragraph 22, www.vatican.va /archive/hist_councils/ii_vatican_council/documents/vat-ii_const_19651207_gaudium-et -spes_en.html.

[32]Pinnock, *Flame of Love,* 200-201.

[33]Van den Toren, "Relationship Between Christ and the Spirit," 268-69.

[34]See for a collection of such stories Don Richardson, *Eternity in Their Hearts* (Ventura, CA: Regal Books, 1981).

This then raises the question of how the activity and presence of the Spirit in other religions is related to the Great Commission, witnessing to Christ as "the way, the truth, and the life" (Jn 14:6) to all because "there is salvation in no one else" (Acts 4:12). In their justified desire to call attention to the proper role of the Spirit in the world of religions, a number of representatives of the "pneumatological turn" have shown a problematic tendency to create a distance between Christ and the Spirit.[35] A number of representatives support the Eastern Orthodox criticism of the *filioque* clause in the Western version of the Nicene Creed, which states that the Spirit proceeds "from the Father *and the Son*." According to these critics, this clause makes the Spirit too dependent on Christ. In his desire to make more space for the Spirit in the world of religions, the Eastern Orthodox theologian George Khodr argues for the "hypostatic independence" of Son and Spirit and talks about a "twofold divine economy" of Son and Spirit.[36] However, the difference between the way God works in Christ and as Spirit, cannot mean that these two persons are working on different projects. As three persons, God is still working out one plan for the salvation of the world and all three persons are perichoretically and intimately related to the work of the others.[37]

This raises a crucial question for the development of a trinitarian theology of religion. How does one find the right balance between the diversity of the three persons and their work on the one hand, and the unity of God and God's purpose for creation on the other? There is a risk here that different positions are simply guided by metaphysical, cultural, or psychological preferences for either a greater unity or a greater diversity. In thinking about this tension, the theologically most responsible way seems to take the history of salvation as the starting point. As expressed in Karl Rahner's principle, "The 'economic' Trinity is the 'immanent' Trinity."[38] We have come to know about God as Trinity not through metaphysical speculation, but because this is how we encounter God's self-revelation in history. In this salvation history, we see an intricate relationship between all three divine persons. The Son came to redeem creation and bring it to its destiny (Col 1:15-20). In salvation history,

---

[35] Amos Yong, "The Turn to Pneumatology in Christian Theology of Religions: Conduit or Detour?," *Journal of Ecumenical Studies* 35, nos. 3–4 (1998): 437-54.

[36] George Khodr, "An Orthodox Perspective on Inter-Religious Dialogue," *Current Dialogue* 19, no. 1 (1991): 25; Khodr, "Christianity in a Pluralist World: The Economy of the Holy Spirit," in *Living Faiths and the Ecumenical Movement*, ed. Stanley J. Samartha (Geneva: World Council of Churches, 1971), 136.

[37] Van den Toren, "Relationship Between Christ and the Spirit," 270-72.

[38] Karl Rahner, *The Trinity*, trans. Joseph Donceel, Milestones in Catholic Theology (New York: Crossroad Publishing, 2005), 22.

the Spirit cannot be subordinated to the Son, as some interpretations of the *filioque* might suggest. Before the Spirit was given by the Son at Pentecost, the Son himself was born through the power of the Spirit and started his ministry in the power of the Spirit (Lk 1:35; 3:22). There is a similar mutuality in their work for the salvation of the world. Western Roman Catholicism and Protestantism has generally stressed that the Spirit always points to Christ and leads to Christ. Yet, the Eastern Orthodox tradition and more recently the Pentecostal tradition have rightly pointed out that in an important sense Christ's work was aimed at the gift of the Spirit. After Christ's death on the cross, the Spirit could be given in view of the redemption of humanity as the "first fruits" of the renewal of creation (1 Cor 15:20; cf. Rom 8:23; Col 1:18). In this respect the Spirit is as much the goal of the work of Christ.[39] At the same time, and here the direction reverses again, it is the desire of the one God "to gather up all things in him [Christ], things in heaven and on earth" (Eph 1:10). This Pauline theme of the *anakephalaiōsis* (gathering up under one head) would play a crucial role in the later theology of the church father Irenaeus of Lyons, who is important for the development of a theology in which Christ and creation were held closely together.[40]

If the Spirit is at work in the world of religions, the discernment of the Spirit (and other spirits) becomes a crucial part of both mission in general[41] and also of apologetic dialogue and witness. Where can we discern the Spirit at work? Where do we discern truths uncovered and desires kindled that can be used as bridges? Or where do we see the truth of God blatantly suppressed or subtly distorted? Kirsteen Kim helpfully proposes four criteria for discerning the Holy Spirit's presence, all drawn from biblical references to the work of the Spirit: (1) The ecclesial criterion of the confessions of Christ as Lord (1 Cor 12:3); (2) the ethical criterion of evidence of the fruit of the Spirit such as love, joy, and peace (Gal 5:22); (3) the charismatic criterion of the practice of the gifts of the Spirit (1 Cor 12:4-11); (4) the liberational criterion of the presence of liberating activities in line with Jesus' proclamation of the good news to the poor (Lk 4:16-21).[42] Looking at signs of the presence of the Spirit in the New

---

[39]Cf. Vladimir Lossky, *The Mystical Theology of the Eastern Church* (London: James Clark &. Co., 1957), 159; Frank D. Macchia, *Baptized in the Spirit: A Global Pentecostal Theology* (Grand Rapids, MI: Zondervan, 2006).

[40]Irenaeus of Lyons. *Against the Heresies*, ed. Matthew C. Steenberg and Michael Slusser, trans. Dominic J. Unger and John J. Dillon (New York: Paulist Press, 1992), bk. III, 16, 6.

[41]Kirsteen Kim, "Discerning the Spirit: The First Act of Mission," *Norsk Tidsskrift for Misjonsvitenskap* 62, no. 1 (2008): 3-21. ·

[42]Kirsteen Kim, *The Holy Spirit in the World: A Global Conversation* (Maryknoll, NY: Orbis, 2007), 168.

Testament, we propose to add a fifth: an experiential criterion of intimacy with God through the Spirit, who invites us to a relationship with God as "Abba, Father" (Rom 8:15; Gal 4:6). As Kim points out, all these criteria (including the fifth we added) follow from Christ as the fundamental criterion, for he is the one who revealed God and God's plans for the world most clearly. This does not actually solve the problem that all criteria have a certain ambiguity. Even the confession of Christ is not decisive, because Jesus himself points out that confessing him as Lord is meaningless (or self-contradictory) when it is not accompanied by true obedience. All other signs have a similar ambiguity.[43] Furthermore, these criteria often point in contradictory directions: What if people invest themselves in the struggle for liberation, but do not show the fruit of the Spirit? What if they experience a certain intimacy with God (as in Sufism and Bhakti movements), but do not confess Christ as Lord, or the one who invites us to call God, "Father"? These criteria can therefore never be used as fixed rules but can be better called "guidelines."[44] A major question in the use of these guidelines will be whether a certain dynamic or movement can be discerned: Do we discern a quest in which we see the Spirit prodding people onward to Christ?[45]

If we engage in apologetic witness in a truly dialogical way, we can combine an openness to the work of the Spirit in unexpected places with a certain relaxedness about the precise value of what we discern. It is in the dialogue itself that the dynamism present in what we might at first perceive as the presence of the Spirit will present itself: Does it in fact contribute to an openness to Christ, to whom the work of the Spirit is directed as we saw above, or does it represent an expression of idolatry and self-righteousness, becoming an obstacle rather than a bridge?

If we perceive intimations of God and discern signs of the presence of the Spirit in other traditions, this may also need to lead to self-criticism. The obstacles for people coming to faith do not just rest in their own tradition, in their own sin, and in the unavoidable scandal of the cross. Sometimes people show a genuine desire for righteousness, a true humility, and a sincere desire for liberation that in fact predispose them against the Christian tradition in the concrete form that they encounter it. No Christian community

---

[43]Kim, *Holy Spirit in the World*, 168-69.

[44]As in Veli-Matti Kärkkäinen, *Spirit and Salvation*, A Constructive Christian Theology for the Pluralistic World 4 (Grand Rapids, MI: Eerdmans, 2016), 175.

[45]Benno van den Toren, "Discerning the Spirit in World Religions: The Search for Criteria," in *The Spirit Is Moving: New Pathways in Pneumatology: Studies Presented to Professor Cornelis van Der Kooi on the Occasion of His Retirement*, ed. Gijsbert van de Brink, Eveline van Staalduine-Sulman, and Maarten Wisse, Studies in Reformed Theology (Leiden: Brill, 2019), 219-21, 226-27.

fully embodies the presence of the Spirit in line with the five criteria listed above, and too often Christian communities can in fact be a counterwitness. Their worship can be stale rather than intimate, they can be self-serving rather than loving, they can be wedded to a style of life that once—and somewhere else—was liberating and holy, but that results in new forms of oppression elsewhere. If the Spirit can be discerned in other traditions, these traditions can also ask us duly critical questions. They can be windows to God that teach us new things, or old things anew about God, and lead us in new ways back to Christ.

4.6 OPENNESS, COMMITMENT, AND CONFIDENCE

When exploring the need and character of true encounter and dialogue, the question of appropriate degrees of openness and commitment is crucial. Some older views of interreligious dialogue claimed that dialogue is only possible when one is completely open to the other religious community and is therefore willing to give up all prior commitments to one's own faith.[46] More recent explorations have, however, argued that true interreligious dialogue is not possible without loyalty and commitment to one's own religious tradition. Without such loyalty, one cannot properly represent one's own community. What is more, the religious traditions of missionaries claim some unique access to truth: How can one belong to such a tradition without taking these claims seriously? More recently, theologians have argued that some degree of openness and some degree of commitment[47] or loyalty[48] are both necessary for engaging in true dialogue, without being able to spell out beforehand what balance between openness and commitment is appropriate.[49] How the two are understood will differ from one religious tradition to another, and within religious traditions. The understanding of the nature of appropriate commitment and openness will be different between, for example, a Hindu in the *Advaita* tradition and an orthodox Sunnite Muslim. It will therefore itself need to be subject to interreligious exchange. It will also need to be questioned in interreligious apologetic dialogue: What is the basis for your commitment and for your openness? Is it warranted?

---

[46]E.g., Langdon Gilkey, "Plurality and Its Theological Implications," in *The Myth of Christian Uniqueness*, ed. John Hick and Paul Knitter (London: SCM Press, 1988), 48.

[47]Catherine Cornille, *The Im-Possibility of Interreligious Dialogue* (New York: The Crossroad Publishing Company, 2008), 59-94.

[48]Volker Küster, "Who, with Whom, about What? Exploring the Landscape of Inter-Religious Dialogue," *Exchange* 33, no. 1 (2004): 92.

[49]Marianne Moyaert, *Fragile Identities: Towards a Theology of Interreligious Hospitality* (New York: Rodopi, 2011), 277.

The Christian understanding of commitment may easily be misunderstood in the West, which currently shows a strong tendency to privatize religious commitments. In the late-modern West, religious commitment may even have become a matter of taste similar to "I prefer vanilla milkshakes," or a question of epistemological loyalty similar to statements such as "I support Ajax as my favorite soccer team."[50] For Christians and many other religious people, this approach makes religion one of the many commodities in our consumer culture. This is therefore not the right way to understand religious difference. Some theological pluralists relativize religions, rather, because of the nature of the divine as unknowable mystery. So the Sri Lankan pluralist theologian can compare religious preference and commitment to a child claiming, "My father is the best in the world."[51] For Christians and many other religionists, however, religious beliefs are not merely a matter of preference; people can be actually wrong about them.[52]

In this respect, religious diversity is more like difference in political opinion or on how to solve social problems: we cannot come up with a definitive argument about the best way to diminish the percentage of school dropouts, for example. Our conclusions may be deeply influenced by ideological biases and by our own social location. Yet, that does not mean these are not issues of truth and error, right and wrong. Politicians and educationalists would definitely debate these issues, supposing that we can and need to carefully reflect on how to adjudicate them.

The difference of opinion is not only about the best way to attain a certain objective. Many political and economic differences go further and also imply a vision of what type of society we should strive for, and what type of society we can realistically hope for. Should we, for example, foster freedom of choice above equality, or should we foster equality even if that means that certain freedoms need to be restrained? Religious choices similarly concern questions of value and even more of ultimate value. They are not conceived as mere preferences ("I prefer this version of the good life above alternatives") but as moral choices ("This is what makes life truly good for everyone"). And they are the type of choices about which we argue.

---

[50]Cf. Miroslav Volf and Matthew Croasmun, *For the Life of the World: Theology That Makes a Difference* (Grand Rapids, MI: Brazos Press, 2019), 25; Tenzin Gyatso [The 14th Dalai lama], "The Bodghaya Interviews," in *Christianity through Non-Christian Eyes*, ed. Paul J. Griffiths (Maryknoll, NY: Orbis Books, 2004), 167.

[51]Wesley S. Ariarajah, *The Bible and People of Other Faiths*. Risk Book Series 26 (Geneva: World Council of Churches, 1985), 21-27.

[52]Griffiths, *Problems of Religious Diversity*, 81-89.

From a Christian perspective, we need to include one further step. We believe that the truth-claim inherent in the Christian faith is not simply a choice we make after considering as honestly as possible all the alternatives of which we are currently aware on the basis of the best evidence we currently have. As argued earlier in this chapter, Christians believe that Christ is God's final self-revelation and decisive inauguration of the kingdom. This is not simply a choice of the best option available, but an acceptance of the decisive revelation of God's plan for this world and our lives that—if true—cannot be surpassed before the final establishment of the kingdom of God. Our relationship to Christ is not limited to commitment and loyalty, but it is a matter of confidence. The difference relates to how we see ourselves as subjects of religious knowledge: it is not that we are committed to what we have to the best of our knowledge discovered, or that we are loyal to the community to which we belong. We are confident that God has decisively spoken here. It is not a knowledge we have acquired, but a knowledge gratefully received.

Within a broader trinitarian theology of religions, this confidence can be combined with a true openness to others: an openness to allow others to present themselves to us as they understand themselves. It also can be combined with an openness to learn more about God. The confidence that God has revealed Godself and salvation definitively in Jesus Christ does not mean that we have uncovered all the riches hidden in him. "For now we see in a mirror, dimly, but then we will see face to face. Now I know only in part; then I will know fully, even as I have been fully known" (1 Cor 13:12). Note the same dynamics as in Philippians 3:11 quoted earlier: "Even as I have been fully known" points to the dynamic, that our limited knowledge is secure in God who knows us fully. There is therefore plenty of opportunity to learn from fellow Christians in other cultural and religious contexts because it is only "with all the saints" that we can fully know "the breadth and length and height and depth . . . [of] the love of Christ" (Eph 3:18-19).[53] There is also a scope for learning from conversation partners in other religious traditions, because they may have acquired specific insights into the nature of God or of human existence. They acquire these insights from the general revelation of God through creation and because God has been leading these individuals or communities by his Holy Spirit who is not confined by the boundaries of the church.[54]

---

[53]Andrew F. Walls, "Ephesian Moment: At a Crossroads in Christian History," in *The Cross-Cultural Process in Christian History: Studies in the Transmission and Appropriation of Faith* (Maryknoll, NY: Orbis, 2002), 72-81.

[54]See Gerald R. McDermott, *Can Evangelicals Learn from World Religions? Jesus, Revelation and Religious Traditions* (Downers Grove, IL: InterVarsity Press, 2000); Ajith Fernando,

Yet, though our knowledge of God is *penultimate* and not complete, we are still confident that in Christ God has revealed his plans decisively and eschatologically in the incarnation, cross, and resurrection of Christ. In our learning, we are therefore constantly directed back to Christ, who is the norm for understanding and evaluating all that God is doing in this world as well as other religious traditions.[55] God's revelation in Christ is the norm, precisely because he is also the goal to which God's universal history—with this world—is moving.[56]

Such a deep confidence in the work and person of Christ may not always be present in the Christian community. It may well be that there is a hesitance to engage in deep and personal encounters with members of other religious communities because believers are worried that they will not know how to share their faith. Believers may even worry that their own faith may be too shaky and may not have any other foundation than the desire to belong to their own community. That is why the encouragement to engage in such encounters needs to go together with a deepening of the faith. This should not only be done *before* we start engaging with others. This confidence may also grow while engaging with others. Theological pluralists often suggest that a greater openness to other religions will naturally result in a diminished commitment to and confidence in the ultimacy of the Christian tradition. Interfaith encounters may, however, also provide opportunities for a growing confidence in the ultimate significance of Christ.

In encountering other religionists, we will of course discover that some of these will have their own reasons for having confidence in the finality of their own religions. This may not be true for all religious traditions. For primal religions, finality may be a foreign concept and for many postmodern spiritual seekers the idea of finality may be rather repulsive. Yet, Muslims will claim finality for Islam on the basis that Mohammed is "the seal of the Prophets" (Qur'an 33:40) and Buddhists may claim that the enlightenment received by the Buddha is in principle unsurpassable. As we have indicated, confidence in the finality of Christ does not depend on a comparison with other claims to finality, because it rests in Christ itself. Yet, such confidence can be challenged when it does encounter other claims to finality. This is why so much is at stake in interfaith encounters—conversion is a real possibility. Just as it can

---

The Christian's Attitude Toward World Religions (Wheaton, IL: Tyndale House Publishers, 1987), 75-76.

[55]Gavin D'Costa, *The Meeting of Religions and the Trinity* (Edinburgh: T&T Clark, 2000), 117-27; Kim, "Discerning the Spirit."

[56]Van den Toren, "Relationship Between Christ and the Spirit," 272-74.

be challenged, belief in the finality of Christ can also be confirmed in inter-faith encounters. This was the experience of Stanley Jones, missionary to India, in the interreligious roundtables he organized: "In every situation the trump card was Jesus Christ. The people who followed him might be spotty and inadequate, but they had hold of the spotless and adequate, or better, he had hold of them."[57]

[57]E. Stanley Jones, *A Song of Ascents: A Spiritual Autobiography* (Nashville, TN: Abingdon Press, 1968), 239-40.

5

APOLOGETICS AS ACCOUNTABLE
WITNESS TO CHRIST

5.1 The Particularity of the Foundation
of the Christian Faith

The Christian faith has no other basis than Jesus Christ: "For no one can lay
any foundation other than . . . Jesus Christ" (2 Cor 4:11). The trinitarian God
is revealed decisively in the history of Jesus of Nazareth. The particularity of
this starting point of the Christian faith is, however, deeply problematic for
Western modernity, which supposes that trustworthy knowledge can only be
based on a universally accessible or acceptable foundation. This has interest-
ing parallels with a trait in many South Asian religions that presuppose that
the divine is equally accessible to each individual soul, and salvation primarily
concerns "the relation between the individual soul and the Eternal."[1] Classic
Western Christian apologetics tried to respond to this challenge by structur-
ing their apologetics according to this universalist foundationalist epistemology. Let us recall that a foundationalist epistemology understands human
knowledge when it is properly structured after the analogy of a building: we
can be sure that we know something if it can be based on a foundation of
rational knowledge or experiences that are universally accessible. A good
apologetic argument would then be an argument that starts from the universal truths of reason or from generally accessible, empirical or religious experiences and gradually argues for Christ. This is problematic for at least three
reasons. As Karl Barth argued, this understanding of apologetics is theologically problematic because the Christian faith is not based on universally
accessible experiences or reasons, but on the self-revelation of God in the
history of Jesus Christ.[2] It is also epistemologically problematic: what we
experience as universally self-evident is in fact deeply shaped by our cultural

---

[1]Lesslie Newbigin, *The Gospel in a Pluralist Society* (Grand Rapids, MI: Eerdmans, 1989), 81.
[2]Karl Barth, *CD* II/1, 8 (1956-1975); van den Toren, *Christian Apologetics,* 77-80.

context (§1.2). It is finally problematic in the context of interreligious dialogue: what people consider the proper basis for trustworthy religious knowledge differs among different religions and often among different streams within these religions: Is it revelation, wisdom, or enlightenment, and how should each of these be understood?[3] The question concerning the proper basis for religious belief should therefore be a central theme of interreligious dialogue rather than being decided beforehand.

In the world of religions and worldviews, the Christian community presents its own understanding of how God can be known most clearly in the history of Jesus Christ. This belief does not arise from some abstract principle, a supposedly universal truth, or a conclusion drawn from a profound meditation on the nature of the universe. "The Christian affirmation about the unique status of Jesus Christ in the midst of the plurality of religions, . . . arises rather from the recognition of the divine nature expressed in actual historical existence."[4] This particular starting point of the Christian faith does not make it less objective than other forms of reasoning. Christians believe that this recognition is the only way we can do justice to the specific nature (the "objectivity") of the object of our faith. Objectivity is not given with a neutral starting point, as many modern thinkers mistakenly claim. Objectivity in the sciences is not a consequence of an a priori agreement on a universally acceptable scientific method, as early modern understandings of science presupposed. Questions concerning the validity of specific research methods are part of the scientific enterprise themselves. The objectivity of scientific research rests in its constant search to do justice to the nature of the reality it researches.[5] The method of the physicist is justified if it does justice to the reality the physicist researches, but that does not mean that physics can be the normative model of all human knowledge. Society should be researched in another way, the human psyche a different way, history a different way, and so forth. History is again done differently, and even in different fields of history one needs to carefully and creatively reflect on how a certain aspect of history can be known: industrial history is studied differently than the history of law. The history of marriage or the history of Christian mission would again demand a different approach. Moreover, it is only after one has engaged

---

[3]Cf. Keith Ward, *Religion and Revelation: A Theology of Revelation in the World's Religions* (Oxford: Clarendon Press, 1994).

[4]Kwame Bediako, "How Is Jesus Christ Lord? Aspects of an Evangelical Christian Apologetics in the Context of African Religious Pluralism," *Exchange* 25, no. 1 (1996): 38.

[5]For an application of this idea with respect to knowledge of God, see Thomas F. Torrance, *Theological Science* (London: Oxford University Press, 1969), 34-43.

in extensive study of a certain aspect of history that one can ask the question whether one has indeed found solid ground for drawing certain conclusions or whether we are simply guessing as to what has happened and how it should be understood.

Theological knowledge can similarly only be objective if it does justice to the reality of God's self-revelation in Christ. Because God has chosen to reveal Godself most clearly in the life, death, and resurrection of Christ, we can only know God properly if there are witnesses who testify to these events and if we receive this witness that has been written down and handed down through a chain of witnesses. This does not make faith an expression of mere subjective opinion. Yet, we need to keep asking ourselves critically whether we are truly encountering a reality beyond ourselves that is imposing itself on us or whether we may be merely dealing with projections of our own imaginations. The question of the trustworthiness of the testimony we hand on has of course particular relevance in a multireligious world. People in different religious traditions believe different, and in significant respects, contradictory religious claims at least initially, because of the testimony of the tradition they have received through their parents and religious teachers. For many modern and postmodern people this is itself sufficient reason to distrust such testimony.[6]

In the following section of this chapter, we will explore what the nature of the object of the Christian faith and the nature of our knowledge relationship with this object entails for Christian apologetic witness and dialogue (§5.2). In line with this, we will explore how this makes witness a crucial category in apologetic dialogue and how the validity and trustworthiness of witness can be a matter of critical discussion (§5.3). We will subsequently apply this to the Christian witness of the resurrection of Christ (§5.4). Yet, while focusing on the resurrection, this chapter will point to a characteristic of *all* Christian apologetic dialogue: Christian apologetics is always witness to Jesus Christ. At the same time, it will address a major apologetic challenge in particular contexts such as Western modernity and South Asian religions: Why do Christians believe a religion that is based on witness to a historical event rather than on some universally accessible experience? And can we confidently entrust ourselves to the human witness of a contingent historical event which places all our earlier perspectives on this world and on life in the balance?

---

[6]See Max Baker-Hytch, "Testimony Amidst Diversity," in *Knowledge, Belief, and God: New Insights,* ed. Matthew Benton, John Hawthorne, and Dani Rabinowitz (Oxford: Oxford University Press, 2018), 183-202.

5.2 THE NATURE OF OUR KNOWLEDGE OF GOD

The grace and scandal of the historicity of this revelation. The fact that God revealed Godself supremely in a particular place and moment in time is sometimes called "the scandal of particularity." This scandal of particularity of God's revelation in Christ, however, is directly related to the greatness of God's gift in Christ. If God and salvation cannot be found in history, this also means that there is no salvation for history and our historical existence. In Hinduism and Buddhism, our historical existence will in the end need to be discarded as illusion and a source of suffering. The resurrection of Christ shows that this God has not abandoned his creation and confirms that this is a good creation rather than an illusion. God redeems history and brings it to its fulfillment. God redeems the suffering bodily existence of Jesus of Nazareth in his resurrected existence and redeems history, humanity, and creation in the resurrection and renewal of creation at the end-time.[7]

This crucial difference between Christianity on the one hand and South Asian religions (and a significant stream of Western modernity) on the other, also relates to a different understanding of what it means to be human. As we saw, from a biblical perspective, human existence is historical and relational (§3.1). When we consider human beings apart from their historical existence in a web of relations and only look at the soul, we do not do so with a real human being, but with an empty ethereal abstraction. Both the greatness and the sinfulness of the human condition are bound up with this historical existence. This is why God's outworking of redemption also happens in history: it does not relate to free-floating souls, but to people existing in history, and in communities that are shaped by historical, cultural, and social conditions.[8] The Son of God incarnated in a specific historical situation, and the gospel continues to be preached to people and communities that are in need of redemption in their historical existence.

The nature of God's relationship to us. The way we come to know God is thus determined by who God is and how God relates to us. This realization is of crucial importance for apologetic dialogue. So often conversation partners may ask for or even demand a certain type of knowledge of God that is simply inappropriate for who this God is. Some people are deeply impressed with the trustworthiness of the knowledge presented by the natural sciences and ask for a similar knowledge of God. Such knowledge cannot be given, not because

---

[7]Vinoth Ramachandra, *The Recovery of Mission: Beyond the Pluralist Paradigm* (Grand Rapids, MI: Eerdmans, 1997), 179-264.

[8]Ramachandra, *Recovery of Mission,* 233; Ramachandra, *Faiths in Conflict? Christian Integrity in a Multicultural World* (Leicester, UK: Inter-Varsity Press, 2000), 97.

God cannot be known adequately, but because this type of knowledge does not fit who God is. God can never be put to the test in a laboratory because God is not an impersonal natural entity or process. God is the Creator of nature and relates to us as a person. Similarly, God should not primarily be sought in our deepest inner selves or through ancestral appearances because of how God, in his grace and sovereignty, decided to make Godself known.[9]

There are four related characteristics of the way we know God in Christ that are crucial for understanding the character of Christian apologetic dialogue and witness, some of which we discussed in earlier chapters. First, our knowledge of God comes through God's revelation in the history of Israel, Christ, and the church. It is therefore a knowledge we receive through witnesses who testify to these events in history (cf. §4.4).

Second, this knowledge of God is therefore also a knowledge mediated to us through a community. Because we cannot find God most clearly in our inner being but depend on God's revelation in history, we depend on a community that witnesses to these events and that embodies the meaning of this message (cf. §2.1). This is related to what Newbigin has called "the logic of election": because God's message of his salvific acts in Christ are of universal significance, God has elected and called the people of Israel and the community of the church to be witnesses to this salvation. Election is therefore not first of all a privilege for the church. It is misunderstood if it is taken to mean that God values Israel and the church above the other nations and communities. It is a calling in view of the entire world.[10]

Third, knowledge of God is always personal knowledge because God invites us into a personal relationship with Godself. That means that it does also involve us personally and that we can never consider this message in an unbiased manner. This again has to do with the nature of the offer. Would we ever expect someone to consider a marriage proposal from a neutral and distant perspective? Whether it is accepted or rejected, it always touches the person concerned deeply. This is compounded by an aspect to which we will return later. Humans are not only created for a personal relationship with God, but as sinners, they also flee from God. They are at enmity with God and afraid of this relationship. God's offer of the gospel therefore always presents itself as both grace and judgment. It is an answer to our deepest needs and longings,

[9]Karl Barth, *Church Dogmatics*, ed. Geoffrey W. Bromiley and Thomas F. Torrance, trans. Geoffrey W. Bromiley et al. (Edinburgh: T&T Clark, 1956–1975), II/1, 63-65.
[10]Newbigin, *Gospel in a Pluralist Society*, 80-88; cf. Ramachandra, *Recovery of Mission*, 229-35; Christopher J. H. Wright, *The Mission of God: Unlocking the Bible's Grand Narrative* (Downers Grove, IL: IVP Academic, 2006).

yet it also confronts us with our pain, our lostness, and sin. Accepting this message is therefore never easy and demands conversion (see further §7.2).[11]

Finally, the personal nature of this message strengthens a characteristic that is also implied in the role of witness in the Christian knowledge of God: accepting this message always demands a measure of trust. Someone who does not want to trust a person or a testimony can always find reason to do so. In that respect, accepting a testimony or the goodness or trustworthiness of a person is very different from accepting the outcome of a mathematical sum or logical derivation. It demands a level of personal judgment. One can always refrain from trusting, yet at a certain moment a lack of trust is no longer intellectually reasonable and may become morally reprehensible. Even if there are still issues that can be brought up to question the trustworthiness of the offer of love, this does not mean that—morally and intellectually—one cannot have confidence in the offer.

5.3 THE APOLOGETIC VALUE OF WITNESS OR TESTIMONY

Witness as a source of knowledge. If the nature of God's self-revelation determines how we can know God, we need to take the role of witness seriously. Some religious traditions, such as Judaism, Christianity, and Islam, have a high regard for witness because of their regard for God's actions in history or God's prophetic words transmitted through the generations. The same would be true for primal or tribal religions with a high regard for the guardians of ancestral traditions. As indicated before, South Asian religions have less regard and need for witness, as is the case with Western modernity. This has to do with an individualist focus: every individual will need to discover the truth which needs to be equally accessible to all. The historical traditions concerning the great Western thinkers, the Vedic traditions, or Gautama the Buddha are therefore considered of secondary importance: they are stories concerning truths everyone will in the end need to discover for themselves.

Western modernity adds another element to the mix. Since René Descartes, there is a strong tendency to privilege doubt over trust or belief: everything that can be doubted should be doubted in order that we may arrive at indubitable knowledge.[12] Sadly, this search for indubitable truth has only led to nihilism, to the inability to believe anything at all with conviction.[13] From a

---

[11]Os Guinness, *Fool's Talk: Recovering the Art of Christian Persuasion* (Downers Grove, IL: InterVarsity Press, 2015), 79-105; van den Toren, *Christian Apologetics*, 80-84.

[12]Lesslie Newbigin, *Proper Confidence: Faith, Doubt, and Certainty in Christian Discipleship* (Grand Rapids, MI: Eerdmans, 1995), 16-28.

[13]Newbigin, *Gospel in a Pluralist Society*, 29-44.

Christian understanding of who we are as created in the image of God, we understand why this is the case: as human beings created in the image of God, we are inescapably part of creation. We can therefore only know the world as part of creation, trusting the way we were created and starting with a fundamental trust in what we learn from the communities to which we belong (§3.1). Of course, this does not mean that we can never be mistaken. Sadly, we do inherit mistaken and even deeply distorted perspectives on reality from the communities to which we belong. We err in our efforts to understand our world and share these misunderstandings with those who trust us. Yet, we cannot deny that we depend on the people around us. Rather than pretend that we can do this alone, we should look for better ways to critically appropriate what we have received and look for communities that transmit perspectives and insights that can be trusted. Even the European Enlightenment and South Asian religions are not made up of free-floating individuals. They form communities in which people are introduced to traditions concerning who they can trust, where truth can be found, and how they can deepen their insights and epistemic practices.

It is therefore not strange that some recent developments in Western philosophy show a new appreciation for the value of witness and testimony.[14] Our entire human life is built on trust in testimony. I would not even know when or where I was born or who my parents are if not by taking it on trust. All learning starts with people telling us what the world is like. Those who will never trust others will not be able to survive and will indeed lead very meager lives. Even learning the sciences, which are supposedly based on experiments, starts with trusting our teachers who tell us what they believe the world is like. Experiments in the classroom only function as illustrations. Only after long years of initiation in the tradition of scientific research by trustworthy witnesses are some allowed to engage in their own experiments. By that time, they are thoroughly socialized in a certain outlook on the world that shapes what they will be looking for. Even the most advanced researchers will need to continue to trust the witness of their colleagues, written down in academic articles. They have to trust the witness of those who have built the complex research equipment they will be using. The most advanced science is now always done in large teams.[15]

---

[14]See, e.g., C. A. J. Coady, *Testimony: A Philosophical Study* (Oxford: Oxford University Press, 1992); Alvin Plantinga, *Warrant and Proper Function* (New York: Oxford University Press, 1993), 77-88.

[15]Alister McGrath, *The Territories of Human Reason: Science and Theology in an Age of Multiple Rationalities*, Ian Ramsey Centre Studies in Science and Religion (Oxford: Oxford University Press, 2019), 89-92.

Apologetics as witness and witness as apologetics. The crucial role of witness in the ordinary processes by which human beings learn and come to believe new things means that we cannot accept a common opposition between apologetics and witness. In one expression of this opposition, it is argued that Christians may believe in God on the basis of biblical witness, but that the apologist cannot simply witness to the truth without arguments based on general experience. Or, conversely, it is argued that because Christian faith in God is based on the Bible that we can only witness to our faith and cannot give an apologetic argument.

This contrast between witness and apologetic argument is foreign to the Christian Scriptures. Think of the four Evangelists. They are of course witnessing to what they have seen and heard when they met Christ—or what they heard from others who personally witnessed these events. But that does not stop them from giving an apology. All four Gospel writers are in their own way also apologists. Matthew argues that Jesus of Nazareth, about whom he witnesses, is indeed the fulfillment of the promises and salvation history of the Old Testament. Luke explains that his testimony is trustworthy because he has collected his stories among the eyewitnesses. In the Gospel of John, the notion of the witness is a recurring theme, as is the assurance that this witness is trustworthy and shows that Jesus is indeed the promised Christ.[16] The Gospel of Mark has been called an "apology for the cross," because it deals with the incomprehension and contempt that the message of a crucified king would inevitably encounter in the Greco-Roman world: it explains why this crucified outcast is indeed God's chosen king.[17]

Apologetic argument and witness are not opposites. Witness is a crucial part of Christian apologetics because of the nature of the Christian message. Witness can be apologetic if it makes an effort to show its trustworthiness and relevance and tries to address potential opposition and incomprehension. Witness is not apologetic if it merely presents its message with "this is what I have to share, take it or leave it," but if it willingly engages in discussions concerning its value and truthfulness. Our recurrent use of "apologetic witness" instead of simply "apologetics" or "witness" is an expression of the desire to keep the two together. Christian apologetics is inherently witness to Christ, and Christian witness to Christ is inherently apologetic, because it is presented with universal intent and with the claim that it is trustworthy and engages everyone.

---

[16]Andrew T. Lincoln, *Truth on Trial: The Lawsuit Motif in the Fourth Gospel* (Peabody, MA: Hendrickson Publishers, 2000).

[17]Robert H. Gundry, *Mark: A Commentary on His Apology for the Cross* (Grand Rapids, MI: Eerdmans, 2000).

The prima facie value of beliefs acquired through witness. The central role of witness to God's salvific actions in Christ in Christian apologetics does not entail that this witness should always be accompanied with elaborate arguments as to why we find these witnesses to be trustworthy and of ultimate importance. Witness as a source of knowledge has the characteristic that it is presented as having *prima facie* value. This Latin expression is a technical term to indicate that we take this source of knowledge "at first sight" (*prima facie*) as trustworthy, unless contrary indications present themselves, making us doubt the witnesses or this particular testimony. Even if we meet a stranger during a long trip who tells us that we should continue carefully because of a particularly bad stretch in the road, we will believe this person prima facie unless we have reason to doubt what they say, for example when that person smells of alcohol and looks particularly disturbed, or when that person tries to extract a significant sum of money for offering themselves as our guide.

Let us consider two further examples. Through my mother, I (Benno) am related to the Bulten family. When I was young, I heard that the Bultens descended from Huguenots who fled France in the seventeenth century, when Protestant Christians where persecuted. This testimony was handed down across many generations, but I had no reason to doubt this witness. I took it as prima facie true and would only doubt it if there were reasons not to believe it. This could be the case when someone would establish a genealogy that went backward, well beyond the seventeenth century, and in which no Huguenot would appear; or if a story came up that a great-granduncle had invented this tradition because of some personal interest. None of this applied. As it happens, a couple of years ago one family member did genealogical research into the Bulten family and discovered that ten generations ago a Huguenot was indeed at the origin of this branch of the family tree.

Or consider the earlier example that I take it on trust that my parents tell me that I am indeed their son. There are of course ancient legends and modern novels based on the premise that someone discovers later in life that the person they thought to be their father or mother was not. This often leads to a major identity crisis, precisely because it was taken on trust. That does not mean, however, that I should not trust my parents in this respect. It is rather unhealthy not to trust the people around us in such basic and fundamental matters, and it would make community life impossible. People can be mistaken and people sometimes consciously mislead us. Yet, trust is essential to life, even while recognizing that we may be mistaken and that we do not live in a fool-proof universe. That is why we need to critically consider who we trust while accepting the risks life necessarily involves.

5.4 THE TRUSTWORTHINESS OF THE RESURRECTION WITNESS

Within the New Testament, the resurrection is the central event that under-girds the Jesus-followers' faith. The resurrection confirmed that he was indeed "both Lord and Messiah" (Acts 2:36). Without the resurrection, Christ's claims to be the Son of God and inaugurator of the eschatological kingdom would have been refuted. Yet, through the resurrection God showed that Jesus was indeed the conqueror over sin and death. Yet, in interreligious dialogue this belief in Christ as the risen Lord will be critically questioned. Just as a call that we should follow someone who promises enlightenment or someone who claims prophethood needs to be tested, in the same way we need to critically ask whether the church's witness to the lordship of Christ as confirmed by his resurrection is warranted.

Different types of objections. Because of the prima facie value of witness as a source of knowledge, apologetic witness can simply present the Christian testimony to the resurrection of Christ and to his life-changing presence in our lives. We do not need to begin with an argument concerning the trust-worthiness of this testimony. We simply present it as prima facie evidence to who Christ is. In certain contexts, this may be enough: our hearers may trust us and their worldview or religion may not present major barriers to this belief. This may be one of the reasons why in Africa, during the modern period, the gospel was relatively easy to accept in primal religious contexts: a resurrection was not considered either impossible or irrelevant, the message of Christ responded to a number of deeply felt needs and anxieties, and missionaries represented a culture that had a high authority.

In other cultural and religious contexts, the witness to the resurrection will provoke more serious questioning. Yet, it is only after such questions are raised that they need to be addressed. This is why one cannot give a Christian apologetic for the resurrection of Christ that is universally helpful. Though the witness to the risen Christ will be part of all Christian witness, the issues that need to be addressed when arguing for the relevance and trustworthiness of this witness will vary from context to context. Though the witness to the resurrection is universally important, Western apologies for the resurrection cannot simply be distributed to other cultures because Western defenses of historicity focus on the questions Westerners (and particularly academically educated Westerners) have with regards to this witness.[18] Modern Westerners may for example ask questions related to the tension between belief in the

---

[18]Varughese John, "A Sense of History and Apologetics in a Hindu Context," *Missiology* 36, no. 2 (2008): 219-26.

resurrection and the modern scientific worldview, or modern and postmodern approaches to historical research that may not be relevant elsewhere. At the same time, Westerners might not ask other questions: How is the resurrection of someone who is not my ancestor relevant for me? How can the resurrection be religiously important if it is part of the world of *māyā* or illusion? Why should we argue about the resurrection if God allowed this prophet Jesus to die on a cross?

When the witness is not accepted as trustworthy, it can be because of one of four reasons. We have already addressed the first type of objection that dismisses witness to historical events as, in principle, religiously meaningless or a second-rate source for religious belief. This is the case for many Buddhist and Hindu thinkers just as it may be for a range of modern and postmodern Westerners. We have argued that witness is a crucial building block for human knowledge in general, and for our knowledge of God in particular, precisely because God has chosen to save humanity and the wider creation through Christ to whom the Scriptures and the Christian community bear witness (§5.2).

A second type of objection concerns the nature of the events that are relayed. Someone may not be convinced—however strong the testimony is—because what is witnessed to is considered impossible. I hear the story of a friend spotting a unicorn, but I will not believe him, however trustworthy I consider him normally, because I believe unicorns are mythical figures that do not exist in our reality. My friend must therefore be mistaken. In the same way, David Hume (1711–1776) thought that no testimony could ever be strong enough to convince him that someone rose from the dead because, the less probable an event, the stronger the testimony needed in order to be convinced. For an event that is infinitely improbable, no amount of strength of witness will ever suffice.[19] In a similar vein, Ernst Troeltsch (1865–1923) argued for the principle of analogy in historical research, according to which one can only have historical knowledge of past events that have analogies in the present.[20] According to this principle, historical knowledge of the incarnation and resurrection of Christ is in principle impossible. This would even be true if we would experience resurrections from the dead in the present, because the resurrection of Christ as the firstborn of the new creation (Rev 1:4) remains unique.

---

[19]David Hume, *Enquiries Concerning the Human Understanding and Concerning the Principles of Morals*, ed. L. A. Selby-Bigge and P. H. Nidditch, 3rd ed. (Oxford: Clarendon, 1975), 115-16.

[20]Stephen C. Evans, *The Historical Christ and the Jesus of Faith: The Incarnational Narrative as History* (Oxford: Oxford University Press, 1996), 187.

A third type of objection to the testimony of the resurrection may be that Christians who believe in the resurrection misinterpret this story. The story should be read as a myth rather than as testimony to a historical event. This is not only an objection to taking the story as testimony, but also a reinterpretation. This reinterpretation may in fact be attractive given that it allows one to salvage some meaning from the study, even if historical events are considered religiously meaningless or even if this event is considered, in principle, impossible. In this case the witnesses are not considered untrustworthy, but rather mistaken about the nature of the stories handed down.

A fourth and final type of objection to the Christian witness to the resurrection—and to witness in general—may be that people consider this witness untrustworthy. This may be because they do not trust this particular person who witnesses. Or they may believe that though generally trustworthy, the person or persons concerned do not have the credentials to testify to this particular event. As I indicated, I may not trust a person warning me about a danger ahead of me if that person looks deranged or seems to act out of self-interest. Similarly, one cannot trust the disciples' witness to the resurrection if one assumes that these people were gullible and would too easily believe in such things because they lived in primitive times. Or one can distrust the scriptural witness, because it is supposed to be vague, contradictory, and written too long after the events. Most Muslims will approach the biblical witness with suspicion because of their understanding of the corruption (*taḥrīf*) of the Jewish and Christian Scriptures,[21] a necessary corollary of the denial of the crucifixion—and therefore resurrection—according to the most common reading in the Qur'an.[22]

A number of stories have been told about how the witness to the resurrection has played a crucial role in some people's conversion to Christ.[23] Many detailed studies have been written and many debates have been held, exploring the trustworthiness of the Christian witness to the resurrection of Christ.[24] This is not the place to engage in an extensive discussion on the

---

[21]Hava Lazarus-Yafeh, "Taḥrīf," in *Encyclopaedia of Islam*, ed. P. Bearman, Th. Bianquis, C. E. Bosworth, E. van Donzel, and W. P. Heinrichs, 2nd ed. (Leiden: Brill, 2000), 111-12.

[22]Brent Neely and Peter Riddell, "Familiar Signs, Altered Concepts: Jesus, Messiah and Resurrection in Islam," in *Jesus and the Resurrection: Reflections of Christians from Islamic Contexts*, ed. David Emmanuel Singh (Oxford: Regnum Books, 2014), 43-64.

[23]E.g., Frank Morison, *Who Moved the Stone?* (New York: The Century Co., 1930).

[24]E.g., Evans, *Historical Christ*; N. T. Wright, *The Resurrection of the Son of God*, Christian Origins and the Question of God 3 (Minneapolis, MN: Fortress Press, 2003); William Lane Craig and Gerd Lüdemann, *Jesus' Resurrection: Fact or Figment?: A Debate between William Lane Craig and Gerd Lüdemann*, ed. Paul Copan and Ronald K. Tacelli (Downers Grove, IL: InterVarsity Press, 2000).

trustworthiness of these historical testimonies and their interpretation. Because of the prima facie character of testimony as a source of warranted belief, people can always propose "rebutting defeaters" or "undercutting defeaters" that intend to undermine the trustworthiness of the evidence or present other reasons why the evidence cannot be trusted.[25] These can then be counteracted by undercutters or rebutters that address these defeaters and so forth. The more people are invested in their particular opinions, the longer the debate can continue. Final agreement will often remain out of reach. What was the extent of the famine caused by Mao's great leap forward and who was responsible? Were Nehru's economic policies a blessing or a disaster? The fact that questioning the evidence can go on endlessly, does not in itself mean that one can never reasonably draw a conclusion. Sometimes conclusions simply need to be drawn, as when an editorial committee decides what does or does not end up in a history manual or when a judge or jury needs to pronounce on the culpability of a defendant.

In what follows, we want to quickly consider the first three of these objections that are of particular importance in intercultural and interreligious apologetic dialogue.

Is it even possible and significant? Whether we are convinced by certain witnesses is not only influenced by our personal stakes in the outcome, but also has to do with our broader cultural and religious worldview. What do we expect to happen? Do we think that certain events are even possible given our view of reality or our experience of what life and humans are like? Or do we consider them highly improbable, even impossible, or simply irrelevant? These concerns relate the first and second type of objections listed above.

As indicated above, the resurrection of Christ simply does not make sense or is outright impossible from certain worldview perspectives. According to an atheistic, naturalistic worldview, miracles do not happen, let alone a resurrection. According to a Hindu or Buddhist worldview, a resurrection to an incorruptible bodily existence does not make sense, because life is rather about escaping the endless rebirths in different forms of embodied existence. According to the majority of Muslims, the resurrection of Jesus or Isa does not make sense because God would never have allowed him to die in the first place.

One characteristic of testimony helps us in this respect. Testimony is almost never witness to a meaningless historical fact. I may witness to a fact to which I cannot give any meaning: "This morning on my way to work, I saw

---

[25]Plantinga, *Warrant and Proper Function*, 40-42.

a man carrying a jar of water on his head." For me this event would not hold any meaning, and those who heard about it would have no reason to tell it to others. It would simply be an oddity. With the story of the man carrying the jar of water in preparation for the Passover, it was different. It was a sign, helping the disciples to find the room wherein they should prepare their final meal with Jesus before he died (Lk 22:7-13).

Similarly, when we share the witness to the resurrection, we do not share a simple historical fact that remains an oddity. We share a story that has a deep meaning, and this meaning comes out in the way we share the story. It is a story about the Creator who has willed our created existence as a blessing and who shows faithfulness to us by conquering death. It is the story of the Son of God who came to share human suffering and thereby conquered it. It is a story that implies that our bodily existence has eternal significance. Christ inaugurates the new creation in which we will exist incorruptibly yet physically and in which the relationship with God, community, and the earth for which we are created will come to its fulfillment. Apologetic dialogue about the resurrection will therefore never be a discussion about an isolated fact which we then subsequently might give theological or religious meaning. It is an invitation to a whole new outlook on life, a whole new relationship with God, ourselves, the world, and our fellow human beings (cf. §6.3).

It is not the case that we must first make people change their worldview before they can start considering the witness of the resurrection. The two go hand in hand, though one of these may take priority in particular conversations. It is a different view of God and the world that helps us make sense of the resurrection of Christ. Yet, the cross and the resurrection of Christ is also an invitation to an entirely different outlook on life. What if these events indeed show that God is not distant from our suffering, but deeply involved? What if these stories indeed confirm an inkling and desire that this physical existence is not meaningless, but something to be cherished as having eternal significance? What if death is not the last word or not part of a long cycle that we need to escape? What if we are indeed heading for a new creation?

John Locke tells a story about a former Dutch ambassador to the king of Siam (now Thailand) that serves as an illustration for how a trustworthy witness should sometimes challenge us with regards to what we consider possible. This ambassador represented the Dutch government in this Asian kingdom, well before the advent of television and even photography. The ambassador became a friend of the king and they spent much time together in conversation. One day, the ambassador said that in the Netherlands, in the winter, it can become so cold that the water becomes hard as rock. Even the elephants would be able to walk over it. This was far beyond what the king could imagine, and he answered, "Hitherto I believed the strange things you have told me, because I took you as a sober, fair man: but now I am sure that you lie."[26] Obviously, the king was not right in letting his own imagination and experience determine what stories he could or could not trust. In this case, the consequences may not be that large, although we do not know what it did to their friendship. Christians would argue that the resurrection of Christ is well beyond what most of us would ever deem possible, but that the trustworthiness of the witnesses invites us to start thinking outside of the boxes that have so far boxed us in, and begin discovering a world that is so much larger and richer than we could so far imagine.

History or myth. Historical arguments are important in a religiously pluralist world because it is easily assumed that the stories concerning the resurrection of Christ represent an example of the formation of mythical stories as we also found around other religious leaders such as Gautama the Buddha.[27] A closer examination of the evidence shows, however, that this interpretation of the resurrection stories as myth does not do justice to the historical evidence. The genre of the New Testament documents is profoundly different from mythical texts, as C. S. Lewis—popular apologist, but by profession a literary theorist—argued in his essay "Fern-Seed and Elephants."[28] Second, the content of the stories is deeply countercultural and was in that context meant and understood as testifying to a bodily resurrection rather than an expression of a belief in the ongoing spiritual significance of a prophet or spiritual leader. For the latter belief, there was other language and imagery readily available in that cultural and religious context.[29] Finally, the short time-lapse between the purported events and the first witnesses, being within one generation, is not enough for the development of mythic traditions and radically different from the timeframe taken in other religions for the growth of mythic traditions concerning their founders.[30] The earliest written testimony extant today occupies a central place in Paul's first letter to the Corinthians, a letter from which the authorship is not seriously contested. It was written in the early half of the first century AD, just over two decades after the

---

[26]John Locke, *An Essay Concerning Human Understanding*, ed. John W. Yolton, 2 vols. (London: Dent, 1961), bk. IV, chap. 15, sec. 5; quoted in Coady, *Testimony,* 180.

[27]John Hick, "Jesus and the World Religions," in *The Myth of God Incarnate*, ed. John Hick, Twentieth Century Religious Thought (London: SCM Press, 1977), 167-84.

[28]C. S. Lewis, *Christian Reflections* (London: Fount, 1981), 191-208.

[29]Wright, *Resurrection of the Son of God*, 32-206.

[30]Peter Kreeft and Ronald K. Tacelli, *Handbook of Christian Apologetics* (Crowborough, UK: Monarch, 1995), 190-91.

events took place. In it, Paul points back to a tradition he had received himself from the first witnesses during his own visit to Jerusalem, well before his mission journeys (1 Cor 15:1).[31]

Concluding remarks. This chapter has shown us that an apologetic truth-finding dialogue about the resurrection plays itself out on at least three different levels: the level of the trustworthiness of the witness and witnesses, the level of worldview, and the level of whether witness itself is a valid and valuable category when discussing truths of ultimate significance. When engaging in such dialogue, it may not be clear at the outset where the most crucial objections lie. Often issues of worldview can, for example, present themselves through the questioning of the trustworthiness of the witness. Only gradually it becomes apparent that there is no real interest in considering the validity of this witness, because it is from the very beginning considered inadmissible for other reasons at the level of worldview. This again underlines the need for attentive listening in apologetic dialogue.

When people find the resurrection or the Christian faith in general hard to believe, this may not only come from intellectual issues but also from emotional barriers or rather from an unwillingness to believe. The leaders of the Sanhedrin did have sufficient evidence when the guards posted at the tomb of Jesus came to them and told them about the earthquake and the appearance of an angel (Mt 28:11-15). They were, however, not interested in the evidence, and they did not go to the tomb to see for themselves what happened. They were much too afraid that it might be true and did not want to believe it. Their problem was not a lack of evidence but an unwillingness to believe. When Jesus appeared to his disciples on the first Easter, Luke notes that "they still did not believe for joy" (Lk 24:41 NKJV). This unbelief did not come from a lack of evidence (they saw the risen Jesus in front of them) nor from an unwillingness to believe. It was rather caused by deep emotional pain and trauma: they were so hurt by the crucifixion that they had lost all hope and had no courage to embrace the risen Christ. It was just "too good to be true." Jesus does not scold them for their unbelief or give them more evidence, but simply allows these disciples to journey with him. He allows them time for their emotional scars, or even trauma, to heal gradually.[32] The role of such "predispositions" at the level of the will or emotion will receive particular attention in chapter seven. For now, we simply need to underline the need that true

---

[31]Cf. Gary R. Habermas and Antony Flew, *Did Jesus Rise from the Dead? The Resurrection Debate*, ed. Terry L. Miethe (San Francisco: Harper & Row, 1987), 23-24.

[32]Os Guinness, *In Two Minds: The Dilemma of Doubt and How to Resolve It* (Downers Grove, IL: InterVarsity Press, 1976), 132-44; cf. Wim Rietkerk, *If Only I Could Believe* (Carlisle, UK: Solway, 1997).

listening is aware of different levels that will play their role in the conversation, be they intellectual, emotional, relational, or at the level of the will.

An awareness of these different levels finally points us back to the importance of the Holy Spirit and of trust in apologetic dialogue and witness: the apologist is in need of the Spirit to carefully listen to and discern what the decisive issues are. Given the multiple barriers, we only engage in such conversations trusting that the Holy Spirit will be able to heal deep hurts and overcome human resistance, while using our apologetic witness simply as an aspect in the multifaceted relationship between God and our conversation partners—because that relationship matters, of course, far more than the relationship between the human conversation partners. Finally, these multiple levels of the conversation do again underline the role of trust in coming to faith. Trust is not only important when it comes to accepting witness, but even more when it comes to entrusting oneself to a God who is able to heal deep hurts and allowing this God to sort out our competing desires and needs.

6

POSSIBILITIES FOR CRITICAL INTERRELIGIOUS DIALOGUE

DURING A YEAR AS SCHOLAR-IN-RESIDENCE at Regent College, Vancouver, I (Benno) met Wonsuk (not his real name), a Buddhist from South Korea. Both of us were visiting scholars, I in theology and Wonsuk in economic history. Both of us were deeply interested in religious questions relating to the meaning of life and the nature of ultimate reality. Both of us also had a deep interest in the other's religious perspective and we ended up meeting on a weekly basis over a period of six months getting to know each other and understanding each other's religious traditions and commitment in increasing depth. In the process, we discovered how much we had in common, being both husbands and fathers, loving our families, our academic jobs, and getting to know other people and cultures.

Yet, we also discovered how profoundly our perspectives and experiences of life and the world differed. This was evident, for example, in how differently we experienced the relationships that were most dear to us: for Wonsuk, these relationships were spiritually problematic attachments and caused suffering. He felt that if he would be able to do so one day, he would need to completely detach from these relationships and leave his family. This would be a necessary step to total detachment, which would lead to liberation into *nirwana* or nothingness. From my own personal history, I was equally aware that love is a source of suffering yet believed that we were created for a loving relationship with and attachment to God and our fellow human beings. I believed that the human relationships most dear to me should not be renounced but were gifts from the God who had created me for relationship. In Christ, God has even shown that Godself accepts the suffering that can come from loss and rejection. Covenant, relationship, and love have ultimate significance and are so precious that we accept the suffering that they bring.

This experience of both deep human connections on the one hand and radically contrasting perspectives on and attitudes toward life on the other is characteristic of many long-term exchanges and friendships across deep differences in religion and worldview. In this chapter, we will think about how apologetic dialogue allows for a critical discussion concerning questions of truth across such radically different perspectives. As such, it builds on §3.3, which discussed the possibility of intercultural and interreligious *understanding*. The ability to understand a radically different perspective, however, does not necessarily imply that it is possible to judge their relative truth. It is *critical* dialogue aimed at persuasion, not by overpowering others rhetorically, emotionally, or otherwise, but by pointing to and critically considering what we have grasped of a truth beyond ourselves. Yet, this is more appropriately called persuasion because it should be done holistically, taking all dimensions of our human existence and the dialogical relationship into account.[1] In this chapter we explore how we can move beyond mutual understanding to critical consideration of what we believe to be true. In chapter seven, we will explore in more depth what it means for such dialogue to be holistic.

This chapter on interreligious and crosscultural persuasion needs to be read in parallel with chapter five, on Christian apologetics as witness to Christ. As we argued in chapter three, human perspectives on the world are deeply shaped by our communities and cultural traditions. If this is the case, one cannot understand the truth of the Christian faith from a neutral perspective, but only in terms of the perspective on the world that was shaped by the decisive events of the life, death, and resurrection of Christ. Christian apologetics is, on the one hand, always witness to Christ, a witness that is transmitted and embodied by the community shaped by these events. Yet, alternative religious traditions equally represent particular perspectives on the world that are embedded in particular cultural traditions and communities. Apologetics is therefore not only *witness* to these particular events but also *dialogue* with different perspectives.

In order to understand the structure of such dialogue, we will first look at the triangular nature of interreligious and intercultural apologetic persuasion. In line with the epistemological insights developed in chapter three, we argue that witness and dialogue always take place in a triangle of relationship with the two conversation partners as two angles of the triangle and the third angle

---

[1]Cf. Glenn G. Scorgie, "Confrontational Apologetics versus Grace-Filled Persuasion," *Perichoresis* 10, no. 1 (2012): 23-39; William Edgar, *Reasons of the Heart, Recovering Christian Persuasion* (Phillipsburg, NJ: Presbyterian and Reformed, 2012); Os Guinness, *Fool's Talk: Recovering the Art of Christian Persuasion* (Downers Grove, IL: InterVarsity Press, 2015).

the reality in which they live and yet understand so differently (§6.1). Then, we will look in greater depth into some of the profound obstacles to addressing questions of truth in interreligious dialogue (§6.2). Subsequently, we will look into three possibilities for engaging in critical dialogue between different perspectives: we will see how the truth and attractiveness of the Christian faith as a whole can function as a pull-factor (§6.3), how contradictions and tensions in alternative worldviews can function as push-factors, motivating people to explore alternatives (§6.4), and how areas of common ground can function as bridgeheads (§6.5). As in other chapters, in the course of this chapter we will illustrate the more general issues discussed with the help of one specific theme that can and should be addressed in interfaith apologetic dialogue—in this case, the theme of the human condition.

This chapter may well come closest to the type of questions and arguments that are traditionally discussed under the heading of apologetics: What type of arguments can be given for the Christian faith, and what type of argumentative bridges can be built to alternative worldviews? Yet, we want to stress again that these types of arguments cannot be understood properly in isolation from whole-life Christian witness embodied in contextual communities, while at the same time maintaining that they are a crucial dimension of such holistic witness.

6.1 THE TRIANGULAR NATURE OF INTERRELIGIOUS DIALOGUE AND PERSUASION

We argued before that though all of us experience and understand the world from a particular cultural and religious perspective, we are not entirely imprisoned in these outlooks (§3.2). These outlooks are not only screens between us and the world—they can also be windows through which we relate to the world as it is. If Christianity is a missionary religion and engages in apologetic witness, it is out of a deep conviction that in Christ we encounter God as God truly is and that the gospel shows our true condition before God and in the world, the greatness to which we are called, and the means of salvation. The value of this perspective therefore depends on its being rooted in a true encounter with God in Jesus of Nazareth, the validity of the insight it provides in the world, and our human existence, as they exist independent from and before our interpretations. This means that Christian interreligious apologetic persuasion always has a triangular structure. This corresponds to what Thomas Torrance argues with respect to what he calls "theological persuasion": "Persuasion of this kind would appear to presuppose that communication involves a triadic relation, that there is an inherent rationality in the nature of things."[2] In intercultural apologetic dialogue, we do not primarily point to the inner logic of our *perspective* on the world or to the meaningfulness of the Christian language game. We point to the inherent rationality of *reality* as revealed in Christ. Our perspectives are presented as pointers to the God we encounter in creation, in Jesus of Nazareth, and as Spirit, to the world in which we live and to the human condition we all share, inviting others to recognize this reality for themselves.

Precisely because our apologetic language points away from ourselves and witnesses to a reality beyond our language and our own understanding, crosscultural persuasion always presents opportunities for learning. We invite others to explore these same realities (Jesus of Nazareth, God, the world, the human condition) using their own perspectives. They may well open up aspects that we so far have missed.[3] It is our confidence in Christ (§4.4) that allows us to be relatively relaxed about the limitations of our own understanding.

We find examples of apologetic persuasion in Scripture:

> [Paul] entered into the synagogue [in Ephesus] and for three months spoke
> boldly, and argued persuasively about the Kingdom of God. When some stub-
> bornly refused to believe and spoke evil of the Way before the congregation,
> he left them, taking the disciples with him, and argued daily in the lecture
> Hall of Tyrannus. This continued for about two years, so that all the residents
> of Asia, both Jews and Greeks, heard the word of the Lord. (Acts 19:8-10)

Note two characteristics of Paul's practice in Ephesus. First, he took his time. He spoke daily for a period of two years—presumably for different audiences, but also because understanding a radically different outlook on life takes time. This type of communication does not sit easily with the late-modern world, where many ideas are expressed in short soundbites or in tweets of 280 characters max. Such soundbites may function as invitations. Yet, it needs to be stressed that radically different perspectives worth discovering take time to explore before people are able to value them for what they are worth.

Second, he spoke "persuasively," a word also picked up in the notion of "interreligious apologetic persuasion" in the title of this chapter. *Persuasion* points to the holistic nature of such apologetic dialogue. It needs to be holistic and address different aspects of our being, not only at the level of our minds

---

[2]Thomas F. Torrance, "Theological Persuasion," in *God and Rationality* (London: Oxford University Press, 1971), 195.

[3]Torrance, "Theological Persuasion," 196-97; cf. Edward Rommen, *Come and See: An Eastern Orthodox Perspective on Contextualization* (Pasadena, CA: William Carey Library, 2013).

but also of our desires and our will. This is needed because, as Torrance continues, "We are psychologically averse to change."[4] This is why this chapter on addressing questions of truth in interreligious and intercultural apologetic dialogue is followed by a chapter on dealing with "predispositions" or motives, on reaching the reasons of the heart (chap. 7). Persuasion needs to keep both aspects in view: on the one hand, truth, reality, and the mind, and on the other, the predispositions of the will and emotions. An appeal to the truth without addressing deeper needs and desires will be powerless and unable to move people. An appeal to emotions, desires, and fears without an appeal to truth and goodness becomes manipulative. The use of *persuasion* here is therefore only understood well if it is seen holistically, in the context of this triangular relationship in which we point to the truth of God and of God's plans for the world beyond ourselves. Otherwise, persuasion just becomes an effort to convince others of my being right and of my community, culture, and perspective claiming superiority over others.

6.2 Obstacles to Interreligious and Crosscultural Persuasion

Before we explore the possibilities for interreligious and intercultural persuasion, we need to be aware of the obstacles we face when engaging in such an enterprise. This is not simply to make us aware of the daunting nature of the task. When we have a better understanding of the way our religious and cultural perspectives have a hold over us, this will help us understand the best ways to overcome these hurdles.

The realist feel and inner coherence of the worldviews we inhabit. In chapter three, we discussed how human beings come to know within the context of a community in which they grow up and are socialized. This is how we learn to understand and explore reality, and this is also why we always come to reality from a certain perspective. When we are younger, we are most often not aware that this is a particular culturally shaped worldview. When I, for example, organize humanity in terms of caste, I will not be aware that "this is how my culture and I myself organize the world"—I will simply experience the world in this way. It will feel natural and have a high degree of realism, even if it may be very painful because I am a *Dalit*, casteless, or "out-cast" person. It is only when we start becoming aware of other perspectives on the world that we see other outlooks on the world are possible. But even then, such outlooks—for example the idea that "all people are born equal"—will in

---

[4]Torrance, "Theological Persuasion," 195.

many cases be experienced as odd, as unrealistic, because they do not correspond to the way the world self-evidently appears to us.

Furthermore, religious outlooks and worldviews are made up of many
building blocks that by and large fit together coherently in a web of beliefs and
therefore support and strengthen each other mutually. From a Western perspective, belief in caste might look deeply unjust and oppressive. But that is
because most Westerners believe that people have only one life to spare, be it
a life that ends at death or a life that prepares us for an eternal destination. If
you believe in reincarnation, this life is just one life in a continuing cycle, and
things may turn out better—or worse—in lives to come. Furthermore, if you
believe in *karma* your current privilege or suffering is not random, but a consequence of the merit or demerit collected in earlier lives. One can therefore
not engage in critical reflection on one aspect of a religious outlook on the
world without critically considering the whole that supports it and with which
it is closely interwoven.

Entanglement of worldview, lifestyle, value, and power. A further reason
why people do not easily question their overall outlook on the world is that
worldviews are closely related to value systems and an *ethos* or lifestyle.[5] If I
live in a Muslim community, my worldview tells me that Allah is the only God
and that I owe complete obedience to his will expressed in the Qur'an and
hadith. If I grow up in such a context, my value system will match the belief
system. I will value obedience, structure, and tradition much more than freedom and self-expression. My community will also embody a lifestyle that
reflects both these beliefs and values and in which I will feel at ease. These
three levels of worldview, values, and *ethos* ideally align and mutually support
each other. The following quote of the anthropologist Clifford Geertz refers
to ethos and worldview, but we can add value as a third component:

> In a religious belief and practice a group's ethos is rendered intellectually
> reasonable by being shown to represent a way of life ideally adapted to the
> actual state of affairs the worldview describes, while the worldview is ren-
> dered emotionally convincing by being presented as an image of an actual
> state of affairs particularly well-arranged to accommodate such a way of life.[6]

These different levels of religion and culture will normally support each other
if one of these is under pressure: if I am uncomfortable with elements of my

---

[5]Benno van den Toren, *Christian Apologetics as Cross-Cultural Dialogue* (London: T&T Clark, 2011),
180; cf. P. G. Hiebert, *Transforming Worldviews: An Anthropological Understanding of How People
Change* (Grand Rapids, MI: Baker Academic, 2008), 25-26.
[6]Clifford Geertz, *The Interpretation of Cultures: Selected Essays* (New York: Basic Books, 1973), 89-90.

lifestyle, I will still do my best to adapt because this lifestyle seems to be best given the way "the world is" and what I consider proper values to live by. Conversely, if I start doubting the realism of this worldview, but I feel at home with my lifestyle and I have imbibed the values (say the late-modern values of freedom and self-expression), I will be motivated to overcome my doubts and shore up my convictions so that I can continue to live the life with which I feel at ease.

Postcolonial analysis has drawn our attention to a fourth factor: the fact that power games influence what communities perceive as truth. Some religious and ideological convictions—and their corresponding values systems and lifestyles—are supported by huge power interests. In the modern world, all forms of marketing cry out both bluntly or subtly that consumption and wealth make us happy. This materialistic outlook on life has support from powerful financial interests that need us to keep consuming more and more, whether we need it or not. Many businesses have huge marketing budgets, and it is hard to compete when the church wants to ask people to reflect on spiritual issues and questions of ultimate meaning. The caste system is of course hugely advantageous for communities that have all sorts of privileges simply because they are born in upper castes. These communities have power, and have significant ideological interests, using their influence to promote the corresponding outlook on the world. As we see in India, Malaysia, or certain Arab countries, governments sometimes have significant interest in presenting one religion as the national religion. Christianity also has been promoted for Western colonial interests.

More radical postcolonial thinkers might conclude that religious truth claims are nothing but bids for power. However, we rather take it that such interests often hinder the human search for truth and limit the space to engage in open and free discussion. An awareness of these ideological interests will help us to unmask such abuse of power in order to increase the space for powers that promote an honest quest for truth, goodness, and beauty.[7]

Tensions, crises, and global flows. Because of the coherence of worldviews and the alignment of worldview, values, lifestyle, and power, critical consideration of individual issues in a religious outlook on the world will often have little to no impact. Individuals may indeed at times wonder about the caste

---

[7]Benno van den Toren, "The Significance of Postcolonial Thinking for Mission Theology," in *Interkulturelle Theologie. Zeitschrift Für Missionswissenschaft* 45, nos. 2–3 (2019): 210-28; Klaas Bom and Benno van den Toren, *Context and Catholicity in the Science and Religion Debate: Intercultural Contributions from French-Speaking Africa*; *Context and Catholicity in the Science and Religion Debate*, Theology and Mission in World Christianity 14 (Leiden: Brill, 2020), 167-69.

system, about the existence of the soul in Buddhism, about the ability of science to cure the human condition, or about certain elements in the Qur'an. Yet, these remain relatively minor issues against the massive amount of beliefs that these individuals—and certainly their communities—hold, and against a way of life with which they feel at ease.[8] Such critical questions may therefore be annoying, but it will take much more to seriously start doubting an entire way of life, let alone start looking for an alternative.

However, there is much more scope for serious questioning than this picture suggests. An older view of cultures, as communally shared homogenous outlooks on the world, has rightly been challenged by more postmodern understandings of culture. Postmodern perspectives have become sensitive to inner tensions within communities, to inner tensions or even contradictions between cultural practices,[9] and the combined existence of themes and counterthemes in worldviews.[10] Certain postmodern approaches may place too high a stress on the "bricolage" character of culture as an eclectic amalgam of unrelated elements. Some cultural outlooks are of course more eclectic than others, but most do present a certain level of integration.[11] Yet, these postmodern analyses show that this integration is never complete and that together with a search for coherence that drives cultural development, concrete cultures are always characterized by a certain level of inner tension. The modern secular Western worldview is far from coherent and is characterized by inner tensions that play out differently in diverse subcultures. The West, for example, simultaneously exports environmental awareness and attitudes that foster the reckless depletion of natural resources.

Often developments in worldviews, values, lifestyles, and power structures are not in sync, and their dynamics may result in deep tensions. This may have been happening in recent decades in Mainland China, where the free-market values that drive the economic boom are no longer in line with the inherited Maoist ideology, which also lost its credibility through the debacle of the Cultural Revolution. This creates space for change and even for conversion to radically different perspectives. Anthropologist Anthony Wallace has noted that crises in societies—sometimes through outside influences, sometimes

---

[8]Benno van den Toren, "Intercultural Theology as a Three-Way Conversation: Beyond the Western Dominance of Intercultural Theology," *Exchange* 44 (2015): 181-82; cf. Michael Polanyi, *Personal Knowledge: Towards a Post-Critical Philosophy* (Chicago: University of Chicago Press, 1962), 288-94.

[9]Kathryn Tanner, *Theories of Culture: A New Agenda for Theology* (Minneapolis, MN: Fortress Press, 1997), 38-58.

[10]Hiebert, *Transforming Worldviews*, 22-23.

[11]Cf. Joel Robbins, "Can There Be Conversion Without Cultural Change?," *Mission Studies* 34, no. 1 (2017): 37-38.

through developments from within—are fertile ground for the development or introduction of religious revitalization movements.[12]

Wallace's analysis of crises leading to religious revitalization movements has been used as an analytic instrument by anthropologists and missiologists,[13] yet Richard Vokes has rightly pointed out that religious renewal and conversion do not only happen because of negative forces or in situations of crisis.[14] In our global world, people are increasingly connected with different parts of the world. The awareness of religious difference diminishes the hold of any one religion over communities and individuals (cf. §1.2). Many people nowadays share, in some way, different identities which allows for ongoing internal questioning and for a freer exploration of alternatives. This may be one of the reasons behind the insider movements, which allow their adherents to embrace Christ while remaining part of the cultural and religious communities into which they were born.[15] Having sketched the challenges that need to be overcome in order to engage in a critical consideration of alternative cultural and religious perspectives, we will use the remainder of this chapter to consider three specific ways to engage in such critical deliberation.

6.3 THE RATIONALITY AND ATTRACTIVENESS OF THE CHRISTIAN PERSPECTIVE AS A WHOLE

The need for discovery and deliberation. Certain forms of apologetics have presupposed that rational argument is only possible when starting from a universally valid common foundation. Yet as we saw, the postmodern and anthropological awareness of how culture powerfully shapes the way we understand the world has undermined this universalist foundationalist epistemology (cf. §1.2; chap. 3). Furthermore, we have also seen that isolated, critical consideration of particular cultural building blocks makes little sense, because of their entanglement with the worldviews of which they are a part. What James Orr concluded already with regard to the apologetic exchange between the Christian faith and modernist naturalism is equally true for the apologetic dialogue with other religious traditions:

> The opposition which Christianity has to encounter is no longer confined to special doctrines or points of supposed conflict with the natural sciences, . . .

---

[12]Anthony Wallace, "Revitalization Movements," *American Anthropologist* 58, no. 2 (1956): 264-81.
[13]Hiebert, *Transforming Worldviews*, 329-32.
[14]Richard Vokes, "Rethinking the Anthropology of Religious Change: New Perspectives on Revitalization and Conversion Movements," *Reviews in Anthropology* 36, no. 4 (2007): 329.
[15]Cf. Harley Talman, *Understanding Insider Movements: Disciples of Jesus within Diverse Religious Communities* (Pasadena, CA: William Carey Library, 2015).

but extends to the whole manner of conceiving the world, and of man's place in it, the manner of conceiving the entire system of things, natural and moral, of which it forms a part. It is no longer an opposition of detail, but of principle.[16]

Yet, this does not mean that such overall religious systems cannot be compared with regard to questions of truth. They can be, but in order to do so, we need to invite our conversation partners to explore the Christian faith as a whole, as an integrated, alternative perspective on reality. While the discussion of isolated themes may make little sense, one can compare the way Christianity, as a whole, makes sense of reality. Its ability to do so is itself a sign of its truthfulness: it is because it allows one to make sense of reality as it appears to us in its multiple dimensions and complexities that we can trust it to be a trustworthy reflection of the inherent structure of the world as it is in itself.

We need to extend the invitation to explore the Christian faith in its entirety so that our interlocutors can come to understand both the realism and attraction of this "strange new world within in the Bible."[17] People not only need to come to know this new world in order to understand its attractiveness and realism, but also in order to know that there is an alternative for the life people are currently living. For most people the way of looking at the world they are used to is the only way they know of—it is the only world there is and the only life they can conceive of. They will not even begin to consider giving this world and life up as long as they are not aware of a valid alternative.

This is the problem with what we might call forms of "battering ram" apologetics: apologetics that focus on attacking others, for example by arguing that their life is meaningless, immoral, or self-contradictory. If this is the only life people can conceive of, such battering ram apologetics will only motivate people to defend what is dear to them. Even if this world is not particularly dear to them, and even if it is experienced as shaky, they will still cling to it for all they are worth, as one will to a rickety raft if the only alternative is the open sea. Such battering ram apologetics also lead to adversarial relationships and, therefore, only diminish the chance that people become genuinely interested in the Christian faith.

This is the main reason why apologetic witness to those experiencing the world from radically different perspectives needs to allow for significant time

---

[16]James Orr, *The Christian View of God and the World: As Centering in the Incarnation*, 3rd ed. (Vancouver: Regent College Publishing, 2002), 4.

[17]Cf. Karl Barth, "The Strange New World within the Bible," in *The Word of God and the Word of Man* (New York: Harper and Brothers, 1957), 28-50.

to discover this new Christian world. They also need time to deliberate its trustworthiness and value, and to consider how it compares to their current way of relating to the world. David Hesselgrave argues that missiological reflection invests too little in understanding this process of discovery and deliberation and how to make it possible.[18] The only context in which this phase is less important may be nominally Christian communities, in which people have a general understanding of the Christian faith and can come to a decision through one decisive sermon or mass meeting. This was of course a widespread phenomenon during the evangelistic meetings of the Great Awakening, which have strongly shaped Western evangelical images of conversion. These situations are, however, rare in interreligious encounter and increasingly in the secular West. People from radically different backgrounds often need extensive time for discovery and deliberation. If people do make relatively quick decisions for Christ in such contexts, as is sometimes the case, discovery and deliberation are not less important, but happen after initial conversion. In such situations an intense period of discipling is crucial, because this becomes the moment of discovery and deliberation, when the recent converts will decide whether they will follow through on their initial decision. They may in this phase also revert to their former religion if Christianity cannot offer what was promised and apparently was not such a good idea after all.[19]

Where to focus? Though Christian witness will need to present the Christian faith as a coherent tapestry, everything can of course not be discussed at once. It is therefore worth asking which areas would require specific attention when dialoguing with a specific audience. Certain foci of the conversation may be given with a certain context, without being universally important. In certain Western academic environments, one will for example need to address the questions of science and religion, but this would not be the same in an African setting, not even in many African university settings.[20] In conversations with Muslims, one may need to address questions surrounding incarnation and Trinity, but these would not be equally important in conversation with Hindus. Hindus might on the other hand find the idea of an ultimate revelation that can be adequately captured in words deeply counterintuitive, while Muslims would have little issue with that aspect of the Christian faith.

We suggest that two clusters of themes are, however, universally important in the dialogical apologetic witness to the Christian faith. First is Jesus Christ.

---

[18]David J. Hesselgrave, *Communicating Christ Cross-Culturally: An Introduction to Missionary Communication*, 2nd ed. (Grand Rapids, MI: Zondervan, 1991), 617-20.

[19]Cf. Hiebert, *Transforming Worldviews*, 327-28.

[20]Cf. Bom and van den Toren, *Context and Catholicity*.

Jesus Christ as Savior and the embodiment of and invitation to life in its fullness is the ultimate pull-factor that is the essence of the attraction of the Christian faith. In Christ, we also encounter a fullness of life that may have been considered impossible or unreachable. Furthermore, Jesus Christ crucified and risen is the primary reality that will not fit our worldviews and religious outlooks, and will therefore invite us to consider that God is entirely different than we have imagined. This is why apologetic dialogue from a Christian perspective is always also witness to Christ.

Apologetic dialogue can often remain barren and abstract when it does not move on to Christ. There may be many triggers for apologetic exchange. We can, for example, be invited to engage publicly or personally on issues such as the existence of God, God and suffering, public morality, religion and freedom, reincarnation, religion and violence, or the possibility of one true religion. Yet, it is important to reflect how such themes might provide an occasion to introduce people to Christ, because Christ is the decisive reason why Christian have come to understand the world differently. There may be a range of reasons why we do not believe in reincarnation, but the crucial reason is that Christ's resurrection shows us that life is not an endless cycle from which we may escape in the end, but that it finds its fulfillment in the resurrection and new creation. There may be a range of reasons why we believe that God and the existence of suffering are not incompatible, but one of the most important reasons is that in Christ we discover that God has not abandoned us in our suffering. And so forth.

A second area that will always need to be addressed in the exploration of the Christian worldview and its alternatives is the range of questions related to who we are as human beings. The discussion of issues related to human nature and the human condition are important because all religions and worldviews address these—how could they be considered relevant if they did not? Furthermore, religions and worldviews differ radically in their estimation of what it means to be human. Are we for example the result of a blind evolutionary process or are we the product of God's love? Is our sense of self and individuality an illusion, or essential to who we are? Is our bodily existence a gift or a curse? A further reason why this area is so important is its existential relevance. Many apologetic questions remain fairly abstract, but these questions touch all of us at a deep level: Who am I? What is the origin of the deep joy and gratefulness I experience when I feel loved or hold my baby? Why is my life such a mess? These existential questions do directly lead to questions of salvation or liberation: What can I hope for? How can it be achieved or received? Is it resurrection, or is it *moksha* through the final liberation from the cycle of reincarnations? Is it *nirvana* or an eternal relationship with God? Do we become truly ourselves through autonomous self-expression, enlightenment, or a divine gift? This is how the questions of who we are will necessarily lead back to the questions of who Christ is.

A final reason for the apologetic value of the questions concerning who we are is that we have the reality we are discussing at hand: everyone has some experience of what it means to be human. Even though Wonsuk and I have a very different understanding of what it means to be human, we share the raw material of our own existence, in which we have so much in common, and that in many ways overlaps. People often run away from reality, preferring to live in their own "phantom worlds."[21] They can run away from God and from Christ for a long time. It is, however, much harder to run away from our own human condition and our own lives. In apologetic dialogue and witness, we should strive to create a level of openness that allows for an honest look at ourselves.

6.4 Tensions in Alternative Approaches to Life

Pull- and push-factors. Jesus Christ represents the principal pull-factor that attracts people, both because of his truth and relevance as Savior, and because he opens up for us the truth of our existence, of the world, and of God. We have stressed the role of this pull-factor, because—apart from situations of extreme crisis—people will not consider leaving where they are if they are not aware of an alternative to their current way of life and making sense of the world. Push-factors, on the other hand, motivate people to look for and explore alternative positions. Without such push-factors many people would probably never begin exploring the meaning of Christ beyond a superficial acquaintance.

Such push-factors often relate to the experience of the human condition, but can take on many different forms. They may have to do with tensions within the community, with an immediate personal or social crisis, or with existential anxiety. Issues of truth are again not the only factors that count, but they do play a significant role. I may feel that the world as I experience it is not treating me well or is not answering my deepest needs. Yet, if this is the only world I know (and therefore the "real world," for all I can see), I may not see a way out. The only option I have is to try harder or to resign to my fate. This is where the question of truth comes in. In addition to the push-factor of an existential unease or even crisis, people will need the pull-factor of the

---

[21]Van den Toren, *Christian Apologetics*, 87.

invitation to another world that is opened up in Christ. There is thus an interplay between push- and pull-factors: it is an awareness of an alternative outlook that makes people more willing to see and consider the weaknesses and
possible blindness (or even deception) in their existing view of life and the
world. Conversely, it is the awareness of such limitations that will motivate
them to explore alternatives.

Anomalies and tensions. An important category of push-factors are inner
tensions within worldviews, or alternatively, between worldviews on the one
hand and the world and life as people experience it on the other. Experiences
of the world do not always neatly fit one's outlook on the world and may even
clash with one's understanding of life. Such tensions are a sign that our understanding of the world is not true or adequate to the world in itself. In science,
these are called *anomalies*: data that do not fit existing theories. The experience of such anomalies is not only a common phenomenon in science, but
also part of our general experience in life. If the number of anomalies keeps
growing and scientific theories are increasingly unable to make sense of such
data, such theories will be put under strain. Scientists will start looking for
alternatives that make better sense of the reality they are researching. This may
even lead to a complete paradigm shift. This is similar with larger worldview
related theories. An increasing sense of discrepancy between our outlook on
the world and the world and life as they present themselves to us will lead to
what MacIntyre calls an "epistemological crisis" (cf. §3.2).[22]

Such an epistemological crisis may well run parallel to the type of crises
which, according to Wallace, form fertile ground for a revitalization movement. However, such a crisis does not automatically lead to a new perspective,
conversion, or revitalization. It may well lead to a further flight from reality,
to a choice to keep defending traditional perspectives, and a condemnation of
those who dare to venture into unknown territory. It can also be taken as an
invitation to view our own human condition with utter seriousness, and to
discover a God who does not disappoint but allows us to embrace ourselves
for what we are and our world for how it presents itself to us.

From a Christian perspective, we would expect worldviews and cultures
that try to shape life without Christ to be characterized by multiple tensions
and anomalies. Christians believe that the human sinful condition is characterized by a denial of our true being as created in the image of God. Human
existence is therefore showing signs of what Swiss theologian Emil Brunner

---

[22] Alasdair MacIntyre, "Epistemological Crises, Dramatic Narrative, and the Philosophy of Science,"
in *Paradigms and Revolutions: Appraisals and Applications of Thomas Kuhn's Philosophy of Science*,
ed. Gary Gutting (Notre Dame, IN: University of Notre Dame Press, 1980).

called "*Der Mensch im Widerspruch*" or, less fluently in English than in German, "The human being in contradiction."[23] If human beings contradict God and revolt against God, they also contradict their true beings and start living in inner contradictions. Furthermore, if human existence and human cultures are created for Christ (Col 1:16) and are intended to find their destination and fulfillment in him, missing Christ as the center and goal of human existence will inevitably lead to inner contradictions.[24]

The Christian faith and life obviously contain their own tensions. Christians, however, understand these to be of a different order. They can be paradoxes that reflect the complexity and multifaceted nature of the human condition and of our relationship to God. They can be part of the call to discipleship and need to keep learning to align our lives with our true being. Or they can be caused by the limits of our grasp of how God relates to us, possibly because our own understanding is distorted by the conceptual frameworks we have adopted from surrounding cultures—frameworks that are not adequate to understand who we are. Apologists for other religions such as Buddhism or Islam would probably respond in kind and say that these inner tensions in the Christian faith are reflections that we have not understood the human condition for what it truly is. These differences in evaluation are therefore an invitation to further apologetic dialogue.

Tensions within worldviews and between worldviews and life itself. Tensions that are important in apologetic dialogue are of two kinds. In the first place, there are tensions inherent in religions and worldviews themselves. An example would be the tension between the denial of the existence of a soul and self in Buddhism with the crucial role of reincarnation and karma. In Buddhism, one can also refer to the tension between the strong moral appeal to live compassionately, and the monist conviction that ultimate reality is beyond good and evil.[25] In Islam one can point to the tension inherent in the belief that God is absolutely one and that God is the creator (see §12.3),[26] or between the fact that Issa (Jesus) as a precursor to Mohammed is less than Mohammed as the later "seal of the prophets," but in other ways surpasses Mohammed because of his special relationship with Allah, his sinless nature,

---

[23]Emil Brunner, 1937; *Man in Revolt: A Christian Anthropology*, trans. Olive Wyon (London: Lutterworth Press, 1939.

[24]Van den Toren, "Intercultural Theology," 165-70.

[25]Cf. P. Williams, *The Unexpected Way: On Converting from Buddhism to Catholicism* (Edinburgh: T&T Clark, 2002), 40-48; Harold Netland, *Encountering Religious Pluralism: The Challenge to Christian Faith and Mission* (Downers Grove, IL: InterVarsity Press, 2001), 303-7.

[26]Cf. Imad N. Shehadeh, "The Predicament of Islamic Monotheism," *Bibliotheca Sacra* 161, no. 642 (2004): 142-62.

and role at the final judgment. In secular humanism, one can point to the deep tension between the evolutionary worldview and the belief that every human being has absolute rights to certain freedoms, to life, and to protection from the other.

Another type of tension is the tension between such worldviews and the world or life itself. With regards to Western materialism, we may point to what can be called the "paradox of hedonism": the harder we search for our own happiness, the less likely we are to achieve it.[27] In African Traditional Religions, one could point to the deep tension between religious practices that invest so much in protecting oneself from evil powers, yet in the process are not able to master them, and continue to feed the fear of and dependence on such powers. These tensions between worldview and life as we experience them are all so powerful because they relate to our human condition. The tensions *within* worldviews often have a similar origin to the tensions between worldviews and life as we experience it. Contrasting elements within worldviews that stand in tension to each other often originate from contrasting aspects of human experience. All religions and worldviews need to grapple in some way with the paradoxical nature of human existence. In the language of the seventeenth-century French scientist, philosopher, and theologian Blaise Pascal, "Man's greatness and wretchedness are so evident that the true religion must necessarily teach there is in man some great principle of greatness and some great principle of wretchedness. It must also account for such amazing contradictions."[28] It was Pascal's conviction that only the Christian faith could give an adequate account of who we are. It explains the "greatness" by referring to our creation in the image of God created for knowing him. It explains the "wretchedness" by our sin which makes us live contrary to who we are and what we are called to be. This makes Pascal's apology so personal, because these questions of truth are at the same time deeply existential. As Pascal indicated, we can try to avoid asking these questions and try to suppress them in our search for "*divertissement*" or distraction, but they cannot be always pushed aside.[29] If they are put on the table in apologetic dialogue, this can indeed be painful, but—because of our knowledge of salvation in Christ—it is ultimately freeing if it allows us to embrace our greatness while remaining realistic about our misery.

---

[27]Alister E. McGrath, *Bridge-Building: Effective Christian Apologetics* (Leicester, UK: Inter-Varsity Press, 1992), 51-58.

[28]Blaise Pascal, *Pensées*, trans. A. J. Krailsheimer (London: Penguin Books, 1995), no. 149.

[29]Cf. Thomas V. Morris, *Making Sense of It All: Pascal and the Meaning of Life* (Grand Rapids, MI: Eerdmans, 1992); Guinness, *Fool's Talk*, 93-105.

6.5 COMMON GROUND

So far, we have stressed the fact that people in other religious communities live, as it were, in a different "world": they perceive and experience the world from different perspectives. The "as it were" is important here. In the critical realist epistemology we used and defended in chapter three, different religions and worldviews represent different perspectives, but perspectives on what is—in reality—the same world. Apologetic dialogue therefore has the triangular structure we pointed out in which both interlocutors relate to the same reality (§6.1). Our perspectives on the world shape how we perceive the world. We can even withdraw from this world in phantom worlds of increasingly imaginary pictures of what we want the world to be like. Yet, we can never entirely create a world to our liking. The pictures we create are always the result of an interplay between our perspectives and the world as it appears to us.

The fact that we can never entirely walk away from this world, or from our own human condition, also means that there are always areas of common ground when two people meet. There are always shared experiences and shared convictions. However, in interreligious encounters our respective understandings of reality do not always overlap in the same place. With Muslims and many African Traditional Religionists, we may share the belief in a creator; with Hindus and Buddhists, the realization that our understanding of the world is darkened and that we need enlightenment; with secular humanists and Muslims, the conviction that every human being has equal value. Yet, though varied, and though not universally present, such shared convictions may be a valid starting point for rich conversations. There may be no convictions that all human beings have in common. And if there are such universal convictions, they are not necessarily and sufficiently rich enough to be a good starting point for apologetic conversation as a foundationalist apologetic would have it. The particular common ground we share with specific conversation partners may be much richer and much more central to their self-understanding and outlook on the world, and therefore a much better starting point for apologetic dialogue.

Common ground is of particular relevance for interreligious apologetic dialogue, because though we look at the world from different perspectives, it allows us to begin with what we have in common, often with shared experiences of what it means to be human. Though apologetic witness always includes an invitation to what is new, such an invitation can be considered more easily when it also relates to what is more familiar. Though apologetic witness inevitably presents challenges to people's lives and outlook on the world, it is important to stress that it is at a deeper level also affirmative: it affirms who we are as creatures. It is only because of this affirmation that people are also invited to conversion, repentance, and the renewal of their minds and life.

7

REACHING THE REASONS
OF THE HEART

7.1 "If It Were the Case That Christianity Were True, Would You Want to Know It?"

In *Seeking Allah, Finding Jesus*, Nabeel Qureshi shares the story of how for years he enjoyed discussing the arguments for and against Islam and Christianity. One day his friend Dave asked, "If it were the case that Christianity were true, would you want to know it?" Dave is aware that the answer is far from self-evident, for "you would have to admit to yourself that you were wrong all those years, and that's not easy. It would also mean you'd have to go back through your entire life and sought out everything you ever thought you knew about God and religion. That's tough, man."[1]

Dave's question was a turning point for Nabeel. He had been discussing Christianity and Islam for a long time, but never seriously considered the option of converting to Christ. Rather, he had discussed these questions in order to sharpen his own arguments and effectiveness as an ambassador for Islam. Pondering Dave's challenge, he at first remained confident that the best representatives of Islam sufficiently argued the corruption of Christianity and its Scripture, and that they would be able to answer all difficulties that may be raised. Yet, from then on, the tone of the conversations changed, because he realized that the truth of God should be allowed to prevail over loyalty to his family, if ever the two would appear to be in tension.[2]

The story of Nabeel shows the power of the deeper drives, attachments, and attitudes all conversation partners have in apologetic dialogue.[3] Our ability and willingness to critically consider the limitations of our current religious

---

[1] Nabeel Qureshi, *Seeking Allah, Finding Jesus: A Devout Muslim Encounters Christianity* (Grand Rapids, MI: Zondervan, 2014), 144.
[2] Qureshi, *Seeking Allah*, 145.
[3] David K. Clark, *Dialogical Apologetics: A Person-Centered Approach to Christian Defense* (Grand Rapids, MI: Baker Books, 1993), 179-204.

outlook and to truly ponder the attractiveness and value of alternatives are profoundly determined by such drives. Some of these drives are simply human, and universally present, such as the desire to remain loyal to one's family and community, as well as the sense of safety that is attached to the understanding of the world to which we are accustomed. Some of these attitudes may be influenced by the social context, such as when Christianity is loathed as the religion of the former colonizers or of new neocolonial powers. Sometimes such attitudes are provoked by the Christian communities encountered, which may appear to belong to an outdated past rather than a promising future. Sometimes attitudes are ingrained through generations of cultural socialization: for example, when Christianity is rejected out of hand because it appears blasphemous with its belief that God has a Son, when religion is considered an affair that relates us to the traditions of our ethnic community, or when religion is seen to be outdated in light of modern science.

Let us call such loyalties, attitudes, drives, and emotions *predispositions*. In this chapter, we will explore the place such predispositions fit in apologetic dialogue and witness. We will first develop a holistic understanding of both the human subject and conversion. We need to recognize the role of the will, of emotions, and of the mind, yet be aware that these cannot be neatly separated as human faculties that can be addressed separately. The human subject can only be understood as an integrated person. This also has important implications for understanding conversion (§7.2). We will subsequently explore how predispositions can be taken into account in apologetic dialogue (§7.3). This will also lead to a consideration of the place of narrative in apologetics because of the power of narrative to touch the entire person (§7.4). If we want to touch a deeper level of the emotions, desires, and commitments, that often remains hidden, the character of the apologist becomes crucial—this will be the subject of the final section of this chapter and of the first part of this book. This will lead us full circle back to the earlier consideration of embodied apologetics in chapter two: just as apologetic witness needs to be embodied in the life of the Christian community, and in real-life encounters, it also needs to become flesh and blood in the person of the witness (§7.5).

7.2 HOLISTIC APOLOGETICS

Beyond faculty psychology. Predispositions can be distinguished from *presuppositions*, which have more to do with how people look at the world. The belief that everything that happens can be explained by laws of nature may be such a presupposition, or the belief that the divine is in principle beyond all defined knowledge. However, one cannot neatly separate presuppositions as intellectual beliefs from predispositions as merely emotional or determined by the will. Attitudes are also expressions of belief, but they are beliefs which also include an evaluative dimension that makes us react positively or negatively.[4] If I feel attracted to religions or religious leaders that promise healing, that attitude reflects both a certain belief that healing is desirable and a deep desire for healing. Someone else may, to the contrary, have a deep mistrust of material blessing and rather be attracted to ascetic religious practices, but this attraction will also be reflected in corresponding beliefs concerning the nature of true salvation.

One cannot therefore neatly distinguish between the mind, the will, and the emotions, as was done in the so-called faculty psychology that was developed in seventeenth-century Europe.[5] This led to an understanding of persuasion and rhetoric that neatly distinguished between apologetics and evangelism: between rational argument that addresses the mind of the hearer and an emotional appeal to a change of attitude or to conversion. This may lead to an idea of apologetics as "pre-evangelism," which takes away intellectual barriers or shows that the Christian faith has at least a good degree of rational justification in order to allow for a subsequent evangelistic call to conversion of the will. Or if one is more aware of the way the will or the emotions are a hindrance to an open consideration of the truth of the gospel, it may lead to an evangelistic practice that dismisses the power of apologetic argumentation and simply launches an emotional call for conversion.

In reality, human feelings, desires, drives, attitudes, thoughts, will, and even the body are profoundly intertwined in processes of change that have a deep existential impact on our self-understanding and the course of our lives.[6] Christians and many other religionists will also add spiritual allegiance and bonds to this mix.[7] This is true most of all for the type of reflection that might lead to religious conversion. As Nabeel's example shows, intellectual exchange on religious truth becomes an inconsequential debate if there is no desire or at least an initial openness to come to know the truth of God or our lives for what they are. Arguments may be exchanged, but, rather than instruments that help us uncover the truth, they serve other purposes: showing off one's intellectual or rhetorical prowess, standing up

---

[4]Clark, *Dialogical Apologetics*, 157-58.

[5]David K. Berlo, *The Process of Communication: An Introduction to Theory and Practice* (New York: Holt, Rinehart and Winston, 1960), 7-10.

[6]David J. Hesselgrave, *Communicating Christ Cross-Culturally: An Introduction to Missionary Communication*, 2nd ed. (Grand Rapids, MI: Zondervan, 1991), 86-91.

[7]David Naugle, *Worldview: The History of a Concept* (Grand Rapids, MI: Eerdmans, 2002), 274-84.

for one's religious community, or simply enjoying the game of a good intellectual discussion. This is of course only the case for those who enjoy such discussions and are confident in engaging in such exchanges. In most religious communities, this is probably only the case for a small number of people, though they may be better represented among some populations, such as university students.

Most people will only engage in serious reflection on questions of religious truth if they see that there are potential benefits that may outweigh the scary process and consequences of conversion. This is why apologetic witness will not only need to consider the truth of the Christian faith, but also its relevance. The dialogue partner will of course understand this relevance primarily in terms of their current religion, worldview, and experience. The significance of the gospel will therefore need to be explained in terms of the felt needs of the listener. These may not be the most fundamental needs that people have, as Christians believe them to be revealed in the Scriptures for what they truly are. But deeper human needs often express themselves near the surface of human self-understanding as felt needs. Felt needs can therefore be a point of contact that shows how both our felt needs and our deepest needs are addressed by the gospel (cf. §6.5; §8.3; §9.3).[8]

It is therefore crucial that apologists listen intently to their conversation partners not only for what is said, but also for what is not said. If appropriate, it is important to try to bring attitudes and desires into the open, both for the conversation partner and the Christian witness: "Could you see yourself as a Christian? What are the most important reasons you would not?" "Do you understand why I myself and other Christians experience Christ and their faith as the greatest blessing there is?" This will obviously require a similar or even greater openness and vulnerability on the side of the Christian conversation partner.

Taking these attitudes, desires, and fears into account should not stop us from taking questions of truth equally seriously. However uninterested people may seem in the truth, their life choices reflect "basic insights into the nature of the real to which [their] practice commits [them]."[9] As we saw previously (§1.4), people in other religious communities will often experience the truth of their own religious perspective as self-evident. They may even be unaware of the fact that their life choices are based on a certain interpretation of reality

---

[8]Hesselgrave, *Communicating Christ,* 598-600.
[9]Kevin Vanhoozer, "The Trials of Truth: Mission, Martyrdom and the Epistemology of the Cross," in *To Stake a Claim: Mission and the Western Crisis of Knowledge,* ed. J. Andrew Kirk and Kevin J. Vanhoozer (Maryknoll, NY: Orbis, 1999), 126.

that can be contested and may be equally unable to understand why Christians could ever accept their faith as true. We will understand this when we think of the dominant non-Christian perspectives in our own contexts. The Western European context is so dominated by modernism and postmodernism that for many any religious truth claim is directly associated with intolerance, while people are unaware of the metaphysical truth claims implicit in the practices of their lives. In majority Muslim or Buddhist societies, the issues with Christianity will be different, but it is equally true that the Christian faith will not be seen as a viable option unless the main reasons people have to dismiss it out of hand will be discussed. A second reason that it will not do to simply appeal to felt needs is that the sharing of the gospel is not a matter of propaganda or advertising in order to fill our churches or strengthen the political weight of our religious community. We invite others to embrace this message because it is true and good. A mere appeal to felt needs would be manipulative and contradictory to the nature of the gospel (cf. §1.4).

Conversion and worldview change. Apologetic conversation is ultimately aimed at persuasion and conversion. In certain cultural contexts, persuasion and conversion have a bad name and are associated with religious and intellectual imperialism and manipulation. We will come back to this later in the chapter (§7.5). For now, it is helpful to note that this criticism is less evident than it seems if we realize that views and values—as well as the mind, will, and emotions—are always intertwined and can never be isolated as neatly separated faculties, as if certain convictions are impartial while others are not. Those who want to forbid Christian mission as a form of proselytizing supporting Western interests have their own interests they are trying to protect and their own agenda of which they try to persuade others. Therefore, the question is not whether persuasion is acceptable, but how we can engage in persuasive dialogue in ways that are not manipulative but rather create space and freedom to consider questions of truth and of what is good for human flourishing.

Apologetic witness and dialogue need to touch the mind, will, and emotions because conversion is such a radical process. Conversion means embracing a new worldview, a new orientation of desires, and a new set of values (cf. §6.2). At the center of these changes is a fundamental change of allegiance to Christ, who from now on will be the linchpin of the new worldview, the object of deepest desire, the guide to what is truly valuable, and the Lord and Liberator of the will. For many this will be a radical change from one allegiance to another because there was another central orientation to this person's allegiance before, be it commitment to one's family, the flourishing of the clan, the search for *nirvana*, submission to the will of Allah, the maximization of personal happiness, or the development of the self. Other people may not have such a single central allegiance but are driven by multiple values and desires that are not always in harmony. This is equally true in the Christian life. Yet, conversion calls all to a commitment to the God we meet in Christ and a willingness to let our value system gradually be reoriented around this new center.

Such conversion—be it gradual or more sudden—does not mean that there is no continuity at all between worldview, values, and desires before and after conversion. Many beliefs and values will remain the same. Through the conversion process, a person may continue to be proud to be from India or desire health and harmony in her family. Before and after conversion many beliefs remain the same and not just trivial ones. A person may continue to believe that every human being has inalienable rights (if indeed he believed so before), that he has a great spouse or bad parents, that human flourishing depends on knowing the will of God, or that China is the nation that holds the keys to world-peace. Yet, such beliefs and desires may find a new place in a reconfigured worldview and value-set that are now oriented around Christ.[10]

Conversion may therefore well be understood in terms of what psychologists call a *Gestalt*-switch, a new way of looking at reality in which everything they saw before is reconfigured and receives a new meaning.[11] Someone may, for example, always have thought that their happiness was their own responsibility and suddenly see that they need to learn to trust other people and live by the grace of God. They will continue to believe many other elements of what made up their outlook on the world, but their overall worldview will receive a new flavor and structure because of the new constellation of these beliefs around these changed central convictions. Often this new perspective is not entirely new and unknown. It generally is a perspective of which someone has been aware for some time. There has been an inner conversation between different potential ways of looking at reality. The mounting awareness of the limitations of one's former worldview, desires, and values may lead to an "inner conflict" (cf. also §6.4)[12] or "epistemological crisis"[13] which finally reaches a tipping point.

---

[10]Cf. Joel Robbins, "Can There Be Conversion Without Cultural Change?" *Mission Studies* 34, no. 1 (2017): 29-52.

[11]Anthony Wallace, "Revitalization Movements," *American Anthropologist* 58, no. 2 (1956): 264-81.

[12]Renford Bambrough, "Fools and Heretics," *Royal Institute of Philosophy Supplement* 28 (1990): 244.

[13]Alasdair MacIntyre, "Epistemological Crises, Dramatic Narrative, and the Philosophy of Science," in *Paradigms and Revolutions: Appraisals and Applications of Thomas Kuhn's Philosophy of Science*, ed. Gary Gutting (Notre Dame, IN: University of Notre Dame Press, 1980).

7.4 ADDRESSING PREDISPOSITIONS

People's predispositions (desires, emotions, values, the will) are therefore not immune to apologetic engagement. Yet, it is not the case that apologetic witness simply provides the best rational argument, preparing a subsequent call to conversion. The call to conversion is indeed an essential part of the process, but of a process in which reasons and predispositions are continually influencing each other.

The apologetic witness will, therefore, from the very beginning, need to invite implicitly or explicitly a true openness to consider the message of Christ. This will happen by positively showing its attractiveness, showing how it responds to people's deepest needs and how it promises true flourishing. It will also need to address desires and emotions that function as barriers to conversion, such as the intuitive and inborn confidence in one's own community, love for those who are most dear, fear for radical change, and so on. The point is not that these loyalties and fears are wrong, but that they can stand in the way. As in the example of Qureshi, addressing such predispositions is needed to free the mind to recognize truth where it can be found. Addressing such predispositions demands at the same time an effort of the mind, because our mind can help us recognize that fear for the unknown, and loyalty to our community is sometimes healthy but at other times a hindrance to finding truth and true flourishing.

A growing openness to truth, therefore, does not demand neutrality and disengagement, as if the ideal would be to rid the mind of all influence of the will and the emotions. The ideal is not *apatheia* or a lack of emotions and desire, but rather the development of appropriate desires and attitudes, the developments of healthy virtues of the mind.[14]

Healthy virtues of the mind include the desire for truth, and the courage to see reality for what it is. This openness to truth demands the growth of a certain confidence—a confidence that reality can be trusted and that such knowledge will in the end help us flourish and be a blessing to those who are most dear to us and to our wider community. Christians, Buddhists, Muslims, and Platonists believe that the truth will make us free and can be known up to a certain level. Many postmodern people believe that the truth cannot be known and that all claims of truth are disguised expressions of self-interest. With this postmodern outlook on reality, it obviously does not make sense

---

[14]Cf. Linda Trinkaus Zagzebski, "Religious Knowledge and the Virtues of the Mind," in *Rational Faith: Catholic Responses to Reformed Epistemology*, vol 10, ed. Linda Trinkaus Zagzebski, Library of Religious Philosophy (Notre Dame, IN: University of Notre Dame Press, 1993), 199-225; Vanhoozer, "Trials of Truth."

to invest oneself deeply in the quest for truth. Many people would echo Pilate's response to Jesus' claim that he "came into the world, to testify to the truth," which Pilate countered with a sad, resigned, and incredulous "What is truth?' (Jn 18:37).

The conviction that truth cannot be found is of course self-confirming. In our world, truth is often hidden and pushed to the margins by sinful and ideological self-interests, and blurred because of different cultural outlooks that shape what people see. If in such a world people do not seek out the truth, there is indeed a good chance that they will not find it. Therefore, an openness to and desire for truth depends on at least an initial belief that truth might be worth pursuing and may show itself. This may demand some argument, but will also reveal that the life of the Christian community and of the apologist show that not everyone is living in a closed world of their own self-interested, tightly guarded perspectives, and that openness to truth and God can lead to a confidence that those who search may indeed find.

With an appeal to the will, we can call ourselves and our interlocutors to rise above their immediate desires, to be more than a passive plaything tossed back and forth between their most immediate needs, desires, and emotions. That humans are not merely or passively pushed by their desires and needs is itself proven by the fact that there is usually not one single desire that dominates all others. We often find ourselves confronted with contradictory desires that force us and give us scope to evaluate the drives and predispositions we encounter. That we have some room in how we relate to our desires is further confirmed by general educational practices in which we teach children to control the desire to gratify their immediate needs, and to "pull themselves together." Beyond these general considerations, there is also a theological reason to give the will a prominent place: God calls people to conversion, a call which presupposes that they can respond: "God elects man in order that he may elect him in return, and therefore on the presupposition that man is capable of this election, not only of desiring, but also of willing, . . . in which he takes up a positive and negative position to his desiring, 'pulling himself together.'"[15]

Some would argue that the noetic influence of sin has a paralyzing effect that imprisons the human mind through sinful desires and therefore makes every appeal to the will and apologetic reasoning powerless.[16] Therefore,

---

[15]Karl Barth, *Church Dogmatics*, ed. Geoffrey W. Bromiley and Thomas F. Torrance, trans. Geoffrey W. Bromiley et al. (Edinburgh: T&T Clark, 1956–1975), III/2, 415.

[16]Cornelius van Til, *The Defense of the Faith*, 3rd ed. (Phillipsburg, NJ: Presbyterian and Reformed Publishing Co., 1967), 46-50.

Christians can in the end only witness to the gospel and leave the task of conviction to the Holy Spirit. This objection creates an unhelpful opposition between witness and apologetics (cf. §5.3). It also misunderstands the work of the Spirit. The Spirit does this miraculous work of conversion most often through natural means of proclamation and dialogue. The biblical prophets and apostles used all their argumentative skill and persuasive power, but all the while depended on the power of the Spirit.[17]

In this section, we keep moving back and forth between values, desires, emotions, and reason, between predispositions and presuppositions, between the soul, the will, and the mind. The language of will, mind, and desires is needed because sometimes the focus of the dialogue and conversation may be more on one of these dimensions rather than on another. Yet, this language might seem to suggest that we have to deal with different faculties of mind, will, and emotions, while they can in practice never be isolated. The biblical language of the heart is helpful in this respect because it brings together all these different elements. The heart in biblical terms is the seat of reason (Deut 29:4), of the will (2 Sam 7:27), of the emotions (Ps 25:7), of our desires (Ps 21:3), yet all these are not necessarily at war because the heart is at the same time seen as the center of human existence,[18] finding its unity in being directed toward God (Ps 86:11).

7.4 NARRATIVE APOLOGETICS

The way mind, emotions, and will are deeply intertwined supports the importance of narrative in apologetic witness. The West has produced a number of Christian thinkers who creatively used stories in their apologetic endeavors, such as G. K. Chesterton, C. S. Lewis, and J. R. R. Tolkien. For many people with a Western mindset, this is counterintuitive because argumentation and storytelling are often seen as two very different types of discourse. Postmodern philosophers and theologians have, nevertheless, rehabilitated narrative and pointed to its importance because of the way narratives shape our lives. This has not necessarily led to a rehabilitation of their use in apologetic witness because narratives are often seen more as a way of shaping reality than of revealing the truth of reality. Postmodern apologists and theologians who major in the use of narrative may sometimes be purposely vague about the truth claims that may or may not be implicitly present in

---

[17]Cf. Hesselgrave, *Communicating Christ,* 584-85; Benno van den Toren, *Christian Apologetics as Cross-Cultural Dialogue* (London: T&T Clark, 2011), 213-14.
[18]Hans Walter Wolff, *Anthropology of the Old Testament* (London: SCM Press, 1974), 55.

their stories.[19] This may of course be a valid rhetorical strategy in a world which sometimes reacts aggressively to truth claims. It is more worrying if this focus on narrative presupposes that all religion is merely a human construction and apologetic narrative no more than a means of showing people the attractiveness of this particular story. As we argued before, it is essential to the Christian faith that it is the true story of life,[20] because Christians live by the grace of what God has done to bring a salvation which far surpasses even the best that human beings are able to construct for themselves (cf. §1.3).

Yet, given this specifically Christian understanding of Christianity as "true story," narrative has a crucial role to play in apologetic witness. This is even more so in cultures that give narrative much more credit in communication and persuasion than the late-modern West. The importance of narrative for apologetics is, first of all, a consequence of the way narrative appeals to the entire person. Narrative does not only engage the intellect by presenting us a new way of looking to the world. It also appeals to our emotions and desires, for it introduces us to different ways of experiencing the world. Many people experience that when reading novels about other cultures. While a factual description of a culture may describe what people believe, it does not easily show us how such a world can be emotionally credible and even appealing. A narrative does just that: it helps me see and feel why people are attracted to an ascetic lifestyle, to the pressure of an urban environment, or rather the quiet of remote communities. Now, I not only imagine but possibly even empathize with why some people become explorers, resistance fighters, faithful spouses, activists, or martyrs. This is apologetically important since, for many outsiders, the Christian faith is not only implausible because of its truth claims but also emotionally unattractive or simply unimaginable. What does it mean to love a Lord who is crucified? And to love a God you cannot see? What does freedom look like when it is only acquired by surrendering one's autonomy? Can one still live in the present while hoping for eternity? How can people forgive their enemies and find hope in pain without denying the reality of suffering? It is through stories that this world can become emotionally plausible and even desirable.

A second strength of narrative as a genre for apologetic witness is that it plunges us right in the middle of a new world. As we saw before, the power of

---

[19]John A. Sims, "Postmodernism: The Apologetic Imperative," in *The Challenge of Postmodernism: An Evangelical Engagement*, ed. David S. Dockery (Grand Rapids, MI: Baker Books, 1995), 334; David K. Clark, "Narrative Theology and Apologetics," *Journal of the Evangelical Theological Society* 36, no. 4 (1993): 508-11.

[20]Lesslie Newbigin, *The Gospel in a Pluralist Society* (Grand Rapids, MI: Eerdmans, 1989), 89-102.

the Christian perspective cannot be seen when it is constantly evaluated in terms of a foreign value system. Its truthfulness and beauty only come out when it is seen in its entirety and according to its own integrity (§6.3). A story or novel allows us to step into the middle of a new world, be it nineteenth-century Orthodox Russia as we discover it in Fyodor Dostoyevsky's great novels, the imaginary world of Middle-earth in J. R. R. Tolkien, or the world of a Japanese Christian pictured by Shusaku Endo. We allow the world of a story to be foreign and do not expect it to be reasonable in terms of the world we know. It is precisely this openness to its foreignness which allows us to discover its own integrity. This creates the space needed to discover how it can, in its own way, be true or even truer to the world and human existence than our current outlook.

There are different types of stories that can be used for different apologetic purposes. Great novels can allow us to imaginatively enter a new universe and discover a new way of life. Short parables can be used to trigger a new insight because it gets past our defenses, just as the prophet Nathan's parable did with king David (1 Sam 12:1-7).[21] Conversion stories from different religious backgrounds to the Christian faith can also play an important role, both in written form and as personal testimony. Such testimonies—like those used in this study—can play a crucial role in showing and addressing the multifaceted struggles that are part of the conversion process. They exemplify what finding Christ in real life may look like. These stories show how felt needs may indeed find unexpected fulfillment when life is reoriented and reconfigured around Christ. Moreover, stories reflect that conversion is a journey and how it works itself out in a gradual process toward and beyond the tipping point of conversion. They make real how a new joy and peace can be found that could not be conceived of previously, outweighing the costs of conversion, even if these costs may be much higher than expected beforehand and higher than their Christian conversation partner may be aware of.

7.5 THE CHARACTER OF THE WITNESS AND THE WITNESS OF CHARACTER

The importance of character. Several strands of our explorations into inter-religious apologetic witness have already pointed to the importance of the character of the apologist. Character is crucial because apologetics is witness to what happened in salvation history and our lives (chap. 5). Appreciating

---

[21]Cf. Robert H. Stein, *An Introduction to the Parables of Jesus* (Philadelphia, PA: Westminster Press, 1981), 35.

the reliability of a testimony will in significant measure depend on the perceived trustworthiness of the character of the witness. We have furthermore seen that people's choices are to a large degree determined by "reasons of the heart," their predispositions, their attitudes, desires, and fundamental life choices. We can only gain the trust needed to reach people at these levels when our behavior and personality invite such openness. In his study of rhetoric, the Greek philosopher Aristotle already noted, "Persuasion is achieved by the speaker's personal character when the speech is so spoken as to think him credible . . . his character must almost be called the most effective means of persuasion he possesses."[22]

The importance of character for persuasion is equally valid for the politician as for the pastor or salesperson.[23] What sort of character is appropriate will, however, depend on the goal of persuasion. Is it simply to convince someone to buy my product, even if they may come to regret it later? Is it to make people trust my can-do personality so that they will give me their vote? Or is it to convince them of the inherent truth and goodness of my message? Different religious outlooks may not demand the same character in their witnesses. A witness that represents a God whose primary attribute is power will do so differently than a witness to the crucified Christ revealing a God whose most fundamental attribute is love. A witness to an inner mystical experience may need to show a reliability of character and testimony differently from a witness to God's liberating presence.

Virtues such as love,[24] gentleness,[25] and personal integrity[26] are important for all apologetic testimony. Some virtues need to be nurtured when engaging in interreligious apologetic dialogue. Earlier we pointed to the importance of the virtues of confidence and openness (§4.6). Here we want to focus on the importance of humility and courage.

Bold humility. Humility is another virtue that needs particular attention in the context of religious pluralism.[27] This is necessary because for the Christian witness the message the Christian shares is not a message that is

---

[22]Aristotle, "Rhetoric," in *Aristotle, Volume II*, ed. Robert Maynard Hutchins, trans. W. Rhys Roberts, Great Books of the Western World 9 (Chicago, IL: Encyclopedia Britannica, 1952), 593-675.

[23]Cf. Clark, *Dialogical Apologetics*, 234.

[24]Arthur Lindsley, *Love, the Ultimate Apologetic: The Heart of Christian Witness* (Downers Grove, IL: InterVarsity Press, 2008); Ajith Fernando, *The Christian's Attitude Toward World Religions* (Wheaton, IL: Tyndale House Publishers, 1987).

[25]Dallas Willard, *The Allure of Gentleness: Defending the Faith in the Manner of Jesus* (New York: HarperOne, 2015).

[26]Van den Toren, *Christian Apologetics*, 225-26.

[27]Cf. John G. Stackhouse, *Humble Apologetics: Defending the Faith Today* (Oxford: Oxford University Press, 2002).

constructed, or a message at their disposal, or a message that has been dis-covered because of their religious genius. The Christian has received this message only by grace, knowing that if left to themselves, they would still be in the dark. Christian witness among the religions therefore has, according to a famous expression of the Sri Lankan theologian D. T. Niles, "One beggar telling another beggar where to get food."[28] It is like the invitation—"Come and see!"—of Philip, who went to Nathanael after he had encountered Jesus. Philip did not share something he possessed, but he invited his friend to check out for himself what he had discovered and received (Jn 1:46).[29] As a consequence, the witness points to a reality that the conversation partners can discover for themselves and on their own terms. Because one culture can never exhaust the riches of the good news we receive in Jesus Christ, the Christian apologist can not only be open, but even expect to discover new things when sharing Christ across religious boundaries, looking at him in new ways.

Humility is needed particularly in the large sectors of society where, because of postmodern and postcolonial sensitivities, virtually all claims to truth are viewed as arrogant. They suggest that the witness places themselves above others and is insufficiently aware of their own cultural location. It may be true that Christian mission has often been conducted in arrogant ways. Yet, we can point to this truth in humility and should do so in recognition of those Christians that have themselves received this message by grace, in imitation of Christ in whom God revealed God's own humility (cf. Phil 2:5-11). It should also be boldly stated that a posture of "not knowing" (or relativism) is not always the humblest stance. If it is indeed true that God revealed Godself in Christ and did this in a way that showed both our human sinfulness and lost-ness, then it takes greater humility to accept this truth of our lives than to hold that truth is all relative.

This humility should also be combined with the virtue of courage. The mis-siologist David Bosch rightly said that Christian mission should be done in "bold humility."[30] This characteristic of mission equally applies to apologetic witness and dialogue, as one aspect of Christian mission. Such "bold humility" is called for particularly in the countries where many groups closely associate

---

[28]Daniel Thambyrajah Niles, *That They May Have Life* (New York: Harper & Brothers, 1951), 96; quoted in Creighton Lacy, "The Legacy of D. T. Niles," *International Bulletin of Missionary Research* 8, no. 4 (1984): 174.

[29]Edward Rommen, *Come and See: An Eastern Orthodox Perspective on Contextualization* (Pasadena, CA: William Carey Library, 2013).

[30]David J. Bosch, *Transforming Mission: Paradigm Shifts in Theology of Mission* (Maryknoll, NY: Orbis Books, 1991), 489.

Christian mission with Western colonialism.[31] Bold humility and humble bold-ness in apologetics are equally needed in the Western contexts, which are char-acterized by a postmodern association of truth claims with power games and imperialism. It demands boldness to challenge the hidden metaphysics of postmodern and pluralist perspectives that have become their own "meta-narratives" to which all other stories will need to adapt if they want to be allowed a hearing.[32] It also demands courage to challenge the deep and sinful predis-positions that incline people to create their own world and meaning autono-mously.[33] Moreover, the Christian apologist will need to show that local stories which do not claim universal adherence, can be equally oppressive.[34] This is all too clear in the many stories that nations in both the West and East tell to shape their identities—stories in which cultural and religious minorities are forced to fit. More positively, the Christian story is precisely a story that has the potential to counteract the abuse of truth claims by those in power. If it is indeed true that there is one God over all, then the weak and marginalized are not at the mercy of the powerful, but they can call to this one God over all for justice and liberation.[35] Furthermore, the Christian message is an inherently anti-imperialist message. At its center stands Jesus Christ who was crucified because he challenged the religious and political powers of his time, by his vulnerable testimony to the truth of this one God and his plans for his creation.[36]

Just as with the earlier pair of virtues, confidence and openness, the virtues of humility and courage present us, at first glance, with a degree of tension. A humble politician, for example, who is well aware of their limitations, may find it difficult to be courageous. A courageous politician on the other hand, who is confident that they can conquer the world, will not easily strike us as humble. Yet, in leadership studies, it has also been pointed out that effective leaders (and therefore effective communicators) need to be both humble

---

[31]David J. Bosch, *The Vulnerability of Mission*, Occasional Paper 10 (Birmingham, UK: Selly Oak Colleges, 1991).

[32]J. Richard Middleton and Brian J. Walsh, *Truth Is Stranger than It Used to Be: Biblical Faith in a Postmodern Age* (Downers Grove, IL: InterVarsity Press, 1995), 76-77; Colin E. Gunton, *The Prom-ise of Trinitarian Theology*, 2nd ed. (Edinburgh: T&T Clark, 1997), 162-67.

[33]van den Toren, *Christian Apologetics*, 76-77; cf. Stephen N. Williams, *Revelation and Reconciliation: A Window on Modernity* (Cambridge: Cambridge University Press, 1995).

[34]Middleton and Walsh, *Truth Is Stranger*, 75.

[35]J. Richard Middleton and Brian J. Walsh, "Facing the Postmodern Scalpel: Can the Christian Faith Withstand Deconstruction?," in *Christian Apologetics in the Postmodern World*, ed. Timothy R. Phillips and Dennis L. Okholm (Downers Grove, IL: InterVarsity Press, 1995), 142, 145-52.

[36]Middleton and Walsh, "Facing the Postmodern Scalpel," 102-7; Vanhoozer, "Trials of Truth"; Rich-ard Bauckham, *Bible and Mission: Christian Witness in a Postmodern World* (Grand Rapids, MI: Baker Academic, 2003), 103-9.

and courageous.[37] From a secular perspective, it is hard to see how the two virtues can be equally nurtured. If we would be either humble or courageous because of our own qualities, they do indeed easily stand in tension. Just as was the case with confidence and openness, we understand how humility and courage in witness can be combined, and even belong together, when we realize that they are both rooted in the believer's relationship with Jesus Christ. If Christ is the basis of our confidence, we have a reason to be courageous. In a pluralist world in which all religious perspectives seem to be relativized, God-self has broken open our imprisonment to our cultural frameworks, by God's self-revelation in this world (cf. Acts 17:30). Yet, we do not own or master this message. We humbly and gratefully receive it by grace before we can share it gracefully. It originates in the sovereign love of God and therefore remains beyond our control. It is revealed in a history of salvation which gives us a solid base for our confidence yet in which God also moves in mysterious ways beyond our grasp.

Further reflection on how these virtues should be expressed in different cultural contexts may be needed. The desire for truth and renunciation of power, for example, needs to be expressed in concrete practices of how one speaks and listens, how arguments are addressed, and how hidden presuppositions, predispositions, and ideological claims are exposed.[38] Such practices may be culturally sensitive, just as the ways in which love, gentleness, integrity, confidence and openness, humility and boldness take concrete cultural shape in the life and witness of different communities. Though these character traits can be expressed in culturally appropriate ways, they will, however, be deeply countercultural. Christian Islam scholar Kenneth Cragg has pointed to the profound difference in attitude toward power between Jesus and Mohammed. Where Mohammed responded to the rejection of his message with political and military power, Jesus went the way of the cross and many of his followers followed suit.[39] We are well aware that in the long history of the church, Christians have often yielded to the temptation of political and even military power for the sake of the Kingdom's advancement. Yet, the normative examples of Jesus and Mohammed remain very different. This means that a Christian renunciation of power and a corresponding

---

[37]E.g., Stephen R. Covey, *The 7 Habits of Highly Effective People* (New York: Fireside, 1989), 217-19; cf. John R. W. Stott, *I Believe in Preaching* (London: Hodder & Stoughton, 1982), 299-337.

[38]Cf. Nancey C. Murphy, "Missiology in the Postmodern West: A Radical Reformation Perspective," in *To Stake a Claim: Mission and the Western Crisis of Knowledge*, ed. J. Andrew Kirk and Kevin J. Vanhoozer (Maryknoll, NY: Orbis Books, 1999), 116-18.

[39]Kenneth Cragg, "The Cross and Power: Parting of Ways," in *Jesus and the Cross: Reflections of Christians from Islamic Contexts*, ed. David Emmanuel Singh (Oxford: Regnum, 2008), 33-46.

renunciation of all manipulation in apologetic witness can, in Islamic contexts, easily be taken as a sign of weakness. However, this should not tempt
us to abandon the practice of humble and vulnerable witness. This humility
is an expression of the attitude of Godself to his world. This humility was
equally mistaken as weakness by many of the political and religious powers
of Jesus' time, yet in his wisdom Jesus knew that only this humble love could
finally overcome the powers of the world. And as the conversion story of the
former Muslim Mark Gabriel shows, an abuse of power in the name of religion undermines its truth claim, for why would the truth need to be anxious
of free exploration and discovery?[40]

Private conversations and public debates. The appropriate mode of expression of the crucial virtues of the Christian apologetic witness is not only
related to the cultural context, but also to the medium and setting of the
encounter. Different settings create their own dynamics, and it is therefore
important to reflect on the advantages and limitations of different media.
When thinking about the setting, it is important to take a moment to reflect
on the difference between private and semi-private conversations on the one
hand and public settings on the other. The deeper drives of dialogue partners
are most easily addressed in private conversation in which mutual trust can
grow, in some cases over a series of meetings or long friendships. In public
apologetic dialogue, conversation partners will find it much harder to be vulnerable and the setting itself will pressure the participants to defend their
position rather than be open about their personal questions.

I (Benno) was once invited to take part in a public apologetic encounter in
a Dutch university city, between an imam, a humanist thinker, and myself (a
Christian theologian). We were invited by a Christian student group, but the
imam had also encouraged the youth of his mosque to join. Because of this
setting, the dialogue turned into the interreligious equivalent of a boxing
match. Although the public followed Dutch cultural etiquette and remained
restrained and quiet, one could sense the different groups cheering inwardly
as they felt that their representative made a good move. In such settings, it is
obviously hard to engage in true dialogue with the people sitting at the table
in front of you. These public speakers may not even be intent on listening, but
are often focused on making their own points and on showing the superiority
of their position. This does not make such settings apologetically irrelevant.
In such conversations the most important audience is not the formal dialogue

---

[40]Mark A. Gabriel, *Jesus and Muhammad: Profound Differences and Surprising Similarities* (Lake
Mary, FL: Frontline, 2004), 11-12; cf. Jean-Marie Gaudeul, *Called from Islam to Christ: Why Muslims Become Christian* (Crowborough: Monarch, 1999), 60.

partners, but the onlookers. There will be Christians who may doubt whether their faith has, in fact, anything to say for itself apart from the fact that they happened to be born in a Christian subculture. They may be interested in learning how it will come out in this conversation. There may be Muslims who are deeply convinced that their religion is intellectually superior to Christianity. For them listening in on an intelligent dialogue may just dent that conviction so that in the future they may be more open to dialogue with Christians. There may of course be a whole range of attitudes from people on both sides, who may be inwardly weighing the options and are truly interested in whether this dialogue will help them make up their mind. These listeners are, as it were, "overhearing" the conversation up front and, precisely because they are not taking part and do not need to take a stand, they have more inner freedom to listen, ponder, and weigh what they hear.[41]

In this case the character of the apologetic witness is also important, but not primary for creating an open conversation with the formal dialogue partner. The character of the witness is important because in public dialogue, one can also win arguments, but lose the audience.[42] It is important because the credibility of the testimony will, to a significant degree, depend on the integrity of the witness. People will listen more intently when they realize that this person up front is there to help them in their quest rather than score points. Yet, the dynamics will be different from a one-on-one conversation. There will be little time for silence to let people ponder. There will be relatively little time to draw people out in order to understand them better. Yet, both in public and in private the apologist is called to be a humble and bold witness of Christ. And in both settings, the witness should not only try to get their point of view across, but invest in deepening mutual understanding, both because God calls us to be loving neighbors and because in both settings people will listen more intently when they feel that this person has a genuine interest in understanding their perspective.

An exploration of public debates on YouTube will show that public exchanges, whether they happen in explicitly dialogical settings or as shorter exchanges in other settings such as talk shows, are fraught with complexities and can easily go wrong. They can easily become boxing matches and demonstrations of religious dominance and prowess. Some religious representatives may even be intent on such exchanges. If one is not careful, film clips of the event can be manipulated. Local Christian communities will need great

---

[41]Cf. Clark, *Dialogical Apologetics,* 223.
[42]Cf. Stackhouse, *Humble Apologetics,* xvi-xvii.

wisdom in whether they should engage in such debates, who should do so, and how to set up or ask for formats that allow for healthy exchange. Yet, though these settings may not be favorable for true personal encounter, they may still be important for the public perception of Christianity. In many countries, the public sphere is dominated by one religious or secular perspective that often consciously or unconsciously puts down other religions as irrational, obscurantist, immoral, or foreign. In such contexts it is important to have winsome representatives of the Christian faith in the public sphere that may create initial openings as well as an initial respectability that will create space for deeper encounters in other settings.

PART 2

CONTEXTUAL APOLOGETIC WITNESS TO PARTICULAR AUDIENCES

IN THE FIRST PART OF THIS INTRODUCTION to apologetic witness among the religions, we have concentrated on generalities. These considerations of the nature of apologetic dialogue and witness in our religiously pluralist world were developed in constant conversation with practical experience and concrete challenges, yet they were structured after the main aspects of the model of interfaith apologetic dialogue developed in this study. In the second part of this book, we will focus on apologetic questions, challenges, and opportunities that come up in the encounter with specific audiences that represent some of the major religious traditions of our world.

These large movements or clusters of movements like Islam or Hinduism present themselves in many cultural forms, theological varieties, and social expressions. They therefore raise a whole range of issues that would need to be addressed in a full-length study of Christian apologetic dialogue with, for example, mystical Islam in Southeast Asia. They all have many facets that require attention, such as their social, political, artistic, psychological, logical, moral, theological, and spiritual dimension. Furthermore, individual members relate to these communities and religious traditions in different ways. For some, adherence is the result of a long religious quest, for others it may be merely an aspect of their cultural or national identity. Some may be ready to engage in conversations and explore alternative answers, others may be defensive. Women will often have a different place in their religious communities than men. One of the primary intentions of this book is to help develop forms of Christian witness that are attentive to such differences. These chapters will therefore also focus on specific expressions of broader religions traditions, for example on African Traditional Religions as a specific cluster of primal religious traditions, on Bhakti Hinduism, and on Theravada Buddhism. These chapters should therefore be read as illustrations rather than as exhaustive, normative, or even typical. Yet, these chapters do provide a crucial elaboration on the first part of the book. They give more elaborate illustrations of what holistic interreligious apologetic witness embodied in community life and embedded in cultural context could look like. They give a first impression of how varied such apologetic dialogue can be, depending on the interlocutors.

In each of the following chapters, we will also elaborate on one aspect of the apologetic approach that we have developed, focusing on the need for inculturation in the discussion of primal religious traditions, and on the importance of "unmasking" in dialogue with secularisms as pseudo-religions. We have chosen these emphases because we believe them to be of particular importance for these specific audiences. Yet, unmasking also needs to happen in the witness to primal religious traditions, just as inculturation is important for apologetic witness to secular cultures. These chapters are therefore not only important for those who engage in apologetic witness to these specific groups but also present further elaboration on more general characteristics of interreligious apologetic witness.

8

INCULTURATION IN DIALOGUE
WITH PRIMAL RELIGIONS

8.1 PERVASIVENESS OF THE PRIMAL IMAGINATION

Primal religions and primal religiosity. "Primal religions" is a term that in recent decades is increasingly used for a cluster of religions that have formerly been referred to with other terms like "ethnic religions" or "tribal religions."[1] The term is used to avoid the negative and demeaning connotations of terms like "primitive religions" and "animism." Though many of these religions are organized along tribal or ethnic lines, this ethnic link is not essential for the relevant form of religiosity to survive in the modern world.[2] The notion of primal religion implies that this form of religion may well be the basic religious expression among humanity and that these religions have preceded all other great religious traditions.[3] We will use the term while remaining cautious with such sweeping generalizations that may need further critical theological reflection.

On all continents, primal religions belong to the oldest known religious traditions. In the modern world, primal religions are retreating in relation to other religions, particularly Christianity and Islam. They do, however, remain an important family of religions with a continuing presence in Africa, among shamanistic groups in Northern Siberia, in the tribal regions of India, on islands in the Indonesian archipelago, among First Nations in North America, and remote tribes in South America. Some religions in this family are relatively new, such as the Brazilian Candomblé religion, which is a blend of

---

[1]E.g., Harold W. Turner, "The Primal Religions of the World and Their Study," in *Australian Essays in World Religions*, ed. Victor Hayes (Bedford Park: Australian Association for World Religions, 1977), 27-37; Andrew Walls, "Primal Religious Traditions in Today's World," in *Religion in Today's World: The Religious Situation of the World from 1945 to the Present Day* (Edinburgh: T&T Clark, 1987), 250-78.
[2]Kwame Bediako, *Christianity in Africa: The Renewal of a Non-Western Religion* (Edinburgh: Edinburgh University Press, 1995), 105.
[3]Turner, "Primal Religions," 28.

traditional religions imported by enslaved African peoples and mixed with elements of Roman Catholicism.

Equally important for the formulation of appropriate apologetic witness among the religions is that most or all world religions—apart from more "pure" expressions—have folk varieties, such as folk Islam, folk Buddhism, and even folk Christianity. These folk varieties combine the more official versions of these religious traditions with many beliefs and practices from primal religious traditions. Roman Catholicism in Latin America has for example incorporated all sorts of traditional religious practices. Many African Muslims can combine Islam with consultations of the *marabut*, a Muslim version of the traditional diviner and healer. In Thailand and Myanmar, we may encounter groups that would be classified as Buddhist, but that in their spirituality and outlook on life would be little different from primal religions. In Christian witness, we do not only reach out to those who adhere to more formal or orthodox versions of their religions but also to those who adhere to these folk-religious varieties.[4]

In the Eurocentric evolutionist view of religions of the nineteenth century, Christianity was seen as furthest removed from primal religions because animism or primitive religions were considered the most basic form of religion on the evolutionary ladder, if they were to be classified as religions at all. Chinese religions and Hinduism were considered slightly higher, then moving from Buddhism to Islam, with Judaism as the religion closest to Christianity. Following Harold Turner, the Ghanaian theologian Kwame Bediako argues, rather, that the Christian faith has a special and close relationship to primal religious traditions.[5] In history, most Christian converts have come from primal religious backgrounds, first in the Greco-Roman world, then among the Germanic and Slavic tribes. In modern times, missions have been most effective among primal religionists in Latin America and Africa. In Asia, Christian missions saw relatively few conversions among Buddhists and Muslims, but much more among the so-called tribals in India and among primal religious communities in Southeast Asia and Oceania. This may well have to do with a certain affinity between the primal worldview and the Christian faith, and why missionaries were sometimes welcomed with the recognition that "this is what we have been waiting for."[6]

---

[4]E.g., Bill Andrew Musk, *The Unseen Face of Islam: Sharing the Gospel with Ordinary Muslims* (Sutherland, Australia: MARC, Evangelical Missionary Alliance, 1989); Paul H. DeNeui, "Contextualizing with Thai Folk Buddhists," in *Sharing Jesus in the Buddhist World*, ed. David S. Lim and Steve Spaulding (Pasadena, CA: William Carey Library, 2003), 121-46.

[5]Bediako, *Christianity in Africa*, 91-108.

[6]Turner, "Primal Religions," 37; quoted in Bediako, *Christianity in Africa*, 96.

In this chapter, we will focus on African primal religions. Given the common structures between primal religions, many of these considerations will be equally important for engaging with aspects of both primal religions and folk religions in other regions of the world, but one needs to be conscious that every primal tradition will have unique features and raise particular challenges.

Characteristics of African primal religions. Primal religions are mainly organized along tribal and ethnic lines, uniting groups of people who share the same ancestors. There are therefore many primal religions in Sub-Saharan Africa. These primal religions do, however, have so much in common that theologians speak about "African Traditional Religion" in the singular[7] or about one African philosophical worldview underlying the various religions.[8] In this section, we will point out a number of crucial characteristics that form a widely shared structure across African religion and many other primal religions that is crucial for understanding the challenges and opportunities for apologetic dialogue. As we shall see, however, these structural themes reveal a certain ambivalence. This means that people can in practice develop different forms of spirituality within this overall structure.[9] This means that apologetic dialogue demands careful attention to how particular individuals or communities live out these primal spiritualities.

The first characteristic that needs our attention is a strong "sense of cosmic oneness" in which all aspects hang together.[10] The primal universe is mystical and spirit-filled. This does not simply mean that there is an extra group of beings people have to account for. Apart from the creator and physical realities, there are also many beings in the "world in between." And it goes further, because this spiritual world also influences all aspects of life. All life events are understood as taking place within this mystical universe and events are therefore never merely physical. The boundary between the physical and spiritual is like a highly permeable membrane.[11] Human actions always have repercussions in relation to the spiritual powers that surround them. Conversely, events that influence human life are never merely events in the physical world but will always be seen to be related to spiritual influences, be they deities, nature spirits, deceased ancestors, or living human beings who try to harm or protect through spells and amulets.

---

[7]Laurenti Magesa, *African Religion: The Moral Traditions of Abundant Life* (Maryknoll, NY: Orbis Books, 1997).

[8]John S. Mbiti, *African Religions and Philosophy* (Nairobi, KE: East African Educational Publishers, 1969).

[9]Walls, "Primal Religious Traditions," 254-55.

[10]John V. Taylor, *The Primal Vision: Christian Presence amid African Religion* (London: SCM Press, 1963), 64; cf. Bediako, *Christianity in Africa*, 93, 95.

[11]We are grateful to Thandi Soko-de Jong for this image.

This spiritual influence also profoundly shapes the experience of illness. Illnesses often are not merely physical but have causes in this spiritual world. In order to deal with illness or other forms of misfortune, one needs to consult a diviner who will be able to discover the spiritual causes of this illness or misfortune and explain how they should be adequately addressed.

Many or most African primal religions have the sense that among or beyond these spiritual powers there is the supreme power of the Creator God. As indicated previously (§1.2), an earlier generation of African theologians invested much energy in tracing these beliefs in the Creator God in order to show that the Christian God was not foreign to Africa.[12] Yet, in African Traditional Religion, there is a certain "ambivalence"[13] in the attitude to this supreme God. This God is recognized as supreme, yet in practice often receives little explicit attention and worship. This leads to opposing interpretations. On the one hand intermediary deities may be seen as manifestations of the Creator God.[14] On the other hand it may be concluded that the focus of attention on the lower spiritual world, in a sense, "eclipses" the Creator.[15] The focus is so strongly on life in this world and on the immediate spiritual influences that shape it, that there is no real need for or interest in a transcendent God.[16] This ambivalence underlines the need to be aware of regional and even individual differences that are open to the possibility that primal religious spiritualities may in practice take on very different forms.

This may be one of the reasons why, in certain African Traditional Religions, belief in the Creator can be completely absent. It is also the reason why the Ugandan philosopher Okot p'Bitek has fiercely criticized Mbiti and his colleagues for "Hellenizing" or Christianizing African primal religions. In order to make African religion acceptable, these theologians made it look more Western or Christian, and thereby did not respect the particular structure of African primal religions when seen from an inside perspective.[17] Bediako argues, against p'Bitek, that this is a misreading of Mbiti. Mbiti should not be read as a cultural anthropological study of African primal religions, but as a

---

[12]John S. Mbiti, *Concepts of God in Africa* (London: SPCK, 1975); Bolaji E. Idowu, *Olódùmarè: God in Yoruba Belief* (London: Longmans, 1962).

[13]Bediako, *Christianity in Africa*, 100.

[14]Bolaji E. Idowu, *Olódùmarè: God in Yoruba Belief* (London: Longmans, 1962).

[15]Keith Ferdinando, "Screwtape Revisited: Demonology Western, African and Biblical," in *The Unseen World: Christian Reflections on Angels, Demons, and the Heavenly Realm*, ed. Anthony N. S. Lane (Grand Rapids, MI: Baker Book House, 1996), 122.

[16]Bediako, *Christianity in Africa*, 100.

[17]Okot p'Bitek, *African Religions in Western Scholarship* (Kampala, UG: East African Literature Bureau, 1970), 80-89.

theological study.[18] Looking from a Christian theological perspective, Mbiti points to traces of belief in the Creator that show God "has not left himself without witness" (Acts 14:17). Mbiti therefore does something similar to what Paul did on the Areopagus, when he positively draws attention to traces of belief in the Creator in the religiosity of his hearers. Even if these traces may not have been as central to his hearers, they formed an appropriate point of contact showing that the Creator has indeed in some ways been recognized.

A final characteristic of these religious traditions that has significant implications for apologetic dialogue is the fact that these religions are this-worldly— a number of observers would also use terms like "anthropocentric" and "pragmatic." This anthropocentrism should not be understood as if the human being could be understood apart from the spiritual universe, but rather in the sense that religious practices are focused on the harmony and blessings they bring to the human beings involved.[19] There is no interest in God for God's own sake, no love for God for who God is, but neither is there for other spiritual powers. The relationships are all focused on what they bring to the worshippers and their community: one engages in religious practices to procure blessings and to protect oneself, or more appropriately the community or clan, from curses. They are therefore pragmatic and the Akan, for example, mostly engaged in them in times of need.[20] Because of this pragmatism and anthropocentrism, recourse to one spirit, the divinity of a human mediator can easily be exchanged for another. If they do not provide what people seek, they can start looking elsewhere, without forsaking any spiritual duty.[21] Their primary religious duty is to their clan and tribe. In that sense, "anthropocentrism" should be nuanced if it can be misunderstood in an individualistic sense: one's primary obligation is to one's family, clan, tribe, and deceased ancestors, rather than to individual progress and flourishing.

Related to this pragmatism is the strong this-worldliness of these religions. Though there is a place for a "hereafter," where good people may go after their death, the focus of spirituality is on the here and now. Spiritual practices should therefore show their value in their ability to fend off curses and dangers, to bring healing, abundant harvest, peace, and welfare in the here and now.

---

[18]Kwame Bediako, *Theology and Identity: The Impact of Culture upon Christian Thought in the Second Century and in Modern Africa* (Oxford: Regnum Books, 1992), 318-19.

[19]Mbiti, *African Religions*, 5, 16; Eloi Messi Metogo, *Dieu peut-il mourir en Afrique? Essai sur l'indifférence religieuse et l'incroyance en Afrique noire* (Paris: Presses de l'UCAC, 1997), 47-65; Magesa, *African Religion*, 69.

[20]Jan Platvoet and Henk J. van Rinsum, "Is Africa Incurably Religious? Confessing and Contesting an Invention," *Exchange* 32, no. 2 (2003): 144.

[21]Metogo, *Dieu peut-il mourir en Afrique?*, 49-50, 67-68.

8.2 APOLOGETIC CHALLENGES AND OPPORTUNITIES

Apologetic challenges from primal religious backgrounds can take many dif-ferent forms. In primal religious contexts, these will often not be raised explicitly as questions of truth (what is the world and God really like?), but, because of the anthropocentric and pragmatic bent, questions are asked in terms of relevance (how does this help me?) and belonging (what does this mean for my community and my relationship to it?). A multiplicity of ques-tions and objections can often be clustered in a limited number of main issues and themes. It is important to see how particular issues raised may be expres-sions of larger often interconnected issues. In this way the apologetic exchange will not be fragmented but be able to relate particular questions to the most crucial issues at hand. Many of the issues brought up in dialogue with African primal religions can be grouped into two clusters.

The first cluster groups issues related to the anthropocentrism, pragmatism, and this-worldliness of primal religions. The Christian faith will be judged on how well it performs in providing blessings and protection from harm. Chris-tianity has often been presented as a message that allows people to go to heaven, but heaven may not easily relate to directly felt needs. If Christianity is joyfully embraced as the way to heaven (which it often is), it may still bear very little relation to the challenges of everyday life. This may well be one of the reasons behind the widespread tendency in Africa to combine an accep-tance of the Christian faith with a continued involvement in traditional reli-gious practices—in order to obtain the protection and blessings needed in the here and now.[22] Christianity is often experienced as an "otherworldly" reli-gion. It has therefore little attraction in terms of what one would originally expect a religion to do. This is part of the attraction of African Instituted Churches (AICs) and more recently African Pentecostal and Charismatic churches that, in this respect, respond to deep needs that earlier missionary churches neglected: blessings here and now, deliverance and healing, and pro-tection in this chaotic spiritual universe.

Christianity is therefore often also experienced as ineffective. It may well be that its effectiveness in providing blessings (for example, through education and hospitals) has been a major factor in the attraction of Christianity. Yet, if one relates to the Christian faith because of its immediate effectiveness, this makes the Christian faith at the same time vulnerable. As one of Benno's stu-dents once asked, "Why is it that if when you are ill, you may go to a pastor

---

[22]Cf. Karl Grebe and Wilfred Fon. *African Traditional Religion and Christian Counseling*, vol. 1, Bamenda-Nkwen (Cameroon: Oasis International, 2006).

and ask for prayer and not be healed, go to a hospital, and still not be healed, and then go to a traditional healer, you may be healed immediately?" It will not do to simply point out that there are many situations in which traditional healers are not able to help. The success of the traditional healer shows for many that at least in this case recourse to primal religious practices was justified and that Christianity failed.

A second cluster of questions is related to Christianity being "the white man's religion." This was probably the most serious challenge against Christianity raised in African literature in the decades before and after independence.[23] There are a number of different elements that feed into this reproach that may have a different weight for particular conversation partners. This reproach may, in the first place, tie in with the issues of the first cluster: the Christian faith in its Western forms (both liberal and conservative) does not really deal with the practical and spiritual issues that are relevant to the daily lives of African communities. A second layer of the problem is related to the fact that Christian worship, church organization, theology, and so many other aspects of the Christian life as originally introduced by Western missionaries did feel deeply foreign. It was hard for many Africans to relate to these at deeper emotional levels. A third layer is the fact that in most contexts in Sub-Saharan Africa, Christianity was introduced together with the arrival of the colonial powers. The relationship between Christian mission and colonial powers was of course complex. Sometimes missionaries colluded with colonial powers; sometimes relations were much more tense because missionaries would side with the interests of the local population. In all cases, the instances of collusion and the simple fact that missionaries and colonizers were from the same cultural background made Christianity not only deeply suspect but feared or hated. A final layer in this cluster is that religious practices in Africa were traditionally tied in with one belonging to a family, clan, and tribe. They were about the harmony and flourishing of the clan and community, about relationships with deceased ancestors. How could a foreign religion contribute to such harmony?

Looking at these two clusters, it becomes clear that these apologetic issues are not merely intellectual. At an intellectual level, the reproach that Christianity is a European religion is relatively easy to answer: this religion originated from the Middle East and Jesus was a Jew. Yet, this intellectual answer does not take away the fact that Christianity in many of its forms seems irrelevant

---

[23]Jesse N. K. Mugambi, *Critiques of Christianity in African Literature: With Particular Reference to the East African Context* (Nairobi, KE: East African Educational Publishers, 1992).

to the daily challenges of African life, or that it is related to a history of colonization that has caused so much pain.

Thankfully, there are not only challenges, but also opportunities. The pragmatic bent of primal religions makes it relatively easy to start exploring other religious practices to see what they have to offer. It is the desire for salvation in African Traditional Religion that may well have been a decisive factor behind many of the conversions—it related positively to what the Christian faith had to offer.[24] Furthermore, particularly in the area of inculturation, much has happened in recent decades, both in theological reflection and in the life of the church. When looking to the pentecostalization of many churches in Africa (also in more traditional denominations), one now encounters a church that looks distinctively African. African Christianity no longer looks like a Western religion but has played a major role in the development of post-Western Christianity.[25]

Apologetic dialogue with traditional religions does of course have many layers and many aspects. All aspects of the general approach developed in the first part of this book will be relevant for apologetic witness to adherents of primal religions: it needs to be embodied, holistic, present the Christian faith as a whole, build bridges, witness to Christ, and so on. In the remainder of this chapter, we will focus on the role of inculturation or contextualization for apologetic dialogue with adherents of primal religions. The relevance of this focus becomes particularly clear in the need to deal with the two clusters of questions and objections just discussed, the idea that Christianity is the white man's religion and that it does not adequately deal with the challenges faced in everyday life in today's Africa.

8.3 POWER, RELEVANCE, AND TRUTH

Power encounters and truth encounters. As missiologist David Hesselgrave points out, "In the context of a tribal worldview, *power encounter* takes precedence over *truth encounter*."[26] This is also reflected in the reality that many conversions that we see today in the context of Hinduism, folk Buddhism, and folk Islam are triggered by experiences of the liberating and healing power of God.[27] A Christian leader from Bhutan shared with us that

---

[24]Cyril C. Okorocha, *The Meaning of Religious Conversion in Africa: The Case of the Igbo of Nigeria* (Brookfield, WI: Avebury, 1987).

[25]Bediako, *Christianity in Africa.*

[26]David J. Hesselgrave, *Communicating Christ Cross-Culturally: An Introduction to Missionary Communication*, 2nd ed. (Grand Rapids, MI: Zondervan, 1991), 231; italics original.

[27]E.g., Chad M. Bauman, "Does the Divine Physician Have an Unfair Advantage? Healing and the Politics of Conversion in Twentieth Century Northern India," in *Asia in the Making of Christianity*, ed. Richard Fox Young and Jonathan A. Seitz (Leiden: Brill, 2013), 297-321; Simon Chan,

his mother was the first to become a Christian in the family, and it happened because she experienced healing when a Christian neighbor prayed for her. This is reflected in one of the conclusions of an elaborate study of conversions among Nigerian Igbo to Christianity: "As a model of religious change, African conversion may be described as a case of 'power encounter' in terms of a confrontation between two or several systems of salvation, resulting in a conscious and rational movement on the part of the people in the direction of power."[28] Note that Okorocha considers this acceptance of Christianity a "conscious and rational movement." It is rational because if two movements claim to be "a power for salvation" (cf. Rom 1:16), then the question whether these religions can indeed deliver what they promise becomes crucial. In that sense, the primal worldview and Christian worldview do have a number of similarities that allow us to evaluate some of their claims according to partially overlapping criteria. It also means that this overlap in a longing for protection, healing, and blessing allows us to unmask a crucial inner tension in the primal worldview: it promises protection from evil forces, yet in practice it never provides full assurance that these forces are conquered. In practice it often increases fear of these powers. It is not able to break their hold. The power encounters are therefore also related to questions of truth: Do these religious mediators have the powers they claim or is their power severely limited because it is at its best only a power from within the created world and at its worst a lie or a usurped power that truly belongs to God?

The question of truth also comes up in another way, namely with regard to the question of how true divine power manifests itself and the nature of the salvation it intends to bring. From the perspective of primal worldviews, the power of Christ may be impressive, but it also has severe limitations. After all, Christ does not always protect us from evil and suffering. From the perspective of many primal religions, much or all serious suffering is caused by some evil influence and shows that the one who suffers is not fully experiencing the blessings of the spiritual world. During a seminar for church leaders among Aka-Pygmies in the Central African rainforest, Benno was once presented the following question by a church leader who said, "My brothers and friends mock me and say: 'What did your Christianity bring you? Two of your children died young. Can you trust

---

Grassroots Asian Theology: Thinking the Faith from the Ground Up (Downers Grove, IL: InterVarsity Press, 2014).

[28]Cyril C. Okorocha, "Religious Conversion in Africa: Its Missiological Implications," *Mission Studies* 9, no. 1 (1992): 174-75.

this God?'" Seeing suffering in the life of Christians was for some a reason not to embrace the Christian faith and, for this church leader, a cause for severe doubt.

Both in apologetic witness and in the discipling of Christians from these backgrounds, questions of truth will need to be raised. It is important to be clear that from a Christian perspective suffering is not always a sign of a curse or that God is not in control. In a Christian confession that was specifically written for the discipling of Christians among Aka-Pygmies, the continued presence of suffering in the life of Christians was explained as follows:

> The powers of sin, of death, and the spiritual and human powers that are in enmity with God continue to be active in this world. God still permits them in order to give to men and women in the whole world the possibility to hear the Good News of the victory of Jesus. The children of God also experience difficulties in this intermediate time. Sometimes they are hungry, they are ill and they die. Yet, they keep courage, for they know that the powers of evil are already conquered. They see the power of God manifest in their lives, when the sick are healed, when evil spirits are thrown out, when oppressed people are set free, when sinners are converted and when they experience the power of God in their weakness. In the most difficult moments, they know that their most precious treasures, the love of God, to be his children, and eternal life, can never be taken from them.[29]

Here, the reality of suffering is explained against the backdrop of a salvation that is much more encompassing than the salvation the traditional Aka religion promised or could even imagine: a salvation from the powers of sin and death, a fullness of life by being adopted as children of God. Another article of this confession concerning Christ's victory over sin and death through his cross and resurrection further explains the basis of this confidence:

> Jesus of Nazareth, the Son of God, suffered for humankind and died on the cross for them. On the cross, he took away the sin of humankind and he broke the power of sin and of the spiritual powers which oppose God and his plan. This victory became manifest after three days, when he rose from the dead and conquered the power of death. Under his protection, we need no longer fear any powers, because he reigns over all.[30]

---

[29]Benno van den Toren, "Growing Disciples in the Rainforest: A Contextualized Confession for Pygmy Christians," *Evangelical Review of Theology* 33, no. 4 (2009): 313.
[30]Van den Toren, "Growing Disciples in the Rainforest," 313.

Relating to felt needs. In the discussion of bridges that can be built between Christ and other religions (§6.5), we have so far given little attention to felt needs. These are an important area of common ground, for worldviews are structured in terms of relevance,[31] and deeply felt needs are near the center of issues that people may experience as most pressing and therefore most immediately relevant. Okorocha suggests that whether it has been explained this way or not, the Igbo understood the Christian message in terms of their own worldview[32] and therefore also in relation to their felt needs of blessing, protection, and salvation. This is also what the first hearers of Jesus' message would have done because this message of the kingdom spoke to the most pressing needs of the people.[33] The New Testament suggests that Jesus and the apostles were, for understandable reasons, most welcomed by those who were aware of their vulnerability and needs (Mk 2:17; 1 Cor 1:26-31).

However, there cannot be a direct correlation between felt needs and the message of the gospel, as in the apologetic correlation between human existential needs proposed by Paul Tillich. Tillich understands correlation as "interdependence of two independent factors" and as "a unity of the dependence and independence of two factors."[34] Thus it would be possible to provide an independent existential analysis of the human condition in order to show only subsequently how the Christian faith answers these needs. Tillich wrote this, however, in the 1950s, before postmodernism and globalization. Clearly colored by his cultural and social context, he was insufficiently aware that his analysis of human existence was not as universal as he believed it to be. One's cultural context, social location, and religious outlook deeply determine which needs are experienced as the most pressing and how they are interpreted. Tillich's understanding of correlation also neglects the influence of sin, which obscures our understanding of our real and deepest needs.

There is indeed a reciprocity between the gospel and human needs, but it is not a direct correlation between gospel and felt needs—it is a critical correlation. The gospel does indeed fulfill our deepest needs but this happens, in the words of Dutch missiologist Hendrik Kraemer, by way of

---

[31]Peter L. Berger and Thomas Luckmann, *The Social Construction of Reality: A Treatise in the Sociology of Knowledge* (Garden City, NY: Doubleday, 1966), 59.

[32]Okorocha, *Meaning of Religious Conversion*, xi; 1992.

[33]Charles H. Kraft, *Anthropology for Christian Witness* (Maryknoll, NY: Orbis Books, 1996), 395, 398 Kraft, *Communicating Jesus' Way*, rev. ed. (Pasadena, CA: William Carey Library, 1999), 53.

[34]Paul Tillich, *Systematic Theology*, vol. 2, *Existence and the Christ* (Chicago, IL: The University of Chicago Press, 1957), 13.

"subversive fulfillment."[35] Thus, the needs of African primal religionists for blessing, protection, and salvation may indeed be fulfilled in one's coming to Christ, but in the process they must also be subverted. Felt needs receive a new meaning in the context of our true human needs as understood in the light of the new "fullness of life" revealed in Christ. It becomes clear that we were created for a destiny that includes, but at the same time surpasses, the immediate needs of our physical and communal existence. Christ furthermore reveals new needs of which we may not have been aware: a need for the God for whom we were created, a need for reconciliation with this God, and a need for sanctification because of our own sinful alienation from God and destructive attitudes toward the community. It will therefore become clear that a fulfillment of our deepest needs will never happen without a conversion away from the ill-directedness, futility, and possibly even self-destructive nature of our search.

Relating the gospel to felt needs is not merely an issue of properly explaining how Christ relates to them. This is a prime area in which apologetics needs to be embodied. People need to be able to see and experience the first fruits of healing and liberation in the Christian community.[36] That the renewal of our relationship with God touches on all areas of life will need to become visible. Of course, this is often not the case. In the context of colonialism, Christianity has been associated with powers that oppress and enslave rather than liberate. Embodied apologetic witness demands that these dark sides of Christian history are recognized, and the Christian community shows a genuine repentance and desire to be a healing presence. It also begins with the recognition that community itself remains in need of healing.

8.4 CRITICAL CONTEXTUALIZATION

One of the crucial characteristics of apologetic witness in a multicultural and multireligious world that we have stressed throughout this book is for apologetic witness to be contextual. According to the Nigerian theologian Osadolor Imasogie, "If this task is to be successfully prosecuted the apologist must take cognizance of the particular spiritual, cultural and intellectual milieu of the non-Christian world to which he addresses himself."[37] Apologetic dialogue

---

[35]Hendrik Kraemer, "Continuity or Discontinuity," in *The Authority of the Faith*, ed. William Paton, Tambaram Series 1 (Oxford: Oxford University Press, 1939), 5; see further §9.3.

[36]Cf. Allan Varghese, "Social Action as Christian Social Apologetics: Through the Lives of Pandita Ramabai and Amy Carmichael," in *Advancing Models of Mission: Evaluating the Past and Looking to the Future*, ed. Kenneth Nehrbass, Aminta Arrington, and Narry Fajardo Santos, Evangelical Missiological Society Series 29 (Littleton, CO: William Carey Library, 2021), 153-68.

[37]Osadolor Imasogie, "Christian Apologetic Theology in a West African Context," *The Journal of the Interdenominational Theological Center* 7, no. 2 (1980): 134.

needs to relate to the specific questions, obstacles, and thoughtforms of the audience in view. It also needs to build bridges between particular alternative religious traditions and concrete people, with their particular histories that have shaped their views and attitudes. This engagement in contextual apologetic dialogue is part of a much broader need for contextualized expressions of Christian theology and Christian discipleship. Conversely, the apologetic encounter with primal religion shows that contextualizing Christian faith and practice is itself a part of, or necessary complement to, apologetic witness. Developing a Christian theology and practice that relates to the concrete experience of local communities is essential to overcoming the obstacle that the Christian faith is experienced as otherworldly and irrelevant to the daily needs and lives of average Africans. Developing an African theology and practice is equally crucial for overcoming the explicit criticism or implicit experience that Christianity is a white man's religion, and thus not for Africans. This is why African theologians have invested so much in developing an "African Christian identity."[38]

There is literature that elaborates on the question of how Christian faith is appropriately contextualized,[39] but these discussions move us beyond the confines of this specific discussion of the contextual nature of apologetic witness. It may be sufficient to stress that contextualization should always be critical contextualization[40] and that in the development of an *African* Christian identity, African Christians find their identity first and foremost in Christ.[41] In contextualization, particular cultural identities are both affirmed and judged from a Christocentric perspective.[42] This does not mean, however, that because the message is in the end about the universal Christ, the process of contextualization can be taken lightly. Christ can only be Lord if his lordship is related to the messages of all others who claim to be lord.[43] Christ can only be truly Savior of the entirety of our concrete human existence if his saving work relates to the needs we experience, reaching into the nooks and crannies of our existence. The question

---

[38]Kwame Bediako, *Theology and Identity: The Impact of Culture upon Christian Thought in the Second Century and in Modern Africa* (Oxford: Regnum Books, 1992).

[39]See for overviews, Stephen B. Bevans, *Models of Contextual Theology* (Maryknoll, NY: Orbis Books, 1992); Scott A. Moreau, "Evangelical Models of Contextualization," in *Local Theology for the Global Church: Principles for an Evangelical Approach to Contextualization* (Pasadena, CA: William Carey Library, 2010), 165-93.

[40]Paul G. Hiebert, "Critical Contextualization," *Missiology* 12, no. 3 (1984): 288-96.

[41]Bediako, *Theology and Identity*, 31-32.

[42]Benno van den Toren, "Kwame Bediako's Christology in Its African Evangelical Context," *Exchange* 26, no. 3 (1997): 218-32.

[43]Kwame Bediako, "How Is Jesus Christ Lord? Aspects of an Evangelical Christian Apologetics in the Context of African Religious Pluralism," *Exchange* 25, no. 1 (1996): 31-32.

is therefore not only how far we are *allowed* to contextualize before we become syncretistic, but how far we *need* to contextualize for Christ to become truly Lord and Savior of our different worlds.

Christianity as an African religion. Precisely because the Christian faith was so often criticized for being a Western and foreign religion, many African theologians and apologists have invested themselves to show that Christianity is also an African religion. This is not to deny that it is a universal religion, but to show that Christianity is at home in Africa and that Africans can find a home in the worldwide Christian family.[44] One cluster of answers given to show that the Christian faith is not foreign to Africa is to draw attention to Africa in the Bible and the history of the early church. In the Old Testament, Africans can, for example, point to the queen of Sheba, as well as references to Egypt, Nubia, and Cush. In the New Testament, they can refer to the temporary home Egypt provided for the young refugee family that fled the murderous king Herod, to Simon of Cyrene carrying the cross of Jesus, to the presence of Egyptians and Libyans among the crowd at Pentecost, and to the Ethiopian Eunuch.[45] From early church history, Africans can refer to the existence of a church in Alexandria (in Egypt) by the end of the first century (according to the tradition established by the evangelist John Mark), to the important role of the church in North Africa in the first centuries of the church, and to the early spread of the church to Ethiopia and southwards along the Nile to Nubia.[46]

The references to Africa in the Bible are of course less apologetically relevant for primal religions in other parts of the world. Yet, church history may equally have apologetic value elsewhere. The early history of the church in countries like Persia, India, and even China is crucial to counteract the idea that Christianity is not a properly Asian religion.[47] It may be equally important to show that many of the Christian heartlands behind the modern mission movement were touched by Christianity relatively late: parts of northern Europe only toward the end of the first millennium, the Americas only from

---

[44]E.g., Reuben Kigame, *Christian Apologetics Through African Eyes* (Nairobi, KE: Posterity Publishers, 2018), 240-74.

[45]David Tuesday Adamo, *Africa and the Africans in the Old Testament* (Benin City, NG: Justice Jeco Press & Publishers, 2005); Edwin M. Yamauchi, *Africa and the Bible* (Grand Rapids, MI: Baker Academic, 2006).

[46]Bengt Sundkler and Christopher Steed, *A History of the Christian Church in Africa* (Cambridge, England: Cambridge University Press, 2000); Thomas C. Oden, *How Africa Shaped the Christian Mind: Rediscovering the African Seedbed of Western Christianity* (Downers Grove, IL: InterVarsity Press, 2007).

[47]Philip Jenkins, *The Lost History of Christianity: The Thousand-Year Golden Age of the Church in the Middle East, Africa, and Asia- and How It Died* (New York: HarperOne, 2008).

the first half of the second millennium. Christianity is by definition a religion that can be translated into different languages and cultural forms, and is not bound to one specific geographic location.[48]

A second cluster of answers aiming to show that the Christian God and Christian message is not foreign to Africa also works for other primal religious contexts. With reference to the work of John Mbiti and others, we already pointed to the traces of belief in the Creator God in traditional Africa. This is then apologetically used as a *preparatio evangelica*, as a sign that the African primal religions were a preparation for the gospel that came in its fullness with Jesus Christ.[49] This understanding of God can be used as a bridge to the proclamation of Christ in a way similar to Paul drawing on the altar "to an unknown god" and the knowledge of the creator "in him we live and move and have our being" in Acts 17 (vv. 23, 28). This passage in Acts 17 is regularly used by African theologians for the formulation of a Christian apologetic in this primal context. It helps to relate to preexisting notions of God and to stress that so far primal religionists have lived in "ignorance" but that "now he commands all people everywhere to repent, because he has fixed a day on which he will have the world judged in righteousness by a man whom he has appointed, and of this he has given assurance to all by raising him from the dead" (v. 30).[50]

The search for parallels is not limited to the recognition of the Creator in traditional Africa. African theologians have given much attention to the study of the Old Testament, which shows so many parallels to the African experience—in its focus on purity and defilement, the sacrificial system and the priesthood, the role of family ties, and the traditional rural context.[51] African traditional culture is in fact much closer to the Old Testament than the modern Western world that introduced Christianity to Africa. Directly related to this love for the Old Testament is the popularity of the epistle to the Hebrews. One can also see the apologetic import of this letter (or sermon). The unknown

---

[48]Lamin O. Sanneh, *Translating the Message: The Missionary Impact on Culture* (Maryknoll, NY: Orbis Books, 1989); Andrew Walls, "The Translation Principle in Christian History," in *The Missionary Movement in Christian History: Studies in the Transmission of Faith* (Edinburgh: T&T Clark, 1996).

[49]John S. Mbiti, *New Testament Eschatology in an African Background: A Study of the Encounter between New Testament Theology and African Traditional Concepts* (London: Oxford University Press, 1971), 189.

[50]E.g., Imasogie, "Christian Apologetic Theology," 139; Bediako, *Christianity in Africa,* 101; Bediako, "How Is Jesus Christ Lord?," 39.

[51]Aloo O. Mojola, "The Old Testament or Hebrew Bible in Africa: Challenges and Prospects for Interpretation and Translation," *Verbum et Ecclesia* 35, no. 3 (2014): 1-7.

author of the epistle compares the Old Testament sacrifices and priesthood to the sacrifice and priesthood of Christ and shows that they are only a shadow of the fullness that is now revealed and become a reality in Christ. It thus provides a model for respecting the value of traditional sacrifices, showing that these do not make Christ's sacrifice superfluous but are, rather, surpassed and fulfilled in the sacrifice of Christ.[52]

A third aspect showing that Christianity is also a religion for Africans is not so much an argument as it is a need to show, in practice, that the Christian faith can be expressed in African cultural forms: song and rhythm, dress and ritual, buildings, and art that reflect African culture. Here, the life of a contextualized community relevant to local needs and expressed in appropriate cultural forms is a crucial aspect of an embodied apologetic. In the last decades, great progress has been made in this area, but this is an area that needs continued attention. This continued attention is needed because so many sources of traditional African culture can still be uncovered and used as treasures to glorify Christ. Continued attention is needed because, like everywhere, African culture is changing. In urban settings, it changes rapidly under the influence of modernization and globalization. Many modern Africans live lives that are still deeply and distinctively African but are at the same time increasingly influenced by Western modernity—modern tastes and modern media that are, in that sense, equally part of a cosmopolitan culture. Christianity also needs contextualized forms that relate to the new urban classes. Part of the success of new Pentecostal and Charismatic churches is precisely that they combine a deep sensitivity to aspects of the traditional spirit-filled worldview—including its need for healing and deliverance—with cosmopolitan expression, and attention to the needs and pressures experienced by the new urban middle class.[53]

A multifaceted Christology. In the first chapter, we defined apologetics as "the reflection on the dialogical witness to the truth and *relevance* of the Christian faith in order to recommend the Christian faith to those who do not yet believe" (§1.5). The aspect of relevance is important in any context but particularly so in the context of religious traditions that have such a strong pragmatic and anthropocentric focus as the primal religions. We indicated that we

---

[52]Imasogie, "Christian Apologetic Theology," 140; Kwame Bediako, "Jesus in African Culture: A Ghanaian Perspective," in *Jesus in Africa: The Christian Gospel in African History and Experience*, Theological Reflections from the South (Akropong-Akuapem, GH: Editions Clé; Regnum Africa, 2000), 25-27.

[53]Joseph Bosco Bangura, "The Charismatic Movement in Sierra Leone (1980–2010): A Missio-Historical Analysis in View of African Culture, Prosperity Gospel and Power Theology" (PhD Thesis, Amsterdam: VU University, 2013), 237-38.

cannot avoid raising questions of truth (§8.3). A position can in the end only be relevant if it helps us to live in the world, as the world truly is, rather than locking us inside our own phantom worlds. Religion can only be relevant if it helps us relate to God as God truly is rather than relating to our own idolatrous projections of what we might want God to be. Yet, in this context, questions of truth can only be addressed via questions of relevance, by showing that these questions of truth are indeed deeply relevant to experienced needs and lives as concretely lived. This issue of relevance is of course one further element in answering the question of Christianity being a foreign religion. One of the reasons it is considered foreign is that it is seen as answering questions Africans are not even asking, while neglecting the needs Africans feel. According to a famous quote of John V. Taylor,

> Christ has been presented as the answer to the questions a white man would ask, the solution to the needs that western man would feel, the Saviour of the world of the European world-view, the object of the adoration and prayer of historic Christendom. But if Christ were to appear as the answer to the questions that Africans are asking, what would he look like?[54]

In the light of the noted this-worldliness of the primal worldview, this means among other things that Christ needs to be related to this-worldly struggles and joys, rather than only to spiritual needs and eschatological fears and hopes. As Okorocha concludes, "The second missiological axiom is that our study of African conversion and religiousness compels us not to place a dichotomy between the gospel, in its 'spiritual' dimension, and social action, as a practical expression of that same gospel, in any given context. Proclamation and action must go together."[55]

The message of the Bible is deeply relevant to the daily needs of people struggling to feed their families, longing for healing, fearful of evil spiritual powers, and in need of reconciliation of broken relationships within the community. The questions from Africa are a call to the Western churches to receive aspects of this message that have for a long time been neglected either because the gospel was too spiritualized and otherworldly, or because daily life was so comfortable and under control that there was little need for God in the practicalities of life. The Christian message in the context of primal religions and folk religions therefore needs to be a message with particular attention to healing, deliverance, protection, and divine providence. This is one of the

---

[54]Taylor, *Primal Vision,* 16.
[55]Okorocha, "Religious Conversion," 176.

reasons that Simon Chan places so much stress on these themes because these relate to the challenges shared by both Christians and non-Christians among the Asian poor.[56]

Building these links to the needs and experiences in the primal religious way of life does of course need to happen in a process of *critical* contextualization. It does need to be stressed because God's projects for us are much bigger than this: God not only wants us to flourish physically and communally, but invites us to fullness of life in a relationship with Godself through his Son (Jn 10:10, 17:3). God not only wants us to flourish within the context of harmonious families, but God has a plan to reconcile all the nations and the entire creation under Christ (Eph 1:10; Col 1:20). He not only wants us to flourish in the short period between birth and death (and for some as ancestors), but has conquered death so that we may become a new creation and share in the eternal life of the risen Lord (1 Cor 15:42-48). We also discover that our deepest problem is not just our human weakness and the disharmony in our families and communities. Our deepest problem is our sin and enmity with God, which required a sacrifice beyond what we imagined. This, ancestors can never provide because they are mortals and sinners like us.[57]

This also points to the apologetic relevance of the question of how Christ is understood and proclaimed. The Christ of Western liberal Christianity— who gives meaning to life—or the Christ of Western conservative evangelicalism—who carries away our sin and guilt—may initially hold little attraction. In primal religions, the deepest problems of life are not relating to meaninglessness, but to powerlessness. The most pressing need is not for divine forgiveness, but for healing. Therefore, images of Christ as victor and healer are much more important in African Christianity than recent Western images of Christ.[58] These images will also have much more attraction in apologetic witness to primal religious communities.

Primal Religious communities invite the worldwide church to rediscover elements of biblical Christology that have been neglected elsewhere. This may

---

[56]Chan, *Grassroots Asian Theology*, 108-13.

[57]Kwame Bediako, "Biblical Christologies in the Context of African Traditional Religions," in *Sharing Jesus in the Two-Thirds World: Evangelical Christologies from the Contexts of Poverty, Powerlessness and Religious Pluralism: The Papers of the First Conference of Evangelical Mission Theologians from the Two Thirds World, Bangkok, Thailand, March 22-25, 1982*, ed. Vinay Samuel and Chris Sugden (Grand Rapids, MI: Eerdmans, 1984), 117; 2000, 26; cf. van den Toren, "Kwame Bediako's Christology," 218-32.

[58]John S. Mbiti, "Some African Concepts of Christology," in *Christ and the Younger Churches*, ed. George F. Vicedom and José Miguez Bonino, Theological Collections 15 (London: SPCK, 1972), 51-62; Imasogie, "Christian Apologetic Theology," 140, 143; Diane B. Stinton, *Jesus of Africa: Voices of Contemporary African Christology* (Maryknoll, NY: Orbis Books, 2004).

be crucial to reach parts of society in the West itself and in other parts of the world that find it harder to relate to the dominant understandings of the Christ of Western churches. This goes beyond the need to rediscover the role of Christ as Conqueror over the powers of evil, and as healer of human weakness and infirmity. It is an invitation to rediscover a much broader range of christological images that help show the relevance of Christ to a great variety of cultures. Christ is also the light of the world, an image that may well relate to those who look for Enlightenment.[59] Christ is also the one who shares and covers our shame, a powerful image in cultures in which shame—not guilt or evil powers—is one of the most decisive experiences and urgent needs.[60]

The need for and possibility of a rediscovery of the multifaceted nature of Christ's salvific work confirms that dialogue with other religions and ideologies can be deeply enriching because it allows us to discover new riches in Christ (§4.4). It also confirms that Christian apologetic persuasion is fundamentally triangular (§6.1): we are not simply sharing ideas; the gospel is not owned by the Christian apologist. We are pointing to a reality beyond ourselves, to a Christ we neither own, control, or fully grasp.[61] When we point our interlocutors to Christ, we ourselves may come to discover new aspects of his work for us and his meaning for our lives. Contextualization in general and contextual apologetic witness have the same structure exemplified in the invitation of Philip to Nathanael: "Come and see" (Jn 1:46). We witness to Christ so that they may discover for themselves who he is and what he means for them in their context.[62]

---

[59]Jey J. Kanagaraj, *The Gospel of John: A Commentary with Elements of Comparison to Indian Religious Thoughts and Cultural Practices* (Secunderabad, IND: OM Books, 2005), 270.

[60]Norman C. Kraus, *Jesus Christ Our Lord: Christology from a Disciple's Perspective* (Scottsdale, PA: Herald Press, 1987), 205; Jackson Wu, *Saving God's Face: A Chinese Contextualization of Salvation through Honor and Shame* (Pasadena, CA: William Carey International University Press, 2012).

[61]Bediako, "How Is Jesus Christ Lord?," 32-34, 39-40.

[62]Edward Rommen, *Come and See: An Eastern Orthodox Perspective on Contextualization* (Pasadena, CA: William Carey Library, 2013).

9

SUBVERSIVE FULFILLMENT
OF THE HINDU QUEST

9.1 THE INTERSECTION OF SOCIAL, POLITICAL, AND RELIGIOUS DIVISIONS

At the end of the five-day Tihar festival sometime in October or November, the Newars in Nepal's Kathmandu Valley celebrate *Bhai Tika*. Bhai Tika, elsewhere known as *Bhai Dooj, Bhaubeej*, or *Bhai Ponta*, is a celebration of family, particularly the relationship between brothers and sisters. Married daughters return to the homes of their parents and brothers. On this final day of Tihar, first a *puja* (worship and prayer) is offered to the gods Ganesh, Janmaraj, and Yamaraj and then the sisters offer their brothers fruits, flower garlands, and the *tika* on their foreheads. One of the garlands is made of the long-lasting amaranth flowers as a sign of longevity. The day is also an occasion for brothers to honor their sisters and to support them economically.[1]

Many Christians in Nepal, after their conversion, no longer participate in such festivals and have effectively been cut off from their community. They considered this part and parcel of their conversion from idolatrous practices or felt it was expected of them by the missionaries and new communities to which they now belonged. This was of course deeply painful and offensive to both their families and themselves as it blocks them from participating in one of the main occasions to celebrate their family ties and their love for their siblings. Hindu religious festivals take very different forms across different regions and communities. Yet, absence of particularly new Christians often occasions tense relationships or simply a significant distance between them and their families, and between Hindu and Christian communities. These festivals are deeply entangled with religious myths and worship, but

---

[1]Cindy Perry, "Bhai-Tika and 'Tij Braka': A Case Study in the Contextualization of Two Nepali Festivals," *Missiology: An International Review* 18, no. 2 (1990): 181.

they are also the prime occasions for celebrating community and reinforcing community values.

This extraction of new converts and separation of Christian communities from their Hindu environment have been characteristic of the modern Christian mission movement in the Indian subcontinent. It has contributed to the experience that Christianity is a foreign religion. This is further strengthened by the fact that the worship and lifestyle of many of the churches established by Western missions are seen as culturally foreign. A third aspect of this foreignness is that Christianity is perceived as the religion of the now former colonizers and neocolonial Western powers. This reproach has a long history but is currently exploited by various Hindu nationalist movements that label Islam as the religion of the Moghul oppressors, and Christianity as the religion of the British colonizers. In reality, Christianity is much older than British colonialism; the relationship between mission and colonialism is much more complex and even tense. There are also significant indigenous Indian Christian movements. Yet the continuing association of Christianity and colonialism remains strong.

The consequences of this for apologetic dialogue and witness can be seen in the ministry of N. V. Tilak (1862–1919). Tilak himself, after a long inner struggle, became a Christian from a Brahmin background. He was initially an example of this "extraction conversion." He discovered that many Hindus had genuine respect for Christ but were unwilling to commit to him. He also encountered situations in which his dialogue partners were fully convinced intellectually of the truth of Christ but then avoided further contact. Becoming a Christian was socially and culturally not an option for them.[2] These were Hindus who had seriously engaged with the Christian faith. Many more are in the same situation as Tilak himself in his earlier life. He was an ardent religious seeker, but because Christianity was so foreign and unattractive, the idea of considering Christ initially never crossed his mind.[3]

This means that forms of apologetic witness that isolate the intellectual challenge of the dialogue with the Hindu worldview from the rest of life will in most cases not be addressing the decisive barriers that need to be overcome. A holistic approach is needed in which questions of worldview are discussed but also combined with inculturation of the gospel message and political engagement. This also means that apologetic engagement will need to address a much wider range of themes than religious truth. Critical engagement with

---

[2] H. L. Richard, *Following Jesus in the Hindu Context: The Intriguing Implications of N. V. Tilak's Life and Thought* (Pasadena, CA: William Carey Library, 1998), 192.
[3] Richard, *Following Jesus*, 191.

different understandings of colonial history,[4] different constructions of
Hindu identity,[5] discussions of the relationship between the religious community and the thorny issue of conversion,[6] of projects for the future of India,[7]
of Independent Indian Christianity,[8] and of the theological value of Hinduism
in its varied forms, are also crucial to it.

In this chapter, we will focus on the theological value of Hinduism, exploring the apologetic value of the idea that Christ is the fulfillment of the Hindu
quest. As with the other chapters in the second part of this volume, these
reflections are also relevant for dialogue with other religious communities. In
the same way, the contributions on contextualization, the confrontation with
reality, idolatry, and so on, from the other chapters are also relevant for the
encounter with Hinduism. This focus on fulfillment is, however, appropriate
because it will explore the possibility of building bridges while maintaining
the decisiveness of God's salvific presence and action in Christ. It will also help
us to deepen some of the implications of the trinitarian theology of religions
developed in chapter four.

In a short introduction to Hinduism, we will explain why we focus—in this
chapter particularly—on the Bhakti traditions (§9.2). We will then critically
introduce the notion of subversive fulfillment, starting with the example of
Sadhu Sundar Singh, who himself represents Bhakti spirituality, both before
and after his conversion (§9.3). In a concluding section, we will consider how
the idea of fulfillment is also concretely embodied in contextual movements
such as the Krista Bhakti and what this might mean for attitudes to Hindu
religious festivals such as Bhai Tika (§9.4).

9.2 HINDUISM AND BHAKTI

Hinduism as a contested notion. In terms of its size, Hinduism is often understood to be the third largest religion in the world, yet the idea that many
religious expressions are brought together under the label of a single religion

---

[4]Vishal Mangalwadi, *Missionary Conspiracy: Letters to a Postmodern Hindu* (Mussoorie, IND: Nivedit Good Books, 1996); Brian Stanley, *The Bible and the Flag: Protestant Missions and British Imperialism in the Nineteenth and Twentieth Centuries* (Leicester, UK: Apollos, 1990).

[5]Vinoth Ramachandra, *Faiths in Conflict? Christian Integrity in a Multicultural World* (Leicester, UK: Inter-Varsity Press, 2000), 47-85.

[6]E.g., Sarbeswar Sahoo, *Pentecostalism and Politics of Conversion in India* (Cambridge: Cambridge University Press, 2018).

[7]Vishal Mangalwadi, *The Book That Made Your World: How the Bible Created the Soul of Western Civilization* (Nashville, TN: Thomas Nelson, 2011).

[8]P. E. Joshua, "Revival and Reformation: The Spirituality of Select Indian Instituted Churches and Their Role, Significance and Implications for Indian Christianity" (PhD Thesis, Amsterdam: VU University, 2013).

is contested. Originally, Hinduism was not a self-description of the people we now call Hindus. Though the use of the term *Hindu* was already used as a religious identification in contrast to *Yavana* (Muslim) as early as the sixteenth century,[9] the modern use of the term was shaped by the British colonizers. They began using it around the 1830s to group together religious expressions in the South Asian subcontinent that could be distinguished from Christianity, Islam, Buddhism, and possibly a number of other smaller religious movements. This use of a Western label resulted in a degree of so-called semitization of South Asian religious expressions. They were understood and described following the template of the Semitic religions (Judaism, Christianity, Islam) known best in the West for having religious scriptures, doctrines, a hierarchy, and so on. This semitization was not only used by outsiders, but also by Hindu reform movements who wanted to represent their religion to the West and in the modern world. This categorization of a broad range of movements as one religion also resulted in the tendency to consider the Sanskritic Brahmin traditions as the paradigmatic expression or even norm for Hinduism, this at the expense of other religious expressions in the region.[10] Alternative religious expressions in the region, such as the *Bhakti* traditions that developed focusing on the devotion to a specific god such as Vishnu,[11] did not necessarily originate as reform movements within this Brahmin religion, but as alternative religious traditions they often developed against the authority of high-caste Brahmins.[12]

Today the situation has become even more complex, as the label "Hinduism" has become an important political tool in Hindu nationalist movements. These nationalists have an interest in presenting themselves as representatives of a wide range of religious movements. As a consequence, diverse religious movements may have an interest in accepting this label in order to find a place within the Hindu nationalist project.

In its current form Hinduism may be seen as a "*family* of culturally similar traditions."[13] This raises a particular challenge for apologetic witness and

---

[9]Gavin Flood, *An Introduction to Hinduism* (Cambridge: Cambridge University Press, 1996), 6.

[10]Axel Michaels, Harald Fischer-Tiné, Patrick Eisenlohr, Adalbert J. Gail, Johannes Lähnemann, and Andrew Wingate, "Hinduism," in *Religion Past and Present: Encyclopedia of Theology and Religion*, ed. Hans Dieter Betz, Don S. Browning, Bernd Janowski, and Eberhard Jüngel, Hea-Jog (Leiden: Brill, 2009), 142.

[11]In Vaishnavism: Ute Hüsken, "Vaiṣṇavism," in *Religion Past and Present: Encyclopedia of Theology and Religion*, ed. Hans Dieter Betz, Don S. Browning, Bernd Janowski, and Eberhard Jüngel (Leiden: Brill, 2013), 255-56.

[12]Joshua, "Revival and Reformation," 163-73.

[13]Julius Lipner, *Hindus: Their Religious Beliefs and Practices* (London: Routledge, 1994), 5; emphasis original.

dialogue. In Christian apologetic exchange with Hinduism, there is a tendency to take one expression as paradigmatic for Hinduism, often the Brahminic *Advaita Vedanta* tradition.[14] This tradition has the strictest monist understanding of reality where only the absolute and ineffable *atman* truly exists. Individual existence and the world which we experience on a daily basis are considered *māyā* or illusion. This *Advaita* movement came to be seen as the ideal expression of Hinduism in part because it was presented as such by a number of intellectuals who became leading voices for Hinduism in the West. One example is Swami Vivekananda (1863–1902), founder of the Ramakrishna Mission who represented Hinduism at the parliament of the world's religions in Chicago (1893). It suited a Western and particularly Protestant tendency to understand religions primarily in terms of its doctrines. It may also have reflected the orientalist tendency to focus on what is most foreign in the Eastern cultures. Among Christian apologists, it was of course an ideal conversation partner for the representatives of worldview apologetics, which stressed the radical difference, inner cohesion, and incompatibility of different religions and worldviews.[15]

Hindu Bhakti. Apologetic dialogue with Hinduism will need to take into account that we encounter this religious family in many forms and shapes. As in any large family, there are family resemblances, but no features will characterize all family members equally. Any particular feature may be absent in at least some of its members. Some family members may even have joined through marriage or adoption. Thus the Lausanne Occasional Paper on "Christian Witness to Hindus" distinguishes philosophical Hinduism, religious Hinduism, popular Hinduism, tribal Hinduism, secular Hinduism, sects and cults—and these forms will each exist in a plurality of overlapping and hybrid forms.[16]

In this chapter, we will focus on apologetic dialogue with *Bhakti* traditions because of the deep religious devotion they express, because of the remarkable combination of both profound difference and resonance with the Christian tradition, and because of the way in which many bhaktas have seen their quest fulfilled in *Krista Bhakti* movements. Paul Joshua argues that Bhakti

---

[14]E.g., C. Fred Smith, "Apologetic Approaches to Hinduism," *UBS Journal* 6, no. 2 (2009): 116-31; Pradeep Tilak, "A Christian Worldview Apologetic Engagement with Advaita Vedanta Hinduism" (PhD Thesis, Louisville, KY: Southern Baptist Theological Seminary, 2013).

[15]E.g., James W. Sire, *The Universe Next Door: A Basic Worldview Catalog*, 5th ed. (Downers Grove, IL: IVP Academic, 2009); cf. Benno van den Toren, *Christian Apologetics as Cross-Cultural Dialogue* (London: T&T Clark, 2011), 208-10.

[16]Lausanne Committee for World Evangelization, "Christian Witness to Hindus," www.lausanne .org/content/lop/lop-14.

cannot be subsumed under Brahminic *Advaita Vedanta* as the normative expression of Hinduism. It is rather an alternative to and critical of this movement and possesses "its own integrity within this family of religions."[17] It focuses on personal love and devotion for the god of choice. It seeks personal mystical union with the divine rather than for a dissolution of one's personhood in the ocean of the impersonal divine. It has a theistic rather than atheistic or pantheistic worldview. As such, it also is more world-affirming than *Advaita Vedanta* which considers the world and history as *māyā* or illusion. *Bhakti* is anti-Sanskrit and anti-Brahmin: prayers are expressed in the vernacular (such as Tamil) and many of the representative poets are non-Brahmin. Furthermore, ignorance is not the only source of evil, as in Vedic theology, but the acknowledgment of sin is crucial to opening oneself up to the grace of God.[18] Bhaktas do not agree among themselves which God is the one God and is therefore most worthy of our devotion. For example, before his conversion to Christianity, Nilakantha Goreh, later Nehemiah Goreh (1825–1885), converted at the age of nineteen from the Shaivism of his upbringing (devoted to Shiva) to Vaishnavism because of his discovery of the supremacy of Vishnu in what he considered the most ancient Hindu texts.[19] Most Indian bhaktas belong to the Vaishnava movement. The International Society for Krishna Consciousness (ISKCON), also known as the Hare Krishna movement, dedicated to Krishna as avatar of Vishnu, may well be the *Bhakti* movement best known in the Western world. Despite the profound differences between the *Bhakti* and *Advaita* traditions in Hinduism, these movements also have significant commonalities, which show that they are part of the same religious "family": the belief that "God has an inexhaustible number of names,"[20] belief in reincarnation as a cycle from which we need to escape in order to attain *moksha* or liberation and an understanding of an *avatar* as the divine appearing in history.

Because of the need for contextual apologetic witness, close attention is needed for understanding their particular riches and challenges of the diverse expressions of Hinduism. Some of the lessons learned in reflecting on *Bhakti* will also be helpful elsewhere and may also be valuable for similar devotional and mystical expressions in other world religions. In the same

---

[17]Joshua, "Revival and Reformation," 163.

[18]Joshua, "Revival and Reformation," 163-73.

[19]Jon Keune, "The Intra- and Inter-Religious Conversions of Nehemiah Nilakantha Goreh," *Journal of Hindu-Christian Studies* 17, no. 1 (2004): 45-46.

[20]Hendrik M. Vroom, *No Other Gods: Christian Belief in Dialogue with Buddhism, Hinduism, and Islam* (Grand Rapids, MI: Eerdmans, 1996), 43-55; cf. Bibhuti S. Yadav, "Vaisnavism on Hans Küng: A Hindu Theology of Religious Pluralism," *Religion and Society* 27, no. 2 (1980): 32-64.

way, certain insights from the chapter on primal religions will be helpful for engaging with popular Hinduisms, elements from the chapter on Buddhism may help for engaging with *Advaita* traditions, and the chapters on secular idols and on late-modern spiritualities may help address secular Hinduism and modern spiritual movements. As a matter of principle, the proposal for contextual apologetic witness in this book does not intend to provide neatly packaged arguments that can be drawn on in precisely described situations. Dialogue and people are never neat and predictable but often rather messy. Our reflections on *Bhakti* are therefore rather meant to continue to develop sensitivity for the art of contextual, holistic, and performative apologetic dialogue and witness.

9.3 Subversive Fulfillment

Sadhu Sundar Singh. We want to introduce the notion of fulfillment with the example of Sadhu Sundar Singh (1889–1929). The Sadhu, as he is often endearingly called, was not an academic theologian, but in his conversion, his personal spirituality, and his ministry, he modeled a form of relating to his religious past and to a reality of God that can enrich critical academic theological reflection.

In Singh we have an example of a Christian convert who did not convert from another religion at its worst, we might say, but at its best.[21] Sundar Singh was born in a Sikh family "but in which the teaching of Hinduism was considered most essential."[22] His religious formation was deeply shaped by *Bhakti* spirituality through his Sikh and Hindu teachers and the spirituality of his mother. As a young man, Sundar Singh had a deep spiritual crisis and contemplated suicide unless God would appear to him to fulfill his deep spiritual yearnings. Very different from what he expected—it was not Krishna, Buddha, or some other *avatara* that appeared—but "the living Christ whom I had counted as dead."[23] His conversion led to a break with his family. In the course of his Christian education he entered St. John's Divinity School in Lahore to train for Anglican ministry, yet he dropped out after a few months because he felt that academic studies did not quench his spiritual thirst, feeling

---

[21]G. Francis S. Gray, "Sadhu Sundar Singh and the Non-Christian Religions," *International Review of Mission* 48, no. 4 (1959): 422.

[22]Sundar Singh, *With and Without Christ: Incidents Taken from the Lives of Christians and Non-Christians Which Illustrate the Difference in Lives Lived with Christ and without Christ* (New York: Harper and Brothers Publishers, 1929), 105.

[23]Singh, *With and Without Christ*, 118; cf. Ivan Satyavrata, *God Has Not Left Himself without Witness* (Oxford: Regnum Books International, 2011), 141.

foreign to his Indian context. By then, he had already opted for life as a *sadhu,* a traditional holy man. Like Justin Martyr († 165) long before him retained his philosopher's robe after his conversion to the Christian faith (as the true philosophy), Sundar Singh fulfilled his preconversion vow to be a *sadhu* because for him Christ was the true goal of the *sadhu's* quest.

In an oft-quoted reference, Sundar Singh says, "Christianity is the fulfillment of Hinduism. Hinduism has been digging channels. Christ is the water to flow through these channels."[24] The *sadhu* has not himself reflected systematically on the precise meaning of this notion, but one can detect a number of elements from his teachings and life. First, the *Bhakti* tradition was the framework that prepared him for his encounter with Christ. This helped shape the theological vocabulary to interpret it both at the time and later in his life.[25] Second, just as Tilak said that he came "by the bridge of [the Tamil bhakti poet] Tukaram to the feet of Christ,"[26] *Bhakti* mystics and seekers were for Sundar Singh both an example of a real quest and a degree of true knowledge of God: "Among its [Hinduism's] teachers were many real seekers after truth and bhaktas or devotees, who had received some measure of light from that God who 'left not Himself without witness' among the nations (Acts 14:16-17)."[27]

A principal example was his own mother, who for him could not simply be called a "heathen" because of her true devotion—a devotion he considered superior to many who called themselves Christians.[28] A third aspect was his choice to be a *sadhu* which was not merely a pragmatic and contextual preference in order to reach people in his culture with the gospel of Christ. Rather "in Sundar Singh's pursuit of Christian discipleship, the cross, the ideal of suffering, and selfless service, finds unique fulfillment in the sadhu idea of self-denial and renunciation for the purpose of God-realization."[29]

Unlike other converts of Hinduism like Krishna Mohan Banerjea (1813–1885) and Nehemiah Goreh (1825–1895), Sundar Singh cannot be considered an apologist.[30] He would probably have frowned at the term. For him argumentation was of limited value as true encounter with Christ was a matter of

---

[24]Burnett Hillman Streeter and Aiyadurai Jesudasan Appasamy, *The Sadhu: A Study in Mysticism and Practical Religion* (London: Macmillan, 1921), 232.

[25]Satyavrata, *God Has Not Left Himself without Witness,* 154-66.

[26]Quoted in R. H. S. Boyd, *An Introduction to Indian Christian Theology* (Madras, IND: The Christian Literature Society, 1969), 117.

[27]Sundhar Singh, *The Search After Reality: Thoughts on Hinduism, Buddhism, Muhammadanism and Christianity* (London: MacMillan and Co., 1925), 22.

[28]Gray, "Sadhu Sundar Singh," 422-23.

[29]Satyavrata, *God Has Not Left Himself Without Witness,* 184.

[30]David Emmanuel Singh, "Sunder Singh and N. V. Tilak: Lessons for Missiology from 20th Century India?," *Dharma Deepika* (December 2010): 10.

immediate experience: "Only those who commune with God in prayer can really know Reality."[31] Yet, we believe that Sundar Singh's insights can and must be integrated into a broader more holistic understanding of apologetics. The *sadhu's* contribution is even essential, for it helps us locate intellectual exchange in the context of a human quest for God. In this sense, Sundar Singh's reflections often closely resemble notions of the innate desire for God in the Western tradition, following Augustine, Pascal, and C. S. Lewis, even where he does not mention their names.[32] On the other hand, religious experiences are not self-authenticating and self-interpreting. Their authenticity can be denied. They can be interpreted very differently, for example, as coming from a named God, from an ineffable divinity, from our own human projections, or from demonic influence. Religious experience is itself a theme in critical interreligious dialogue. If some religious experiences might indeed be self-authenticating, experience suggests that these are not given to all.

Fulfillment. One major metaphor or model that has been used to understand the relation between Christianity and the different religious traditions of the world is fullfilment[33]—as, for example, in John Nicol Farquhar's understanding that Christianity is *The Crown of Hinduism.*[34] Differently from Sundar Singh's formulation that "Christianity is the fulfillment of Hinduism," we would prefer to speak of *Christ*, rather than Christianity, as the fulfillment. We would furthermore see Christ primarily as fulfillment of the *deepest human longings* that are part of the driving forces behind the religious quest. Only secondarily can we also speak of Christ and Christianity as the fulfillment of other religions, and only insofar as these traditions are true to these deepest human longings, and insofar as Christianity is true to these longings and to Christ. It is important to distinguish between the ontological orientation or "desire" of every human being to God's love in Christ and the many desires that shape human life and human religion. The latter are rooted in this ontological desire but take multiple shapes, some healthy, some destructive, some appropriate, and some misguided.[35] Insofar as religious traditions reflect this original religious longing, they can be fulfilled in Christ. But, because that is not always case (and often it is not), we also need other metaphors and models for understanding the relationship between Christ and the religions.

---

[31]Singh, *Search After Reality*, 9.

[32]E.g., Singh, *Search After Reality*, 21, 34, 58-59.

[33]Paul F. Knitter, *Introducing Theologies of Religions* (Maryknoll, NY: Orbis Books, 2002), 61-106.

[34]J. N. Farquhar, *The Crown of Hinduism* (London: Oxford University Press, 1913); cf. Satyavrata, *God Has Not Left Himself without Witness*, 47-90.

[35]Cf. Klaas Bom, "Directed by Desire: An Exploration Based on the Structures of the Desire for God," *Scottish Journal of Theology* 62, no. 02 (2009): 135-48.

While respecting these limitations, it is important to take this notion of fulfillment seriously. According to Ivan Satyavrata, there is "a widespread appropriation of the fulfilment concept as a unifying phenomenon among [former Hindu] converts."[36] We may not be able to universalize his estimation, as he focuses mainly on converts from a high-caste Hindu background. Yet our estimation is that the fulfillment structure will also be recognized by many converts from other religious traditions, such as primal religions and Islam. Given the value of insights from conversion stories for apologetic witness and dialogue, we want to explore this notion in more depth.

The fulfillment approach has its roots in the New Testament, where Jesus said, "Do not think that I have come to abolish the law or the prophets; I have come not to abolish but to fulfill" (Mt 5:17). This was a programmatic statement at the beginning of the Sermon on the Mount concerning his relationship with earlier Jewish religious traditions. The notion of fulfillment in the Jewish tradition is central to the Gospel of Matthew but equally present in most other New Testament authors (e.g., Lk 4:21; Heb 1:1-4). The relationship of Jesus Christ to the Jewish tradition is of course particular because of the role of the Jewish people in the history of salvation. The New Testament, however, also uses a fulfillment type structure in its relationship with the Gentile religions. In the text of Acts already quoted above by Sundar Singh, Paul tells his Gentile audience in Lystra that "in past generations he allowed all the nations to follow their own ways; yet he has not left himself without a witness in doing good— giving you rains from heaven and fruitful seasons, and filling you with food and your hearts with joy" (Acts 14:16-17). In Lystra, he was unable to finish his address, but from his speech in Athens recorded in Acts 17, he used quotes from Greek altars, poets, and philosophers as a bridge to talk about the new times that have now come with the arrival and resurrection of Christ (Acts 17:22-31; cf. §4.4).[37]

Some of the early Greek church fathers, such as Clement of Alexandria, used a similar fulfillment theory to build bridges to Greek philosophy. Drawing on the Gospel of John and Stoic philosophy, they undergirded this with a logos Christology. They argued that Christ as logos has been present and active since the beginning of creation and could therefore have been partially known thus preparing for his incarnation in the fullness of time. The Fathers therefore universalized salvation history: God not only prepared for the full- ness of time in the history of Israel, but all human history was destined to

[36]Satyavrata, *God Has Not Left Himself without Witness*, 26.
[37]Satyavrata, *God Has Not Left Himself Without Witness,* 204-5.

reach its fullness in the incarnation of the Son, bearing the traces of that destiny. They were, however, careful to distinguish between "different kinds of participation in the *Logos* by the pagan, Jew and the Christian."[38] They had a more critical attitude to pagan traditions than to the Hebrew Bible but understood both in the light of God's self-revelation in Christ.

Beyond the fulfillment of Jewish salvation history and the logos model of the church fathers, Satyavrata distinguishes a third model: the nineteenth-century European approach that works with a Darwinian evolutionary model. This model places religions on an evolutionary scale, with the lowest religions (such as animism) at the bottom gradually progressing through other religions such as Hinduism and Islam to (liberal Protestant) Christianity at the top or beyond Christianity. This model also influenced Farquhar's *Crown of Hinduism*.[39] We see the apologetic value of the fulfillment model in the first two versions described here, as used in the New Testament and church fathers. Some variety of the logos model can be further developed in relation to Hinduism. However, we have serious questions concerning the evolutionary model of fulfillment theology, because it implies that humanity is progressing in a gradual line with Christians and Christianity on a higher stage than other religionists. This seems to be inappropriate given the many wise and beautiful people we encounter in other religions, the corruption that equally distorts many expressions of Christianity, and the theological recognition that we have nothing that we have not received by grace in Christ.

A trinitarian theology of religions as developed in chapter four is a better framework for fulfillment theology than an evolutionary framework. If the Father created the universe and humanity for the Son, our created existence is not accomplished in itself, but is open to and in need of Christ. In as far as religions (and their scriptures) are true to what they can perceive of the Creator in creation and properly recognize the deepest longings of the human heart, they may point beyond themselves (§4.3). The Holy Spirit who is universally present is always the Spirit of Christ. This Spirit will kindle this desire for an openness to God's future. The Spirit will seek to lead individuals and communities in various ways, to live in accordance with what is revealed in creation, and in view of the glorious future for which humanity is created (§4.5). Yet, Christ is not a direct fulfillment of all human desires. In Christ, we also discover that human religiousness is not only an expression of a desire for God, but also a flight from God, an effort to create surrogates and often a

---

[38]Satyavrata, *God Has Not Left Himself Without Witness*, 13.
[39]Satyavrata, *God Has Not Left Himself Without Witness*, 14-15, 69.

tool of oppression and self-aggrandizement. As was pointed out with reference to Barth and Kraemer, this is equally true for Christianity as a human
enterprise that is open to all sorts of distortions, reflecting human sin and
weakness. Christians need to constantly return to Christ and open themselves
up to the Spirit for the fulfillment of their lives and the pruning of their all too
human religiousness (§4.3).

This trinitarian model also helps us address another question regarding the
fulfillment model, concerning the direction of the fulfillment: In what direction does this fulfillment take place? Is it only Christ and Christianity that
fulfills other religious aspirations or is Christianity in some way itself fulfilled
in its ongoing encounter with other religions? B. F. Westcott, for example, suggests a mutual fulfillment approach.[40] John Cobb proposes a radical pluralism
in which each religion "in faithfulness to its past [searches] to be enriched and
transformed in its interaction with other religious traditions."[41] It is beyond
the scope of this study to discuss this complex question in detail. We have
argued, however, that Christ is God's final and, in principle, unsurpassable
self-revelation and how creation was from its origin intended to find its destiny in him (§4.4). If this is the case, the fulfillment relationship cannot be
symmetric: Christ is uniquely unique because of who he is and what he
accomplishes. It is, however, not inconceivable that Christians learn from
other religions and that there might be mutual learning.[42] The spiritual journey of Sadhu Sundar Singh suggests that he did indeed enrich the Christian
tradition by bringing in lessons and practices from the traditions of the *sadhu*.
Mission historian Andrew F. Walls famously argued, "Christ himself actually
grows through the work of mission."[43] Since the gift of the Spirit at Pentecost,
the message of Christ is translated in ever new cultural forms; it takes on new
meanings that enrich the Christian understanding of Christ.[44] If we cannot
neatly distinguish culture from religion, the new cultures the global church
encounters on its mission journey will also be influenced by the dominant
religious traditions. If our understanding of the gospel is enriched by other

---

[40]Satyavrata, *God Has Not Left Himself Without Witness*, 23.

[41]John Cobb, "Beyond 'Pluralism,'" in *Christian Uniqueness Reconsidered: The Myth of a Pluralistic Theology of Religions*, ed. Gavin D'Costa (Maryknoll, NY: Orbis, 1990), 92; quoted in Satyavrata, *God Has Not Left Himself Without Witness*, 239.

[42]Cf. Gerald R. McDermott, *Can Evangelicals Learn from World Religions? Jesus, Revelation and Religious Traditions* (Downers Grove, IL: InterVarsity Press, 2000).

[43]Andrew F. Walls, introduction to *The Missionary Movement in Christian History: Studies in the Transmission of Faith* (Edinburgh: T&T Clark, 1996), xvii.

[44]Andrew F. Walls, "Ephesian Moment: At a Crossroads in Christian History," in *The Cross-Cultural Process in Christian History: Studies in the Transmission and Appropriation of Faith* (Maryknoll, NY: Orbis, 2002), 72-81.

cultures, it will equally happen through encounters with religious traditions that shape them, as the pilgrimage of Sundar Singh and other Indian converts have shown. Enrichment in religious encounter will therefore be reciprocal, but not symmetrical, for God's decisive revelation in Christ will always remain the principal criterion by which we can judge where the Spirit is leading the church (cf. §4.5). It is under Christ that God intends to bring all humanity together and to Godself (Eph 1:10; Col 1:15-20).[45]

Subversion. Christ can thus be seen as the fulfillment of the Hindu religious quest, as seen in the stories of Tilak and Sundar Singh. Yet, our reflections on the role of sin in the human religious enterprise show that Christ and the belief in the trinitarian God are also critical of human religion. This can be expressed with the notion of "subversive fulfilment," which we borrow from Hendrik Kraemer.[46] Fulfillment of the human religious quest is never merely a direct answer in line with the quest, as if Christ is simply the last step in a continuous religious evolution. First, Christ is always different than expected. Accepting the divine response to the human religious quest always demands some form of conversion, a turning around. It may be too dogmatic to presuppose that there is one way in which such conversion may be needed and to suppose, for example, that "all human-made religion is self-centered," "all human-made religions is a form of self-justification," or "all human religion is a form of salvation by our own efforts." Sometimes this may not be the case because of common grace and the work of the Spirit already present. Yet, such aberrations often characterize the religious quest (including the quest of many Christians), and it may be wise to suppose that the finding of fulfillment also demands some form of criticism of the direction or form of the quest itself. Sometimes earlier devotion will even need to be exposed as idolatry, be it idolatrous nationalism, the idolatrous secular gods, or religious idol worship (cf. §12.2). Yet, even when subversion is most radical, there are always traces of truth and of valid desires that may need to be redeemed, finding fulfillment in Christ. Second, subversion has a political connotation. True religious fulfillment can never happen if the oppressive social structure of the caste system, that is part of many and perhaps most streams within Hinduism, remains intact. This is one of the criticisms of

---

[45]Benno van den Toren, "The Relationship Between Christ and the Spirit in a Christian Theology of Religions," *Missiology: An International Review* 40, no. 3 (2012): 272-74.

[46]Hendrik Kraemer, "Continuity or Discontinuity," in *The Authority of the Faith*, ed. William Paton, Tambaram Series 1 (Oxford: Oxford University Press, 1939), 5; cf. also Michael W. Goheen, "Is Lesslie Newbigin's Model of Contextualization Anticultural?," *Mission Studies* 19, no. 2 (2002): 136-58.

fulfillment theology from Dalit theologians. They see it as a theology of high-caste Christians who want to maintain as much continuity with a religious system that Dalit experience as deeply oppressive. This explains why a confrontational approach to Hinduism was more effective among Dalit communities.[47] Fulfillment of our deepest religious desires in Christ must always be subversive of the ways in which religions, including Christianity, have been used to support social inequality.

To these aspects of subversion, we can add two points of discontinuity between Christ and human religions (in a more general sense). There is a third discontinuity despite the continuity because, as we see in Sundar Singh's testimony, the *Bhakti* devotional quest has not been able to produce Christ out of its own riches. Christ is a radically new gift from God, and Christ can be the only answer to this quest.[48] This answer is always a gift of grace and can never be the natural outcome of the quest. Fourth, Christ is never in continuity with all aspects of the former religion. Many aspects of the religion will need to be criticized in light of the new faith in Christ. Thus, Sundar Singh gave a new meaning to the vocation of a *sadhu*. He no longer understood the ascetic practices as salvific in themselves, because for him creation was a good gift of his heavenly Father. Furthermore, this renunciation was no longer a path to self-realization, but rather "renunciation for the purpose of selfless service of the poor."[49] Because of this fourfold discontinuity and subversion, Christ is not only the fulfillment of the religious quest, but "the crisis of all religions," including the Christian religion in as far as it is also a tainted human project.[50]

This notion of "subversive fulfillment" allows us to understand why some conversion stories, such as Sundar Singh's, can stress continuity, while others such as Rabindranath Maharaj in *Death of Guru*, stress the radical discontinuity: "There was no compromise, no possible blending of Hinduism and true Christianity. They were diametrically opposed."[51] The two aspects come together in the conversion story of Michael Graham, a former follower of the guru Muktananda who in one place can say, "Walking with Christ was not an extension or a magnification of the old or a *fulfillment* of something familiar. . . . It wasn't a further development on an

[47]Satyavrata, *God Has Not Left Himself without Witness*, 240-41.

[48]Satyavrata, *God Has Not Left Himself without Witness*, 171, 176.

[49]Satyavrata, *God Has Not Left Himself without Witness*, 181.

[50]Hendrik Kraemer, *The Christian Message in a Non-Christian World* (London: Edinburgh House Press, 1938), 110.

[51]Rabi R. Maharaj, *Death of a Guru: A Remarkable True Story of One Man's Search for Truth* (London: Hodder & Stoughton, 2004), 134.

already existing evolutionary trajectory. There was a hiatus. Michael Graham then died and a vestigial new being began to arise and take shape."[52]

Yet, in the same book he argues that "the Easterner's spiritual quest [finds] in Jesus Christ . . . it's [sic] object and in him the entire quest is fulfilled."[53] The notion of subversive fulfillment allows one to approach different expressions of Hinduism and other religions with openness and without a preconception of which one of the two aspects dominates. Those who stress continuity will stress the fulfillment, and those who stress the discontinuity will stress the subversion.[54] In the Bible, the attitudes toward the religion of those outside the covenant community differ greatly, as can be seen in the difference between the attitude to the mysterious Melchizedek in Genesis 14 and the attitude to Baal worship. Because of the realities of creation, logos, and Spirit on the one hand, and human finitude and sin on the other, both aspects will be there. Yet, because every community and human being is unique—because of the subtlety of sin and because the Spirit works in mysterious ways—we cannot know in advance how this will work out in concrete situations. Within the range of religious expressions grouped under the label of Hinduism, we therefore should not look for one way in which Christ fulfills a single quest, but rather a range of relationships in which subversion and fulfillment relate in various ways.

The dialectic of subversive fulfillment also helps us respond to one of the enduring criticisms of the fulfillment theory—that there are in fact no such desires in Hinduism to which the Christian faith responds. Hinduism responds to its own needs; Christianity brings an entirely new hope that could not be imagined before.[55] However, the issue is not whether these longings can be seen as an arrow directly pointing to the as yet unknown Christ. It is from the perspective of Christ and of the new life in him that the former desires and quest can be seen as originating in our being created for Christ—even though often misdirected and distorted. With a critical realist epistemology presupposed in our approach, "elements of the old paradigm can be incorporated in the new, but because they are part of a new configuration, they take on new meanings."[56]

---

[52]Michael Graham, *From Guru to God: An Experience of the Ultimate Truth* (Hyderabad, London: Authentic Books, 2007), 165.

[53]Graham, *From Guru to God,* 199-200.

[54]D. Strange, "For Their Rock Is Not as Our Rock: The Gospel as the 'Subversive Fulfillment' of the Religious Other," *Journal of the Evangelical Theological Society* 56, no. 2 (2013): 379-95.

[55]Alfred G. Hogg, "'The Crown of Hinduism' and Other Volumes [Review]," *International Review of Mission* 3, no. 4 (1914): 171-74; Kraemer, "Continuity or Discontinuity," 6; Satyavrata, *God Has Not Left Himself without Witness,* 72-76.

[56]P. G. Hiebert, *The Missiological Implications of Epistemological Shifts: Affirming Truth in a Modern/ Postmodern World* (Harrisburg, PA: Trinity Press International, 1999), 79.

Sadhu Sundar Singh has been criticized for not giving sufficient attention to the discontinuity between the desired mystical union with the divine in *Bhakti* and the historical revelation of God in Jesus Christ—therefore, his Christ is considered docetic.[57] This is a crucial issue given the centrality of the value of salvation history as one of the principal areas of discontinuity between Hinduism and the Christian faith. It is also a crucial theme in Hindu-Christian encounter. It is indeed true that for Sundar Singh the direct experience of Christ sometimes overshadows the crucial place of the witness to the salvific events in Jesus of Nazareth as the center of history (cf. chap. 5). For example, he says, "If all men had the receptive spirit and the ready ear and could hear the voice of God speaking to them, it would not be necessary for Evangelists and Prophets to go about proclaiming the will of God."[58]

On the other hand, the *sadhu* took the historical facts of the life of Jesus Christ rather literally.[59] This tension in his formulations may be one of the consequences of the fact that the *sadhu* was, first of all, a mystic and evangelist, not a systematic theologian. The role of the historical Christ, however, needs particular attention in the apologetic encounter with Hinduism. This is not only here that the crucial difference between Jesus Christ and a Hindu *avatar* becomes clear, but it is also related to the Christian understanding of salvation—not as salvation from history, but of our embodied historical existence.[60] This does not mean that we need a Western style historic apologetic to the resurrection. These Western apologies tend to respond to specifically modern Western historical criticism, itself partially a product of Christianity as a historical religion. What we need is a joyful witness to what it means that God entered our history in Christ.[61] Critical historical objections only need to be responded to if and when they come up (see further §5.3).

The fulfillment model as the end of true dialogue? One can see how the fulfillment model allows for apologetic dialogue that seeks for what is best in Hinduism, for an openness that allows for mutual enrichment. At the same time, it recognizes the decisive place of Christ in the history of

---

[57]Kaj Baagø, *Pioneers of Indigenous Christianity*, Confessing the Faith in India Series 4 (Bangalore, IND: Christian Institute for the Study of Religion and Society and the Christian Literature Society, 1969), 62-63.

[58]Sundar Singh, *Reality and Religion: Meditations on God, Man and Nature* (London: MacMillan and Co., 1924), 11.

[59]Singh, *Search After Reality*, 60-66; cf. Satyavrata, *God Has Not Left Himself Without Witness*, 177.

[60]See further Vinoth Ramachandra, *The Recovery of Mission: Beyond the Pluralist Paradigm* (Grand Rapids, MI: Eerdmans, 1997), 240-56.

[61]Cf. Varughese John, "A Sense of History and Apologetics in a Hindu Context," *Missiology* 36, no. 2 (2008): 219-26.

salvation and explains why Christians want to share this precious gift and truth. Yet, the fulfillment model also has its critics who argue that no true dialogue is possible if one party is already convinced that the relative value of the other's perspective can only be measured in relation to a criterion that one sets in advance—in this case Jesus Christ as witnessed in the Christian Scriptures.[62] For this context it is particularly relevant to consider the criticism of the fulfillment theology of the early Hans Küng in *Freedom Today*, by the Vaishnavist philosopher and theologian Bibhuti Yadav.[63] According to Küng, God is present and speaks in the religions, but since humanity is created for Christ, all religions will eschatologically find their fulfillment in him. Yadav experiences this, understandably, as deeply offensive. He scathingly evaluates, "The uniqueness of this God is to enslave religions in the name of 'loving' them, to not be bored with repeating what was done 'once for all.'"[64] For Yadav, this conception is incompatible with true openness to other religions. Though he does not use the term, he would probably evaluate it as a continuation of the European colonial attitude toward India and its religions.[65] He would probably have said the same of the position we represent in this book.

Yadav is critical of Küng's manner of interpreting Hinduism and other religions from a particular Christian perspective on God's relationship to the world. The first part of the response is that Yadav himself does the same from his Vaishnavist Hindu perspective. In line with the Vaishnavist philosopher Vallabhacharya (1479–1531), he proposes a sophisticated understanding of the nature of the divine, of divine speech, and of human religious texts from which he argues that "all the scriptures of all the religions are true because God has spoken them all."[66] His position provides an illustration of D'Costa's argument, that true pluralism is an impossible position. Even a supposedly pluralist theology of religions also represents a theological and religious position that excludes others.[67] Yadav could argue that he at least does not consider Vaishnavism and its scriptures superior to Christianity. Yet, his own position is itself shaped by a particular Vaishnavist understanding of the divine and by an understanding of the human condition from which salvation is needed. According to Yadav, "God comes to people . . .

---

[62]Knitter, *Introducing Theologies of Religions*, 103-4.

[63]Hans Küng, *Freedom Today*, Theological Meditations (New York: Sheed and Ward, 1966), 109-61.

[64]Yadav, "Vaisnavism on Hans Küng," 39.

[65]Paul J. Griffiths, ed., *Christianity through Non-Christian Eyes* (Maryknoll, NY: Orbis, 2004), 235.

[66]Yadav, "Vaisnavism on Hans Küng," 56.

[67]Gavin D'Costa, "The Impossibility of a Pluralist View of Religions," *Religious Studies* 32, no. 2 (1996): 223-32.

because he knows there is no man-made solution to the man-made problem *that is history.*[68]

A second and closely related part of the answer is that the Christian understanding of the uniqueness of God's presence and salvific acts in Christ is intrinsically related to the Christian understanding of the human predicament and of the nature of salvation. Christian salvation is not salvation *from* history, as for Yadav and other strands of Hinduism. God saves humanity in Christ, in history and creation, in view of a resurrected existence in the new creation.[69] Both the Christian and Vaishnavist position will need to be appreciated on their own merits. We have explained why Christians can be humble, vulnerable, and open in such a conversation while remaining confident in what they have received in Christ (§4.6). A third step would be to explore the relevance and realism of the Christian understanding of the human predicament and of salvation, and to explore the reasons to have confidence in Christ rather than in other or all revelations. This raises particular issues for Yadav's and similar "pluralist" positions. As Newbigin argues, religions offer different and often contradictory understandings of salvation. The question of whether some understandings of the nature of the human predicament and of salvation are more truthful than others cannot be avoided if we expect any guidance from religion in these matters.[70]

9.4 CONCLUDING REFLECTIONS

As in the other chapters, the exploration of the subversive fulfillment of the Hindu quest is only exemplary and exploratory—it can be developed in many different directions. The purpose of this chapter is not to present one normative model for apologetic exchange with Hinduism, but rather to nurture an expectation that there are desires (even when partially distorted or misdirected), partial truths, and intimations in diverse streams within Hinduism and other religious traditions that can be related to God in Christ. We have focused our attention on the religious desire as nurtured in the *Bhakti* tradition. One could, for example, further explore the notion of sacrifice both in the Rigveda, as used by Banerjea,[71] and in many day-to-day Hindu practices, the recognition of the moral requirements of the human being in

---

[68]Yadav, "Vaisnavism on Hans Küng," 58; italics ours.

[69]Lesslie Newbigin, *The Gospel in a Pluralist Society* (Grand Rapids, MI: Eerdmans, 1989); Ramachandra, *Recovery of Mission.*

[70]Lesslie Newbigin, "Religion for the Marketplace," in *Christian Uniqueness Reconsidered: The Myth of a Pluralistic Theology of Religions,* ed. Gavin D'Costa (Maryknoll, NY: Orbis, 1990), 142f.

[71]Satyavrata, *God Has Not Left Himself Without Witness,* 105-12.

the *Bhagavad-Gita*,[72] or the belief and expectations related to the *avatar*. In all cases, talk of fulfillment will need to be accompanied by an awareness of the subversion that is part of the same process.

There are of course areas in which opposition and tension are more pronounced than continuity, as reflected in the Dalit criticism of the caste system. Yet Pandita Ramabai (1885–1922) and other examples show that one can be deeply critical while at the same time keeping as close as possible to contextually relevant and recognizable expressions of worship and action, in the search for a Christian *Bhakti marga* (the way of devotion) and *karma marga* (the way of action). Using these terms suggest that contextual witness will also demand a Christian *jnana marga*, the third of the three ways to salvation that Hinduism often distinguishes: "The way of knowledge." In Christ all these three ways will find their destiny, though conversion will always be part of the process.

The possibility of fulfillment of at least some elements in Hindu traditions in Christ also allows for a more positive social relationship than the examples of "extraction conversion" we have encountered in this chapter. In recent decades such new relationships have been expressed in the development of Christian *Bhakti* movements. These indigenous movements have remained much closer to the Hindu cultural and religious expression than the Christianity imported by foreign missionaries. Examples include the Indian Bible Mission[73] or other *Krista Bhakti* movements.[74] Such movements have also become places of refuge for converts to Christ, who in a later stage of their spiritual journey seek to relate their newfound faith to their cultural and religious roots.[75]

These insider movements are often discussed as examples of dual religious belonging because they help their members maintain ties with their religious communities of origin. Part of the problem with the term "dual religious belonging" is that it can cover a range of ways one relates to these different communities. Dual or double religious belonging can on the one hand be used for people who try to combine different religious paths, but on the other hand also for those fully committed to Christ who nevertheless try to maintain their social identification within their original religious

[72]Varughese John, "The Ethical Requirement in Hinduism and Christianity," *Doon Theological Journal* 17, no. 1 (2020): 58-74.

[73]Joshua, "Revival and Reformation," 161-98.

[74]E.g., Jonas Adelin Jørgensen, *Jesus Imandars and Christ Bhaktas: Two Case Studies of Interreligious Hermeneutics and Identity in Global Christianity* (Frankfurt am Main: Peter Lang, 2008).

[75]Raghav Krishna, "From 'Krishna Bhakti' to 'Christianity' to 'Krista Bhakti,'" *International Journal of Frontier Missiology* 24, no. 4 (2007): 173-77.

community.[76] Because of the primacy of Christ in God's plan of salvation, such dual belonging should, in line with the notion of subversive fulfillment, also be a "subversive belonging." Yet, precisely when Christian converts continue to belong, to some degree, to their religious communities of origin, they can be a subversive presence witnessing to their new Lord.

Recognizing the values of certain Hindu beliefs and practices may also help to find ways of negotiating religious and cultural rituals, and thereby restore broken community ties. An example is Sahadev, a deacon of a respected church in the Kathmandu Valley. After extended personal reflection he decided to no longer separate himself from the family during the *Bhai Tika* celebrations. He clearly indicated to his family how he could participate and where he could not, for example in the *pujas* or in accepting *prasad* offered to idols. Yet, even with these limitations he was gladly welcomed by his family.[77] In rebuilding his family ties, he could become a much more effective witness and recognize what remained of value in the *Bhai Tika* ceremony: the celebration and strengthening of the relationships between brothers and sisters.

Such participation may not be equally possible for all. This may depend on someone's status in the family, the attitude of the family, the time-lapse since conversion, and the spiritual maturity of the Christian.[78] The measure of appropriate involvement will obviously be a matter of pastoral concern and theological debate. Similar debates will happen when relating the Christian *marga* to other aspects of the *Bhakti marga, karma marga,* and *jnana marga.* Here insiders and outsiders will both have their role to play. Intercultural theological conversation within the global church is therefore crucial to finding faithful and relevant forms of holistic contextual apologetic witness.[79]

[76]Kang-San Tan, "Dual Belonging: A Missiological Critique and Appreciation from an Asian Evangelical Perspective," *Mission Studies* 27, no. 1 (2010): 24-38.

[77]Perry, "Bhai-Tika and 'Tij Braka,'" 181.

[78]Perry, "Bhai-Tika and 'Tij Braka,'" 182.

[79]Cf. Benno van den Toren, "Intercultural Theology as a Three-Way Conversation: Beyond the Western Dominance of Intercultural Theology," *Exchange* 44 (2015): 123-43; Kevin J. Vanhoozer, "'One Rule to Rule Them All?' Theological Method in an Era of World Christianity," in *Globalizing Theology: Belief and Practice in an Era of World* Christianity, ed. Craig Ott and Harold A. Netland (Grand Rapids, MI: Baker Academic, 2007), 85-126.

10

BUDDHISM CONFRONTS REALITY

10.1 THE WORLD OF BUDDHISM

Buddhism is the fourth largest world religion in terms of its size. According to the Pew-Templeton Global Religious Futures project in 2020, around 511 million people or 6.6 percent of the global population self-identify as Buddhists, though this number is expected to decline slowly both percentage-wise and in absolute terms in the coming decades, mainly because of demographic reasons.[1] The Buddhist-run Dhammawiki does, however, present a number of 1,089 million for 2016.[2] Dhammawiki gives a much higher percentage of Buddhists in populous nations such as China and Japan, and this may well point to a complexity in classifying religionists as Buddhists. Many people combine elements of Buddhism with other religious influences such as primal religious practice, Confucianism, or Taoism. Unlike traditional forms of Christianity and Islam, Buddhism can easily be one component of a multireligious identity. Kang-San grew up in a Chinese-Malaysian family that combined Buddhist, Taoist, and Confucian teachings.

Like Christianity and Islam, Buddhism has from the time of the Buddha himself been a missionary religion. This was part of its self-understanding, because Gautama Buddha's insight into the nature of the human condition is understood to be true and salvific for all. From its early years in the fifth century BC, it started spreading out, mainly to the East. Like Christianity, Buddhism is not the main religion in the place it originated (in Nepal and on the border of Northern India), but is now the dominant religion in Sri Lanka and a number of Southeast Asian countries (Thailand, Myanmar, Laos, Cambodia) and has a significant presence in China, Japan and other East Asian countries in the region. In recent decades, it has gained a substantial following in the traditionally Christian countries in the West. Unlike Islam, this is not mainly

---

[1] Pew-Templeton Global Religious Futures Project, n.d., http://globalreligiousfutures.org /explorer#.
[2] "Buddhists in the World—Dhamma Wiki," n.d.

through migration and intermarriage, but through a significant amount of conversions among those who formerly considered themselves either Christian or atheist. The spiritual journey of Emma Slade "from banking to Buddhism in Bhutan" is one of many examples.[3] Many Western intellectual spiritual seekers consider Buddhism an attractive spirituality without the need to believe in a God or accept an authoritative revelation. The wider cultural appeal in our globalizing world can be seen in the Buddha statues found in many Western homes and gardens.

The success of Buddhist missions in the West seems to be mirrored by a lack of impact of Christian mission in Buddhist countries. Korea and China are of course significant exceptions, but after centuries of Christian missions in Japan, Thailand, Myanmar, Laos, and Vietnam, the number of Christians under the traditionally Buddhist populations remains below one or two percent. One major factor is that Buddhist affiliation is not merely a spiritual reality, but also represents a cultural, familial, and often national identity, while the Christian call to conversion is too often understood as a demand to sever all such ties. In a city like Yangon, Myanmar, it is difficult to find Christian communities where seekers with a Burmese cultural background would feel at home culturally. This demands critical missiological reflection on forms of dual religious belonging from a Christian perspective. Thus, how far can one retain cultural and social ties with one's former religious community after conversion?[4]

As with all major religious traditions discussed in these chapters, Buddhism exists in many different forms and shapes. There is the major division between Mahayana and Theravada Buddhism. There are a number of subtraditions that have had a great international prestige, such as Japanese Zen-Buddhism through the influence of its meditative practices and philosophical voices, and Tibetan Buddhism through the diplomacy of the Dalai Lama. Furthermore, there are significant differences in how Buddhism is lived out among monastics, for example, and laypeople. There are different degrees to which many laypeople may combine Buddhism with modern materialism on the one hand or folk-religious practices on the other. Buddhism is well able to integrate such a range of commitments because of its understanding of the

---

[3]Emma Slade, *Set Free: A Life-Changing Journey from Banking to Buddhism in Bhutan* (London: Summersdale, 2017).

[4]Kang-San Tan, "Dual Belonging: A Missiological Critique and Appreciation from an Asian Evangelical Perspective," *Mission Studies* 27, no. 1 (2010): 24-38; Tan, "The Inter-Religious Frontier: A 'Buddhist-Christian' Contribution," *Mission Studies* 31, no. 2 (2014): 139-56; Peter Thein Nyunt, *Missions Amidst Pagodas: Contextual Communication of the Gospel in the Burmese Buddhist Context* (Carlisle, UK: Langham Monographs, 2016), 108-19.

path to liberation as an extended process that normally demands a long series of rebirths. A virtuous life following lower religious practices may therefore count as valid preparation for a later rebirth that may allow one to tread the Buddhist path to Enlightenment more fully—perhaps as a Buddhist or even as a Buddhist monk. There are also important differences between modernized forms of Buddhism that are adapted to Western modernity, or to the influence of globalization and modernity in the East[5] over against more traditional expressions.

At the same time, it seems justified to speak about Buddhism in general as well as in the singular, as is also reflected in many studies with "Buddhism" in the title, whether written by Buddhist representatives,[6] by Christian conversation partners,[7] or from a religious studies perspective.[8] This is justified by the fact that, like Christians and Muslims, Buddhists understand themselves as followers of a single founder, belonging to a unified *Sangha* (religious community), even if they may vehemently disagree about which Buddhist teachings are true or what is the best Buddhist lifestyle. In this chapter, we will mainly focus on Theravada Buddhism, the Southern tradition that is dominant in Sri Lanka and Southeast Asia, but limit ourselves as much as possible to the more general traits of Buddhism. Because of this choice, we also use *Pāli* Buddhist terminology unless otherwise indicated, because Theravada Buddhism especially values the more limited and older *Pāli* canon. We will bring other Buddhist expressions into the conversation in as much as we consider them relevant for exploring challenges and possibilities in apologetic dialogue and witness. Like the other chapters, the conversation has an illustrative character inviting our readers to explore and do justice to the specific forms of Buddhism they will encounter.

As in dialogue with primal religions, apologetic witness to Buddhists needs to be contextually sensitive and come alive in contextually embedded Christian communities that present a locally relevant and understandable "hermeneutic of the gospel." Like we did in the exploration of Bhakti Hinduism, it is possible to present Christ as the fulfillment of the religious quest that, in a different way, is expressed in Buddhism. In this chapter we want to focus on another challenge in the interreligious encounter between Christianity and

---

[5]Gottfried Rothermundt, "Apologetic Tendencies in Modern Buddhism," *Bangalore Theological Forum* 11, no. 2 (1979): 109-21.
[6]K. Dhammananda, *What Buddhists Believe* (Kuala Lumpur: Buddhist Missionary Society, 1987).
[7]Keith E. Yandell and Harold A. Netland, *Buddhism: A Christian Exploration and Appraisal* (Downers Grove, IL: IVP Academic, 2009).
[8]Thomas Oberlies, "Buddhism," in *The Brill Dictionary of Religion*, ed. Kocku von Stuckrad, trans. Robert R. Barr (Leiden; Boston: Brill, 2006), 208-15.

Buddhism. Too often Christian encounters with and outreach to Buddhists do not take sufficient time to understand the great strength and attraction of Buddhism from an insider perspective. It does not sufficiently probe the appeal of Buddhism in both the depth of its *Dhamma* (*Dharma* in Sanskrit) or teaching, and the attraction of its proposed *magga* (*mārga in Sanskrit)* or path to liberation and enlightenment. It also does not always show sufficient awareness of Buddhism's profound difference with the Christian worldview. There is limited fundamental overlap between the two worldviews. If religious traditions are understood primarily as cultural and linguistic constructs of the community, then there is limited scope for an apologetic conversation starting from shared fundamental presuppositions. In line with the critical realist epistemology developed in chapter three, we want to argue that despite the radically different understandings of reality and attitudes to reality between Christianity and Buddhism, neither Christians nor Buddhists can in the end avoid the reality that exists beyond the worlds we create for ourselves. This being the case, we will explore how an honest dialogue between two radically different worlds of experience is possible, and how we relate to a reality of a shared existence and a shared world. The belief that we live in such a shared world is, for Christians, given with the belief in the way God created us yet is also reflected in a general experience: that in intercultural conversations we can point to a reality beyond ourselves that we can never entirely force into the mold of our cultural perspectives. We can invite each other to take this reality seriously—and we are on other occasions painfully confronted with the fact that reality will resist the way we understand it, shaping our lives and hopes accordingly. We understand this conversation thus as triangular relationship where both communities do not just relate to each other, but also to this reality beyond their respective perspectives as the third angle (cf. §6.1). As dialogue partners we will discover both elements where we agree concerning the diagnosis of human suffering as well as profound disagreements in our respective understanding of the nature of salvation, including the path to it. In search for deeper understanding of the complexities of suffering, there will be mutual learning as well as contrast and competition in how to make sense of the world we share.

In the following section, we will explore how we can do justice to the radical difference between Christian and Buddhist understandings of reality as well as the human condition, noting many shared sensitivities between the two religions (§10.2). In the next section, we will raise an important apologetic challenge: how Buddhism presents itself as a rational religion without a need to believe in revelation or doctrine (§10.3). In the final two sections, we will explore how we may engage in a constructive conversation rooted in the shared reality in which we live, both the reality of our human condition (§10.4) and the reality of the trinitarian God through and for whom we exist (§10.5).

10.2 RESONANCE AND DIFFERENCE

When we compare the teachings of Christianity and Buddhism, there is a striking combination of deep resonances and radical differences. Christians will resonate with the prince Siddhartha Gautama's deep grief about the manifold suffering in the world and his desire for liberation. It was this awareness of suffering that led the prince to abandon his family and choose the life of a wandering ascetic. Yet, after six years of ascetic renunciation following various masters and schools, he discovered that it had not brought him any nearer to the experience of liberation from suffering, so he sat down under a peepal tree with the commitment to not get up before he received enlightenment. According to the tradition, in his enlightenment experience, he received the insight that is summarily expressed in the four noble truths[9] and the noble eightfold path.[10] The four noble truths are (1) that the whole of existence is *dukkha* or suffering. This is not only true for experiences of pain or grief, but also for experiences of joy, as all these remain impermanent and passing. (2) The cause of this suffering is craving or selfish desire: because humans are attached to the world and everything they desire, they suffer and cause suffering to others. This desire traps them within the cycle of rebirths. (3) The end of suffering is therefore only possible when one can end all craving, as is reached in the state of *nibbana* (*nirvana* in Sanskrit). (4) The final noble truth is the way leading to the end of *dukkha*, which is the noble eightfold path. This eightfold path is a combination of three moral practices (right speech, right action, right livelihood), of three mental practices (right effort, right mindfulness, and right concentration) and two aspects of wisdom (right understanding and right thoughts).

Christians will value the crucial insight that was part of Buddha's enlightenment experience, that craving is the root cause of suffering. At the same time a crucial difference comes out: Christians do not believe that all craving out of need is wrong, as the Buddha did, but only misdirected and sinful desire. Christians would again resonate with the insight of the Buddha that understanding of the true nature or life and reality is crucial for attaining liberation. Yet, here too, while recognizing the similarities, we need to be simultaneously

---

[9]Dhammananda, *What Buddhists Believe*, 74-78.
[10]Dhammananda, *What Buddhists Believe*, 78-85.

aware of the deep differences: for Christians, the cause of suffering is not only a problem of the mind and of lack of insight but as much a problem of the will. Insight is therefore not enough to attain liberation—we need forgiveness, freedom from sin, and liberation from death.

When we come to the Buddha's understanding of the true nature of reality, crucial for attaining salvation, the focus on *anicca* or impermanence, also has a certain resonance with the Judeo-Christian tradition. The Christian Scriptures repeat that the human being is like grass that soon withers (Job 14:2; Ps 103:15; Is 40:6; 1 Pet 1:24). With the grief about suffering, the realization of the corruption of human desire, and the awareness of the transitory nature of life and the world, Buddhism presents a crucial reminder—and at times prophetic criticism—of particularly forms of Western Christianity: this includes forms of prosperity theology that consider human flourishing virtually a right, having a strong focus on the value and expression of the self.[11] The final Buddhist doctrine that needs mentioning here is the idea of *anattā* or no-self. This is a fundamental difference from Hinduism, that sought the deliverance of the self through a long cycle of rebirths. Though Buddhism also seeks deliverance from *samsara* or the cycle of rebirths, a significant aspect of the deliverance is the realization of no-self: the self is an illusion and there is therefore no continuity of the self through the cycle of rebirths.

It is precisely these insights into the nature of reality that are crucial for attaining liberation. On a visit to the Maha Vihara temple in Brickfields, Kuala Lumpur, our guide explained the role of the candles and the flowers on the altar. Their meaning did not reside in their beauty but in their impermanence: in meditating on their imminent decay, we become aware of their and our own transience, to which we should not become attached. A meditation in the candle flame helps us realize that as soon as we are aware of the flame, the same flame has already gone and what we perceive is a new reality. If there is no self to be lost and no goal to be reached, I cannot miss it.

I am like a leaf in the wind, and who knows where the wind goes? I see where I am going; I live every moment consciously, yet without attachment or desire. I will not be disappointed because my desires are extinguished. I cannot become lost, for I have no goal.[12]

There is some resonance between the idea of no-self and the Pauline realization that human fallenness has to do with our attachment to the self from which

---

[11]Cf. Gerald R. McDermott, *Can Evangelicals Learn from World Religions? Jesus, Revelation and Religious Traditions* (Downers Grove, IL: InterVarsity Press, 2000), 133-56.

[12]Hendrik M. Vroom, *No Other Gods: Christian Belief in Dialogue with Buddhism, Hinduism, and Islam* (Grand Rapids, MI: Eerdmans, 1996), 15.

we need to be liberated, through the discovery that "it is no longer I who live, but it is Christ who lives in me" (Gal 2:20). Yet, this is at the same time one of the places where a radical difference between Christianity and Buddhism comes to the fore. Christianity believes that though the self can be distorted by being turned inwards onto itself (as Luther also said), as a created reality the self is nonetheless real and precious. Similarly, though the Scriptures are aware of the transience of the created world—they show creation is a real and valuable gift of God. The existence of God finally points to the third difference. Buddhism can recognize the existence of gods as part of the transient reality of *samsara* in which we live, but even the gods have no permanent existence. Liberation is only possible if we come to recognize the impermanence of even the gods so that we will not attach ourselves to them. This is the most fundamental difference from which the other differences flow. Christians believe in the reality rather than the non-reality of the world and the self because this world and the self are willed and created by God. Furthermore, they are included in God's salvific plan in which they have eternal meaning and an eternal destiny.

With respect to the understanding of the nature of God, the self, and the world, Buddhism is far removed from Christianity.[13] Efforts by religious pluralists[14] to harmonize both worldviews are not doing justice to the radical difference.[15] This also means there is a real risk of misunderstanding in interreligious apologetic dialogue. Even where there are important parallels, as in, for example, the joint interest in compassion for those who suffer, similar terms may have profoundly different meanings. Buddhists would aim for a compassion without attachment. As the term says, Christian "*com*-passion" means that we help others because we feel and suffer *with* them, just as Jesus experienced deep grief over the death of Lazarus (Jn 11:35). Jesus is not a peaceful smiling Buddha but with us in his agony on the cross. Yet, for Buddhists, such suffering with others would still be an unhealthy form of attachment over against the ideal of complete detachment, in which their pain cannot touch us.[16]

---

[13]So Alex G. Smith, "The Christian Response to Buddhism," in *Christian Witness in Pluralistic Contexts in the 21st Century*, ed. Enoch Yee-nock Wan, Evangelical Missiological Society Series 11 (Pasadena, CA: William Carey Library, 2004), 135-68.

[14]Perry Schmidt-Leukel, "'Light and Darkness' or 'Looking through a Dim Mirror'? A Reply to Paul Williams from a Christian Perspective," in *Converging Ways? Conversion and Belonging in Buddhism and Christianity*, ed. John D'Arcy May (St. Ottilien, Edinburgh: Eos Klosterverlag, 2007), 67-88.

[15]As argued by Paul Williams, "Buddhism, God, Aquinas and Morality: An Only Partially Repentant Reply to Perry Schmidt-Leukel and José Cabezón," in *Converging Ways? Conversion and Belonging in Buddhism and Christianity*, ed. John D'Arcy May (Edinburgh: T&T Clark, 2007), 117-54.

[16]Vroom, *No Other Gods*, 29, 36.

We need to be aware that even behind partial recognition there can be a fundamental and ultimate disagreement. This can be seen in the Buddhist appreciation for many Christian practices and in the warm attitude of many Buddhists to the Christian faith. This will often be rooted in the Buddhist idea of "skillful means": how different religions can have a value at a certain stage in the long journey to liberation that will take many rebirths and many lives. So even the Dalai Lama—often considered a champion of pluralism in the West—believes that Christianity can be welcomed as a skillful means at a certain stage on the way[17]: "If Buddhists themselves have to wait, perhaps many lifetimes, for their goal, why should we expect that it be different for non-Buddhists?"[18] Yet, in the end, "liberation in which 'a mind that understands the sphere of reality' is a state that only Buddhists can accomplish."

Here, the Dalai Lama shows that he is not a religious pluralist, but rather a Buddhist inclusivist for whom the value of other religions is measured in the context of the Buddhist metanarrative of salvation. This is of course as legitimate as it is for Christians to value other religions in the light of how they have come to know God in Christ. It demonstrates, however, that the hard work of asking which religious understanding of reality is actually true is unavoidable if we want to take religious quests and claims seriously.

A theology of religions that focuses on shared human religious nature and the universal presence of the Creator and the logos will tend to stress the parallels between the two religions,[19] while a theology of religions focusing on human sin and the need for Christ will focus on the differences.[20] A trinitarian understanding of religious pluralism (chap. 4) invites us to take the two aspects with equal seriousness. As the missionary work of Karl Ludvig Reichelt among Buddhist monks in China exemplifies,

> We will approach these religious people in a sympathetic way, using the points of contact which exist in all the greater systems of religion, at the same time faithfully laying stress on the uniqueness of Christianity, showing them that their highest aspirations may be fulfilled in Jesus Christ, the all-embracing

---

[17]Ernest M. Valea, *Buddhist-Christian Dialogue as Theological Exchange: An Orthodox Contribution to Comparative Theology* (Eugene, OR: Wipf and Stock, 2015), 14-15.

[18]Tenzin Gyatso [The 14th Dalai lama], "The Bodghaya Interviews," in *Christianity through Non-Christian Eyes*, ed. Paul J. Griffiths (Maryknoll, NY: Orbis Books, 2004), 169.

[19]E.g., Schmidt-Leukel, "Light and Darkness."

[20]E.g., Smith, "Christian Response to Buddhism"; Bruce Nicholls, *Building Bridges: From Asian Faiths to Jesus in the Gospels* (Oxford: Regnum, 2019), 73-113.

Word of God, the Eternal Logos, which "shineth in the darkness" and "lighteth every man that cometh into the world."[21]

10.3 A NONDOCTRINAL YET RATIONAL RELIGION

A further apologetic challenge in the Buddhist-Christian conversation is related to how Buddhism presents itself as a religion for "free thinkers." In a brochure of the Maha Vihara temple in Kuala Lumpur, Sri Dhammananda critiques people who "try to introduce their religious concepts and beliefs and practices by . . . appealing to divine messages." He recommends Buddhism because "the Buddha has given full freedom for man to think freely without depending on the concept of a god, a Buddha or a teacher to understand the truth."[22] The Dalai Lama equally presents Buddhism as "not a path of faith but a path of religion and knowledge."[23] This is also part of its attraction in the West. It is a practical religion that helps to live life consciously and with compassion but without the burden of belief in God or revelation. For Slade, the attraction of Buddhism is that it is fundamentally a form of "Kindhism" (her term): "This is the point. The robes help, the shaven head helps, renouncing desire helps, but Buddhism has taught me what I wanted to learn: how to be a kinder person."[24]

This relativizing of doctrine over life and liberation is clear from the story of the monk and the raft ascribed to Gautama the Buddha himself. Doctrine is compared to a raft that a monk decides to carry with him on his head because it has helped him to cross a river. That would of course not be practical. Like the raft, doctrine only becomes a burden if it is not relinquished when it is no longer needed, after it has helped us to find freedom.[25] In line with the idea of the Dalai Lama above that different religions may have a role to play on the long trajectory to final liberation, this also means that theist doctrine

---

[21]Karl Ludvig Reichelt, "Buddhism in China at the Present Time and the New Challenge to the Christian Church," *International Review of Mission* 26, no. 2 (1937): 61; cf. Rory MacKenzie, "Lessons from the Life of Karl Reichelt," in *Contextualisation and Mission Training: Engaging Asia's Religious Worlds*, ed. Jonathan Ingleby, Kang-San Tan, and Tan Loun Ling (Oxford: Regnum Books, 2013), 59-73.

[22]K. Dhammananda, *Buddhism and the Free Thinkers* (Kuala Lumpur: Sasana Abhiwurdhi Wardhana Society, 2016), 12.

[23]Tenzin Gyatso, *Universal Responsibility and the Good Heart* (Dharamsala: Library of Tibetan Works and Archives, 1980), 8; quoted in P. Williams, *The Unexpected Way: On Converting from Buddhism to Catholicism* (Edinburgh: T&T Clark, 2002), 69; cf. Rothermundt, "Apologetic Tendencies."

[24]Slade, *Set Free*, 302.

[25]Cf. Kang-San Tan, "Genesis 1-11 and Buddhist Scripture: How the Gospel Can Transform Buddhist Worldviews," in *Communicating Christ in the Buddhist World*, ed. Paul H. De Neui and David S. Lim (Pasadena, CA: William Carey Library Publishers, 2006), 34-36.

can support spiritual growth for a season in life or even for a lifetime. This is of course attractive in a religiously pluralist context. It also resonates with postmodern attitudes toward life and the world that understand religions primarily as a set of practices, as a cultural construct or language game. It seems to allow for the possibility of a legitimate plurality of such practices and avoids the burden of metaphysical beliefs.

Yet, the question of religious truth cannot be avoided. First, such claims about the nature of religious language do fit with certain religious traditions and not with others. For example, they do not cohere with Muslim and Christian beliefs that God is at the origin of the world, of human existence, of language, or that knowledge of God's will is essential to human flourishing. It does not cohere with a Christian understanding that the telos of human life is to be found in a personal relationship with a God who is not a human construct precisely because we are God's handiwork and rest in God's embrace. Furthermore, Buddhism itself cannot do without metaphysical commitments. As we saw above with reference to the Dalai Lama, the possibility of respecting the relative validity of other religious paths—as rafts with a temporary value—rests in a particular understanding of ultimate liberation.

> Buddhists clearly regard certain claims as simply true, in a fairly straightforward sense, and other as equally evidently false . . . there is a long tradition of anti-theistic apologetics within the tradition. [For] theism is ultimately a barrier to the attainment of Nirvana and thus . . . Christians must, finally, be disabused of their adherence to it.[26]

In dialogue with Buddhists, it is equally important to stress that Christians do not believe people are saved by true doctrinal beliefs. Salvation happens through a relationship with the living Christ. Doctrine is merely a window on that relationship and an explanation of how and why salvation takes place. Yet, it is at the same time essential for understanding how we can receive this gift and what that relationship entails, just as Buddhists will hold that certain insights into reality are crucial for attaining liberation.

10.4 THE REALITY OF THE SELF AND THE WORLD

Missional and apologetic encounters between Christians and Buddhists need to happen at a number of integrated levels.[27] It needs to be embodied in the

---

[26]Paul J. Griffiths, ed., *Christianity through Non-Christian Eyes* (Maryknoll, NY: Orbis, 2004), 137-38.
[27]Cf. Kang-San Tan, "Elements of a Biblical and Genuine Missionary Encounter with Diaspora Chinese Buddhists in South-East Asia," in *Sharing Jesus in the Buddhist World*, ed. David S. Lim and Steve Spaulding (Pasadena, CA: William Carey Library, 2003), 22-27.

life of a community where people can experience the love of God for a suffering world. Of course, many Buddhists are not detached from the experiences of suffering and need in their day-to-day life. This is why folk-Buddhism temples are also a place for recourse to the pressing needs of health, family, school, work, and spiritual oppression. With respect to these needs, the message and experience of Christ as healer and liberator is crucial, as it is in primal religious contexts.[28] Missional outreach needs to happen with awareness of postcolonial realities of oppression—where Christianity is often seen as the violent religion of the former colonizers.

Apologetic exchange also needs to happen at the level of logical argument, precisely because Buddhist philosophers have developed such a sophisticated understanding of language and metaphysics. The practical witness of a lively church will have little attraction for philosophically inclined Buddhists. It will need to be accompanied by sophisticated philosophical exchange as for example between Paul Williams (a Christian convert from Buddhism)[29] and José Cabezón (himself a Buddhist).[30] If not, the liveliness of the church will be suspect, a clinging to community, doctrine, and the material world. While all that may be attractive and good, it is seen as a penultimate blessing that in the end is still bound to the cycle of *samsara*. There are a number of fundamental, logical conundrums related to the central tenets of Buddhist belief that can function as triggers to explore alternative perspectives on reality. Consider the fact that the Gautama's belief that all is impermanent does in itself also undermine his central religious message. Even the message that everything is impermanent needs to be relativized, as it is itself impermanent, rather than the only absolute truth. This is a problem that parallels every absolutized expression, relativism, or skepticism. There is also another fundamental tension between the doctrine of *anattā*, or no-self—the idea of rebirth—and the idea that the self needs to engage on a quest for improvement and purification.

Precisely because of the sophistication of Buddhist philosophy, argument alone will have limited impact. Buddhist scholars have elaborately discussed these issues and different schools have come up with a range of answers. Furthermore, people can always decide that certain questions cannot be answered, or at least not for now. The pressing question concerning the

---

[28]Cf. Simon Chan, *Grassroots Asian Theology: Thinking the Faith from the Ground Up* (Downers Grove, IL: InterVarsity Press, 2014), 108-17.

[29]Williams, *Unexpected Way*, 2007.

[30]José Ignacio Cabezón, "A Buddhist Response to Paul Williams's The Unexpected Way," in *Converging Ways? Conversion and Belonging in Buddhism and Christianity*, ed. John D'Arcy May (St. Ottilien, Edinburgh: Eos Klosterverlag, 2007), 89-115.

reason for the existence of this fleeting transient world motivated the former Buddhist Paul Williams in his quest for God, resulting in his conversion to Roman Catholicism. Yet many other Buddhists are content to accept that this is a question that can never be answered because there simply is no further ground for the existence of this world.[31] Whether secular or religious, we all live with a number of deep riddles in our lives. The question is not why we live with these riddles and mysteries, but why we accept living with certain riddles rather than others.

We want to suggest that a crucial aspect of the apologetic encounter with Buddhism is the confrontation with the reality as it exists beyond our own interpretations and projections. Logically, the Buddhist worldview has a high degree of coherence and is developed with much sophistication. The logical strength of the worldview is that it can withdraw from any of the questions that immediate experience raises by declaring them illusionary and part of the transient world. At the same time Buddhism draws on a limited range of powerful experiences, such as the experience of suffering and the awareness of the existence of cravings that bind us. In this sense, Buddhism has similarities with the postmodern view of reality, according to which all reality is constructed. Constructivist postmodernism may hide its own metaphysical commitments even more effectively than Buddhism. It similarly has a high internal coherence because it does not easily permit the world out there to challenge its theoretical outlook. It builds on a limited but important range of experiences of reality which suggest that humanity is able to construct worlds according to its own image and often does so driven by ideological interests.

Buddhism, secular postmodernism, and Christianity all present worldviews that have an all-inclusive take on reality and are therefore not easily challenged by a limited range of experiences. Yet, they can be compared with each other as integrated outlooks on reality (cf. §6.3). Furthermore, aspects of our experience of reality can point us to the unsatisfactory nature of such integrated worldviews and set us out on a pilgrimage for a better understanding, opening us to consider or embrace other worldviews if they make more sense of reality and of our lives. We noted that such tensions between our worldview and our experience of the world can be push-factors that motivate us to critically review our understanding and commitments (§6.4). This is a fact of life about which Christianity, Buddhism, and many religious traditions would agree: they share notions of spiritual quest or pilgrimage triggered by new experiences of the life that people have so

---

[31]Williams, *Unexpected Way,* 30-40.

far resisted. The Christian worldview makes sense of this phenomenon, that we do indeed construct worlds according to our fundamental presuppositions and predispositions. Yet, it also helps us understand that we cannot entirely shape the world to our liking and are thereby motivated to not settle where we are but set out on this quest. From a Christian perspective, we can never know from nowhere, because as creatures we are part of the world. Our beliefs are always shaped by our place in the world and the traditions of the community to which we belong. But because we are creatures—and part of a world that is larger than us—we cannot entirely shape an image of the world to our liking. If we try, we will harm those around us, damage the world in which we live and stunt the flourishing of our own lives (cf. §3.1).

This is also one of the reasons that arguments matter. They have power because they can create phantom worlds or bring out the beauty (or the horror) in the world as it is—often they do a bit of both. That is also how words and arguments can have real power: if they are not mere intellectual discussions but are spoken to make sense of the world and our lives, and to give meaning and hope. They are existentially relevant. This is why we plead for a form of apologetic witness that is, as we have said, *triadic*. It is a dialogue between radically different perspectives but also with and about the world in which we live. This is of course true for all apologetic exchange, but the issue has a special weight in the dialogue with Buddhism. On the one hand, Buddhism will agree with Christianity that ultimate truth matters, yet on the other hand experiences of the world around us do seem to carry little weight because of their transience and the illusionary nature of experience, of which we become aware when we realize our nature as no-self. Yet, arguments are powerful precisely when they do not remain intellectual word games, but when they are existentially relevant, and relate our beliefs to the world in which we live.

Let us consider two experiences that show how reality will resist being molded by the Buddhist worldview. Os Guinness tells the story of the Japanese poet Issa (1762–1826) who suffered greatly in his life. His five children all died and then he also lost his wife. In his grief, he sought support from a Zen-master. After a long silence, the Zen-master told him, "The world is dew." The world is dew that soon evaporates. Our grief is a sign that we are not yet able to liberate ourselves from our attachment to this passing world. In response to this Buddhist perspective on his grief, Issa wrote the following *haiku*, a short Japanese form of poetry[32]:

---

[32]Os Guinness, *The Dust of Death: A Critique of the Establishment and the Counter Culture—and a Proposal for a Third Way* (Downers Grove, IL: InterVarsity Press, 1973), 225.

The world is dew–
The world is dew–
And yet,
And yet . . .

Issa understood the logic of the Zen-master, but the experience of grief was simply too real to believe that in the end it should be looked upon as a passing phenomenon of no real consequence. Behind this experience of suffering is the more fundamental reality that we experience the self as something deeply valuable, unique, and irreplaceable (rather than *anatta*). We therefore experience loss of others and relationships as real.

We already pointed to another tension Paul Williams experienced between his religious worldview and the experience that played a crucial role in his conversion (§6.4). After trying the Buddhist path to liberation for decades, he discovered that he was now only further away from the goal: "What does Buddhism offer the one who tried but honestly cannot make any progress?"[33] The difficulty for human beings—to save themselves from themselves—is reflected in the Mahayana Buddhist tradition of the *bodhisattva*, the enlightened person who delays entry into *nibbana* in order to help others on their path.[34] This awareness is most radically reflected in the deep insight of the Jodo-Shin (Pure Land) and Jodo-Shin-Shu (True Pure Land) currents in Buddhism. They state that humanity cannot save itself, but is dependent on the power of a savior, Buddha Amitābha: "Among the great Buddhist thinkers, Shinran [the founder of Jodo-Shin-Shu] alone, . . . with his vivid awareness of his own tendency to egoism, really takes this on board."[35]

There are at least two reasons behind the arduousness of the Buddhist path to salvation through many rebirths, that Williams and others discover to be impassable. First, there is the rigidity of the doctrine of *kamma* (Sanskrit: *karma*) that demands that we all carry the weight of our own mistakes and of our past lives because no one else can do it for us. As the Buddha says, "There is no place to hide in order to escape from kammatic results."[36] Second, and perhaps more fundamentally, there is the inherent tension between the need to take on oneself the responsibility for one's salvation—investing oneself entirely in this quest—and the need to lose oneself, to forget oneself, to realize no-self. According to the Sri Lankan theologian Lynn de Silva:

---

[33]Williams, *Unexpected Way*, 99; cf. Nyunt, *Missions amidst Pagodas*, 102-4.
[34]Cabezón, "A Buddhist Response," 106.
[35]Williams, *Unexpected Way*, 99.
[36]Quoted in Dhammananda, *What Buddhists Believe*, 91; cf. Nyunt, *Missions amidst Pagodas*, 107.

Here is one of the deepest dilemmas in Buddhism. What is the self that denies the self and at the same time asserts that it alone can save the self? If the doctrine of *anattā* is taken in all its seriousness we must reach the conclusion that man has no power within himself to work out his own salvation. To deny the self and to affirm self-sufficiency is a contradiction.[37]

Of course, these experiences do not prove that Buddhism is inconsistent and cannot be true. It is possible to say that the poetry of Issa simply shows how he is still grieving because he has not been able to make the decisive step. It is possible to argue that Williams should have tried harder and hoped for a future life where he may be better placed to make some progress. It is possible that the conundrum de Silva points out is or will be solved in other Buddhist schools, or that it belongs to this passing world and will finally be solved in the ultimate reality that is beyond human logic. Yet, such antinomies and profound tensions between the religious perspective and the world as it is experienced can function as a trigger to start exploring radically different understandings of the world and different paths to salvation. Furthermore, they are not mere logical riddles but point to existential problems. What if there is a possibility to recognize the depth of suffering without sacrificing the value of the individual or relationships? What do I do when I am constantly thrown back on my own responsibility to save myself and, in the process, I am only discovering my inability to do so? It was one of the triggers that set Williams on the path to explore the arguments for theism and the resurrection of Christ, because "the Church was not set up for saints, the virtuous ones. It was set up for sinners (see Matthew 9:13). I am wicked. I am a sinner. It seems that I should feel very much at home in the Catholic Church."[38]

Our worldviews shape the way we perceive reality, but we cannot simply "beat nature into line" if it does not fit what we want it to be.[39] If our views crash head-on with the world around us, we can, in the words of the sociologists of knowledge, suffer an acute "breakdown in reality,"[40] a breakdown in our experience of the realness of our worldview, of its adequacy to outline reality as it is.

---

[37]Lynn A. de Silva, "Good News of Salvation to the Buddhists," *International Review of Mission* 57, no. 228 (1968): 450-51.

[38]Williams, *Unexpected Way,* 99.

[39]Cf. Thomas S. Kuhn, *The Structure of Scientific Revolutions,* 3rd ed. (Chicago: University of Chicago Press, 1996), 135.

[40]Peter L. Berger and Thomas Luckmann, *The Social Construction of Reality: A Treatise in the Sociology of Knowledge* (Garden City, NY: Doubleday, 1966), 175.

10.5 THE REALITY OF GOD IN CHRIST

The riddle of the grandeur and misery of human existence is, in itself, not sufficient to point to the limits of the Buddhist understanding of the world. Maybe suffering can in the end not be overcome. Maybe the suffering that accompanies deep relationships does not weigh up against the fleeting moments of meaning we experience in loving relationships. Maybe detachment is therefore the most reasonable way forward.

Christians do indeed agree with Buddhists that attachment to others in a fallen world all too often leads to suffering. It leads to suffering because people disappoint or even betray us. It leads to suffering because we lose our loved ones to death. It leads to suffering, because we often try to use others to fill deep existential needs that they never can. Yet, Christians believe that the deep value and joy we find in relationships is worth both the risk and the cost of the pain involved. This is related to three central traits of the Christian worldview.

First, Christians believe that our experience of ourselves and others is not an illusion and that we become most truly ourselves when we live in relationships. Our relationality is a consequence of our creation as persons by a trinitarian God who exists as an eternal relationship of love. In this respect, Christianity differs as much from Buddhism as it would from an evolutionary materialist understanding of the universe, in which personhood, love, and relationship are the byproducts of either mental processes or blind evolution. In distinction to both, the Christian faith maintains that personhood, relationship, and love are at the origin of the universe because they belong to the nature of Godself. Personhood, relationship, and love therefore have ultimate significance. De Silva argues that Christians can build positive bridges to the Buddhist awareness that human beings are shackled by their attachment to their own selves. From a Christian perspective, this is indeed true, but we can only truly lose a wrong attachment to our own self when God becomes the object of our desires, and when this God in Christ liberates us from ourselves.

> The loss of individuality (*anattā*) which constitutes the fulfilment of personality, is the essence of the experience of love. Eternal life in this sense is participation in the individuality-negating, personality-fulfilling love which is created in us when we are confronted by the perfect manifestation of such love in the life of Jesus Christ—"the man for others"—in Whom we are summoned into a responsible relationship with others. This involves dying to self (*anattā*) and living for others.[41]

---

[41] De Silva, "Good News," 456.

A second difference relates to the right ordering of human love. Christians and Buddhists agree that wrongly directed desire is the cause of suffering. Yet, where Buddhists believe that all desire out of need is wrong, Christians believe that such desire should be well-directed and well-ordered. We should only love what is truly worth loving.[42] Furthermore, we should only love what we love in accordance with its true nature.[43] This is why we should love God above everything and everyone else because only God can fill our deepest needs. Using a well-known image from Pascal, we are created with a space in our lives that can never be filled by anything else but God.[44] This is why our deepest needs will never be fulfilled if we search for them in material objects or when we search for it in other persons. But when we search for our greatest treasure in God, we can find a treasure that is large enough to fill this need, a treasure that cannot be lost because God is both eternal and faithful. Once we have come to love God for who God is, we can also desire and love our fellow human beings and the created world for what they are. We can love them without clinging excessively to them, because our identity and destiny is secure in God. We indeed need to love and desire well: we need to learn to love the created world as an object of both enjoyment and care, as gift from God and pointer to God. We need to love human beings as our equals and never as mere objects to be used for our needs. We need to love in ways appropriate to the relations we have, so that we love spouses in ways that are different from the ways we love parents, or children, friends, or the needy neighbor placed on our path.

A third difference between the Christian and Buddhist evaluation of suffering and of the selves relates to the hope Christians find in Christ. Christianity and Buddhism agree that human life is marked by deep suffering. When we look at the world itself, there seems to be no way to decide whether the experience of love weighs up against the reality of the suffering it brings with it. Buddhists also share with many Western atheists a profound questioning of the goodness of the Creator, in light of the radical evil in the world: "If God is absolutely good, what is the origin of evil in the world?"[45] Christian apologists have developed a whole range of answers to this question of evil, and which answer is most important will often depend on the experiences that

---

[42]James K. A. Smith, *You Are What You Love: The Spiritual Power of Habit* (Grand Rapids, MI: Brazos Press, 2016).

[43]Cf. John Burnaby, *Amor Dei: A Study of the Religion of St. Augustine* (London: Hodder and Stoughton, 1938).

[44]Blaise Pascal, *Pensées*, trans. A. J. Krailsheimer (London: Penguin Books, 1995), no. 148.

[45]Masao Abe, "Self-Awakening and Faith—Zen and Christianity," in *Christianity through Non-Christian Eyes*, ed. Paul J. Griffiths (Maryknoll, NY: Orbis Books, 2004), 177; cf. Yandell and Netland, *Buddhism*, 185-88.

drive specific lines of questioning.[46] Answers to the logical problem of the existence of both a good, almighty God and evil do not necessarily reach the depth of the existential experience of evil that people like the poet Issa encounter. Christians believe, however, that Christ's cross and resurrection show that God is deeply involved with this suffering world, and that suffering and decay have been overcome and will be overcome. The cross and resurrection of Christ have shown that human sin can be trumped by forgiveness, and death trumped by life. In the end the victory of Christ is an essential element of the Christian answer to suffering and the human condition in general. In this respect, Karl Barth points to a crucial difference between Pure Land Buddhism and the Christian faith. His *Church Dogmatics* section on "The Revelation of God as the Abolition of Religion" gives little attention to non-Christian religious traditions, apart from a remarkable excursus on Pure Land Buddhism. He sees its teachings on the need for grace and faith as noteworthy parallels to the Christian faith. However, he rightly points out that this does not undermine the uniqueness of the Christian message about Christ. We are not saved by the *idea* of grace or faith. We are saved by Christ. The preponderance of the notions of grace and faith in the Christian tradition are a consequence of the *reality* of the saving activity and presence of Christ.[47] Christ himself is the answer to human suffering. Christ himself is the ultimate answer to the human craving for love and relationship. Christ himself is the answer to sin and death. Without Christ, there might be no answer to the deep reality of suffering that set Gautama off on his quest. Without Christ, detachment might indeed be the most reasonable way to solve the riddle of human greatness and misery. Yet, the suffering of loss and desire for love seems too real to settle for the Buddhist message. In the end, only an encounter with a personal God, the message of hope in the history of Israel, and the person of Jesus Christ provide confidence that there is another path. Apologetic dialogue with Buddhism will therefore always need to be apologetic witness to the God whom we have met in Jesus Christ.

---

[46]Benno van den Toren, *Reasons for My Hope: Responding to Non-Christian Friends* (Oxford: Monarch Books, 2010), 40-57.

[47]Karl Barth, *Church Dogmatics*, ed. Geoffrey W. Bromiley and Thomas F. Torrance, trans. Geoffrey W. Bromiley et al. (Edinburgh: T&T Clark, 1956–1975), I/2, 340-44.

11

ISLAM AND THE INTEGRITY
OF THE CHRISTIAN FAITH

11.1 THE PARTICULARITY AND MULTIDIMENSIONALITY OF THE MUSLIM-CHRISTIAN ENCOUNTER

Among the world religions, Islam presents one further apologetic challenge that is unrelated to the ones discussed so far. It is the only major world religion that has post-Christian origins. It is therefore the only major world religion that, as part of its traditions, includes a view of Jesus (as a prophet, but not as the Son of God), of the Christian Scriptures (as originally prophetic, but later corrupted), and of Christians (as a related religious community, but as culpable of *shirk*, of idolatry by associating Jesus with God). This means that their religious commitment also commits them directly to a view on Christianity. The view that Islam largely surpasses what Christianity has to offer is inherently part of their religious tradition. In practice this may result in a range of attitudes, from vehement rejection to welcoming collaboration.[1]

This means that the relationship between Christianity and Islam is particular in two respects that at first sight seem to be contradictory. Apart from Judaism as the third "Abrahamic religion," no religious tradition has as much in common with the Christian faith as Islam. When exploring points of contact or common ground, allowing for constructive dialogue, Islam presents us with quite a list: belief in one God, in creation, in a final judgment, in God sending his prophets, in shared personalities in the respective Scriptures, a recognition of the unique role of Jesus, the value of obedience to God, and so on (cf. §6.3). At the same time, there may be no religious tradition with which the relationship is more tense and historically loaded (again, possibly apart from Judaism). There is no other world religion with such a fierce anti-Christian apologetic tradition.

---

[1]David Marshall, "Heavenly Religion or Unbelief? Muslim Perspectives on Christianity," *Anvil* 23, no. 2 (2006): 89-100.

Like any other world religion, Islam presents itself to us with many faces. It can present itself as a group of boys studying the Qur'an diligently in Arabic in a madrassa in Northern Pakistan, as an oppressed people group in the Xingjian region in Northwest China, as women demonstrating for the freedom to wear a veil in France, as legal scholars discussing how the Sharia should be applied in today's Aceh in Indonesia, as a huge demonstration when cartoons of Mohammed in Denmark provoke indignation on the other side of the globe, as a Muslim student association engaging with the challenges of Western life in Britain, and as dancing dervishes, an expression of Sufi mysticism. These variations are partly due to major theological differences between Sunnis and Shiites and different theological schools, partly to cultural difference between the Arab heartlands and Urdu expressions in South Asia, and partly between different political social contexts, such as the contrast between Muslim majorities in Islamic nations and the Islamic diaspora in secular nations in Europe.

For apologetic dialogue and witness, it is important to realize that individual Muslims will live and understand their Islam in very different ways—also, where it concerns their understanding of its relationship with the Christian faith. Some have embraced Islam with conviction and find satisfaction in its beliefs and practices. Others may have embraced its truths but see themselves as failures or fakes when it comes to their obedience to the divine will or their ability to fit in with the social, religious norms and expectations.[2] Some may have a strong sense of communal Muslim identity, which leads them to embrace Islamic beliefs as a matter of course. Others may just be nominal adherents because this is what is culturally expected. Others may even feel a deep sense of dissatisfaction with central tenets of the faith or with the dominant expressions in the communities or countries to which they belong. They may be on a genuine spiritual quest. Some may see Christianity as a kindred religion "of the book" while others may see Christianity as the greatest enemy of Islam or as the religion responsible for the moral degradation and colonial interests of the Western world.

This means that apologetic dialogue needs to be holistic and that witness and encounter need to happen at many levels. One of the aspects that may need particular attention in Christian-Muslim encounters is the political dimension. These encounters are loaded with collective memories of violence between the two communities: in the early expansion of Islam, in the

---

[2]Cf. Miriam Adeney, *Daughters of Islam: Building Bridges with Muslim Women* (Downers Grove, IL: InterVarsity Press, 2002), 146-49.

Crusades and European Colonization, in Christian support for and Muslim attacks on the state of Israel, in Islamic terrorism and Western responses. There is, rightly or wrongly, a strong perception on both sides that Christianity and Islam, as the two largest religions, are caught in a struggle for dominance.

As with all the chapters in part two of this book, this chapter focuses on one particular aspect of apologetic witness that is also important in dialogue with other religious traditions. Here, we focus on one of the possibilities for crosscultural and interreligious apologetic witness that we set out in chapter six: the possibility of showing the relevance and truth of the Christian faith in its integrity, as a whole. Other aspects of the apologetic approach developed in the first half of this book are equally relevant to the dialogue with Islam, but this aspect of the approach has a particular importance, precisely because the many parallels between Islam and Christianity often seem to make it harder rather than easier to understand what the Christian faith stands for.

In the next section we will look at one particular apologetic challenge Islam presents to the Christian faith: it understands itself as the most natural, realist, and sensible religion as well as the natural religion of humankind (§11.2). It will therefore be crucial to help Muslims discover the rationality and warrant the Christian faith has from an inside perspective. We will explore what such an invitation may look like by focusing on the Christian understanding of God as Trinity, one of the focal points of Islamic criticism, yet at the same time one of the richest gifts Christians can share (§11.3). In a concluding section, we will come back to the notion of Islam as the "natural religion" of humankind, pointing out how what comes most naturally to us religiously—and appears at first sight most sensible—may in the end downsize the sovereign God to the limits of our human imagination and perceived needs (§11.4). This chapter therefore has a strong theological focus. This is appropriate in an apologetic encounter with Muslims because, while recognizing the weight of the political context, both conversation partners will understand that many of the decisive issues are theological in nature: What does it mean that there is only one God? How does God relate to us? What is the predicament of humanity in this world? What is the nature of salvation?

11.2 ISLAM AS THE NATURAL RELIGION OF HUMANITY

An apologetic dialogue. In 2006, Wycliffe Hall, an Anglican college within Oxford University, where Benno was teaching at the time, had the privilege of hosting a Muslim-Christian dialogue. When three Muslim scholars from the Al-Azhar University in Cairo visited us for one day, we organized a meeting in which we hoped we could be open about our deepest convictions, open to claims to finality of our respective religions, and open to exchange, with both sides willing to listen to serious arguments as a way to explore questions of truth. Both the guests from Al-Azhar and the three representatives of Wycliffe Hall had apologetic interests and felt that we could pursue these while fully respecting the other dialogue partners.

As a Christian doctrine tutor participating in this dialogue, Benno found himself confronted with tough questions that defied any tendency to give quick answers: "Why do your Gospels contain all those stories about Jesus, instead of the words of Jesus to us?" "If you believe that Jesus is the Son of God, how could God allow him to suffer so terribly on the cross?" "Why couldn't God simply forgive our sins and why did he ask for the sacrifice of his Son?" "If Jesus was the Son of God, why did he pray to God in heaven?" "If Jesus was God himself, why did he not agree with God in the Garden of Gethsemane?" "How could he then cry on the cross: 'My God, My God, why have you forsaken me?'" "When someone commits a murder, asks for forgiveness and is immediately forgiven, doesn't that give him the liberty to do it again?"

We could add other questions put before Christians by Muslims that similarly suggest the sensibility and rational superiority of Islam over Christianity. The criticism of the counterintuitive doctrine of the Trinity is an obvious one. More practical is the criticism of the Christian understanding of morality. The Christian moral stance, as exemplified in the Sermon on the Mount, seems to ask for a holiness and lifestyle that is utterly unattainable and impractical. Because it seems an impossible ideal, it gives little guidance for everyday life. Because it stresses our constant need for forgiveness, it can easily be used to downplay graver sins that should never be allowed to happen. Furthermore, it is difficult to build a society on the basis of commandments: to love your enemies and to forgive without limit. Though Jesus left a code of morality, he refrained from giving a clear blueprint of how society should be organized.[3]

Our three guests from Al-Azhar knew more about the Christian faith than the average Muslim. They had looked beyond the crudest caricatures of Jesus, being the physical son of Mary and Son of God, and did not come up with the obvious reproaches about the Crusades, immorality in the West, or the North-Atlantic invasion in Iraq—which was a huge issue at the time. They had made an effort to

---

[3] Alain Besançon, Préface in *Jacques Ellul, Islam et judéo-christianisme: texte inédit*, by Jacques Ellul, ed. Alain Besançon (Paris: Presses Universitaires de France, 2004), 20-24; Seyyed Hossein Nasr, "The Islamic View of Christianity," in *Christianity through Non-Christian Eyes*, ed. Paul J. Griffiths (Maryknoll, NY: Orbis Books, 2004), 130-31.

discuss what we would consider the essential convictions of the Christian faith. Yet, these simply did not make sense to them in any straightforward manner.

From the Christian side of the dialogue, we talked about the cost of real forgiveness, about Jesus being fully human and divine at the same time, about the consequences of sin, about the joy of knowing a God who knows our suffering, about forgiveness as an invitation to know God rather than as a carte blanche to continue sinning. Yet, we were often talking with the help of metaphors, to refer to a reality which we cannot easily grasp. We were referring to mysteries beyond our understanding, and we knew that our words were inadequate to grasp the complex realities we were trying to communicate. For us as Christians, this seemed a perfectly appropriate way to talk about God. Yet, it was not hard to guess that our guests found these answers rather hesitant and vague compared with the clear-cut concepts Islam presented them with.

The rationality, sensibility, and realism of Islam. For many modern people from the West, attraction to Islam as a sensible and rational religion may be hard to understand, for Islam has a number of traits that modern and postmodern Westerners find particularly hard and unattractive. It seems to have a rather crude and literalist understanding of revelation and scriptural authority; it seems authoritarian and oppressive for women; its Sharia law and conception of the state strikes many modern Westerners as backward or even medieval. Islam seems so crudely supernatural, and its concept of divine law leaves so little space for human freedom.

We should realize however that for many non-Westerners these issues are far less offensive. Many are more appreciative of authority and more open to supernatural events and interventions. Given those parameters, to many Islam indeed seems a fairly rational religion. Its doctrines are easier to understand than the Christian faith: just one God, rather than a Trinity; God sending prophets, rather than the mind-baffling idea of an incarnation; God forgiving because God simply can, rather than atonement; a Qur'an that is presented as the direct expression of the word of God, rather than the Bible, which contains many different human voices and genres; sin as simple disobedience rather than the morally problematic notion of "inherited sin"; a God whose sovereignty and power is never compromised rather than a God who allows his divine Son to suffer on the cross.[4]

Furthermore, Islam presents a religion that provides clear guidance for organizing society and has an ethic that is, at first glance, much more sensible and

---

[4]E.g., Joram van Klaveren, *Apostate: From Christianity to Islam in Times of Secularisation and Terror* (The Hague: 't Kennishuys, 2019), 40-50.

feasible: praying five times a day, one month of fasting and the regular giving of alms is—at least if one has a reasonable position in society—so much more doable than precepts like "pray without ceasing," "sell all your possessions," or "love your enemies." This rational character is consistently demonstrated in Islamic theology[5] and apologetics, as in the widely influential apologetic booklets and clips of the South African apologist for Islam, Ahmad Deedat.[6]

In apologetic dialogue with Muslims, the Christian witness may experience unease about the difficult Christian concepts and the unreasonable demands of the Christian life. It is in fact a step toward deeper exchange when we understand why Muslims consider their religion far superior. For Muslims, this eminent rationality, sensibility, and realism of Islam is also related to the conviction that Islam is the natural human religion. According to the influential Sunni preacher Bilal Philips, "Every child is born with a natural belief in Allah and an inborn inclination to worship Him alone."[7] It is only through socialization in other religious traditions that this natural purity is distorted or lost.

11.3 Invitation to an Inside Perspective

The sovereignty and primacy of God in revelation. Christians need to face this claim of Islam as the natural, rational, and sensible religion, for it is almost always there in the background of Islamic-Christian dialogue. It needs to be challenged, for it presupposes a certain concept of rationality and of how religion should be rational. According to this concept, Christian morality seems too demanding, and its doctrines fly in the face of what is conceivable with straightforward human rational concepts. Yet, there are good reasons to challenge this understanding of rationality and reasonableness, not just because we are Christians, but because this approach to the rationality of religion may not be adequate to deal with the reality of life and with the reality of God as he encounters us.

First of all, the primacy of God in his revelation, a conviction shared by Muslims and Christians, can function as common ground in the dialogue and can help move the dialogue forward. Because revelation originates in God and because God sovereignly decides how and when to reveal Godself, we cannot approach revelation with preconceived notions of what it should

---

[5]E.g., Sayyid Qutb, "That Hideous Schizophrenia," in *Christianity through Non-Christian Eyes*, ed. Paul J. Griffiths (Maryknoll, NY: Orbis Books, 2004), 80-81.

[6]David Westerlund, "Ahmad Deedat's Theology of Religion: Apologetics through Polemics," *Journal of Religion in Africa* 33, no. 3 (2003): 263-78.

[7]Abu Ameenah Bilaal Philips, *The Fundamentals of Tawheed: Islamic Monotheism* (Birmingham, UK: Al-Hidaayah Publishing and Distribution, 1982), 14.

look like.[8] In their dialogue with Muslims, Christians will need to stress that complex doctrines, such as those of the Trinity, the nature of Christ, the atonement, and the nature of the Scriptures, do not stem from some desire to be vague, complex, or mystical, or because of some inability to express ourselves univocally. These doctrines were basically forced on the Christian community because of the nature of the reality of God they encountered in Jesus Christ. This reality simply did not fit with any given understandings of the divine and of how the divine interacts with the world. The encounter with us God initiated in Christ provoked a complete rethinking of our understanding of God. It took the church centuries to work out the right concepts for a proper understanding of the nature of God and of Jesus Christ.

A good case can be made that this is the way we should approach God and reality in general. Rather than forcing God into our preconceived rationalities, we need to adapt our rationalities to this unexpected reality. This is a simple consequence of the primacy and sovereignty of God in revelation: "Revelation is God's sovereign action upon man or it is not revelation."[9] We can of course debate with Muslims whether God is really revealed in Jesus of Nazareth, as the Gospels witness, just as we need to ask if there are good reasons to accept Mohammed's claim to be God's final envoy. Yet, when God takes the initiative in revealing Godself, humans cannot expect God to fit any of their preconceived notions. Rather, we need to be willing to change, adapt, and expand these notions when our encounter with God invites us to do so. When we discover that the reality of God in Christ indeed wrecks our preconceived "natural" concepts of the divine and reality, this should not amaze us. If God exists, if there is indeed an uncreated source of the created universe, it is to be expected that this God will not fit neatly into our rational concepts that have been developed in interaction with the created world.

One step toward this recognition is how many aspects of the created world invite us to expand our preconceived notions. Do we not find ourselves stammering when we try to formulate how Christ on the cross was both God and human? It is not clear whether contemporary philosophy has already found an adequate understanding of the relationship and interaction between the mind and the brain. But even when science is not capable of providing an adequate understanding, and it has not been able for centuries, this is no reason to doubt that we have both a mind and a brain. As an analogy to the

---

[8]Benno van den Toren, *Christian Apologetics as Cross-Cultural Dialogue* (London: T&T Clark, 2011), 77-80.

[9]Karl Barth, *Church Dogmatics*, ed. Geoffrey W. Bromiley and Thomas F. Torrance, trans. Geoffrey W. Bromiley et al. (Edinburgh: T&T Clark, 1956–1975), I/2, 295.

two natures of Christ, people have sometimes pointed to the fact that light can be described as both waves and particles, and that we cannot make a mental picture of how the two go together, though they do. If we need to stretch our preconceived concepts so much in our encounter with created reality, how much more so should we expect it when we encounter God and when we try to work out how God relates to and enters into creation?

We need to steer a careful course here. It may be an easy cop-out to call for the limitation of our human understanding when we come up to questions we cannot answer. We need to make clear that it is rather the reality we encounter that invites us to such a reconsideration of our preconceived ideas. Such a reconsideration does not, however, allow us to accept anything unreasonable. It is rather a question of adapting our reason to the reality we encounter, and it is this reality that determines how we should use human reason. This is implied in the critical realist epistemology that underlies the awareness of the cultural embeddedness of human reasoning and dialogue developed in chapter three. Because of who God is, a Christian theologian will need to steer a middle course between a tendency to master God with human reason and a tendency to let God dissolve into a complete ineffable reality. If the unknown God reveals Godself and created us in God's image so that we might know God, this means that we can have adequate knowledge of God, a knowledge that stretches us out of ourselves, beyond what we ever considered possible.

A second step needs to be taken. Realizing that the reality we meet when God encounters us is beyond the limits of our preconceived rationalities and sensibilities does not need to be the final word. When we encounter this reality, we enter a whole new world.[10] Yet, this world has a rationality and sensibility of its own. After a closer look the inner logic of this world makes much more sense of reality and gives a much deeper sense to life than our preconceived thought patterns ever could. For Muslim-Christian apologetic dialogue, this means that we should not simply stress how Christian beliefs take us beyond our natural human conceptions, but show that they actually make better sense of life, showing a more profound and "realistic" rationality than the Islamic concepts that are superficially so much easier to grasp. For some postmodern Western Christians, this desire to show the rationality of the faith may sound passé. Whatever the truth may be for Western Christians, we need to realize that most Muslims have not passed through and beyond modernity as many Westerners have—Muslims demand a rational justification of the faith. The

---

[10]Karl Barth, "The Strange New World within the Bible," in *The Word of God and the Word of Man* (New York: Harper and Brothers, 1957), 28-50.

model of holistic and embodied apologetic witness and dialogue developed here allows us to take this need for a rational defense seriously while avoiding reductionist and narrowly rationalist approaches.

The Trinity. Showing how this can be done goes beyond the scope of this chapter, for it would amount to a presentation of all the great doctrines of the Christian faith, in order to show how they make sense of life and the God whom we encounter in Christ and in the Scriptures. This is a particularly daunting undertaking precisely because these doctrines go beyond many of the flat, one-dimensional concepts of the natural human mind, of natural religion. There are no quick answers to the many difficult questions our Muslim dialogue partners ask us, or answers to match the clear-cut concepts they present us. As one crucial example, we will limit ourselves to giving some indication of what Christian apologetic witness to the doctrine of the Trinity might entail.

I (Benno) was once invited to give a talk about the Christian belief in the Trinity for a Shiite community in Northwest England. The leaders of the community may have extended this invitation with varied motives. Some may have been genuinely interested; others may have thought that this was the safest doctrine to ask a Christian to speak about because it is so obviously irrational (three persons—one God, really?) and it so obviously undermines the greatness of the one God. It was of course a major challenge to speak on this doctrine that contrasts or even contradicts the doctrine of *tawheed* or the oneness of God—a doctrine so central and dear to Islam.[11] While the doctrine of *tawheed* is by its very nature considered simple and obvious, the doctrine of the Trinity is seen as irrational, contradictory, and nonsensible. Consider the Islamic preacher Shabbir Akhtar's reflections:

Assuming that there is only one God, the Trinity implies:

i.	Christ must be his own Father and his own Son;

ii.	The Holy Spirit is neither Father nor Son yet he is both;

iii.	The Son was begotten by the Father but existed before he was begotten;

iv.	Christ is as old as his Father;

v.	The Father is as young as his Son;

vi.	The Holy Spirit proceeded from the Father and Son but he is as old as his "parents."

These are absurd propositions.[12]

---

[11]Philips, *Fundamentals of Tawheed.*
[12]Shabbir Akhtar, *Islam as Political Religion: The Future of an Imperial Faith* (London: Routledge, 2010), 163.

I considered it a privilege to speak about the Trinity because it brings us to the heart of what Christians believe about who God is and who God is for us. Yet, I was also aware that I would never be able to convincingly counter the critical questions I would encounter as long as the audience would keep looking at this doctrine at a distance, from within the framework of an Islamic understanding of God. I therefore opted to invite my hearers to explore this doctrine from the inside, and to try to understand why it made sense to Christians. This was of course much less threatening and precisely the sort of step that allows discovering the strength of the Christian faith without feeling the need to directly abandon one's own position (§6.3).[13]

In my introduction—and the extensive conversations which took us over two hours—I hoped to make at least three things clear. First, I wanted to show that Christian theologians did not wake up one morning and propose to devise such a complex and counterintuitive doctrine. According to the Christian understanding, this doctrine is a response to the history of God's self-revelation: they knew God as the Creator of the universe and subsequently encountered God's personal presence in Jesus of Nazareth, as God among us. They also encountered God as Spirit, who lived in them as the down payment of the new creation, renewing them from the inside out, rather than only giving them guidance from the outside. This led to a long process of describing who God is, because Christians, Muslims, and Jews agree that God is one. This oneness needs to be stressed constantly. Yet, they discovered that the oneness of God is much richer than a mathematical oneness. It is a oneness of love.[14]

A second step was to show the beauty and attraction of this doctrine. The doctrine of the Trinity is directly related to a profound difference between two understandings of how God relates to humankind. According to orthodox and majority Islam (Sufism is different in this respect), "God does not reveal Himself. He does not reveal Himself to anyone in any way. God reveals only His will."[15] This corresponds to the different master metaphors in the relationship between God and humankind. For Islam, this relationship is understood as a relationship between a master and a slave, or a king and his subjects, in which the primary call to the human is to submit and obey. These metaphors are not foreign to the Bible, yet they are combined with metaphors of the

---

[13]Benno van den Toren, *A Pocket Guide to Christian Belief* (Oxford: Lion Hudson, 2009), 19-21.

[14]Cf. André Manaranche, *Le monothéisme chrétien* (Paris: Cerf, 1985); Jason J. Yoder, "The Trinity and Christian Witness to Muslims," *Missiology* 22, no. 3 (1994): 339-46.

[15]Isma'il Raji al-Faruqi, "On the Nature of Islamic Da'wah," *International Review of Mission* 65, no. 260 (1976): 405; cf. Colin Chapman, *Cross and Crescent: Responding to the Challenge of Islam* (Leicester, UK: Inter-Varsity Press, 1995), 220.

relationship between a father and his children, a groom and his bride, or even between friends or lovers. This relationship presupposes that God lets Godself be known for who God is in Godself.

If God only reveals the divine *will*, and if this will is unrelated to who God is in Godself, this raises the question of how we can know whether God is trustworthy, particularly if God's sovereignty and freedom mean that God can change God's will.[16] More important than this downside of the Muslim model is the attractiveness of the Christian understanding: Would it not be marvelous if God indeed invites us to relate to God as children and to know God's love rather than only God's will? Muslims do, of course, know from experience both types of relationships: the relationship between a master and a servant, on the one hand, and loving relationships such as between friends, parents, children, husband, and wife on the other. We estimate that many Muslims would, at the human level, experience the latter category of relationships as richer and intrinsically more valuable than relationships centering on obedience and submission. Granted that it is staggering to consider that the God of the universe invites us to such a relationship of love (without denying the absolute difference between the parties), would it not be great if we could have such a relationship with God? In contrast, would it not be slightly odd if the richest relationships we experience have no reflection in our relationship with God, but in that relationship both we and God need to settle for less?

In a third step, I tried to show that this understanding of God indeed stretches our reason and imagination but that at a deeper level it makes lots of sense. It has a rationality of its own, a rationality that has great depth. In the above, I pointed to a number of issues: the fact that if God reveals God's personality and heart rather than only God's will, we know that this revealed will can be trusted. If God invites us to be God's children and bride, we know that what we understand to be our deepest relationships point to our intended relationship with God, rather than only more superficial ones such as our relationships with masters and rulers. Furthermore, it provides an explanation for our experience that "personality" is one of the most basic realities in the universe, maybe *the* most basic reality: Godself is eternally personal and eternally loving, allowing creation to mirror that aspect of God's being.[17]

The doctrine of the Trinity also helps answer a logical conundrum that characterizes what we may call "absolute numerical monotheism." If God is

---

[16]Imad N. Shehadeh, "The Predicament of Islamic Monotheism," *Bibliotheca Sacra* 161, no. 642 (2004): 156-59.

[17]Stanley J. Grenz, *The Social God and the Relational Self: A Trinitarian Theology of the Imago Dei* (Louisville, KY: Westminster John Knox Press, 2001).

absolutely one and undivided, why would God create a universe apart from Godself? There seem to be two possible answers. One is that God is in need of the universe; otherwise, God remains lonely or in some other way unfulfilled. For both Christianity and Islam, this is unacceptable because God is sovereign and does not need us. The other possible answer is that creating or not creating is completely arbitrary to God; it does not mean anything to Godself. If so, it is hard to explain why God created this world. But, more importantly, it seems existentially unsatisfactory: Is our existence completely inconsequential for God? Does the entire universe and humanity mean nothing to God? The doctrine of the Trinity presents us with an answer. God is an eternal relationship of Father, Son, and Spirit. Though God does not need to relate to anything beyond Godself, this love can freely overflow and be shared with something yet to be created. The closest human parallel we may know is the love of marriage: the mutual love of the couple may be fulfilling. They may need nothing beyond each other to be fully loved, but they can decide to share this love with children, loving these children without needing anything in return.[18]

We might consider taking a fourth step in this apologetic presentation of the Trinity. The final question is of course whether we have good reasons to believe that God is most clearly visible in Christ—or whether God spoke most clearly through Mohammed as the "seal of the prophets" (Surah 33:40).[19] If we believe that God's self-revelation should be the starting point of our search to understand God as God, we cannot avoid asking where God is known most clearly. The spiritual quests of Mark Gabriel[20] and Nabeel Qureshi[21] show that at some moment in their journey the question of the trustworthiness of the messages of Jesus and Mohammed became unavoidable. In my presentation for this Muslim audience, I avoided addressing this question directly. Indirectly, I touched on it by explaining why Christians believe that the doctrine of the Trinity is not a late development, but deeply rooted in the New Testament itself.[22] I also gave some indications why Christians believe that the

---

[18]Huw Parri Owen, *Christian Theism: A Study in Its Basic Principles* (Edinburgh: T&T Clark, 1984), 24; Manaranche, *Le monothéisme chrétien*, 229-31.
[19]Muhammad A. S. Abdel Haleem, trans. *The Qur'an* (Oxford: Oxford University Press, 2010), 269.
[20]Mark A. Gabriel, *Jesus and Muhammad: Profound Differences and Surprising Similarities* (Lake Mary, FL: Frontline, 2004).
[21]Nabeel Qureshi, *Seeking Allah, Finding Jesus: A Devout Muslim Encounters Christianity* (Grand Rapids, MI: Zondervan, 2014).
[22]E.g., Max Turner, *The Holy Spirit and Spiritual Gifts: Then and Now* (Carlisle, UK: Paternoster, 1996), 169-80; Richard Bauckham, *God Crucified: Monotheism and Christology in the New Testament* (Grand Rapids, MI: Eerdmans, 1999).

New Testament we currently have is a trustworthy text going back to the sources of early witnesses of Jesus Christ, thus implicitly refuting the notion of the corruption of the Christian Scriptures. A direct attack on the trustworthiness of the Qur'an would not have been very productive and only created the type of opposition which would make it much harder to allow the audience to gain an inside view of what the Trinity means for Christians—and why Christians trust that this is indeed a trustworthy understanding of God. As indicated in chapter six, it is generally only after people know that there is a trustworthy alternative understanding of God and the world that they will allow themselves the mental and existential space to critically consider their former perspectives.

11.4 CONCLUDING REFLECTIONS

Many centuries of exchange between Islam and Christianity, both in the dialogue of life and in the dialogue of the mind (cf. §2.2), have seen only little fruit. In his overview of movements from Islam to Christ, the first major movement in the history of this exchange happened through the evangelistic work of Radin Abas Sadrach Surapranata, the "apostle to Java" (c. 1835–1924) in the late nineteenth century.[23] Amazingly, Garrison is able to identify many such movements (defined as at least one thousand new believers or one hundred churches in a two-decade period) in the final decades of the twentieth century and in the first twelve years of the twenty-first century, when he finished his research. He studied eighty-two of these movements spread out across what Garrison calls the "nine rooms" of the house of Islam, representing all major cultural regions in which Islam has spread. The sensitive nature of the material does of course not allow for broad quantitative research methods and for publicly accessible data. Yet, the trend sketched here is confirmed by what others have noted in studying "insider movements" in different parts of the world, movements of Muslims who become followers of Jesus without leaving the Islamic cultures and communities to which they belong.[24] We may well be entering a new era of Christian outreach to Muslims that makes the question of how we share the truth of Christ appropriately all the more important.

---

[23]V. David Garrison, *A Wind in the House of Islam: How God Is Drawing Muslims Around the World to Faith in Jesus Christ* (Monument, CO: WIGTake Resources, 2014), 13-14; cf. Emanuel Gerrit Singgih, "A Postcolonial Biography of Sadrach: The Tragic Story of an Indigenous Missionary," *Al-Jami'ah: Journal of Islamic Studies* 53, no. 2 (2015): 367-86.
[24]See, e.g., Harley Talman, *Understanding Insider Movements: Disciples of Jesus Within Diverse Religious Communities* (Pasadena, CA: William Carey Library, 2015).

As we have seen, Islam presents itself as the eminently rational, sensible, and realistic religion. In the Muslim view, this shows that it is indeed the natural religion, the religion that human beings would naturally embrace unless they are led astray. Christians may agree that Islam does, in a number of ways, reflect aspects of natural religion in line with the power and majesty of the Creator that is visible in creation (Rom 1:20; cf. §4.3). This is also one of the reasons why a number of positive bridges can be built between Muslim and Christian understandings of God. Here we can draw on insights of the positive use of natural revelation, natural reason, and natural theology developed particularly in the Roman Catholic tradition following Thomas Aquinas.[25]

However, the Protestant theologians in the tradition of Barth have developed another understanding of natural religion and natural theology that is a crucial correction and complement to the Thomist understanding. Here natural religion is criticized because it downsizes God to human measurements, to the limits of the human imagination. This understanding also criticizes natural religion because it presents us with twisted pictures of God so that this god becomes less of a threat for sinful human existence.[26] Our reflections on the Trinity suggest that the Muslim criticism of this idea indeed results in the downsizing of the greatness of God and the astonishing nature of God we come to know in the history of salvation, centering in the incarnation of Jesus Christ and the gift of the Spirit. Part of the Muslim criticism of the Christian faith may therefore also be natural religion and natural theology in this second critical sense. We see here a domestication of God and religion so that it is less of a challenge to human reason and sinful human existence. Muslim ethics, for example, may be good at organizing society, precisely because they are so pragmatic and sensible. Yet for the same reason, it may not be able to expose the depth of human sin. For the same reason, it may also be less able to expose the profound oppressive structures in societies and interhuman relations that can continue even when some basic moral rules are respected.

In this chapter we showed how these challenges can be answered if we help our listeners understand the proper integrity of the Christian faith with its inherent rationality, relevance, and beauty. If God cannot be made to fit the dimensions of what we consider sensible and reasonable, we need to let our understanding of who God is be shaped by God's chosen means of revelation. The

---

[25]So Besançon, preface in *Jacques Ellul.*
[26]Barth, *CD* II/1, 155-58.

need to do so is implied by the freedom and sovereignty of God in God's self-revelation, a central conviction that many Christian and Muslim theologians share. Our reflections on the Trinity propose that the God we encounter in the history of salvation indeed surpasses our wildest expectations, but this faith also has an unexpected rationality and is at the same time deeply attractive. This message makes profound existential and intellectual sense.

These reflections on the Trinity will need to be extended with similar explorations on the Christian understanding of salvation, original sin, the cross, revelation, and the Scriptures. It is our conviction that in all these cases an argument can be built that these doctrines far exceed what we naturally believed to be possible. These doctrines, at the same time, reflect a deep sense of life, our deepest needs, and our most noble desires, and are the only way we can do justice to how God made Godself known in the history of salvation. This means that a growing understanding of Christian doctrine is an essential part of an apologetic witness that intends to show the integrity and ground of the Christian faith. In this sense David Ford is right that "the best apologetics is good systematics."[27] Yet, we should not stop there. This is not necessarily the type of systematic theology that focuses on all the finer details of precise logical distinctions, though this may sometimes be needed. We need systematic theology that shows the inner coherence of the Christian faith and how it presents, in its entirety, an attractive and deeply insightful perspective on reality. The apologist needs a systematic theology that shows how the central Christian doctrines are the outcome of a sustained attention to the nature of God's self-revelation in history.

We may conclude that Islam may seem more sensible than the Christian faith. Christians can claim that this is precisely because it is an expression of natural religion, a religion on a human scale. For the same reason, its doctrines fall short of the far greater and deeper reality of God which we encounter in Christ. They fall short of the goal that God has set for humanity: to share in the divine life through our adoption as his children. And they fall short of the complexity of life as it reveals itself on closer inspection. This richer and more realistic rationality has not gone unperceived by Muslims. Some Muslims have actually been drawn to Christ precisely because they found Islam rationally unsatisfying and stultifying. In Christ, they encountered a deeper, more rational, and realistic understanding of God, reality, and themselves.[28]

---

[27]David F. Ford, "'The Best Apologetics Is Good Systematics': A Proposal about the Place of Narrative in Christian Systematic Theology," *Anglican Theological Review* 67, no. 3 (1985): 232-54.

[28]Jean-Marie Gaudeul, *Called from Islam to Christ: Why Muslims Become Christian* (Crowborough, UK: Monarch, 1999), 77-83.

For Barth, natural religion was not primarily a concept used to reflect on other religions. He lived in a nominally Christian culture and saw many forms of Christianity as expressions of natural religion[29] just as his criticism of religion as "unbelief" (see §4.3) was primarily a critical tool to look at the problematic aspects of the Christian religion as a human enterprise.[30] It is indeed true that Christians share this tendency to downsize the Christian faith to something that fits more comfortably within our limited imagination and is less of a challenge to our self-chosen lifestyles. This downsized Christianity often looks in many ways like some of the central tenets of mainstream Islam. God is primarily seen as the Creator, and there is little understanding of the Trinity. Jesus is primarily seen as a divine envoy who teaches us how to live according to the will of God. Such Christianity is not about radical discipleship but about being decent people. We do our best and hope that God will forgive the rest. If the dominant form of Christianity that Muslims encounter is such a downsized Christianity, they will rarely perceive the deeper rationality and existential depth of the Christian faith. Islam is indeed more sensible than such a Christianity. When there is little understanding of the richness of our knowledge of God as Trinity, it simply becomes a theological enigma. When Christ is primarily a prophet or some demigod, seeing him die for the sin of others makes no sense and should even be rejected as unjust and cruel. When our forgiveness is some form of cheap grace, it becomes a license to sin. When the Bible is seen as a book directly dictated from heaven, then it is indeed messy and contaminated by all sorts of human interactions.

The Christian encounter with Islam, therefore, is what Kenneth Cragg terms "a call to retrieval."[31] It is a call to rediscover the uniqueness and depth of the Christian message over against the downsized forms of Christianity which Mohammed likely encountered and which many Muslims still encounter today. This call to retrieval is not only a call to retrieve certain doctrines such as the doctrine of the Trinity, the incarnation, the cross, the Holy Spirit, and salvation history. It is also a call to retrieve a Christian lifestyle, one that reflects the Christian understanding of God—or rather our being grasped by this God. The value of the Trinity will need to be embodied in a community that shows the joy of relationship and love, rooted in the Trinity and allowing for a new experience of God as loving Father.[32] It is a

---

[29]E.g., Barth, *CD* II/1, 141-42.
[30]Barth, *CD* I/2, 300.
[31]Kenneth Cragg, *The Call of the Minaret*, 2nd ed. (Maryknoll, NY: Orbis, 1985), 218-42.
[32]Yoder, "Trinity and Christian Witness," 242-344.

call for a radical Christian discipleship so that Muslims can be amazed by this God and the grace they meet in Christ. The Christian community should reflect a willingness to follow the way of the cross of Christ, showing how this place of shame, foolishness, and weakness is the wisdom and power of God, and how the cross allows a new experience of God's forgiveness and redemption.[33]

---

[33]Cf. Ida Glaser, "Cross-Reference Theology: Speaking, Thinking and Living the Cross in the Context of Islam," in *Jesus and the Cross: Reflections of Christians from Islamic Contexts*, ed. David Emmanuel Singh (Oxford: Regnum, 2008), 151-55.

12

UNMASKING SECULAR IDOLS

12.1 MODERN PSEUDO-RELIGIONS

The special relationship between Christianity and modernity. From its inception, Christianity was a globalizing movement, both in its missionary zeal to reach the "ends of the earth" and in its desire to not simply replace other cultures, but enter in and engage with ever-new cultural contexts. As a globalizing movement, Christianity stands in an uneasy and ambiguous relationship with modernity. The spreading of Western modernity has been a significant vehicle for the spread of the Christian faith, just as the Jewish diaspora and Roman roads were in the early centuries of the church. At the same time, modernity is one of the strongest competitors to the Christian faith, either replacing it with its secularist worldview or so deeply transforming Christianity that it risks losing its distinctive message and bite. This happens, for example, when Christianity is presented within a late-modern consumerist framework, without challenging its core values.[1]

That Christianity risks losing its identity in its engagement with Western modernity is an example of the general challenge to the contextualization—or inculturation—of the Christian faith. On the one hand, the Christian faith needs to enter into a culture so that it becomes truly indigenous, so that its relevance can be seen. On the other hand, the Christian faith needs to remain sufficiently countercultural, so that it will not be imprisoned by the local culture—it should be able to convey its radically new and liberating message (see also §8.4).[2] Beyond this general issue, the relationship between Christianity and modernity presents Christian mission and witness with an additional challenge that accompanies every contextualization process. This

---

[1]Os Guinness, "Mission Modernity: Seven Checkpoints on Mission in the Modern World," in *Faith and Modernity*, ed. Philip Sampson, Vinay Kumar Samuel, and Chris Sugden (Oxford: Regnum Books, 1994), 322-31.

[2]Cf. Andrew Walls, "The Gospel as Prisoner and Liberator of Culture," in *The Missionary Movement in Christian History: Studies in the Transmission of Faith* (Edinburgh: T&T Clark, 1996), 3-15.

additional challenge is rooted in the close relationship between Christianity and modernity. In important respects, Western modernity is the child of Europe's Christian history—or possibly the child of the marriage between the biblical faith of the Old and New Testament and Classical Greek culture. Modern belief in progress has developed out of the Christian understanding of history as linear rather than cyclical, moving from creation toward the new heaven and new earth. Modern science and the modern attention to ordinary life have grown out of the faith in God as the Creator. Modern individualism has grown out of the Christian faith, namely the ultimate value of the individual who has a unique value for God. These fruits of modernity have grown from its Christian roots, but these fruits have also turned sour: the value of the individual has morphed into an individualism, a belief in absolute autonomy; the gift of science has turned into scientism; the respect for creation has turned into secularism, leaving no place for God; the belief in progress has been severed from the Christian hope so that humanity has itself become the only creator of its future. In this sense, modernity can be called "a systematic Christian *heresy*."[3] This close relationship is also at the root of what Os Guinness calls the "gravedigger thesis": "The Christian church contributed to the rise of the modern world; the modern world, in turn, has undermined the Christian church. Thus, to the degree that the church enters, engages and employs the modern world uncritically, the church becomes her own gravedigger."[4]

Part of the ongoing debate between Christianity and modernity is how this development should be interpreted. Is secular modernity the child of Christianity, of which the umbilical cord is rightly cut, so that it can come of age and flourish? (Note that the use of this image presupposes the modern Western value that independence from one's parents is seen as a good thing.) Or is modernity like a tree which is cut off from its roots so that its fruits will wither and die? Will modernity in the end even undermine the good gifts of Christianity when the originally beautiful fruits turn sour, when belief in freedom becomes a destructive war of everyone against everyone, when individualism spells the end of true community, when materialism means the end not only of transcendence but also of morality? There are powerful arguments for the latter view. Without denying the great gifts of modernity to the world, they lose their splendor and mooring when cut off from God the Creator.

---

[3] Cf. Vinoth Ramachandra, *Gods That Fail: Modern Idolatry and Christian Mission* (Downers Grove, IL: InterVarsity Press, 1996), 22.
[4] Guinness, "Mission Modernity," 324, full quote italicized in original; cf. Guinness, *The Gravedigger File: Secret Papers on the Subversion of the Modern Church* (London: Hodder and Stoughton, 1983).

The close relationship between Christianity and Western modernity has an additional dimension. Because secular modernity is a post-Christian movement, modern people feel that Christianity belongs to the past rather than to the future. Moreover, modernity has inherited many gifts from the Christian faith, such as the significance of daily life, belief in progress, and the value of the individual. Secularists are not so easily impressed by these values, which had a profoundly liberating impact in other contexts where Christianity first arrived. Even when these gifts have lost some of their luster in the modern world, possessing them as second-hand goods tends to make these heirs less interested in the God from whom they originate.

These apologetic challenges linked with modernity are not only encountered in Western cultures, but all over the world. Though explicit atheism and secularism may not be as widely present outside the North Atlantic, they have spread to other parts of the world—for example, through secular higher education and through the spread of the Marxist criticism of religion to countries as varied as China, Nepal, and Peru. The translation of Richard Dawkins's works in Arabic is a remarkable phenomenon,[5] partly triggered by the religious abuse of political power. Modern attitudes to life have also spread to other parts of the world without the secular worldview that is so often its Western counterpart.[6] This may partly be the case because aspects of modernity can easily link up with the this-worldly focus of African Traditional Religions[7] or with religious individualism and liberating *gnosis* in South Asian religions.[8] "Materialism as a cult of acquisition and ostentatious consumption is as prominent in the cities of Asia as it is in Europe."[9] This means that the Christian witness encounters a similar "secularization of desire," as we will discuss below, in all continents of the world, both in explicitly secular communities and among religionists (including Christians). Finally, some of the gifts of the Christian faith have also spread around the world through Christian mission—the painful reality of colonization, modernization, and globalization—even where Christianity itself has not been embraced. Thus, the Hindu renaissance has in its effort to

---

[5]Depapriya Chatterjee, "Arabic Translation of 'The God Delusion' Downloaded 10 Million Times," *Atheist Republic* (June 16, 2016), www.atheistrepublic.com/news/arabic-translation-god-delusion-downloaded-10-million-times.

[6]Benno van den Toren, J. Bosco Bangura, and Dick Seed, eds., *Is Africa Incurably Religious? Secularization and Discipleship in Africa*, Regnum Studies in Mission (Oxford: Regnum, 2020).

[7]Benno van den Toren, "African Neo-Pentecostalism in the Face of Secularization: Problems and Possibilities," *Cairo Journal of Theology* 2 (2015): 103-20.

[8]Cf. Vinoth Ramachandra, *The Recovery of Mission: Beyond the Pluralist Paradigm* (Grand Rapids, MI: Eerdmans, 1997), 244-50.

[9]Ramachandra, *Gods That Fail*, 19.

modernize Hinduism incorporated a number of modern Christian values,[10] and certain strands of Buddhism have through their encounter with Christianity integrated elements of social responsibility. Christians can be grateful that these gifts are recognized beyond the boundaries of the Christian community. Yet, it presents a challenge if we recommend the divine Giver in situations where people have already been enjoying some of these gifts, such as the value of the individual, human rights, and the hope for a better future. Given the waning confidence in some of the central values of modernity—such as open communication and honest exploration—a reconnection with the Giver may be crucial for the future of some of the most valuable gifts of modernity itself.

Secular quasi-religion. The apologetic challenges and opportunities presented by modernity in its secular and religious forms are numerous. Important studies have been written on the epistemological challenges raised by the modern idolatry of science and reason.[11] Other apologetic studies have given serious attention to the explicit criticism of religion by the ideological atheists, such as Marx, who saw religion as the opium of the poor; Freud, who saw God as an infantile illusion; and Nietzsche, who saw Christianity as the most debased version of a slave-morality that detracts from the will-to-power.[12] It seems appropriate that in this study on Christian apologetic witness among the religions, we focus on secular modernity as a quasi-religion. Apologetic dialogue with modernity is not all that different from critical dialogue with the great religious traditions of our world. As we have seen in the chapters above, every great religious tradition presents its unique apologetic challenges; so does secular modernity. Secular modernity, and not only in its militant atheist guise,[13] presents itself as the one rational alternative to religious traditions, which are all based on irrational faith in supernatural beings. However, secular modernity makes its own metaphysical assumptions about the nature of ultimate reality, and it has its own fundamental beliefs about what makes life worth living. Only when these quasi-religious beliefs are brought out in the open, can we create a level playing field for dialogue. Only then can we help our secular partners create some distance from their deepest commitments. Only then can we help them find the freedom to ask whether these

---

[10]Vinoth Ramachandra, *Faiths in Conflict? Christian Integrity in a Multicultural World* (Leicester, UK: Inter-Varsity Press, 2000), 78-79.

[11]E.g., Ramachandra, *Gods That Fail*, 136-95.

[12]E.g., Hans Küng, *Does God Exist? An Answer for Today* (Garden City, NY: Doubleday, 1980); D. L. Avis, *Faith in the Fires of Criticism: Christianity in Modern Thought* (Eugene, OR: Wipf & Stock, 2006).

[13]Richard Dawkins, *The God Delusion* (London: Random House, 2006); Christopher Hitchens, *God Is Not Great: How Religion Poisons Everything* (New York: Twelve, 2007).

commitments are really as self-evident and healthy as they are often presented and whether they are indeed worth living (and dying?) for.

Classifying secular modernity as a pseudo-religion demands that we return to our definition of religion. We have already pointed out that defining religion is notoriously difficult (§4.1). Whatever characteristic we use to define the essence of religion is present in some of the phenomena we call religion, but not in others. A well-known example is philosophical Buddhism, which is atheistic and does not directly worship a divine being. We have avoided this conundrum so far by simply using religion without precision, in a generally recognizable way, and by using Ninian Smart's seven dimensions of religion (§2.1). Another proposal for a way around the problem of defining the essence of religion (as in substantive definitions) is providing a "functionalist definition." A functionalist definition focuses on the function religion has in a society or in someone's personal life. A well-known example of a sociological functionalist definition comes from Emile Durkheim, who studied religion in terms of the contribution it makes to the social cohesion of society.[14] An example of a more individualist functionalist definition can be found in the existential theologian Paul Tillich, who defined religion in terms of "ultimate concern": what is of ultimate concern to me, surpassing all relative interests, is my religion, be it God or some secular ideal.[15]

In this respect, Luther's understanding—from his *Larger Catechism*—is worth pondering:

> What does "to have a god" mean, or what is God? Answer: A "god" is the term for that to which we are to look for all good and in which we are to find refuge in all need. Therefore, to have a god is nothing else than to trust and believe in that one with your whole heart. As I have often said, it is the trust and faith of the heart alone that make both God and an idol.[16]

This is an example of a functionalist definition: something or someone other than the true God can also have the role of God in my life if this is (1) from which I expect all good and (2) to which I take refuge in distress. These are two of the three elements central to the biblical understanding

---

[14]Emile Durkheim, *The Elementary Forms of the Religious Life*, trans. Joseph Ward Swain (London: Georg Allen & Unwin, 1968).

[15]Paul Tillich, *Systematic Theology*, vol. 1, *Reason and Revelation, Being and God* (Chicago, IL: The University of Chicago Press, 1951).

[16]Martin Luther, "The Large Catechism," in *The Book of Concord: The Confessions of the Evangelical Lutheran Church*, ed. Robert Kolb and Timothy J. Wengert, trans. Charles P. Arand, Eric Gritsch, Robert Kolb, William Russell, James Schaaf, Jane Strohl, and Timothy J. Wengert (Minneapolis, MN: Fortress Press, 2000), 386.

of idolatry.[17] When idols take the place of God, they become the object of our love and devotion ("to look for all good" in Luther), so that the worship of idols in the Old Testament can be compared to spiritual idolatry, a metaphor introduced in Exodus (34:15-16) and used extensively in the prophets Hosea, Amos, and Ezekiel. A second element of the biblical concept of idolatry is trust and confidence, of taking "refuge in all need," in Luther's language. People bow down to idols saying, "Save me, for you are my god" (Is 44:17). A third element in the biblical notion of idolatry is the notion of service and obedience: an idol is a master which I serve. If I worship an idol, be it a statue of a god or something else, this reality becomes my master: "No one can serve two masters; for a slave will either hate the one and love the other, or be devoted to the one and despise the other. You cannot serve God and [the god Mammon or] wealth" (Mt 6:24).

This biblical notion of idolatry presents a helpful analytical tool to detect the hidden religiosity in secular worldviews. If secular people make certain aspects of the created reality the highest reality—be it money, success, or the state, which they love, trust, and obey above anything else—these become idols and take the place that only belongs to the true God. Sociologists might in this respect speak of quasi-religion because certain behaviors and attitudes do have implicit religious characteristics, even though they lack other characteristics which we would normally attribute to religion when using substantive definitions, such as belief in spiritual beings.[18] From a theological perspective, we could also label this a pseudo-religion: people are involved in semireligious practices by giving certain aspects of created reality absolute authority (such as the state), to give them love and devotion above anything else (such as the love of money, success, hedonist pleasure, or family), or to expect their ultimate security to come from such created realities (be it the security the state provides or the protection I expect in return for the loyalty to my clan). In all these situations, these worshippers "exchanged the truth about God for a lie and worshipped and served the creature rather than the Creator" (Rom 1:25).

Such idolatry is an affront to God. As our Creator and Redeemer, God is the only one who deserves our love, trust, and obedience. What makes the notion of idolatry such a powerful apologetic tool, however, is that it does not stop at the debunking of idols. It is, first of all, a loving and liberating message. The problem of idols is that they cannot deliver what they promise. The problem

---

[17]Brian S. Rosner, *Greed as Idolatry: The Origin and Meaning of a Pauline Metaphor* (Grand Rapids, MI: Eerdmans, 2007), 140-48, 159-65.

[18]Malcolm Hamilton, "Implicit Religion and Related Concepts: Seeking Precision," *Implicit Religion* 4, no. 1 (2001): 5-13.

with serving Mammon or the god of money is that he ultimately cannot fulfill our deepest needs or protect us from the real dangers in our lives. Mammon fools us with empty promises and is not worth our love, trust, and obedience. Idols will need to be unmasked for what they truly are in order to present the true God for who God is.

This unmasking—illustrated in this chapter—will be an aspect of the overall holistic apologetic approach developed in this book. The unmasking reflects the most critical aspect of the holistic apologetic model, reflecting the reality that human religion is not only an expression of a deep quest for God and salvation, but can also be an expression of the sinful human tendency to replace God with what is not God and work out salvation on one's own strength (cf. §4.3)—it often may be both at once. We have chosen to illustrate this aspect with respect to the cultural context to which both of us are a part, in order to express our awareness that idolatry is not merely something one should look for in "pagan societies" but that it happens everywhere—Christians are also vulnerable to it.

12.2 UNMASKING SECULAR IDOLS

Modernity's monotheism and postmodernity's polytheism. When we look to modernity and postmodernity through the hermeneutical lens of true religion and idolatry, we recognize that modernity and postmodernity (or late modernity) represent forms of idolatry and pseudo-religion. There is, however, an important difference between the religiosity of modernity and postmodernity. Modern worldviews are more like monotheist religions in that they replace the one true God with one alternative focal point of life that is considered the highest authority to be obeyed, the greatest good to be sought after, and the most secure source of help in trouble. This idol can be variously conceived: as reason and science, as a communist paradise at the end of history, or as unlimited consumption to be achieved through capitalism. These modern idols are each set in a different metanarrative, an encompassing story that is supposed to explain all of life.

Postmodernity has been described as the end of all metanarratives that claimed to be able to provide a unified understanding of life and the universe.[19] From a Christian perspective, it is not surprising that these grand narratives have failed. Taking God out of the picture necessarily leads to a universe

---

[19]Jean-François Lyotard, *The Postmodern Condition: A Report on Knowledge*, trans. Geoffrey Bennington and Brian Massumi, Theory and History of Literature 10 (Minneapolis: University of Minnesota Press, 1984).

without a center and a life without coherence. God is the one Creator, Reconciler, and Goal—the origin of unity in the universe and of coherence in our lives. This is one of the theological explanations as to why modernity gave way to postmodernity.

In an important sense, postmodernity resembles polytheism more so than monotheist worldviews, where one God guarantees the unity of existence. Postmodern society does, in this respect, share important traits with the Greco-Roman world in which the unique lordship of Christ was first proclaimed. In the Greco-Roman world, there were, on the one hand, regional religions for every city or tribe. These gods did not have much authority or great value beyond those who lived in and around these cities, or for those belonging to the tribes.[20] This is not unlike the postmodern and postliberal understanding, according to which religions have value for those societies or groups that organize their lives according to a specific religion, yet do not claim value and truth beyond the boundaries of these communities.[21]

Additionally, the Greco-Roman world knew of many gods that people could opt for because of their specific needs, as when one was ill or traveling. They also knew a group of religious practices—"mystery religions," such as Mithraism—that people adhered to because of personal preference, but neither were considered of universal value.[22] Another expression of the postmodern attitude to religion has parallels to these personal gods or mystery religions. They consider religious adherence as a matter of choice and personal preference, but, again, not as a matter of universal truth as with monotheism and modernity. Just like in the Greco-Roman world, secular postmodern people consider the religious lifestyles of others—and their own secular lifestyles—to be ways of life that are either particular to their community or opted for out of personal preference or need. Like in the ancient world, the more socially mobile sectors of society may feel comfortable combining a number of religious practices (in the case of polytheism), or a number of lifestyles and their ideals (as in the case of postmodernism). Because there is supposedly no ultimate unity at the basis of the universe or life, this is not necessarily seen as inconsistent or unhealthy. At one point in my life, I may go all out for my economic career; at another point, for my love life or family; and later in life, I may discover volunteering, travel, or yoga give meaning to my life. I may

---

[20]James S. Jeffers, *The Greco-Roman World of the New Testament Era: Exploring the Background of Early Christianity* (Downers Grove, IL: InterVarsity Press, 1999), 92.

[21]Cf. George Lindbeck, *The Nature of Doctrine: Religion and Theology in a Postliberal Age* (Philadelphia, PA: Westminster Press, 1984).

[22]Jeffers, *Greco-Roman World*, 96-100.

even combine these, not bothered by how they fit together, just as an ancient Hellenistic city dweller might combine worship of the gods of the city, of their trade, or their ethnic group with some divinity of personal choice.

The apparent polytheism of many ancient religions and the apparent pluralism of postmodernity are, however, deceptive. Often there is behind (or above) the polytheist universe a unifying force or highest authority that assigns the smaller deities their appropriate place. In the Greco-Roman world, the authority of the Roman Empire surpassed the authority of the cities and tribal leaders, even if they had a degree of independence. In the later Roman Empire this became explicit in the required worship of the emperor: other religions might be tolerated as long as they did not undermine the supreme authority of the emperor.[23] That is why the later refusal of Christians to sacrifice to the emperor showed that this society was not truly pluralistic. Furthermore, many polytheistic religions have an underlying worldview that unified these diverse religious expressions and that could not easily be challenged by adding another religious practice. The Christian faith with its worship of only one God fell outside the range of what was acceptable, even more so than Judaism, which could up to a certain level been accommodated as an ethnic religion.[24] In the Greco-Roman world, this was detectable in the belief in the three *moirai*, the goddesses of destiny that determined the destiny of all, even of the other gods. In ancient German mythology, *wurd* or fate plays a similar role, as a force to which even the gods are subject.[25] In a similar vein, behind the many gods of modern Hinduism that can be chosen for personal devotion stands a worldview in which these gods need to fit so that the worshippers can be good citizens of this polytheist universe.

Both in the ancient and postmodern world, the proclamation of the absolute lordship of Christ exposes the hidden absoluteness of this polytheist universe. Today's postmodernism presents at a certain level tolerance and respect, but more often than not, this tolerance and pluralism is itself restricted by a framework that assigns all other gods their place within an overall metaphysics, and that allows different worldviews their respective places in so far as they do not challenge the postmodern worldview that is considered superior. This happens, for example, when all religious convictions are made private and a

---

[23]Cf. Jeffers, *Greco-Roman World*, 100, 105.

[24]Larry W. Hurtado, *Destroyer of the Gods: Early Christian Distinctiveness in the Roman World* (Waco, TX: Baylor University Press, 2016), 15-36.

[25]Cf. G. Ronald Murphy, *The Saxon Savior: The Germanic Transformation of the Gospel in the Ninth-Century Heliand* (New York: Oxford University Press, 1989), 33-53; K. H. Miskotte, *Edda en Thora; een vergelijking van Germaanse en Israëlitise religie* (Nijkerk, NL: Callenbach, 1970), 142-59.

secular worldview (or neoliberal ideology) claims the public domain for itself. It also happens when postmodernism claims to end all metanarratives, but becomes a new metanarrative itself, setting the limits for all other stories.[26] In apologetic dialogue, our conversation partners need to be made aware of the particularity of their own presumedly universal perspectives.

Leaps of faith. If both secular modernism and secular postmodernism represent forms of idolatry and pseudo-religion, one of the tasks of apologetic witness is to "unmask" the secular gods.[27] It is helpful to distinguish different aspects in this process of unmasking, though in concrete dialogues, these are often intertwined.

A first aspect of this unmasking is to show that modernism and postmodernism are indeed pseudoreligious worldviews. Secularism will often explicitly or implicitly claim to be the only sober and rational attitude to life in contrast to religious attitudes. The latter are superstitious and can therefore be no more than private opinions. Postmodernism may claim to refrain from any claim to truth and seem even more sober and measured. These worldviews and lifestyles do, however, imply their own truth claims that are central to their attitude to life. If secularism claims that there is nothing more to life than can be seen, it is dogmatic rather than critical. If it claims that science is the only trustworthy avenue to truth, it clings religiously to science, rather than respecting the necessary limits that the scientific method sets for what it can deliver. Even if what science tells us about reality is by and large trustworthy, science itself cannot answer how important science is for understanding the meaning of life. Science will find its place in an encompassing worldview. Such worldviews are based on faith commitments and in that respect secular worldviews are on par with religious commitments. Both need to be looked at equally and critically. Postmodernism often makes its own absolute claims with its hidden metanarrative, which is equally faith-based and needs to be looked at with a critical eye. There are of course forms of modernism and postmodernism that are well aware of these deeper religion-like worldview commitments—commitments that are foundational to their outlook on life and the world. These people may be more amenable conversation partners because they will neither absolutize their own certainties nor their own doubts.

Secularisms not only need to be unmasked as pseudoreligious because of their faith commitments at the foundation of their outlook on life. We also

---

[26]William Edgar, "No News Is Good News: Modernity, the Postmodern and Apologetics," *Westminster Theological Journal* 57 (1995): 359-82.

[27]Cf. Nancy Pearcey, *Finding Truth: 5 Principles for Unmasking Atheism, Secularism, and Other God Substitutes* (Colorado Springs, CO: David C. Cook, 2015).

need to unmask their idolatry: those realities in which they trust in the face of danger, which they seek as their highest good, and whose authority needs to be obeyed above all else. Such idolatry is most clearly perceptible in the grand narratives of modernity, such as the narrative of scientific optimism, the narrative of a revolutionary journey toward the Marxist utopia, the story of inevitable progress in liberal societies, and more individualistic narratives of finding one's true self through absolute autonomy or adequate psychothera- peutic insight. These again are faith statements. The problem with such state- ments is often not that they are too critical, but rather that they are too credu- lous. The problem with many modern people is not that they believe too little, but that they believe too much. Superstition is not only a problem in the world of religions, but also among many secular people. What robust basis do we have for our belief in a Marxist utopia, in the ability of science and psycho- therapy to solve our deepest problems, and for our belief that unhindered economic growth will produce a better world? In an honest conversation, people may be much more realistic. They may recognize that their conviction— that this lifestyle is the best bet for a good life, a better world, and for protec- tion against life's greatest evils—is just that, a best bet. If so, they should also be open to those who have religious worldviews. They have no reason to dis- miss out of hand the Christian witness to the true God, and how life in its fullness can be found in Jesus Christ.

Gods that fail. A second aspect of the unmasking process is one step beyond the recognition that the modern and postmodern confidence in secu- lar values and hopes is also a matter of faith. Unmasking also means that these are "gods that fail"[28]; they are "counterfeit gods"[29] that are unable to contrib- ute to true flourishing in the way that only the true God can.

Idolatry means that human beings give the glory and honor due to the true God to an aspect of created reality that is divinized (Rom 1: 23, 27). Such aspects of the created world as romantic love, consumption, children, wealth, freedom, or life in harmony with nature become idolized and are seen as the source of absolute fulfillment. Other aspects of the created world can also be seen as the solution to humanity's deepest problems, be it the state, the econ- omy, science, or psychotherapy. This leads, of course, to great tensions between our deepest needs and what we can realistically expect. We can move in differ- ent directions to deal with this tension. We can either try to negate the deep dissatisfaction, postpone fulfillment, and hope that the future will be better

---

[28]Cf. Ramachandra, *Gods That Fail.*
[29]Timothy Keller, *Counterfeit Gods: When the Empty Promises of Love, Money, and Power Let You Down* (London: Hodder & Stoughton, 2010).

than today. Or we can seriously downgrade our expectations in life and settle for the limited joys that this life provides while bracing for the inevitable uncertainties and anxieties that are part of life. It seems that modernity erred more on the side of keeping high expectations and postponing fulfillment, hoping that one day the world at large would find a solution to today's problems. Late- and postmodernity have a stronger tendency to downgrade expectations and embrace uncertainty, risk, failure, and disappointment as part of life.

For both moderns and postmoderns there is a significant collateral cost to these psychological strategies: they settle for the limited joy this life may have to offer while neglecting the plight of the huge swaths of society for whom even the limited joys of this world are out of reach. For many, even such limited contentment is out of reach because they belong to the oppressed masses of their societies, because they happen to be born in parts of the world that are torn apart by drawn-out civil wars, or because they simply cannot cope with the pressures of life. From a Christian perspective, there cannot be true hope unless it can be presented as such to all God's children.

Gods that diminish human beings. A third aspect of this unmasking process is that these gods not only fail but are too small for what humans are meant to be. Though the language of unmasking sounds critical and negative, Christian witness should keep seeking words, images and the right tone to express how it is essentially positive and life-affirming. It can affirm how all that it encounters is true and good. It can affirm all the opportunities human beings—created in God's image—have received to make something beautiful out of their lives, as well as this rich and multifaceted creation. The problem is not that these gifts are not good in themselves, but that they are part of creation and can never replace the Giver who infinitely surpasses his gifts. The biblical notion of the "image of God" (Gen 1:27) has a multilayered meaning, but one aspect is that humankind is created in a special relationship with God,[30] created to find ultimate fulfillment in a loving covenant relationship with God, made possible in the gift of God's Son who is the image of God par excellence (Col 1:15), in whom we are also recreated into God's image (Col 3:10).[31]

The problem with secular idols is that these ideologies think too highly of humankind, as if humanity can be its own savior and find its destiny in itself. Yet, the bigger problem may be that it thinks too little of humanity, as if there

---

[30]Henri Blocher, *In the Beginning: The Opening Chapters of Genesis* (Downers Grove, IL: InterVarsity Press, 1984), 85; Claus Westermann, *Genesis 1–11: A Continental Commentary* (Minneapolis, MN: Fortress Press, 1994), 158.

[31]Benno van den Toren, *Christian Apologetics as Cross-Cultural Dialogue* (London: T&T Clark, 2011), 106-8.

is nothing more to life that humankind can achieve on its own steam. The difference between Christianity and secular modernity/postmodernity concerns not only a different view of God, but also a fundamentally different view of what it means to be human. As John Calvin classically stated, the knowledge of ourselves and of God is closely related and mirror each other.[32] According to a classic formulation of Augustine of Hippo, "You inspire us to take delight in praising you, for you have made us for yourself, and our hearts are restless until they rest in you."[33] Augustine's disciple Blaise Pascal expressed this with a helpful image that has rich apologetic potential. He notes that human beings all through history keep seeking a fulfillment they cannot find. He sees the root of this continuing quest in the fact that human beings find in themselves an "infinite abyss [which] can only be filled by an infinite and immutable object, that is to say, only by God Himself."[34]

This does not mean that humans wherever they find themselves only need some introspection to discover that they are created for an eternal relationship with God. Augustine writes about this unrest with *hindsight*. It was only after he had come to know God in Christ that he became fully aware that God had all the time been guiding and drawing him and that the unrest he sometimes only vaguely (and sometimes more acutely) felt was caused by his being created for a covenant relationship with God.

Furthermore, as the psalmist already noted of those who worship idols (Ps 135:18),

Those who make them
and all who trust them
shall become like them.

In the language of James K. A. Smith, "You are what you love."[35] If individuals and communities for long periods of time—and even for generations—live with substitutes for what only the true God can offer, this will shape their lives accordingly. As a consequence, they will become less and less aware of a goal of life that transcends what their culture considers the highest achievable goal. This is strengthened by a psychological process that Blaise Pascal described

[32]John Calvin,. *Institutes of the Christian Religion*, trans. Henry Beveridge, 2 vols. (Grand Rapids, MI: Eerdmans, 1983), para. I, I, 1.

[33]Augustine, *Confessions Books 1–8*, trans. Carolyn J.-B. Hammond, Loeb Classical Library 26 (Cambridge, MA: Harvard University Press, 2014), bk I, I.1; 3.

[34]Blaise Pascal, *Pensées*, trans. A. J. Krailsheimer (London: Penguin Books, 1995), no. 148.

[35]James K. A. Smith, *You Are What You Love: The Spiritual Power of Habit* (Grand Rapids, MI: Brazos Press, 2016); cf. Ps 115:8; G. K. Beale, *We Become What We Worship: A Biblical Theology of Idolatry* (Downers Grove, IL: InterVarsity Press, 2008).

aptly in the seventeenth century, yet that seems even stronger in the media-saturated societies of the twenty-first century: *divertissement* or distraction. The unrest people experience in their lives and the abyss they glimpse from time to time can of course be deeply disconcerting. Many people flee from this recognition by seeking all sorts of distraction.[36] This may lead to a superficial satisfaction with life as it is and a seeming indifference toward life's deeper questions. Therefore, the apologist not only needs to unmask idolatry, but also these forms of distraction or, more positively, self-protection. When considering this formidable challenge, we can learn from the fact that the writings of some of the greatest apologists such as Augustine, Pascal, and later Søren Kierkegaard not only brought rational clarity to the task, but also showed psychological wisdom. The Christian witness will in this respect be listened to most attentively if they show an awareness of the temptation to replace the true God with a counterfeit, and the tendency to let ourselves be distracted from issues that really matter—both are equally present in the Christian community and in one's own live.

Part of the task of Christian witness, therefore, is to rekindle the flame of desire that may have been smothered under layers of ash; the desire for more that has almost been extinguished because of the hardship of life or the shallowness of a culture. Yet, when this flame is kindled it becomes apparent that there is a deep desire for more in the human life, for life "to the full" (Jn 10:10 TNIV). This desire can be dismissed as a helpful though misleading evolutionary trait,[37] but is so much greater. It is indeed a hunger that is meant to be satisfied by living our created life deeply earthed yet in a loving covenant relationship with the Creator.[38]

12.3 Cultural Hermeneutics

This chapter so far has been an exercise in "cultural hermeneutics." Where biblical hermeneutics is concerned with the interpretation of the meaning of the Christian Scriptures, cultural hermeneutics is asking how we should interpret our culture at large and specific cultural phenomena in particular.[39]

---

[36]Thomas V. Morris, *Making Sense of It All: Pascal and the Meaning of Life* (Grand Rapids, MI: Eerdmans, 1992), 31-45; Os Guinness, *Fool's Talk: Recovering the Art of Christian Persuasion* (Downers Grove, IL: InterVarsity Press, 2015), 99-105.

[37]As Erik J. Wielenberg, *God and the Reach of Reason: C. S. Lewis, David Hume, and Bertrand Russell* (Cambridge: Cambridge University Press, 2008), 115-19.

[38]Cf. C. S. Lewis, "The Weight of Glory," in *The Weight of Glory and Other Addresses* (New York: Macmillan Company, 1949), 25-46.

[39]Kevin Vanhoozer, "What Is Everyday Theology? How and Why Christians Should Read Culture," in *Everyday Theology: How to Read Cultural Texts and Interpret Trends*, ed. Kevin J. Vanhoozer, Charles A. Anderson, and Michael J. Sleasman (Grand Rapids, MI: Baker Academic, 2007), 15-60.

According to John Stott, a Christian should always be involved in "double listening," in an effort to understand both the Scriptures and the world in which they live.[40] This has been characteristic of all the chapters in part two: they all intend to understand different religious traditions according to their inner logic and also ask how to interpret these different religious traditions from a Christian perspective, in light of God's self-revelation as Father, Son, and Spirit.

This chapter proposes a reading of the secular worldview and lifestyles with the help of the notion of idolatry as an interpretative key, showing how secular modernity hides its own religious convictions, even from itself. Therefore, this reading invites us to a countercultural stance in the contextualization process because it shows that modern secular culture is not a neutral background for the proclamation of the gospel; rather, it presents an alternative metanarrative with alternative accounts of hope and salvation.[41] However, that the biblical story is countercultural does not mean that it is anticultural.[42] If the gospel is critical of modern culture, it does so in order to value and liberate everything that is true and good, so that it might find its fulfillment in the context of the kingdom. However, this fulfillment is, according to missiologist Hendrik Kraemer, a subversive fulfillment, because it can only happen when the idols of our times are at the same time unmasked and challenged (cf. §9.3).

Such cultural hermeneutics are not only needed in view of understanding the deeper structures of cultures, worldviews, and religions at large. They are also needed with regard to concrete cultural phenomena as varied as the insurance industry, modern educational theory, Starbucks, Facebook, and the newest influencers or television series. This is the case because Christian discipleship needs to be lived out amidst the big challenges and humdrum of daily life, which encompasses all the above and so much more. It is equally needed because these cultural phenomena reflect the worldviews, desires, and longings of our culture, shaping the lives of the people we encounter, including the Christian community.[43] They not only reveal the idolatry that needs to be unmasked but also reveal the deeper desires and longings of our culture,

---

[40]John Stott, *The Contemporary Christian: An Urgent Plea for Double Listening* (Leicester, UK: Inter-Varsity Press, 1992).

[41]Lesslie Newbigin, *Foolishness to the Greeks: The Gospel and Western Culture* (London: SPCK, 1986); Stephen B. Bevans, *Models of Contextual Theology* (Maryknoll, NY: Orbis Books, 1992), 117-37.

[42]Lesslie Newbigin, "The Gospel and Our Culture: A Response to Elaine Graham and Heather Walton," *Modern Churchman* 34, no. 2 (1992): 1-10; contra Elaine Graham and Heather Walton, "A Walk on the Wild Side: A Critique of 'The Gospel and Our Culture,'" *Modern Churchman* 33, no. 1 (1991): 1-7.

[43]E.g., Smith, *You Are What You Love*, 46-53.

providing positive points of contact that can be reinterpreted in the light of the gospel.[44]

One of the added benefits of such cultural hermeneutics is that is can be great fun. Benno and his wife Berdine were, for a number of years, members of a "secular" book club in which they discussed the newest literary novels, inviting the participants—in a natural way—to serious conversations about the deeper questions of life. Others have had similar experiences with film clubs, in which students engage with recent films that reflect the deep longings of our time, but also often present only limited answers to the profound questions that are raised, evoked, or hinted at.[45] What to think of a discussion of hope on the basis of a film such as *Gladiator*?[46] The question is not simply what the director Ridley Scott (or the scriptwriters, actors, or producers) wanted to convey with this film. Films may point beyond their original intent because the greatest questions of life cannot be straightjacketed so easily. Scott himself speaks of "mortality" as the central theme of *Gladiator*. Michael Sleasman shows that the film points beyond mortality to glimpses of an afterlife which motivate Maximus, the central character of the film, at crucial moments in the story.[47] One may even ask critically whether the liberating actions of Maximus would have been credible without this "eschatological" perspective.

Christians are called to become competent interpreters of both popular and more erudite expressions of culture. This is a massive undertaking that can only be taken on as a community. This allows each of us to contribute by trying to understand the cultural expressions we know best—and possibly also those which we enjoy most. It helps us to see the great gifts in culture that often speak unexpectedly of deep human longing and may also provide glimpses of salvation. Some of these cultural voices have themselves begun the work of unmasking the limited or misleading gospels on offer. These may also help Christians remain critical of their cultures—cultures that present such a constant, humming background noise that Christians are no longer aware how the messages of culture shape their own desires and hopes.

---

[44]Theodore A. Turnau III, "Popular Culture, Apologetics, and the Discourse of Desire," *Cultural Encounters* 8, no. 2 (2012): 25-46.

[45]Turnau III, "Popular Culture."

[46]Ridley Scott, *Gladiator* (Universal Pictures Germany GmbH, 2000).

[47]Michael J. Sleasman, "Swords, Sandals, and Saviors: Visions of Hope in Ridley Scott's Gladiator," in *Everyday Theology: How to Read Cultural Texts and Interpret Trends*, ed. Kevin J. Vanhoozer, Charles A. Anderson, and Michael J. Sleasman (Grand Rapids, MI: Baker Academic, 2007), 141-43, 148.

13

INNER TENSIONS
IN LATE-MODERN SPIRITUALITIES

13.1 ORIGINS AND INTERACTIONS

For most of the twentieth century, the dominant view among sociologists was that Europe and North America would, under the influence of modernity, become increasingly secular. Religions would be pushed toward the margins, both in numbers and influence. This was partly due to a perception of decreasing religious participation, but possibly more to an ideological presupposition that modernity and religious adherence cannot be harmonized. The increasing influence of science, open communication, and individual freedom was supposed to automatically lead to a decreasing influence of religion. The influence of modernity in other regions of the world would supposedly also lead to secularization.

Only in the final decade of the twentieth century, this secularization thesis came increasingly under pressure. It became evident that rather than just declining, religion was transforming in the late-modern era.[1] Under the influence of colonialism—and after its demise—some of the great non-Western religious traditions experienced a renaissance rather than a decline. Though atheism and agnosticism grew rapidly in the first three quarters of the twentieth century, its percentage share in the world population has been declining for some decades.[2] In the West itself, religion became less institutional and more a matter of personal religious experience. Religion in the West also received new impulses through the influx of Christians from other parts of the world, through immigration of Muslim and other religious minorities, in the wake of the Western counterculture of the 1960s and 1970s, and through

---

[1] Peter L. Berger, ed., *The Desecularization of the World: Resurgent Religion and World Politics* (Grand Rapids, MI: Eerdmans, 1999); Charles Taylor, *A Secular Age* (Cambridge, MA: Belknap Press, 2007).
[2] G. A. Zurlo, T. M. Johnson, and P. F. Crossing, "World Christianity and Mission 2020: Ongoing Shift to the Global South," *International Bulletin of Mission Research* 44, no. 1 (2020): 8-19.

the dissemination of ideas from South Asian religions (particularly Hinduism and Buddhism).[3]

Part of this religious resurgence or "reenchantment" of the world is a cluster of religious movements that can be variously labeled as New Age, new religious movements, new spiritualities, or sometimes disparagingly, as cults. The term "New Age" was popular in the sixties and seventies. In its narrower sense, it refers to a group of religious movements that expected a new spiritual age, the age of Aquarius, which at the end of the second millennium would replace the former age dominated by Christianity. In a wider sense, New Age was a label for a broader collection of religious movements inspired by older European and North American esoteric movements (such as theosophy and Christian Science) and influenced by Asian religions, most of all Hinduism.[4] Since the eighties and nineties, the label New Age has fallen into disrepute,[5] but these spiritualities are still very alive. It is a cluster of eclectic spiritual movements without a central organization, without central spiritual texts, and without a doctrinal orthodoxy.

In "Late Modern Spiritualities," we will discuss a cluster of religious movements and sensitivities that shares a number of characteristics with the earlier New Age movement. This spirituality is now present in certain aspects of Western mainstream culture, as seen in the popularity of yoga and certain eco-spiritualities in parts of the environmental movement. It can be seen in the popularity of Buddha statues, spiritual retreats, and healing crystals among people who might not consider themselves religious and would not want to align themselves with a movement. These spiritualities can be called late-modern in that this form of religiosity, with its consumerist and individualistic approach to religions, fits the Western capitalist world particularly well. We prefer the term *spiritualities* rather than religions or even religious movements, because many of its expressions need not necessarily function as organized religions. They are incredibly varied, so that it is impossible to identify clear characteristics—it is fluid, what does and does not belong to this spirituality. For every characteristic there will also be particular examples that do not fit the mold. Yet, these spiritualities by and large present a number of traits and sensitivities that allow one to group them together. They

---

[3]Cf. Os Guinness, *The Dust of Death: A Critique of the Establishment and the Counter Culture—and a Proposal for a Third Way* (Downers Grove, IL: InterVarsity Press, 1973).
[4]Olav Hammer, "New Age," in *The Brill Dictionary of Religion*, ed. Kocku von Stuckrad, trans. Robert R. Barr, III (Leiden: Brill, 2006), 1313-15.
[5]John P. Newport, *The New Age Movement and the Biblical Worldview: Conflict and Dialogue* (Grand Rapids, MI: Eerdmans, 1997), xi.

also present specific challenges and possibilities for apologetic witness and dialogue.

The movement has a complex relationship with South and East Asia.[6] Its adherents constantly refer to older spiritual traditions, which are mainly Asian, but may also include shamanistic traditions of First Nations in North America and elsewhere. In the process of their reception in the West, these Eastern religious traditions have been transformed in ways that we will further discuss below. For example, the Western reception of Hinduism by Helena Blavatsky and Annie Besant as well as through the study of Asian religions in Western academia, has in turn influenced the Hindu renaissance in India.[7] There are therefore important parallels between Western New Age-type religions and Indian authors such as Abdul Kalam,[8] and Osho (also known as Bhagwan Shree Rajneesh).[9] Today Western New Age authors are also published in India.[10]

The great variety of views and expressions within these new spiritualities underlines the importance of attentive listening stressed throughout this book. A Christian conversation partner should never presuppose that they know where their interlocutor comes from but should always try to understand how individuals create their own eclectic spirituality in a manner that fits their personal history. It does mean, at the same time, that a number of reflections in this chapter are equally valuable when reflecting on other post- or late-modern expressions that may in certain respects have a different focus, a different worldview, and different spiritual practices. Because they are part of the late-modern cultural context, they may still share a number of the same sensitivities and values that can raise similar barriers, but also provide similar opportunities for deep conversation and encounter. A prime example are neo-pagan movements such as Wicca, Druidry, and Heathenism.[11] They

[6]Andrea Grace Diem and James R. Lewis, "Imagining India: The Influence of Hinduism on the New Age Movement," in *Perspectives on the New Age*, ed. James R. Lewis and J. Gordon Melton, SUNY Series in Religious Studies (Albany, NY: State University of New York Press, 1992), 48-58; Irving Hexham and Karla Poewe-Hexham, "New Religions as Global Cultures," in *Encountering New Religious Movements: A Holistic Evangelical Approach*, ed. Irving Hexham, Stephen Rost, and John W. Morehead (Grand Rapids, MI: Kregel, 2004), 91-111.
[7]Hexham and Poewe-Hexham, "New Religions," 104-5; Vinoth Ramachandra, *Subverting Global Myths* (London: SPCK, 2008), 234-38.
[8]E.g., A. P. J. Abdul Kalam, *Transcendence: My Spiritual Experiences with Pramukh Swamiji* (New York: Harper Element, 2016).
[9]E.g., Osho, *Christianity the Deadliest Poison & Zen the Antidote to All Poisons* (Pune, IND: Osho Media International, 2014).
[10]E.g., Russ Michael, *Feeling Good Is Feeling God* (New Delhi: Good Times Books, 2011).
[11]Matthew D. Rogers, "Paganism/Neopaganism," in *The Brill Dictionary of Religion*, ed. Kocku von Stuckrad, trans. Robert R. Barr, vol. III (Leiden: Brill, 2006), 1393-96; Paul Cudby, *The Shaken Path:*

tend to have a stronger spirituality of nature and will often tend to embrace the brevity of individual existence rather than hope for reincarnation that characterizes New Age movements influenced by Hinduism. Yet, they will share the focus on experience, the nondoctrinal and noninstitutional approach to religion, and a panentheistic worldview (God is in everything). We could also see other parallels in the post-Christian spiritualities of many church-leavers: for example, in a movement that in the Netherlands is called "somethingism," but has parallels elsewhere ("I believe in something, but you may call it differently").[12]

According to John Drane, "Effective mission within New Spirituality is probably a specialist ministry."[13] This is indeed the case for outreach in specifically targeted contexts such as booth ministries in Mind and Spirit festivals.[14] Throughout this chapter, we will encounter a whole body of specialist literature supporting those ministries, both in the traditional "heresy-rationalist," anti-cult tradition, and in line with more recent holistic approaches. Yet, apart from specialized ministries, ministers in local congregations will, on a regular basis, encounter these spiritual seekers in both the West and in the Indian subcontinent as well as in many late- or postmodern cosmopolitan settings across the globe. Moreover, in certain contexts, some of the general features of these spiritualities may be so widely present, that Christian communities must be helped to develop their own faith and discipleship so that they can adequately witness to their family, friends, colleagues, and neighbors. This is part of missionary discipleship itself, being good friends to fellow spiritual pilgrims. It is also part and parcel of deepening the contextually rooted understanding of the unique and unsurpassable gift of salvation we have received in Christ.

After further analysis of the character of these movements (§13.2) and of the specific apologetic challenges they present (§13.3), we will again choose one apologetic angle to approach these movements: the exploration of the inner tensions that characterize these lifestyles (§13.4). Apologetic witness

---

A Christian Priest's Exploration of Modern Pagan Belief and Practice (Lanham, UK: John Hunt Publishing, 2017); Philip Johnson and John Smulo, "Reaching Wiccan and Mother Goddess Devotees," in Encountering New Religious Movements: A Holistic Evangelical Approach, ed. Irving Hexham, Stephen Rost, and John W. Morehead (Grand Rapids, MI: Kregel, 2004), 209-25.

[12]E.g., G. D. J. Dingemans, Ietsisme: een basis voor christelijke spiritualiteit? (Kampen, NL: Kok, 2005).

[13]J. W. Drane, "New Age," in New Dictionary of Christian Apologetics, ed. Gavin McGrath, Walter Campbell Campbell-Jack, C. Stephen Evans, and S. Carter (Downers Grove, IL: InterVarsity Press, 2006), 484.

[14]Cf. Philip Johnson, "Discipling New Age and Do-It-Yourself Seekers through Booth Ministries," in Encountering New Religious Movements: A Holistic Evangelical Approach, ed. Irving Hexham, Stephen Rost, and John W. Morehead (Grand Rapids, MI: Kregel, 2004), 227-42.

always needs to be multidimensional and holistic. Most of the angles chosen in earlier chapters such as the need for contextualization, the importance of the integrity of the Christian faith, the notion of fulfillment, and so on, are also relevant for engaging these movements apologetically. A focus on the inner tensions (cf. §6.4) allows us to move beyond earlier apologetic models developed in relation to these spiritualities.

13.2 NEW SPIRITUALITIES AS WORLDVIEWS AND LIFESTYLES

Late-modern spiritualities cannot be easily described and analyzed, as with a worldview or cluster of overlapping worldviews. Because of their eclectic nature, they can combine—into continuously reshaped late-modern constellations—components of older Western esoteric traditions with elements from South Asian religions and older pagan and shamanistic traditions in the Northern Atlantic world. Though it has integrated important elements from Hinduism, it would be a misrepresentation to see these movements, even in its New Age form, as representing a "strong unity of ideas"[15] or the resurgence of old religions, be it Gnosticism, Paganism, or Hinduism. "Ideas that help create new religions travel as fragments of traditions, not distinct traditions."[16] This being said, one can detect a number of central ideas in most of these new spiritualities, giving them their family resemblance.

A broadly shared central idea is a pantheistic (all that exists is divine) or panentheistic worldview (the divine is in everything). This also means that every human being has a divine spark and is, in fact, already divine. Spiritual growth means becoming aware of this spark or of one's fundamental divine identity. Because all is divine, this also links the individual deeply with all that exists, both on this earth and in the entire material and spiritual universe. This can be combined with a monistic view of reality: only what is eternal and divine really exits, the rest is only illusion. Thus Russ Michael shares that when he was enlightened, "I knew absolutely that my own 'I Am' awareness was real, eternal and all-encompassing, yet all of the intense human drama, human suffering and limitations or lack experienced on earth that seemed so real while I was immersed in them were only empty dreams."[17] An alternative to monism is a radical dualism in which evil is no illusion, but an eternal reality which exists in parallel to the true and good. Both this radical monism and dualism are difficult to square with the more positive views to material and historic

---

[15]Contra John P. Newport, *The New Age Movement and the Biblical Worldview: Conflict and Dialogue* (Grand Rapids, MI: Eerdmans, 1997), 3.

[16]Hexham and Poewe-Hexham, "New Religions," 92.

[17]Michael, *Feeling Good,* 42.

existence that dominate the modern era. Many late-modern spiritualities embrace more mediating positions in which material existence is not entirely evil, but a lower form of existence that, at some point, will need to be left behind.[18]

A central attitude to life is seekership: human beings are on this earth to discover who they really are.[19] There is no need for salvation because the fundamental problem of humankind is not sin or death but ignorance. One needs to strive for enlightenment, and in this search, the seeker looks for gurus, wise guides, or spiritual mediums who can channel messages from friendly spiritual beings who want to help the seeker along. This search does not need to end in this life but may have been going on for many lives (or forms of existence) in the past, continuing through many reincarnations in the future. This is one of the reasons there is no strong desire to convert others. Everyone will need to discover the truth for themselves and, unlike in the Christian faith, there is no sense that this one life has decisive significance. Individuals can continue to grow gradually thorough many lives to come. As we saw earlier with reference to Buddhism (§10.2), people cannot just tolerate but embrace the existence of multiple religions. Maybe for others, existence as a Christian is the right thing on the current leg of their journey.

Such monism (radical or moderate), and the belief in reincarnation and karma, show the links between New Age, late-modern spiritualities, and South Asian religions such as Hinduism and Buddhism. There are, however, also significant differences, so that New Age is not simply a Western form of Hinduism. For example, in the West reincarnation is positively valued, as a hopeful expectation in the face of death. In Hinduism and Buddhism, the cycle of reincarnations is seen as a cycle of suffering from which one hopes to escape. Furthermore, these Western spiritualities tend to have a more positive view of earthly life. Rather than escaping from it through ascetic practices, it can be enjoyed and cherished. Michael combines this castigating of life as a dream with a strong sense of ecological responsibility: "We on Mother Earth . . . are assigned to be conscious, collective co-creators of our planetary Earth body and the kind of world we co-create within her highly advanced beautiful bright 'Inner Earth' civilization or upon her end times drastically over-industrialized surface."[20]

---

[18]Cf. Wouter J. Hanegraaff, *Western Esotericism: A Guide for the Perplexed* (London: Bloomsbury Academic, 2013), 73-85.

[19]John P. Newport, *The New Age Movement and the Biblical Worldview: Conflict and Dialogue* (Grand Rapids, MI: Eerdmans, 1997), 11.

[20]Michael, *Feeling Good*, 64.

These Western movements hope for a better world and feel called to work for it, unlike classical Hinduism which desires for escape.[21] The valuation of the inner spiritual being and the embodied life can be seen in Osho, who promotes a spirituality of "Zorba the Buddha" (a reference to Zorba the Greek), representing earthly joy and the need to be deeply rooted in materialism: "Zorba is the roots in the earth, and the Buddha is a longing to fly into ultimate freedom, to reach to the space which is unbounded."[22] This appreciation for nature is particularly pronounced in various forms of Neopaganism, such as Wicca and Druidry. Like New Age-type movements, neo-pagan spiritualities are post-institutional and post-doctrinal. They desire to move beyond mechanistic, scientist, and naturalist understandings of reality and see all nature as in-spirited. These religions are, however, less about personal salvation, be it through reincarnation or otherwise. Neo-pagan spirituality is primarily "about celebrating one's place in the natural world" rather than aiming for a higher existence.[23]

As a lifestyle of seekership, new spiritualities can be embodied in various ways. It can lead to entry into more sectarian communities in the margins of society, but aspects of it can also be combined with respected roles in wider society. In virtually all of its Western expressions, these spiritualities are individualized. On the one hand this can be understood as an antiestablishment attitude that seeks to discover religion free from institutional limitations and societal norms.[24] From another perspective, this can be seen as a form of religion which fits our secular late-modern societies, which do not want religious interference. These societies are welcoming to religion and spirituality as long as they do not present a radical challenge to individual autonomy and to the late capitalist society controlling the secular domain.

13.3 Challenges for Apologetic Witness

Theological appreciation. From a Christian theological perspective, the New Age movement and other late-modern spiritualities can invite rather

---

[21]Newport, *New Age Movement*, 14.

[22]Osho, *Christianity the Deadliest Poison & Zen the Antidote to All Poisons* (Pune: Osho Media International, 2014), 22; cf. Osho, *Zorba the Buddha*, Darshan Diary Series (Antelope, OR: Rajneesh Foundation International, 1982); Hugh B. Urban, *Zorba the Buddha: Sex, Spirituality, and Capitalism in the Global Osho Movement* (Oakland, CA: University of California Press, 2015).

[23]C. H. Partridge, "Pagan and Indigenous Religions," in *New Dictionary of Christian Apologetics*, ed. Gavin J. McGrath, Walter Campbell Campbell-Jack, C. Stephen Evans, and S. Carter (Leicester, UK: Inter-Varsity Press, 2006), 527.

[24]John A. Saliba, *Christian Responses to the New Age Movement: A Critical Assessment* (London: Geoffrey Chapman, 1999), 230.

contrasting appreciations. On the one hand, they can be embraced as an ally against secular modernity. On the other hand, one can underline the radical dissimilarities: these spiritualities have no understanding of the radical difference between the Creator and creation, and have no concept of sin or salvation from death and sin: "When exposed in the light of God's revelation in Christ and the Scriptures, even those parts of another religion that might appear to be lofty and uplifting prove to be parts of a whole that is under the judgment of God."[25]

Chapter four, which developed a Christian theology of religions, invited us to a more nuanced understanding of the relationship between the trinitarian God and the world of religions: in Christ, religions are indeed exposed as human constructs that not only express the need for God, but also as efforts to live life without the true God, to flee from his presence, his demands, and to organize life in ways that contradict God's good will for humanity and for his creation (§4.4). Vinoth Ramachandra rightly notes, "Therapeutic religion, pandering to the narcissism of the modern self, seems to be the opium of the ruling classes."[26] Because of their openness to spiritual realities, religions are also open to manipulation by evil spiritual powers.

Yet, religions are also a response to God's majesty revealed in creation, to an inborn need for God (§4.3). If the Spirit is at work everywhere, in order to bring creation, cultures, and humanity to their destiny under the one headship of Christ, then the world of religions cannot be excluded from this activity (§4.5). Then we are allowed to draw attention to an awareness of God's presence our conversation partners already have, as Paul did on the Areopagus (§4.6).[27]

Because of this dual attitude toward religion, the Christian faith does not automatically side with religion over against secularism and atheism. Secularism itself is partly a consequence of the Judeo-Christian belief in a Creator God. This belief disenchants creation: the world and humanity are no longer divine but created.[28] God's Spirit may breathe through and enliven creation (against the dead and mechanized universe of the Enlightenment), but creation itself is no longer divine, and humankind is not at the mercy of the

---

[25]David Hesselgrave, "Traditional Religions, New Religions, and the Communication of the Christian Faith," in *Encountering New Religious Movements: A Holistic Evangelical Approach*, ed. Irving Hexham, Stephen Rost, and John Morehead (Grand Rapids, MI: Kregel, 2004), 148.

[26]Vinoth Ramachandra, *Gods That Fail: Modern Idolatry and Christian Mission* (Downers Grove, IL: InterVarsity Press, 1996), 41.

[27]Cf. Loren Wilkinson, "Circles and the Cross: Reflections on Neo-Paganism," *Evangelical Review of Theology* 22 (1998): 36-37.

[28]Cf. Lesslie Newbigin, *Honest Religion for Secular Man* (London: SCM Press, 1966), 19-30.

spiritual forces of this world (against panentheisms and magic understandings of life). In a certain way, the Christian faith finds itself at an equal distance from atheism on the one hand, and mystical and pagan religion on the other. As Karl Barth indicated: both atheism and mysticism are equal consequences of a rejection of the God of the Bible,[29] but they may both also contain positive points of contact (cf. §6.5).

This nuanced approached allows for creative interaction in which varying sensitivities and insights into these new spiritualities are embraced, yet critically challenged in the light of the God whom we encounter in Christ. Even though in this process Christ is the norm, Christ is not our possession—he is always ahead of us. The Spirit guides the Christian community in ever new territory and toward new insights. As a number of authors have recognized, these new religious movements may also expose weaknesses of forms of Christianity that are themselves deeply shaped by Western modernity. As it used to be said of older heresies and cults, these new religious movements represent, in a number of ways, the unpaid bills of the church.[30] "Evangelicals need to realize that New Age is the mirror in which we find ourselves reflected for all the theological issues we have neglected in our time."[31] New Age-type movements reflect the fact that a number of modern Christian traditions neglected sacramental understandings of reality that stress how God can be encountered and even touched in liturgy and in nature. They often neglected the rich Christian mystical tradition. The church has often suppressed individual freedom and creativity in the name of the authority of tradition. Neo-pagan movements also confront the church with its neglect of nature, of the human body, and of female aspects of spirituality.[32] Christians have much to learn in these encounters—while joyfully pointing to the incarnation, cross, and resurrection of Christ—giving this nature and body spirituality a new depth and solid foundation. We will return to this in the final section of this chapter.

---

[29]Karl Barth, *CD* 1956–1975, I/2, 314024; cf. H. Berkhof, "Theologiseren in een a-theïstisch tijdperk," in *Bruggen en bruggehoofden: een keuze uit de artikelen en voordrachten van prof. dr. H. Berkhof uit de jaren 1960–1981, verzameld en uitgegeven ter gelegenheid van zijn afscheid als kerkelijk hoogleraar te Leiden*, ed. E. Flesseman-van Leer, F. O. van Gennep, and W. E. Verdonk (Nijkerk, NL: Callenbach, 1981), 59-74.

[30]Lausanne Committee for World Evangelization, "Religious and Non-Religious Spirituality in the Western World," Lausanne Occasional Paper 45 (25), Pattaya, 2004, www.lausanne.org /content/lop/religious-non-religious-spirituality-western-world-lop-45.

[31]Philip Johnson, "The Aquarian Age and Apologetics," *Lutheran Theological Journal* 34, no. 2 (2000): 58.

[32]Philip Johnson and John Smulo. "Reaching Wiccan and Mother Goddess Devotees," in *Encountering New Religious Movements: A Holistic Evangelical Approach*, ed. Irving Hexham, Stephen Rost, and John W. Morehead (Grand Rapids, MI: Kregel, 2004), 201.

Beyond heresy-rationalist apologetics. The fluidity and eclectic character of these movements present one of the major challenges for an older evangelical apologetic approach that was characteristic of the anti-cult or countercult movement. In line with the critical analysis of John Morehead and others, an important strand of this apologetic can be properly called "heresy rationalist apologetics."[33] This approach treats these new religious movements as "cults" in the sense of heretical movements that draw on the Christian tradition, but do not do justice to orthodox Christian faith. Furthermore, they stress the inner coherence of the orthodox Christian faith over against the inconsistency of cultic New Age alternatives. This apologetic approach may have some validity with respect to older Western esoteric movements that functioned within the broader Christian society.[34] They may also function as a defensive apologetic strategy in helping Christians see why these movements may seem attractive yet do not present a valid alternative to orthodox Christian faith.

However, this apologetic strategy has limited effect—for a number of reasons—in witness to and conversation with adherents of these new religious movements. The first reason they have little effect is that these movements give relatively little weight to the coherence of their worldview. They would rather criticize both secular worldviews and Christianity for being too rationalistic; for them the most valid access points to the deepest truth of our lives is experience and feeling. Second, these movements can, in most cases, not be labeled cults in the theological sense of heretical movements that distort the Christian faith. Rather they should be conceived as alternative religious movements that have a certain coherence in themselves. The fact that these movements depart from orthodoxy is not in the least disconcerting for their adherents. Orthodox Christianity belongs to the Old Age; it is an institutional, doctrinal, and therefore oppressive and restrictive, form of religion that needs to be left behind.[35]

The Lausanne group on "Religious and Non-Religious Spirituality in the Western World" and a team of missiologists and practitioners around Johnson, Hexham, and Morehead (which represent partly overlapping groups) have therefore argued that we should not treat these new spiritualities as cults but as cultures.[36] They should be treated as religious traditions in themselves.

---

[33]John W. Morehead, "Conclusion: Where Do We Go from Here? Transforming Evangelical Responses to New Religions," in *Encountering New Religious Movements: A Holistic Evangelical Approach*, ed. Irving Hexham, Stephen Rost, and John W. Morehead (Grand Rapids, MI: Kregel, 2004), 286-87.

[34]Cf. Hanegraaff, *Western Esotericism*, 139.

[35]Johnson, "Aquarian Age," 52.

[36]Morehead, "Conclusion: Where Do We Go from Here?," 298; Lausanne Committee for World Evangelization, "Religious and Non-Religious Spirituality."

Their members and communities should be approached holistically with all the tools and sensitivities that have been developed in crosscultural mission, with a deep awareness of how the way people see reality is colored by their worldview, as well as how their choices are shaped by their value system, history, social location, and needs as they experience them. These sensitivities are well in line with the general approach developed in this book.

Late modernity and the question of truth. When we look at these movements as dynamic subcultures, and to these spiritualities as embedded in broader cultural contexts, we note a couple of characteristics that pose a particular challenge to missional outreach and apologetic dialogue. First, as already noted, these movements are post-Christian. They see institutional Christian religion as belonging to the past and not fit for our globalizing world. Furthermore, because they are post-Christian, they have integrated many of the great gifts Christianity provides the world (similar to what we saw with secular modernity), such as the value of individual freedom and of our created existence—though the place of creation is somewhat ambivalent. As a post-secular movement, they have seen the limitations of secular modernity, with its lack of depth, yet they feel that all Christianity has to offer as a religion is integrated in their own eclectic spirituality.

Second, these movements and spiritualities do, in many respects, fit late-modern culture, far better than traditional Christianity. It fits the late capitalist culture in which religious symbols and practices are simply objects of consumption[37] and are "vulnerable to co-optation, bricolage, and mass commodification."[38] "They offer an attractive synthesis of Western consumerism and Eastern Mystery."[39] And in our globalizing context of competing and sometimes warring religions, spiritualities that promise an assemblage of the best of all religious traditions are highly attractive.

In the third place, it is difficult to address questions of truth in dialogue with these late-modern spiritualities. When we considered the theological rationale behind the call to Christian apologetic witness among the religions (§1.3), we pointed to the fact that according to the Christian faith, the God of Jesus Christ is the God of all humanity—this message is true independent of us, because God can only save us if God is not just our projection or construction. Finally, this God can, in some ways, be known through the human intellect, not fully, but at least adequately, and that this truth can be communicated

---

[37]Hanegraaff, *Western Esotericism*, 141.

[38]William Dinges, "The New (Old) Age Movement: Assessing a Vatican Assessment," *Journal of Contemporary Religion* 19, no. 3 (2004): 278.

[39]Ramachandra, *Gods That Fail*, 41.

with others. All these aspects that undergird the importance of apologetic dialogue and witness are not easily communicated with late-modern spiritual seekers. If there is a God for all, this is not a God out there, but a God of which we all are a part, whom we will not find by looking outside or by listening to others, but by looking inside. Within ourselves, we find all that is needed to find salvation, or rather enlightenment, from our religious ignorance. A second reason classic apologetic forms of argumentation about questions of truth are not seen to be important is that these movements have a strongly pragmatic and therapeutic approach to religion: religious practices and views are good because they work; they help us feel better. We can note a certain parallel here with Buddhism (§10.3). "Feeling good is feeling God."[40] Whether it works is much more important than whether ideas are consistent, a criterion important in much Western apologetics but which holds little weight, and is easily sidelined as a relic of Western modernity. A third reason is that these movements play on the psychologization of life and of religion in the West. In a certain sense, they turn the modern Feuerbachian approach—that religion is just human projection—on its head: Would it matter if our religious views result from our inner beings, particularly if our inner beings connect us to the divine? The sacred is thus psychologized and, in the same movement, psychology is sacralized. In many instances, questions of truth will be left open without a sense of unease. The boundaries between fact and fiction are deliberately blurred, as remnants of a defunct modern Western view of reality.[41] A final reason why apologetic dialogue would be frowned upon is that it is intuition or feeling that is considered the primary (or only) access to the divine in ourselves.[42] Intellectual discussions will necessarily remain at the surface and only feeling will reveal the truth of reality. No one else can do that for us, for this knowledge is incommunicable.

13.4 Apologetic Dialogue

Witness as fellow pilgrims. In his book *Dialogical Apologetics*, David Clark stresses the need for "a person-centered approach to Christian defense," very much in line with the approach we elaborate in this book. Clark shares that his favorite question to open a dialogue is, "Would you mind telling me about your spiritual journey?"[43] This and similar questions seem particularly

---

[40]Russ Michael. *Feeling Good Is Feeling God* (New Delhi: Good Times Books, 2011).

[41]Hanegraaff, *Western Esoterism*, 135-39.

[42]Hanegraaff, *Western Esoterism*, 87-89.

[43]David K. Clark, *Dialogical Apologetics: A Person-Centered Approach to Christian Defense* (Grand Rapids, MI: Baker Books, 1993), 216.

apt for postmodern spiritual seekers, precisely because they perceive themselves as seekers. It is not just a simple trick to open a dialogue, though it
may help if we do not know where to start. If it is a genuine question, it sets
the dialogue up in a particular way: (1) It asks for permission, showing an
awareness that these conversations demand a certain vulnerability, (2) it
gives the other permission to speak about themselves, a subject about which
they have unique insight, and (3) it presupposes that the other is on the move,
not yet arrived, and therefore invites one implicitly to an openness toward
further discovery.

Such conversations tap into the "informality and flexibility" of these spiritualities.[44] "We [therefore] need a new vocabulary about conversion that
emphasizes pilgrimage, journey and processes of spiritual growth."[45] For such
an encounter to be genuine, we need to understand ourselves as "fellow-
pilgrims."[46] This mutual recognition as fellow pilgrims gives us freedom to
share what we have received in Christ and explain why we believe that what
we have received in his incarnation, cross, and resurrection is utterly unique.
Yet, it also demands an awareness that our own understanding of God, even
of God in Christ, is still partial ("For now we see in a mirror, dimly," 1 Cor
13:12) and that we long to grow in our knowledge of God and always desire to
be more attuned to the Spirit.

This of course does not mean that discernment is no longer necessary.
Doreen Virtue, formerly a well-known New Age writer, notes that she discovered after her conversion to Christ, "I didn't realize that it was vital to 'test the
spirits,' as the Bible says (1 Jn 4:1-6). I had an open-door policy, and unfortu-
nately the open door can invite in unwanted beings."[47] Paul Cudby notes that
in neo-Pagan spirituality "a spiritual experience is often taken at face value. 'It
is what it is.'"[48] Yet, he also notes that "pagans with any degree of experience
know for themselves that not every spirit that they encounter is either harmless or whishes them goodwill."[49] This is an important point of contact, because
spiritual messages do send us in different and sometimes opposite directions.

---

[44]Lausanne Committee for World Evangelization, "Religious and Non-Religious Spirituality in the Western World," 26.

[45]Lausanne Committee for World Evangelization, "Religious and Non-Religious Spirituality in the Western World," 29.

[46]Lausanne Committee for World Evangelization, "Religious and Non-Religious Spirituality in the Western World," 64.

[47]Doreen Virtue, "About Doreen's Conversion to Christianity," DoreenVirtue.Com (blog), March 12, 2018, www.angeltherapy.com/2018/03/12/about-doreens-conversion-to-christianity/.

[48]Cudby, *Shaken Path*, 29.

[49]Cudby, *Shaken Path*, 30.

Even without directly asking questions of absolute truth and goodness, one can, with the apostle Paul, begin to tap into the general therapeutic desire for what works: "'All things are lawful for me,' but not all things are beneficial. 'All things are lawful for me,' but I will not be dominated by anything" (1 Cor 6:12). Or in seeker-speak: "We should take all spiritual intuitions and messages seriously, but they may not all help us equally in our spiritual journey."

Inner tensions. We already indicated that pointing out rational inconsistencies in the worldview of new spiritualities may have little weight, because of the distrust of rational argument over against intuition and feeling. Furthermore, it is possible to develop monism as a rationalist system in a virtually consistent manner. It may have fewer apparent contradictions than the Christian faith, which, for many who look at it from the outside, at first glance seems to have counterintuitive ideas: God Three-in-One, Jesus as fully divine and fully human, an all-powerful and all-good God who permits evil to exist? Particularly if you consider all experience of the world illusionary, inconsistencies do not easily appear. Though such monism might be consistent, it does not mean that it is existentially satisfactory. More promising than pointing to logical contradictions may therefore be to point to the experience of tensions within these worldviews and within a life shaped by these spiritualities. Such tensions may function as push-factors motivating people for alternative ways to understand and live their lives (cf. §6.4). The tone should not be "You are not allowed to believe this because it is inconsistent," but rather "How do you face these life experiences that seem to be inherent to the way you understand reality and life?" In the chapter on Buddhism, we focused more on the tensions between the worldview or spirituality and reality beyond our conceptions that prove resistant to the mold of our religious perspective. In this chapter, we focus primarily on tensions that are inherent to spirituality itself and a life lived in line with it. Note, however, that tensions within a worldview or spirituality are often related to tensions between central traits of the worldview and the world as it is (from which we cannot flee). Let us point to four of these inner tensions, though more could be added.

The first tension is related to the notions of *karma* and reincarnation. The belief that we need to suffer the consequences of our evil actions—and lifestyles that constantly drag us in spiritually unhealthy directions—should not be automatically denied. The Bible also accepts that "you reap whatever you sow" (Gal 6:7). The need for forgiveness is not a denial of that belief, but rather a recognition that this should be the normal and just order. However, many people will, if they are honest with themselves, come to the recognition that if they need to suffer all the consequences, life may not turn out well for them—a multitude of reincarnations may still not be able to deal with the way they are setting themselves up. The belief in *karma* may therefore become a stepping-stone for sharing the joy of forgiveness.[50]

The impossibility of overcoming *karma* over many lives is a consequence of the second tension: the more direct experience of making significant spiritual progress within a single lifetime. In *From Guru to God*, Michael Graham describes his quest for spiritual insight and liberation through *Siddha Yoga*, and the personal improvement course business in which he is active. After a long journey, he discovers, "As if pressed on me from outside myself was the conviction that everything I had done, the thousands of hours of meditation, cognitions, realizations, spiritual experiences, had added up to a *huge fat zero!* It was as though I'd been trying to draw water from an empty well . . . it was as though a 28-year-investment had gone bust."[51] This is all the more remarkable in light of the apparent gift for both ecstatic experiences and disciplined practice Graham showed over these years. People can only discover for themselves the futility of their spiritual investment. When others try to point this out, it may be counterproductive. Yet, when we create an openness in sharing our spiritual quests and failures, the importance of the Christian message of grace and salvation offered may well be seen in a new light, as happened to Graham himself.

In his analysis of Neopaganism, Loren Wilkinson points to a third tension with similarities to other postmodern spiritualities. On the one hand, these spiritualities place great stress on the importance of living in harmony with the entirety of humanity and with the universe, both material and spiritual, because we/it all share the same divine being. On the other hand, there is a deep postmodern perception that I create my own reality. We encountered this in the psychologization of religious beliefs, but it is equally linked with the creative powers that are attributed to the divine self. This points to a deep-running tension in the worldview itself: "Either there is a reality outside the self to which one must be conformed-or there is not, and the world is simply an extension of myself, waiting to be brought under the influence of my power."[52]

Beyond the issue of rational coherence are the tensions this raises in life: we experience how the universe and other people beyond ourselves are not simply an extension of our own inner selves and that we cannot manipulate them by

---

[50]Newport, *New Age*, 599.

[51]Michael Graham, *From Guru to God: An Experience of the Ultimate Truth* (Hyderabad, London: Authentic Books, 2007), 154; italics in the original.

[52]Loren Wilkinson, "Circles and the Cross: Reflections on Neo-Paganism," *Evangelical Review of Theology* 22 (1998): 35.

our own spiritual powers. Even if we could, we need to ask whether this would lead to deep harmony: a world that is simply a projection of myself may be easy to live in, but can we call this harmony—is it so attractive? It is not a world in which I can experience true love from people around me or from God, nor a true welcome by an earth that was created to be my home. These are, after all, only products of my own imagination or willpower. This means, first, that if we want to live in harmony with the universe, the people around us, and with God, we need to be open to discover who they are and be real enough to recognize that they may be different, more resistant to my project, but possibly also far more beautiful than I could have imagined. This means, furthermore, that we may well discover that a significant part of the problem of living in harmony with the people, the world, and with Godself is not simply due to my lack of willpower or imagination, but to what Christians call sin: my inability and unwillingness to live my life in the loving relationships for which we are created.

> The circle of our selfhood has for sinful human beings been not only the arena of our freedom, creativity, and uniqueness; it has also become a voracious and devouring circle, a kind of inner "black hole" with Hell at its centre. The only place we see proper human selfhood is in Christ. The pattern is drawn by Paul in Philippians 2: "Do nothing out of selfish ambition or vain conceit . . . look not only to your own interests but to the interests of others." This is impossible for us; we see it only in Christ, equal with God beyond all worlds, but known in the self-emptying death on a cross.[53]

One of the complexities of the apologetic use of the three tensions just developed is that they demand our conversation partners have or develop an awareness of their own shortcomings: of the risk or reality of building up negative *karma*, or the reality that our own life choices contribute significantly to the lack of harmony in nature, humanity, and with the divine. Wiser conversation partners may have this awareness, but others may find these suggestions offensive. Because they touch on their self-image, we can often not go further than a gentle prodding. An aggressive pointing to others' failures will often result in defensiveness and in the pulling up of drawbridges, making the type of open dialogue that allows for new discoveries and change virtually impossible.

There is a fourth inner tension in many of these spiritualities that does not have this drawback and will draw much more on elements that everyone in the conversation will experience as positive. We already noted this tension when we pointed out that late-modern spiritualities will often combine the

---

[53]Wilkinson, "Circles and the Cross," 44.

monist worldview of South Asian religions with a positive view of nature, the body, individual human existence, and even the future of the natural world. In terms of the history of ideas, this is probably part of the Christian heritage assimilated in these movements, partly mediated through Western modernity, having also integrated a number of Christian values. It is of course the question whether one can be so positive about the natural world if one no longer accepts the doctrine of creation and states that all is illusion or an eternal cycle. We can equally question whether one can be so positive about bodily existence and its ultimate value without belief in the incarnation and resurrection. One may even argue that in as far as these gifts of the Christian tradition are incorporated without the underlying basis of belief in creation, incarnation, and resurrection, these newer spiritualities are inconsistent and parasitic on Christianity in ways similar to certain neo-Hindu movements.[54] It would, however, not be very productive to begrudge our conversation partners these Christian values. These spiritual movements embrace their eclectic nature and feel free to pick and choose what they see as the best gifts of other religious traditions. As Christians, we should be grateful for traces of the gifts of Christ elsewhere, rather than enviously believe that we are the only rightful owners of these gifts.

The joy of the cross and resurrection. A more positive way might be to recognize and embrace these values: What gives us this confidence? On what basis do we believe that I am a unique and irreplaceable individual if I am going through an endless cycle of reincarnations after which I will dissolve as a drop into the ocean of divinity? What gives me confidence that our embodied existence is beautiful even when people succumb to ugly illnesses? What gives me hope for the future of this planet, even if spirituality keeps being marginalized by the powers of a capitalist economy? Can we have a hope for the world that is not only valuable for the well-to-do middle classes in London or New Delhi—those looking for a bit of spiritual depth—but have their physical existence well in order? Can we have a hope that is also good news to Rohingya refugees, people caught between warlords in eastern Congo, and girls trafficked for the sexual pleasures of others? And can we have hope for those in the middle classes of the world who do not want to close their hearts to the suffering of others? This is where Christ's cross and resurrection provide real answers. The cross and resurrection do not take us away from the goodness of creation—as indeed some Christian practices may have suggested—but rather they happen in the middle of creation and history, for the sake of

---

[54]Cf. Vinoth Ramachandra, *Faiths in Conflict? Christian Integrity in a Multicultural World* (Leicester, UK: Inter-Varsity Press, 2000), 78-79.

our redemption. "The bodily resurrection of Jesus, seen as the 'firstfruits,' demonstrates God's concern not only for one's 'spirit' but also for the totality of the New Spirituality concept of humanness—mind, body, and spirit."[55]

This is indeed beautifully expressed in the symbol of the Celtic cross: a Christian cross in the midst of the circle of the world or cosmos. This image explains how Christ can speak to both neo-pagans and a variety of late-modern spiritualities that are more world-denying. In both cases the universe is conceived of as a circle in which everything hangs together, and in which life progresses through endless cycles. The appreciation of unity and harmony is precious, but such views do not have an answer to real evil in the world and in our own lives, apart from declaring them illusionary or marginal. These two answers are, at certain times in life, blatantly trite and unsatisfactory. The cross of Christ stands in the midst of history and reaches into the reality of suffering and evil. But the arms of the cross break through the circle and show a future that does not abandon this world, but rather brings it to its fulfillment.[56]

A concept that can help build these bridges between the circle and the cross—and between Christians and late-modern spiritual seekers—is the idea of the "story of Christ [as] true myth," which was so important in C. S. Lewis's conversion story.[57] Lewis was at first bothered by the many parallels between Christianity and ancient pagan myths; for example, dying and rising gods. Late modernity shows—in film, novels, and computer games—a great interest in myths and the mythic, both classic myths and modern epic stories. From a Christian theological perspective, these can be seen as an expression of a deep human desire for God, an awareness of lostness, and a need for redemption. These mythic symbols can therefore become bridges to the Christian faith in which, according to Lewis, is "myth become fact."[58] These mythical images are signs that creation and history point beyond themselves to what is now no longer a faint or even unrealistic hope, but a reality in Christ's cross and resurrection.[59] In this way, "there is still a role [and sometimes a need] for historical and legal evidences . . . provided this traditional apologetic is reframed."[60]

---

[55]Ross Clifford, "Reframing a Traditional Apologetic to Reach 'New Spirituality' Seekers," in *Encountering New Religious Movements: A Holistic Evangelical Approach*, ed. Irving Hexham, Stephen Rost, and John W. Morehead (Grand Rapids, MI: Kregel, 2004), 199.

[56]Wilkinson "Circles and the Cross," 43-44.

[57]Roger Lancelyn Green and Walter Hooper, *C. S. Lewis: A Biography* (London: Collins, 1974), 118.

[58]C. S. Lewis, "Myth Became Fact," in *God in the Dock: Essays on Theology and Ethics*, ed. Walter Hooper (Grand Rapids, MI: Eerdmans, 2014), 54-60.

[59]Cf. Philip Johnson, "Apologetics and Myths: Signs of Salvation in Postmodernity," *Lutheran Theological Journal* 32, no. 2 (1998): 62-72.

[60]Clifford, "Reframing a Traditional Apologetic," 194.

Conclusion

LOOKING BACK AND FORWARD

WE HAVE COME TO THE END OF THE EXPLORATION in the second part of this study, in which we encountered a dazzling variety of religious and secular approaches to life, embedded in specific historic, cultural, and social contexts and embodied in communities and practices. In this way we illustrated what the contextual, holistic, and embodied apologetic dialogue and witness developed in the first part can look like. Yet, these chapters are not merely illustrations. They are also case studies that support our proposal for this model of interfaith apologetics. They show that we need to take these religious and secular traditions seriously, as culturally embedded and embodied attitudes to life in which worldview, values, deep quests, and the emotive layers of existence are intertwined. These examples also show that such religious and cultural frameworks are not self-sufficient or enclosed worlds that pass each other like rafts on an open sea.[1] Interfaith conversations can indeed have a triadic shape in which both parties are not merely trying to understand each other. Together, we are relating to a world beyond ourselves, a God beyond ourselves, whom Christians believe is supremely revealed in Jesus of Nazareth. Because of this shared world, we can communicate, bridges can be built, and we can be reminded of the inadequacy of our own views and attitudes toward life. For Christians themselves, much is at stake in this enterprise, as Stanley Jones expressed when looking back to the interreligious roundtable conversations he organized in India in the early decades of the twentieth century: "And we Christians who came with what we call a gospel—would it sound like a gospel here? When we had stripped our religious life of overgrown verbiage, how much would we have

---

[1] Cf. Ernest Sosa, "The Raft and the Pyramid: Coherence Versus Foundations in the Theory of Knowledge," *Midwest Studies in Philosophy* 5, no. 1 (1980), 3-25; Benno van den Toren, *Christian Apologetics as Cross-Cultural Dialogue* (London: T&T Clark, 2011), 132-36.

left? Would our gospel ring true to reality? . . . Would it face life and answer it?"[2]

In the process we were reminded that Christianity is an eccentric religion that does not find its anchor in the depth of the soul nor in the richness of a religious tradition or community, but in the triune God who—as Creator, Son, and Spirit—is before, among, and ahead of us. In the process we have again and again been surprised by this Jesus and this God in whom Christian faith and assurance rests. It is not the tradition or the depth of our experience, but this God who gives us the confidence to engage in this dialogue, in humility and vulnerability, with reverence for the people and gifts we encounter. In the words of Jones:

> I found myself not particularly interested in the victory, as such, of one religious system over another. . . . The crusaders conquered Jerusalem and found in the end that the Christ was not there. . . . More proselytization partakes of these methods and share the same barrenness of results. . . . The final issue is not between the systems of Christianity and Hinduism or Buddhism or Islam. . . . The final issue is between Christ and other ways of life.[3]

We are all too aware that apologetics can become a battle for the victory of one intellectual system over another. Yet, apologetics can also be a dialogue that is attentive to others and a witness to a truth we do not own. Therefore, apologetic dialogue is also an antidote to forms of religious or secular self-defense, or propaganda that are merely based on social and cultural power, or of prestige that so easily drowns out the still small voice we have heard and encountered in Christ. We would like to invite the readers to join us on this journey of dialogue, witness, exploration, and discovery.

---

[2]E. Stanley Jones, *Christ at the Roundtable*, rev. ed., The 21st Century in Our Times Series (n.p.: E. Stanley Jones Foundation, 2019), 35.

[3]Jones, *Christ at the Roundtable*, 24.

STUDY QUESTIONS AND
FURTHER READING

1. APOLOGETIC DIALOGUE IN A MULTICULTURAL WORLD
Questions for discussion and personal reflection

1. Have you read apologetic books or articles, or listened to apologetic talks? What are the strengths and limitations of the apologetics you have encountered so far for your particular context?

2. What are the main secular and religious groups in your context to which the Christian community is called to witness to Christ? What are the major challenges for witnessing to the truth of the good news of Jesus Christ in this particular environment? What are the issues with which you would like to be helped while studying this book?

3. Is your context mainly characterized by cultural and religious relativism or rather by fundamentalisms? Or is there one religion or worldview that strongly imposes itself on your context?

4. "The work of the Holy Spirit is central in evangelism and in people coming to faith. Yet, the Holy Spirit also works through ordinary human means, also ordinary means of how we come to know and judge different truth-claims" (§1.3). Do you agree? What has been the place where you considered the truth of the Christian faith in your own coming to faith, or in remaining faithful to the faith you received from your parents or educators?

5. Which one of the three missiological motivations for engaging in apologetic witness is most relevant for your context? Would you want to add a further motivation?

Further reading

Griffiths, Paul J. "An Apology for Apologetics." *Faith and Philosophy* 5 (1988): 399-420.

Netland, Harold A. *Encountering Religious Pluralism: The Challenge to Christian Faith and Mission.* Downers Grove, IL: InterVarsity Press, 2001, esp. 247-83.

Van den Toren, Benno. *Christian Apologetics as Cross-Cultural Dialogue*. London: T&T Clark, 2011, esp. 1-92.

2. Embodied Apologetics

Questions for discussion and personal reflection

1. What do you consider the strength of the Christian community to which you belong (as a "hermeneutic of the gospel")? How easily can a non-Christian understand the gospel as it is embodied in the life of this Christian community? Can its readability be improved?

2. What are the most natural encounters in which members of your Christian community share their lives with non-Christians? Do you see possibilities for bringing more depth to these encounters in the regular "dialogue of life"?

3. Consider your place in the different cultural scales developed by Erin Meyer. Were you able to locate yourself in relation to other communities in the communication scale between "low context" and "high context"? How do you normally express disagreement? What is your preferred argumentation pattern: starting with universal values, pragmatic, or holistic? What makes you trust other people: skill and knowledgeability or relationship? In which of these areas might you need to become more aware of differences between you and your conversation partners?

Further reading

Meyer, Erin. *The Culture Map: Decoding How People Think, Lead, and Get Things Done across Cultures*. New York: Public Affairs, 2015, esp. chaps. 1, 3, 6, 7.

Newbigin, Lesslie. "The Congregation as Hermeneutic of the Gospel." In *The Gospel in a Pluralist Society*, by Lesslie Newbigin, 222-33. Grand Rapids, MI: Eerdmans, 1989.

3. The Cultural Embeddedness of Belief

Questions for discussion and personal reflection

1. What are the three decisive characteristics of what it means to be created in the image of God, according to this chapter? How is this important for understanding how people will come to know the truth? Do you recognize elements of this in your own experience?

2. Can you come up with an example in your own life where your outlook on life or God has been changed because of experiences you've had or because the world you encountered did not sit well with your earlier

understanding of life and the world? This may be either an experience that contributed to your conversion to Christ or an experience that helped (or forced?) you to grow in your understanding of the Christian faith.

3. Can you mention an example of a foreign cultural practice or view that you have encountered that at first seemed very odd but made sense after you came to better know the people involved?

4. What is the ideological or religious outlook on life that you know best apart from the Christian faith? Do you have a particular calling to witness in this context?

5. Is there a religious or cultural group that is foreign to you to which you feel called to serve? What may be next steps to come to know better what their outlook on life looks and feels like from an inside perspective?

Further reading

MacIntyre, Alasdair. "Epistemological Crises, Dramatic Narrative, and the Philosophy of Science." In *Paradigms and Revolutions: Appraisals and Applications of Thomas Kuhn's Philosophy of Science*, edited by Gary Gutting, 54-74. Notre Dame, IN: University of Notre Dame Press, 1980.

Van den Toren, Benno. "'Everyone is Entitled to Their Opinion': The Culture of Relativism." In *Reasons for My Hope: Responding to Non-Christian Friends*, 58-74. Oxford: Monarch Books, 2010.

4. GOD'S PRESENCE AND TRUTH IN THE WORLD OF RELIGIONS

Questions for discussion and personal reflection

1. Which of the three perspectives of a trinitarian theology of religions (a focus on the Creator, Christ, or on the Spirit) tends to dominate in your own thinking about the relationship between the Christian faith and other religions? What are the strengths and weaknesses of this perspective?

2. Which of the three perspectives might you have neglected, or requires more attention, when thinking about God's presence in the world of religions?

3. If you believe that Christ is God's final revelation, what is the basis for this faith? Which element for having confidence in the finality of Christ that is discussed here can deepen your understanding?

4. Do you find it easier to be committed and confident, or to be open in the relationship between Christians and other religionists? What would you need to learn in this respect?

Further reading

Kärkkäinen, Veli-Matti. *Trinity and Religious Pluralism: The Doctrine of the Trinity in Christian Theology of Religions.* Burlington, VT: Ashgate, 2004.

McDermott, Gerald R., and Harold A. Netland. *A Trinitarian Theology of Religions: An Evangelical Proposal.* Oxford: Oxford University Press, 2014.

Van den Toren, Benno. "The Relationship between Christ and the Spirit in a Christian Theology of Religions." *Missiology* 40, no. 3 (2012): 263-80.

5. Apologetics as Accountable Witness to Christ

Questions for discussion and personal reflection

1. The Christian knowledge of God has specific characteristics related to who God is and how God makes Godself known. This knowledge is, among other characteristics, (1) based on testimony; (2) transmitted by a community; (3) personal and asks for commitment; and (4) requires trust. Which of these characteristics is most problematic for non-Christians in your particular context? How could this misunderstanding or mistrust be overcome?

2. What are decisive factors for people in your context to consider testimony trustworthy—or not? Can these factors be used or overcome in apologetic witness to Christ?

3. In your context, what are the most important obstacles to trusting the witness to the resurrection of Christ? Which issues discussed in this chapter can help you overcome these? Are there also obstacles that need further attention? Where would you look for further answers?

Further reading

Coady, C. A. J. *Testimony: A Philosophical Study.* Oxford: Oxford University Press, 1992, esp. chaps. 1–3, pp. 1-75.

Van den Toren, Benno. "'Why Jesus?': The Reliability of Christ." In *Reasons for My Hope: Responding to Non-Christian Friends,* 125-53. Oxford: Monarch Books, 2010.

6. Possibilities for Critical Interreligious Dialogue

Questions for discussion and personal reflection

1. Which barriers to crosscultural persuasion do you consider most important to address? It will be helpful to focus on obstacles that are

particularly relevant to apologetic persuasion, not to evangelistic witness in general.

2. In the context where you are living and working, what are areas, apart from the focus on Jesus Christ and the human condition, that need particular attention in apologetic dialogue? Can you find creative ways to show how these issues point us back to issues related to either questions concerning Christ or concerning the human condition? Would it be worth exploring these links or would they feel artificial?

3. Consider the quote from Pascal in §6.4:
"Man's greatness and wretchedness are so evident that the true religion must necessarily teach there is in man some great principle of greatness and some great principle of wretchedness. It must also account for such amazing contradictions."

   a. How does the religion or worldview with which you are most acquainted (apart from the Christian faith) account for (1) the greatness (2) and the wretchedness of the human condition, (3) as well as the tension between the two?

   b. Does this interpretation do justice to (our experience of) the human condition?

4. Consider again the religion or worldview, apart from Christianity, with which you are acquainted most. Can you think of other areas of common ground than those that have been mentioned here? How could they be the starting point of an apologetic conversation?

Further reading

Clark, David K. "Apologetics as Dialogue." In *Dialogical Apologetics: A Person-Centered Approach to Christian Defense*, 102-26. Grand Rapids, MI: Baker Books, 1993.

Torrance, Thomas F. "Theological Persuasion." In *God and Rationality*, 195-206. London: Oxford University Press, 1971.

7. Reaching the Reasons of the Heart

Questions for discussion and personal reflection

1. Can you recount a story in your own life where strong feelings or desires limited your ability to face reality for what it was? How might that help you to sympathize with the struggles of someone like Nabeel Qureshi?

2. Communities and cultures as well as individuals can in their own way be shaped by certain predispositions (emotions, desires, commitments).

What are specific predispositions present in a community to which you are called to witness? How do they form a barrier to properly hearing the message of the gospel? Are there also desires and such that might predispose people positively to considering the truth of the Christian message?

3. Can you think of stories, either fictional or real, that might help people face the predispositions discussed under question two?

4. Do you agree that Christian apologetic witness should be characterized by "bold humility"? Why? What might it look like in your context, given cultural understandings and expressions of courage and humility?

Further reading

Fernando, Ajith. *Sharing The Truth in Love*. Uhrichville, OH: Discovery House, 2001, esp. chaps. 1–4, pp. 17-83.

Guinness, Os. *Fool's Talk: Recovering the Art of Christian Persuasion*. Downers Grove, IL: InterVarsity Press, 2015.

Stackhouse, John G. *Humble Apologetics: Defending the Faith Today*. Oxford: Oxford University Press, 2002.

8. INCULTURATION IN DIALOGUE WITH PRIMAL RELIGIONS

Questions for discussion and personal reflection

1. Do you perceive influence of the primal worldview in the world religions with which you are best acquainted (folk Islam, folk Buddhism, folk Christianity, etc.)?

2. How do you understand the relationship between power encounters and truth encounters in Christian mission?

3. In light of the apologetic calling of the church to be contextually relevant, where do you perceive the most critical need for the contextualization of the practice or the message of the church in your context?

4. For the people in your context, what aspects of Christ's work are crucial for understanding his relevance and indispensability?

Further reading

Bediako, Kwame. "The Primal Imagination and the Opportunity for a New Theological Idiom." In *Christianity in Africa: The Renewal of a Non-Western Religion*, 91-108. Edinburgh: Edinburgh University Press, 1995.

Hesselgrave, David J. "Communicating Christ into the Tribal Worldview." In *Communicating Christ Cross-Culturally: An Introduction to Missionary Communication*, 221-36. 2nd ed. Grand Rapids, MI: Zondervan, 1991.

Imasogie, Osadolor. "Christian Apologetic Theology in a West African Context." *The Journal of the Interdenominational Theological Center* 7, no. 2 (1980): 129-44.

9. Subversive Fulfillment of the Hindu Quest
Questions for discussion and personal reflection

1. How would you look at *Bhakti* Hinduism in light of the trinitarian understanding of religions developed in chapter four? What would an analysis in light of the doctrine of creation (or a patrological perspective), a christological perspective, and a pneumatological perspective contribute to a theological understanding of this cluster of movements?

2. Among the major world religions, Hinduism is probably the religion that, from its own perspective, believes it can most easily accommodate worshiping Jesus. Why is this the case? Would you consider that a bridge or an obstacle for apologetic dialogue? Why?

3. Do you think Christ can be understood more appropriately as the fulfillment of Hinduism or of the Hindu quest? If so, why? Where can you see fulfillment? Where would you see subversion?

4. Is the notion of "subversive fulfillment" also a helpful concept for understanding other religious movements? If you choose a particular example, in what way can Christ be understood as its fulfillment or its subversion?

Further reading
Graham, Michael. *From Guru to God: An Experience of the Ultimate Truth*. London: Authentic Books, 2007.
Ramachandra, Vinoth. "Hinduism and the Search for Identity." In *Faiths in Conflict? Christian Integrity in a Multicultural World*, 47-85. Leicester, UK: Inter-Varsity Press, 2000.
Satyavrata, Ivan. *God Has Not Left Himself without Witness*. Oxford: Regnum Books International, 2011.

10. Buddhism Confronts Reality
Questions for discussion and personal reflection

1. From a Buddhist perspective, we should distrust the way reality appears to us because it can easily mislead and distract us from our true destiny. How would you evaluate that attitude from a Christian perspective?

2. Buddhism presents itself as a "non-doctrinal, yet rational religion." Buddhism is of course not alone in this respect and, like other nondoctrinal

spiritualities, it has an advantage over Christianity as a doctrinal religion. How can a Christian respond to this challenge?

3. Do you think that the idea developed in this chapter—that the Buddhist believer cannot entirely shape reality according to its own presuppositions and in its own image—is helpful? Why or why not?

4. For other religious traditions with which you are familiar, do you think this concept can also be used in an apologetic dialogue? Can you give examples?

5. This approach can also have critical implications for Christians, as Christians may also try to walk away from the world as it appears to us. Can you give examples of this tendency among Christians? How can Christians in this respect grow in maturity?

Further reading

Tan, Kang-San. "The Power of the Kingdom in Encountering Buddhist Worldviews." In *Sharing Jesus Holistically in the Buddhist World*, edited by David S Lim and Steve Spaulding, 13-51. Pasadena, CA: William Carey Library, 2005.

Williams, Paul. *The Unexpected Way: On Converting from Buddhism to Catholicism*. Edinburgh: T&T Clark, 2002.

11. Islam and the Integrity of the Christian Faith

Questions for discussion and personal reflection

1. How do you encounter Islam in your context? What do you consider the principal challenge that needs to be overcome in the apologetic dialogue with Muslims?

2. Do you recognize the complexity of explaining the Christian faith to Muslims from your own experience? If so, how have you dealt with this? What is the strength and what are the limitations of this approach?

3. In Christian communities or in your own context, do you recognize the image of "popular Christianity" as sketched in this chapter? If so, how does it hinder apologetic witness to Muslims or to other audiences?

4. Do you experience the Christian understanding of God as Trinity as one of the gifts of the Christian faith to Muslims and other audiences or as a problem or embarrassment that we should keep in the background for as long as we can until our conversation partners are willing to consider it seriously? What aspect of the proposed way of explaining

the Trinity to Muslims in this chapter do you find most helpful for your context?

Further reading

Gaudeul, Jean-Marie. *Called from Islam to Christ: Why Muslims Become Christian.* Crowborough, UK: Monarch Books, 1999. (esp. 57-86)

Qureshi, Nabeel. *Seeking Allah, Finding Jesus: A Devout Muslim Encounters Christianity.* Grand Rapids, MI: Zondervan, 2014.

Shehadeh, Imad N. "The Predicament of Islamic Monotheism." *Bibliotheca Sacra* 161, no. 642 (April–June 2004): 142-62.

12. Unmasking Secular Idols

Questions for discussion and personal reflection

1. In your context, where do you see a positive relationship between the Christian faith and the values of modernity? Where do you see a negative relationship? How can this shape the dialogue between the Christian faith and modernity?

2. Do you believe the notion of idolatry to be helpful in addressing secular conversation partners? If you want to avoid using the concept of idolatry, because of its negative connotation, how can you use the relevant ideas?

3. Do you agree that a secular worldview also demands a "leap of faith"? If so, how can this notion help you in apologetic dialogue in your context?

4. The notion of unmasking is more widely applicable than in conversation with the secular world. Can you give examples of how it may be used in religious contexts?

Further reading

Keller, Timothy. *Counterfeit Gods: When the Empty Promises of Love, Money, and Power Let You Down.* London: Hodder & Stoughton, 2010.

Ramachandra, Vinoth. *Gods That Fail: Modern Idolatry and Christian Mission.* Downers Grove, IL: InterVarsity Press, 1996.

13. Inner Tensions in Late-Modern Spiritualities

Questions for discussion and personal reflection

1. Can you think of spiritual movements in your context or people you know who share some traits of the late-modern spiritualities discussed in this chapter? What aspects of their spirituality would you consider

a bridge to the Christian faith? Where do you see obstacles for constructive apologetic dialogue and witness?

2. As with many other religious traditions, these new spiritualities represent both a worldview and a lifestyle. You could initially engage in dialogue at one of those levels, though a holistic approach will mean that both aspects will become part of the conversation. Can you think of questions that would invite the people discussed in question one into a conversation (a) starting with their worldview and (b) concerning their lifestyle?

3. New religious movements can be seen as the "unpaid bills of the church," exposing some of the weaknesses in current expressions of the Christian faith. What are areas in which you believe the Christian faith should be deepened or broadened in order to witness more effectively to spiritual seekers?

4. What do you think of the idea of "Christianity as true myth"? Do you see examples of myths or mythic symbols in your cultural context that can be used in apologetic conversations?

Further reading

Hanegraaff, Wouter J. *Western Esotericism: A Guide for the Perplexed*. London: Bloomsbury Academic, 2013.

Hexham, Irving, Stephen Rost, and John W. Morehead, eds. *Encountering New Religious Movements: A Holistic Evangelical Approach*. Grand Rapids, MI: Kregel Academic, 2004.

Lausanne Committee for World Evangelization. "Religious and Non-Religious Spirituality in the Western World." Lausanne Occasional Paper 45. Pattaya, 2004. www.lausanne.org/content/lop/religious-non-religious-spirituality-western-world-lop-45.

BIBLIOGRAPHY

Abdel Haleem, Muhammad A. S., trans. *The Qur'an*. Oxford: Oxford University Press, 2010.

Abe, Masao. "Self-Awakening and Faith—Zen and Christianity." In *Christianity through Non-Christian Eyes*, edited by Paul J. Griffiths, 172-80. Maryknoll, NY: Orbis Books, 2004.

Abū Qurrah, Thāwdhūrus. *Theodore Abū Qurrah*. Translated by John C. Lamoreaux. Library of the Christian East 1. Provo, UT: Brigham Young University Press, 2005.

Adamo, David Tuesday. *Africa and the Africans in the Old Testament*. Benin City, Nigeria: Justice Jeco Press & Publishers, 2005.

Adeney, Miriam. *Daughters of Islam: Building Bridges with Muslim Women*. Downers Grove, IL: InterVarsity Press, 2002.

Akhtar, Shabbir. *Islam as Political Religion: The Future of an Imperial Faith*. London: Routledge, 2010.

al-Faruqi, Isma'il Raji al-. "On the Nature of Islamic Da'wah." *International Review of Mission* 65, no. 260 (1976): 391-409.

Anderson, Bernhard. "The Babel Story: Paradigm of Human Unity and Diversity." *Concilium* 121 (1977): 63-70.

Ariarajah, S. Wesley. *The Bible and People of Other Faiths*. Risk Book Series 26. Geneva: World Council of Churches, 1985.

Aristotle. "Rhetoric." In *Aristotle, Volume II*, edited by Robert Maynard Hutchins, translated by W. Rhys Roberts, 593-675. Great Books of the Western World 9. Chicago, IL: Encyclopedia Britannica, 1952.

Auffarth, Christoph, and Hubert Moher. "Religion." In *The Brill Dictionary of Religion*, edited by Kocku von Stuckrad, translated by Robert R. Barr, III, 1607-19. Leiden: Brill, 2006.

Augustine. *Confessions Books 1–8*. Translated by Carolyn J.-B. Hammond. Loeb Classical Library 26. Cambridge, MA: Harvard University Press, 2014.

Avis, D. L. *Faith in the Fires of Criticism: Christianity in Modern Thought*. Eugene, OR: Wipf & Stock, 2006.

Baagø, Kaj. *Pioneers of Indigenous Christianity.* Confessing the Faith in India Series 4. Bangalore: Christian Institute for the Study of Religion and Society and the Christian Literature Society, 1969.

Baker-Hytch, Max. "Testimony Amidst Diversity." In *Knowledge, Belief, and God: New Insights,* edited by Matthew Benton, John Hawthorne, and Dani Rabinowitz, 183-202. Oxford: Oxford University Press, 2018.

Bambrough, Renford. "Fools and Heretics." *Royal Institute of Philosophy Supplement* 28 (1990): 239-50.

Bangura, Joseph Bosco. "The Charismatic Movement in Sierra Leone (1980–2010): A Missio-Historical Analysis in View of African Culture, Prosperity Gospel and Power Theology." PhD Thesis, Amsterdam: VU University, 2013.

Barth, Karl. *Church Dogmatics.* Edited by Geoffrey W. Bromiley and Thomas F. Torrance. Translated by Geoffrey W. Bromiley et al. 4 vols. Edinburgh: T&T Clark, 1956–1975.

———. "The Strange New World within the Bible." In *The Word of God and the Word of Man,* 28-50. New York: Harper and Brothers, 1957.

Bauckham, Richard. *Bible and Mission: Christian Witness in a Postmodern World.* Grand Rapids, MI: Baker Academic, 2003.

———. *God Crucified: Monotheism and Christology in the New Testament.* Grand Rapids, MI: Eerdmans, 1999.

Bauman, Chad M. "Does the Divine Physician Have an Unfair Advantage? Healing and the Politics of Conversion in Twentieth Century Northern India." In *Asia in the Making of Christianity,* edited by Richard Fox Young and Jonathan A. Seitz, 297-321. Leiden: Brill, 2013.

Beale, G. K. *We Become What We Worship: A Biblical Theology of Idolatry.* Downers Grove, IL: InterVarsity Press, 2008.

Bediako, Kwame. "Biblical Christologies in the Context of African Traditional Religions." In *Sharing Jesus in the Two-Thirds World: Evangelical Christologies from the Contexts of Poverty, Powerlessness and Religious Pluralism: The Papers of the First Conference of Evangelical Mission Theologians from the Two Thirds World, Bangkok, Thailand, March 22-25, 1982,* edited by Vinay Samuel and Chris Sugden, 81-121. Grand Rapids, MI: Eerdmans, 1984.

———. *Christianity in Africa: The Renewal of a Non-Western Religion.* Edinburgh: Edinburgh University Press, 1995.

———. "How Is Jesus Christ Lord? Aspects of an Evangelical Christian Apologetics in the Context of African Religious Pluralism." *Exchange* 25, no. 1 (1996): 27-42.

———. "Jesus in African Culture: A Ghanaian Perspective." In *Jesus in Africa: The Christian Gospel in African History and Experience,* 20-33. Theological Reflections from the South. Akropong-Akuapem, Ghana: Editions Clé; Regnum Africa, 2000.

———. *Theology and Identity: The Impact of Culture upon Christian Thought in the Second Century and in Modern Africa.* Oxford: Regnum Books, 1992.

Berger, Peter L., ed. *The Desecularization of the World: Resurgent Religion and World Politics*. Grand Rapids, MI: Eerdmans, 1999.

———. *The Heretical Imperative: Contemporary Possibilities of Religious Affirmation*. Garden City, NY: Doubleday, 1980.

Berger, Peter L., and Thomas Luckmann. *The Social Construction of Reality: A Treatise in the Sociology of Knowledge*. Garden City, NY: Doubleday, 1966.

Berkhof, H. "Theologiseren in een a-theïstisch tijdperk." In *Bruggen en bruggehoofden: een keuze uit de artikelen en voordrachten van prof. dr. H. Berkhof uit de jaren 1960–1981, verzameld en uitgegeven ter gelegenheid van zijn afscheid als kerkelijk hoogleraar te Leiden*, edited by E. Flesseman-van Leer, F. O. van Gennep, and W. E. Verdonk, 59-74. Nijkerk, NL: Callenbach, 1981.

Berkouwer, Gerrit C. *General Revelation*. Studies in Dogmatics. Grand Rapids, MI: Eerdmans, 1955.

Berlo, David K. *The Process of Communication: An Introduction to Theory and Practice*. New York: Holt, Rinehart and Winston, 1960.

Besançon, Alain. "Préface." In *Jacques Ellul, Islam et judéo-christianisme: texte inédit*, by Jacques Ellul, edited by Alain Besançon, 9-29. Paris: Presses Universitaires de France, 2004.

Bevans, Stephen B. *Models of Contextual Theology*. Maryknoll, NY: Orbis Books, 1992.

Blocher, Henri. *In the Beginning: The Opening Chapters of Genesis*. Downers Grove, IL: InterVarsity Press, 1984.

Boersma, Hans. *Heavenly Participation: The Weaving of a Sacramental Tapestry*. Grand Rapids, MI: Eerdmans, 2011.

Bom, Klaas. "Directed by Desire: An Exploration Based on the Structures of the Desire for God." *Scottish Journal of Theology* 62, no. 02 (2009): 135–48.

Bom, Klaas, and Benno van den Toren. *Context and Catholicity in the Science and Religion Debate: Intercultural Contributions from French-Speaking Africa*. Theology and Mission in World Christianity 14. Leiden: Brill, 2020.

Bosch, David J. *Transforming Mission: Paradigm Shifts in Theology of Mission*. Maryknoll, NY: Orbis Books, 1991.

———. *The Vulnerability of Mission*. Occasional Paper 10. Birmingham, UK: Selly Oak Colleges, 1991.

Boyd, R. H. S. *An Introduction to Indian Christian Theology*. Madras: The Christian Literature Society, 1969.

Brunner, Emil. *Der Mensch im Widerspruch: Die christliche Lehre vom Wahren und vom wirklichen Menschen*. Zürich: Zwingli Verlag, 1937.

———. *Man in Revolt: A Christian Anthropology*. Translated by Olive Wyon. London: Lutterworth Press, 1939.

"Buddhists in the World—Dhamma Wiki." n.d. Accessed May 1, 2020. dhammawiki.com /index.php/Buddhists_in_the_World.

Burnaby, John. *Amor Dei: A Study of the Religion of St. Augustine*. London: Hodder and Stoughton, 1938.

Cabezón, José Ignacio. "A Buddhist Response to Paul Williams's The Unexpected Way." In *Converging Ways? Conversion and Belonging in Buddhism and Christianity*, edited by John D'Arcy May, 89-115. St. Ottilien, Edinburgh: Eos Klosterverlag, 2007.

Calvin, John. *Institutes of the Christian Religion*. Translated by Henry Beveridge. 2 vols. Grand Rapids, MI: Eerdmans, 1983.

Chan, Simon. *Grassroots Asian Theology: Thinking the Faith from the Ground Up*. Downers Grove, IL: InterVarsity Press, 2014.

Chapman, Colin. *Cross and Crescent: Responding to the Challenge of Islam*. Leicester, UK: Inter-Varsity Press, 1995.

Chatterjee, Depapriya. "Arabic Translation of 'The God Delusion' Downloaded 10 Million Times." *Atheist Republic*. June 16, 2016. www.atheistrepublic.com/news/arabic -translation-god-delusion-downloaded-10-million-times.

Clark, David K. *Dialogical Apologetics: A Person-Centered Approach to Christian Defense*. Grand Rapids, MI: Baker Books, 1993.

———. "Narrative Theology and Apologetics." *Journal of the Evangelical Theological Society* 36, no. 4 (1993): 499-515.

Clifford, Ross. "Reframing a Traditional Apologetic to Reach 'New Spirituality' Seekers." In *Encountering New Religious Movements: A Holistic Evangelical Approach*, edited by Irving Hexham, Stephen Rost, and John W. Morehead, 193-208. Grand Rapids, MI: Kregel, 2004.

Coady, C. A. J. *Testimony: A Philosophical Study*. Oxford: Oxford University Press, 1992.

Coakley, Sarah. *God, Sexuality and the Self: An Essay "on the Trinity."* Cambridge: Cambridge University Press, 2013.

Cobb, John. "Beyond 'Pluralism.'" In *Christian Uniqueness Reconsidered: The Myth of a Pluralistic Theology of Religions*, edited by Gavin D'Costa, 81-95. Maryknoll, NY: Orbis, 1990.

Colwell, John. *Promise and Presence: An Exploration of Sacramental Theology*. Waynesboro, GA: Paternoster, 2005.

Cornille, Catherine. *The Im-Possibility of Interreligious Dialogue*. New York: The Crossroad Publishing Company, 2008.

Covey, Stephen R. *The 7 Habits of Highly Effective People*. New York: Fireside, 1989.

Cragg, Kenneth. *The Call of the Minaret*. 2nd ed. Maryknoll, NY: Orbis, 1985.

———. "The Cross and Power: Parting of Ways." In *Jesus and the Cross: Reflections of Christians from Islamic Contexts*, edited by David Emmanuel Singh, 33-46. Oxford: Regnum, 2008.

Craig, William Lane, and Gerd Lüdemann. *Jesus' Resurrection: Fact or Figment?: A Debate between William Lane Craig and Gerd Lüdemann*. Edited by Paul Copan and Ronald K. Tacelli. Downers Grove, IL: InterVarsity Press, 2000.

Cudby, Paul. *The Shaken Path: A Christian Priest's Exploration of Modern Pagan Belief and Practice*. Lanham, UK: John Hunt Publishing, 2017.

Cullmann, Oscar. *Christ and Time: The Primitive Christian Conception of Time and History*. Translated by Floyd V. Filson. Philadelphia, PA: Westminster, 1964.

Dawkins, Richard. *The God Delusion*. London: Random House, 2006.

D'Costa, Gavin. "The Impossibility of a Pluralist View of Religions." *Religious Studies* 32, no. 2 (1996): 223-32.

D'Costa, Gavin. *The Meeting of Religions and the Trinity*. Edinburgh: T&T Clark, 2000.

DeNeui, Paul H. "Contextualizing with Thai Folk Buddhists." In *Sharing Jesus in the Buddhist World*, edited by David S. Lim and Steve Spaulding, 121-46. Pasadena, CA: William Carey Library, 2003.

de Silva, Lynn A. "Good News of Salvation to the Buddhists." *International Review of Mission* 57, no. 228 (1968): 448-58. doi.org/10.1111/j.1758-6631.1968.tb01996.x.

Dhammananda, K. *Buddhism and the Free Thinkers*. Kuala Lumpur, MY: Sasana Abhiwurdhi Wardhana Society, 2016.

————. *What Buddhists Believe*. Kuala Lumpur: Buddhist Missionary Society, 1987.

Diem, Andrea Grace, and James R. Lewis. "Imagining India: The Influence of Hinduism on the New Age Movement." In *Perspectives on the New Age*, edited by James R. Lewis and J. Gordon Melton, 48-58. SUNY Series in Religious Studies. Albany, NY: State University of New York Press, 1992.

Dingemans, G. D. J. *Ietsisme: een basis voor christelijke spiritualiteit?* Kampen, NL: Kok, 2005.

Dinges, William. "The New (Old) Age Movement: Assessing a Vatican Assessment." *Journal of Contemporary Religion* 19, no. 3 (2004): 273-88.

Drane, J. W. "New Age." In *New Dictionary of Christian Apologetics*, edited by Gavin McGrath, Walter Campbell Campbell-Jack, C. Stephen Evans, and S. Carter, 482-85. Leicester, UK; Downers Grove, IL: Inter-Varsity Press; Intervarsity Pres, 2006.

Dulles, Avery. *A History of Apologetics*. Modern Apologetics Library. San Francisco, CA: Ignatius Press, 2005.

Durkheim, Emile. *The Elementary Forms of the Religious Life*. Translated by Joseph Ward Swain. London: Georg Allen & Unwin, 1968.

Edgar, William. "No News Is Good News: Modernity, the Postmodern and Apologetics." *Westminster Theological Journal* 57 (1995): 359-82.

————. *Reasons of the Heart, Recovering Christian Persuasion*. Phillipsburg, NJ: Presbyterian and Reformed, 2012.

Ensminger, Sven. *Karl Barth's Theology as a Resource for a Christian Theology of Religions*. T&T Clark Studies in Systematic Theology 28. New York: T&T Clark, 2014.

Evans, C. Stephen. *The Historical Christ and the Jesus of Faith: The Incarnational Narrative as History*. Oxford: Oxford University Press, 1996.

Farquhar, J. N. *The Crown of Hinduism*. London: Oxford University Press, 1913.

Ferdinando, Keith. "Screwtape Revisited: Demonology Western, African and Biblical." In *The Unseen World: Christian Reflections on Angels, Demons, and the Heavenly Realm*, edited by Anthony N. S. Lane, 103-32. Grand Rapids, MI: Baker Book House, 1996.

Fernando, Ajith. *The Christian's Attitude Toward World Religions*. Wheaton, IL: Tyndale House Publishers, 1987.

———. *Sharing the Truth in Love*. Grand Rapids, MI: Discovery House Publishers, 2001.

Flett, John. "Alasdair MacIntyre's Tradition-Constituted Enquiry in Polanyian Perspective." *Tradition and Discovery: The Polanyi Society Periodical* 26, no. 2 (1999): 6-20.

Flew, Antony. *There Is a God: How the World's Most Notorious Atheist Changed His Mind*. New York: HarperOne, 2007.

Flood, Gavin. *An Introduction to Hinduism*. Cambridge: Cambridge University Press, 1996.

Ford, David F. "'The Best Apologetics Is Good Systematics': A Proposal about the Place of Narrative in Christian Systematic Theology." *Anglican Theological Review* 67, no. 3 (1985): 232-54.

Gabriel, Mark A. *Jesus and Muhammad: Profound Differences and Surprising Similarities*. Lake Mary, FL: Frontline, 2004.

Garrison, V. David. *A Wind in the House of Islam: How God Is Drawing Muslims around the World to Faith in Jesus Christ*. Monument, CO: WIGTake Resources, 2014.

Gaudeul, Jean-Marie. *Called from Islam to Christ: Why Muslims Become Christian*. Crowborough, UK: Monarch, 1999.

Geertz, Clifford. *The Interpretation of Cultures: Selected Essays*. New York: Basic Books, 1973.

Gehlen, Arnold. *Man, His Nature and Place in the World*. New York: Columbia University Press, 1988.

Geisler, Norman L. *Christian Apologetics*. Grand Rapids, MI: Baker Book House, 1976.

Gellman, Jerome I. *Experience of God and the Rationality of Theistic Belief*. Ithaca, NY: Cornell University Press, 1997.

Gilkey, Langdon. "Plurality and Its Theological Implications." In *The Myth of Christian Uniqueness*, edited by John Hick and Paul Knitter, 37-52. London: SCM Press, 1988.

Glaser, Ida. "Cross-Reference Theology: Speaking, Thinking and Living the Cross in the Context of Islam." In *Jesus and the Cross: Reflections of Christians from Islamic Contexts*, edited by David Emmanuel Singh, 137-55. Oxford: Regnum, 2008.

Goheen, Michael W. "Is Lesslie Newbigin's Model of Contextualization Anticultural?" *Mission Studies* 19, no. 2 (2002): 136-58.

Goldingay, John. *God's Prophet, God's Servant: A Study in Jeremiah and Isaiah 40–55*. Exeter, UK: Paternoster Press, 1984.

Gosler, Andrew G. "Surprise and the Value of Life." In *Real Scientists, Real Faith*, edited by R. J. Berry, 173-89. Oxford; Grand Rapids, MI: Monarch, 2009.

Graham, Elaine, and Heather Walton. "A Walk on the Wild Side: A Critique of 'The Gospel and Our Culture.'" *Modern Churchman* 33, no. 1 (1991): 1-7.

Graham, Michael. *From Guru to God: An Experience of the Ultimate Truth*. Hyderabad, London: Authentic Books, 2007.

Gray, G. Francis S. "Sadhu Sundar Singh and the Non-Christian Religions." *International Review of Mission* 48, no. 4 (1959): 421-26.

Grebe, Karl, and Wilfred Fon. *African Traditional Religion and Christian Counseling*. Vol. 1. Bamenda-Nkwen, Cameroon: Oasis International, 2006.

Green, Roger Lancelyn, and Walter Hooper. *C. S. Lewis: A Biography*. London: Collins, 1974.

Gregory, Brad S. *The Unintended Reformation: How a Religious Revolution Secularized Society*. Cambridge, MA: Belknap Press, 2012.

Grenz, Stanley J. *The Social God and the Relational Self: A Trinitarian Theology of the Imago Dei*. Louisville, KY: Westminster John Knox Press, 2001.

Griffiths, Paul J. *An Apology for Apologetics: A Study in the Logic of Interreligious Dialogue*. Maryknoll, NY: Orbis Books, 1991.

———, ed. *Christianity through Non-Christian Eyes*. Maryknoll, NY: Orbis, 2004.

———. *Problems of Religious Diversity*. Malden, MA: Blackwell Publishers, 2001.

Guinness, Os. *The Dust of Death: A Critique of the Establishment and the Counter Culture—and a Proposal for a Third Way*. Downers Grove, IL: InterVarsity Press, 1973.

———. *Fool's Talk: Recovering the Art of Christian Persuasion*. Downers Grove, IL: InterVarsity Press, 2015.

———. *The Gravedigger File: Secret Papers on the Subversion of the Modern Church*. London: Hodder and Stoughton, 1983.

———. *In Two Minds: The Dilemma of Doubt and How to Resolve It*. Downers Grove, IL: InterVarsity Press, 1976.

———. "Mission Modernity: Seven Checkpoints on Mission in the Modern World." In *Faith and Modernity*, edited by Philip Sampson, Vinay Kumar Samuel, and Chris Sugden, 322-52. Oxford: Regnum Books, 1994.

Gundry, Robert H. *Mark: A Commentary on His Apology for the Cross*. Grand Rapids, MI: Eerdmans, 2000.

Gunton, Colin E. *The Promise of Trinitarian Theology*. 2nd ed. Edinburgh: T&T Clark, 1997.

Gyatso, Tenzin [The 14th Dalai lama]. "The Bodghaya Interviews." In *Christianity through Non-Christian Eyes*, edited by Paul J. Griffiths, 166-70. Maryknoll, NY: Orbis Books, 2004.

———. *Universal Responsibility and the Good Heart*. Dharamsala: Library of Tibetan Works and Archives, 1980.

Habermas, Gary R., and Antony Flew. *Did Jesus Rise from the Dead? The Resurrection Debate*. Edited by Terry L. Miethe. San Francisco: Harper & Row, 1987.

Hackett, Stuart C. *The Resurrection of Theism: Prolegomena to Christian Apology.* Grand Rapids, MI: Baker Book House, 1982.

Hamilton, Malcolm. "Implicit Religion and Related Concepts: Seeking Precision." *Implicit Religion* 4, no. 1 (2001): 5-13.

Hammer, Olav. "New Age." In *The Brill Dictionary of Religion*, edited by Kocku von Stuckrad, translated by Robert R. Barr, III, 1313-15. Leiden: Brill, 2006.

Hanegraaff, Wouter J. *Western Esotericism: A Guide for the Perplexed.* London: Bloomsbury Academic, 2013.

Heim, S. Mark. *The Depth of the Riches: A Trinitarian Theology of Religious Ends.* Grand Rapids, MI: Eerdmans, 2001.

Hesselgrave, David J. *Communicating Christ Cross-Culturally: An Introduction to Missionary Communication.* 2nd ed. Grand Rapids, MI: Zondervan, 1991.

——. "Traditional Religions, New Religions, and the Communication of the Christian Faith." In *Encountering New Religious Movements: A Holistic Evangelical Approach*, edited by Irving Hexham, Stephen Rost, and John Morehead, 137-56. Grand Rapids, MI: Kregel, 2004.

Hexham, Irving, and Karla Poewe-Hexham. "New Religions as Global Cultures." In *Encountering New Religious Movements: A Holistic Evangelical Approach*, edited by Irving Hexham, Stephen Rost, and John W. Morehead, 91-111. Grand Rapids, MI: Kregel, 2004.

Hick, John. "Jesus and the World Religions." In *The Myth of God Incarnate*, edited by John Hick, 167-84. Twentieth Century Religious Thought. London: SCM Press, 1977.

——. "The Non-Absoluteness of Christianity." In *The Myth of Christian Uniqueness*, edited by John Hick and Paul Knitter, 16-36. London: SCM Press, 1988.

Hiebert, Paul G. "Critical Contextualization." *Missiology* 12, no. 3 (1984): 288-96.

——. *The Missiological Implications of Epistemological Shifts: Affirming Truth in a Modern/Postmodern World.* Harrisburg, PA: Trinity Press International, 1999.

——. *Transforming Worldviews: An Anthropological Understanding of How People Change.* Grand Rapids, MI: Baker Academic, 2008.

Hiebert, Theodore. "The Tower of Babel and the Origins of the World's Cultures." *Journal of Biblical Literature* 126, no. 1 (2007): 29-58.

Hitchens, Christopher. *God Is Not Great: How Religion Poisons Everything.* New York: Twelve, 2007.

Hofstede, Geert, and Gert Jan Hofstede. *Cultures and Organizations: Software of the Mind.* 2nd ed. New York: McGraw-Hill, 2004.

Hogg, Alfred G. "'The Crown of Hinduism' and Other Volumes [Review]." *International Review of Mission* 3, no. 4 (1914): 171-74.

Hume, David. *Enquiries Concerning the Human Understanding and Concerning the Principles of Morals.* Edited by L. A. Selby-Bigge and P. H. Nidditch. 3rd ed. Oxford: Clarendon, 1975.

Hurtado, Larry W. *Destroyer of the Gods: Early Christian Distinctiveness in the Roman World*. Waco, TX: Baylor University Press, 2016.

Hüsken, Ute. "Vaiṣṇavism." In *Religion Past and Present: Encyclopedia of Theology and Religion*, edited by Hans Dieter Betz, Don S. Browning, Bernd Janowski, and Eberhard Jüngel, 255-56. Leiden: Brill, 2013.

Idowu, E. Bọlaji. "God." In *Biblical Revelation and African Beliefs*, edited by Kwesi A. Dickson and Paul Ellingworth, 17-29. London: Lutterworth Press, 1969.

———. *Olódùmarè: God in Yoruba Belief*. London: Longmans, 1962.

Imasogie, Osadolor. "Christian Apologetic Theology in a West African Context." *The Journal of the Interdenominational Theological Center* 7, no. 2 (1980): 129-44.

Irenaeus of Lyons. *Against the Heresies*. Edited by Matthew C. Steenberg and Michael Slusser. Translated by Dominic J. Unger and John J. Dillon. New York: Paulist Press, 1992.

Jeffers, James S. *The Greco-Roman World of the New Testament Era: Exploring the Background of Early Christianity*. Downers Grove, IL: InterVarsity Press, 1999.

Jenkins, Philip. *The Lost History of Christianity: The Thousand-Year Golden Age of the Church in the Middle East, Africa, and Asia—and How It Died*. New York: HarperOne, 2008.

Johansson, Lars. "New Age—A Synthesis of the Premodern, Modern and Postmodern." In *Faith and Modernity*, edited by Philip Sampson, Vinay Kumar Samuel, and Chris Sugden, 208-51. Oxford: Regnum Books, 1994.

John, Varughese. "The Ethical Requirement in Hinduism and Christianity." *Doon Theological Journal* 17, no. 1 (2020): 58-74.

———. "A Sense of History and Apologetics in a Hindu Context." *Missiology* 36, no. 2 (2008): 219-26.

Johnson, Philip. "Apologetics and Myths: Signs of Salvation in Postmodernity." *Lutheran Theological Journal* 32, no. 2 (1998): 62-72.

———. "The Aquarian Age and Apologetics." *Lutheran Theological Journal* 34, no. 2 (2000): 51-60.

———. "Discipling New Age and Do-It Yourself Seekers through Booth Ministries." In *Encountering New Religious Movements: A Holistic Evangelical Approach*, edited by Irving Hexham, Stephen Rost, and John W. Morehead, 227-42. Grand Rapids, MI: Kregel, 2004.

Johnson, Philip, and John Smulo. "Reaching Wiccan and Mother Goddess Devotees." In *Encountering New Religious Movements: A Holistic Evangelical Approach*, edited by Irving Hexham, Stephen Rost, and John W. Morehead, 209-25. Grand Rapids, MI: Kregel, 2004.

Jones, E. Stanley. *Christ at the Roundtable*. Revised edition. The 21st Century in Our Times Series. n.p.: E. Stanley Jones Foundation, 2019.

———. *A Song of Ascents: A Spiritual Autobiography*. Nashville, TN: Abingdon Press, 1968.

Jørgensen, Jonas Adelin. *Jesus Imandars and Christ Bhaktas: Two Case Studies of Inter-religious Hermeneutics and Identity in Global Christianity*. Frankfurt am Main, DE: Peter Lang, 2008.

Joshua, P. E. "Revival and Reformation: The Spirituality of Select Indian Instituted Churches and Their Role, Significance and Implications for Indian Christianity." PhD Thesis, Amsterdam: VU University, 2013.

Kaiser, Christopher B. *Creation and the History of Science*. Grand Rapids, MI: Eerdmans, 1991.

Kalam, A. P. J. Abdul. *Transcendence: My Spiritual Experiences with Pramukh Swamiji*. New York: Harper Element, 2016.

Kanagaraj, Jey J. *The Gospel of John: A Commentary with Elements of Comparison to Indian Religious Thoughts and Cultural Practices*. Secunderabad, India: OM Books, 2005.

Kärkkäinen, Veli-Matti. *An Introduction to the Theology of Religions: Biblical, Historical, and Contemporary Perspectives*. Downers Grove, IL: InterVarsity Press, 2003.

———. *Spirit and Salvation*. A Constructive Christian Theology for the Pluralistic World 4. Grand Rapids, MI: Eerdmans, 2016.

———. *Trinity and Religious Pluralism: The Doctrine of the Trinity in Christian Theology of Religions*. Aldershot, UK: Ashgate, 2004.

Kellenberger, James. "The Language-Game View of Religion and Religious Certainty." *Canadian Journal of Philosophy* 2, no. 2 (1972): 255-75.

Keller, Timothy. *Counterfeit Gods: When the Empty Promises of Love, Money, and Power Let You Down*. London: Hodder & Stoughton, 2010.

Kelsey, David H. *Eccentric Existence: A Theological Anthropology*. Louisville, KY: Westminster John Knox Press, 2009.

Keune, Jon. "The Intra- and Inter-Religious Conversions of Nehemiah Nilakantha Goreh." *Journal of Hindu-Christian Studies* 17, no. 1 (2004): 45-54.

Khodr, George. "Christianity in a Pluralist World: The Economy of the Holy Spirit." In *Living Faiths and the Ecumenical Movement*, edited by Stanley J. Samartha, 131-42. Geneva: World Council of Churches, 1971.

———. "An Orthodox Perspective on Inter-Religious Dialogue." *Current Dialogue* 19, no. 1 (1991): 25-27.

Kigame, Reuben. *Christian Apologetics Through African Eyes*. Nairobi: Posterity Publishers, 2018.

Kim, Kirsteen. "Discerning the Spirit: The First Act of Mission." *Norsk Tidsskrift for Misjonsvitenskap* 62, no. 1 (2008): 3-21.

———. *The Holy Spirit in the World: A Global Conversation*. Maryknoll, NY: Orbis, 2007.

Knitter, Paul F. *Introducing Theologies of Religions*. Maryknoll, NY: Orbis Books, 2002.

Kombo, James Henry Owino. *The Doctrine of God in African Christian Thought: The Holy Trinity, Theological Hermeneutics, and the African Intellectual Culture*. Leiden: Brill, 2007.

Kraemer, Hendrik. *The Christian Message in a Non-Christian World*. London: Edinburgh House Press, 1938.

——. "Continuity or Discontinuity." In *The Authority of the Faith*, edited by William Paton, 1-23. Tambaram Series 1. Oxford: Oxford University Press, 1939.

——. *Why Christianity of All Religions?* Translated by Hubert Hoskins. London: Lutterworth, 1962.

Kraft, Charles H. *Anthropology for Christian Witness*. Maryknoll, NY: Orbis Books, 1996.

——. *Communicating Jesus' Way*. Revised edition. Pasadena, CA: William Carey Library, 1999.

Kraus, C. Norman. *Jesus Christ Our Lord: Christology from a Disciple's Perspective*. Scottsdale, PA: Herald Press, 1987.

Kreeft, Peter, and Ronald K. Tacelli. *Handbook of Christian Apologetics*. Crowborough, UK: Monarch, 1995.

Krishna, Raghav. "From 'Krishna Bhakti' to 'Christianity' to 'Krista Bhakti.'" *International Journal of Frontier Missiology* 24, no. 4 (2007): 173-77.

Kuhn, Thomas S. *The Structure of Scientific Revolutions*. 3rd ed. Chicago: University of Chicago Press, 1996.

Küng, Hans. *Does God Exist? An Answer for Today*. Garden City, NY: Doubleday, 1980.

——. *Freedom Today*. Theological Meditations. New York: Sheed and Ward, 1966.

Küster, Volker. "Who, with Whom, about What? Exploring the Landscape of Inter-Religious Dialogue." *Exchange* 33, no. 1 (2004): 73-92.

Lacy, Creighton. "The Legacy of D. T. Niles." *International Bulletin of Missionary Research* 8, no. 4 (1984): 174-78.

Lausanne Committee for World Evangelization. "Christian Witness to Hindus." Lausanne Occasional Paper 14. Pattaya, 1980. www.lausanne.org/content/lop/lop-14.

——. "Religious and Non-Religious Spirituality in the Western World." Lausanne Occasional Paper 45. Pattaya, 2004. www.lausanne.org/content/lop/religious-non-religious -spirituality-western-world-lop-45.

Lazarus-Yafeh, Hava. "Taḥrīf." In *Encyclopaedia of Islam*, edited by P. Bearman, Th. Bianquis, C. E. Bosworth, E. van Donzel, and W. P. Heinrichs X, T-U: 111-12. 2nd ed. Leiden: Brill, 2000.

Lewis, C. S. "Fern-Seed and Elephants." In *Christian Reflections*, edited by Walter Hooper, 191-208. London: Fount, 1981.

——. "Myth Became Fact." In *God in the Dock: Essays on Theology and Ethics*, edited by Walter Hooper, 54-60. Grand Rapids, MI: Eerdmans, 2014.

——. "The Weight of Glory." In *The Weight of Glory and Other Addresses*, 25-46. New York: Macmillan Company, 1949.

Lincoln, Andrew T. *Truth on Trial: The Lawsuit Motif in the Fourth Gospel*. Peabody, MA: Hendrickson Publishers, 2000.

Lindbeck, George A. "The Gospel's Uniqueness: Election and Untranslatability." *Modern Theology* 13, no. 4 (1997): 423-50.

———. *The Nature of Doctrine: Religion and Theology in a Postliberal Age*. Philadelphia, PA: Westminster Press, 1984.

Lindsley, Arthur. *Love, the Ultimate Apologetic: The Heart of Christian Witness*. Downers Grove, IL: InterVarsity Press, 2008.

Lipner, Julius. *Hindus: Their Religious Beliefs and Practices*. London: Routledge, 1994.

Livermore, David A. *The Cultural Intelligence Difference: Master the One Skill You Can't Do without in Today's Global Economy*. New York: AMACOM, American Management Association, 2011.

Locke, John. *An Essay Concerning Human Understanding*. Edited by John W. Yolton. 2 vols. London: Dent, 1961.

Lossky, Vladimir. *The Mystical Theology of the Eastern Church*. London: James Clark & Co., 1957.

Luther, Martin. "The Large Catechism." In *The Book of Concord: The Confessions of the Evangelical Lutheran Church*, edited by Robert Kolb and Timothy J. Wengert, translated by Charles P. Arand, Eric Gritsch, Robert Kolb, William Russell, James Schaaf, Jane Strohl, and Timothy J. Wengert, 377-480. Minneapolis, MN: Fortress Press, 2000.

Lyotard, Jean-François. *The Postmodern Condition: A Report on Knowledge*. Translated by Geoffrey Bennington and Brian. Massumi. Theory and History of Literature 10. Minneapolis, MN: University of Minnesota Press, 1984.

Macchia, Frank D. *Baptized in the Spirit: A Global Pentecostal Theology*. Grand Rapids, MI: Zondervan, 2006.

MacIntyre, Alasdair. "Epistemological Crises, Dramatic Narrative, and the Philosophy of Science." In *Paradigms and Revolutions: Appraisals and Applications of Thomas Kuhn's Philosophy of Science*, edited by Gary Gutting, 54-74. Notre Dame, IN: University of Notre Dame Press, 1980.

———. *Whose Justice? Which Rationality?* Notre Dame, IN: University of Notre Dame Press, 1988.

MacKenzie, Rory. "Lessons from the Life of Karl Reichelt." In *Contextualisation and Mission Training: Engaging Asia's Religious Worlds*, edited by Jonathan Ingleby, Kang-San Tan, and Tan Loun Ling, 59-73. Oxford: Regnum Books, 2013.

Magesa, Laurenti. *African Religion: The Moral Traditions of Abundant Life*. Maryknoll, NY: Orbis Books, 1997.

Maharaj, Rabi R. *Death of a Guru: A Remarkable True Story of One Man's Search for Truth*. London: Hodder & Stoughton, 2004.

Manaranche, André. *Le monothéisme chrétien*. Paris: Cerf, 1985.

Mangalwadi, Vishal. *The Book That Made Your World: How the Bible Created the Soul of Western Civilization*. Nashville, TN: Thomas Nelson, 2011.

————. *Missionary Conspiracy: Letters to a Postmodern Hindu*. Mussoorie, IND: Nivedit Good Books, 1996.

Marshall, David. "Heavenly Religion or Unbelief? Muslim Perspectives on Christianity." *Anvil* 23, no. 2 (2006): 89-100.

Masood, Steven. *Into the Light: A Young Muslim's Search for Truth*. Carlisle, UK: OM, 1986.

Mbiti, John S. *African Religions and Philosophy*. Nairobi: East African Educational Publishers, 1969.

————. *Concepts of God in Africa*. London: SPCK, 1975.

————. *New Testament Eschatology in an African Background: A Study of the Encounter between New Testament Theology and African Traditional Concepts*. London: Oxford University Press, 1971.

————. "Some African Concepts of Christology." In *Christ and the Younger Churches*, edited by George F. Vicedom and José Miguez Bonino, 51-62. Theological Collections 15. London: SPCK, 1972.

McDermott, Gerald R. *Can Evangelicals Learn from World Religions? Jesus, Revelation and Religious Traditions*. Downers Grove, IL: InterVarsity Press, 2000.

McDermott, Gerald R., and Harold A Netland. *A Trinitarian Theology of Religions: An Evangelical Proposal*. Oxford: Oxford University Press, 2014.

McGrath, Alister E. *Bridge-Building: Effective Christian Apologetics*. Leicester, UK: InterVarsity Press, 1992.

————. *The Territories of Human Reason: Science and Theology in an Age of Multiple Rationalities*. Ian Ramsey Centre Studies in Science and Religion. Oxford: Oxford University Press, 2019.

Metogo, Eloi Messi. *Dieu peut-il mourir en Afrique? Essai sur l'indifférence religieuse et l'incroyance en Afrique noire*. Paris: Presses de l'UCAC, 1997.

Meyer, Erin. *The Culture Map: Decoding How People Think, Lead, and Get Things Done Across Cultures*. New York: Public Affairs, 2015.

Michael, Russ. *Feeling Good Is Feeling God*. New Delhi: Good Times Books, 2011.

Michaels, Axel, Harald Fischer-Tiné, Patrick Eisenlohr, Adalbert J. Gail, Johannes Lähnemann, and Andrew Wingate. "Hinduism." In *Religion Past and Present: Encyclopedia of Theology and Religion*, edited by Hans Dieter Betz, Don S. Browning, Bernd Janowski, and Eberhard Jüngel, Hea-Jog: 142-52. Leiden: Brill, 2009.

Middleton, J. Richard, and Brian J. Walsh. "Facing the Postmodern Scalpel: Can the Christian Faith Withstand Deconstruction?" In *Christian Apologetics in the Postmodern World*, edited by Timothy R. Phillips and Dennis L. Okholm, 131-54. Downers Grove, IL: InterVarsity Press, 1995.

————. *Truth Is Stranger than It Used to Be: Biblical Faith in a Postmodern Age*. Downers Grove, IL: InterVarsity Press, 1995.

Miskotte, K. H. *Edda en Thora; een vergelijking van Germaanse en Israëlitise religie.* Nijkerk, NL: Callenbach, 1970.

Mojola, Aloo O. "The Old Testament or Hebrew Bible in Africa: Challenges and Prospects for Interpretation and Translation." *Verbum et Ecclesia* 35, no. 3 (2014): 1-7.

Montgomery, John Warwick. *Faith Founded on Fact: Essays in Evidential Apologetics.* Nashville, TN: Nelson, 1978.

Moreau, A. Scott. "Evangelical Models of Contextualization." In *Local Theology for the Global Church: Principles for an Evangelical Approach to Contextualization,* 165-93. Pasadena, CA: William Carey Library, 2010.

Morehead, John W. "Conclusion: Where Do We Go from Here? Transforming Evangelical Responses to New Religions." In *Encountering New Religious Movements: A Holistic Evangelical Approach,* edited by Irving Hexham, Stephen Rost, and John W. Morehead, 279-304. Grand Rapids, MI: Kregel, 2004.

Morison, Frank. *Who Moved the Stone?* New York: The Century Co., 1930.

Morris, Thomas V. *Making Sense of It All: Pascal and the Meaning of Life.* Grand Rapids, MI: Eerdmans, 1992.

Moyaert, Marianne. *Fragile Identities: Towards a Theology of Interreligious Hospitality.* New York: Rodopi, 2011.

Moynagh, Michael. *Church for Every Context: An Introduction to Theology and Practice.* London: SCM, 2012.

Mugambi, Jesse N. K. *Critiques of Christianity in African Literature: With Particular Reference to the East African Context.* Nairobi, KE: East African Educational Publishers, 1992.

Murphy, G. Ronald. *The Saxon Savior: The Germanic Transformation of the Gospel in the Ninth-Century Heliand.* New York: Oxford University Press, 1989.

Murphy, Nancey C. "Missiology in the Postmodern: A Radical Reformation Perspective." In *To Stake a Claim: Mission and the Western Crisis of Knowledge,* edited by J. Andrew Kirk and Kevin J. Vanhoozer, 96-119. Maryknoll, NY: Orbis Books, 1999.

Musk, Bill Andrew. *The Unseen Face of Islam: Sharing the Gospel with Ordinary Muslims.* Sutherland, Australia: MARC, Evangelical Missionary Alliance, 1989.

Nash, Ronald H. *Worldviews in Conflict: Choosing Christianity in a World of Ideas.* Grand Rapids, MI: Zondervan, 1992.

Nasr, Seyyed Hossein. "The Islamic View of Christianity." In *Christianity through Non-Christian Eyes,* edited by Paul J. Griffiths, 126-34. Maryknoll, NY: Orbis Books, 2004.

Naugle, David. *Worldview: The History of a Concept.* Grand Rapids, MI: Eerdmans, 2002.

Neely, Brent, and Peter Riddell. "Familiar Signs, Altered Concepts: Jesus, Messiah and Resurrection in Islam." In *Jesus and the Resurrection: Reflections of Christians from Islamic Contexts.,* edited by David Emmanuel Singh, 43-64. Oxford: Regnum Books, 2014.

Nemoianu, V. Martin. "Pascal on Divine Hiddenness." *International Philosophical Quarterly* 55, no. 3 (2015): 325-44.

Netland, Harold A. *Dissonant Voices: Religious Pluralism and the Question of Truth.* Grand Rapids, MI: Eerdmans, 1991.

——. *Encountering Religious Pluralism: The Challenge to Christian Faith and Mission.* Downers Grove, IL: InterVarsity Press, 2001.

Newbigin, Lesslie. *Foolishness to the Greeks: The Gospel and Western Culture.* London: SPCK, 1986.

——. "The Gospel and Our Culture: A Response to Elaine Graham and Heather Walton." *Modern Churchman* 34, no. 2 (1992): 1-10.

——. *The Gospel in a Pluralist Society.* Grand Rapids, MI; Geneva: Eerdmans; WCC Publications, 1989.

——. *Honest Religion for Secular Man.* London: SCM Press, 1966.

——. *The Open Secret: An Introduction to the Theology of Mission.* Grand Rapids, MI: Eerdmans, 1995.

——. *Proper Confidence: Faith, Doubt, and Certainty in Christian Discipleship.* Grand Rapids, MI: Eerdmans, 1995.

——. "Religion for the Marketplace." In *Christian Uniqueness Reconsidered: The Myth of a Pluralistic Theology of Religions,* edited by Gavin D'Costa, 135-48. Maryknoll, NY: Orbis, 1990.

Newport, John P. *The New Age Movement and the Biblical Worldview: Conflict and Dialogue.* Grand Rapids, MI: Eerdmans, 1997.

Nicholls, Bruce. *Building Bridges: From Asian Faiths to Jesus in the Gospels.* Oxford: Regnum, 2019.

Niles, Daniel Thambyrajah. *That They May Have Life.* New York: Harper & Brothers, 1951.

Nyunt, Peter Thein. *Missions amidst Pagodas: Contextual Communication of the Gospel in the Burmese Buddhist Context.* Carlisle, UK: Langham Monographs, 2016.

Oberlies, Thomas. "Buddhism." In *The Brill Dictionary of Religion,* edited by Kocku von Stuckrad, translated by Robert R. Barr, 1 A-D: 208-15. Leiden; Boston: Brill, 2006.

Oden, Thomas C. *How Africa Shaped the Christian Mind: Rediscovering the African Seedbed of Western Christianity.* Downers Grove, IL: InterVarsity Press, 2007.

Okorocha, Cyril C. *The Meaning of Religious Conversion in Africa: The Case of the Igbo of Nigeria.* Aldershot, UK; Brookfield, WI: Avebury, 1987.

——. "Religious Conversion in Africa: Its Missiological Implications." *Mission Studies* 9, no. 1 (1992): 168-81.

Orr, James. *The Christian View of God and the World: As Centering in the Incarnation.* 3rd ed. Vancouver: Regent College Publishing, 2002.

Osho. *Christianity the Deadliest Poison & Zen the Antidote to All Poisons.* Pune, IND: Osho Media International, 2014.

——. *Zorba the Buddha.* Darshan Diary Series. Antelope, OR: Rajneesh Foundation International, 1982.

Owen, Huw Parri. *Christian Theism: A Study in Its Basic Principles*. Edinburgh: T&T Clark, 1984.

Paley, William. *Natural Theology: Or, Evidences of the Existence and Attributes of the Deity, Collected from the Appearances of Nature*. Farnborough, UK: Gregg, 1970.

Panikkar, Raimon. *The Intra-Religious Dialogue*. New York: Paulist Press, 1999.

Pannenberg, Wolfhart. *Anthropology in Theological Perspective*. Translated by Matthew J. O'Connell. Philadelphia, PA: Westminster Press, 1985.

———. *Jesus, God and Man*. Translated by Lewis L. Wilkins and Duane A. Priebe. Philadelphia, PA: Westminster Press, 1968.

Partridge, C. H. "Pagan and Indigenous Religions." In *New Dictionary of Christian Apologetics*, edited by Gavin J. McGrath, Walter Campbell Campbell-Jack, C. Stephen Evans, and S. Carter, 523-28. Leicester, UK: Inter-Varsity Press, 2006.

Pascal, Blaise. *Pensées*. Translated by A. J. Krailsheimer. London: Penguin Books, 1995.

Patel, Rahil. *Found by Love: A Hindu Priest Encounters Jesus Christ*. Watford, UK: Instant Apostle, 2016.

p'Bitek, Okot. *African Religions in Western Scholarship*. Kampala, UG: East African Literature Bureau, 1970.

Paul VI. "Gaudium et Spes: Pastoral Constitution on the Church in the Modem World, Promulgated by His Holiness, Pope Paul VI on December 7, 1965." www.vatican.va/archive/hist_councils/ii_vatican_council/documents/vat-ii_const_19651207_gaudium-et-spes_en.html.

Pearcey, Nancy. *Finding Truth: 5 Principles for Unmasking Atheism, Secularism, and Other God Substitutes*. Colorado Springs, CO: David C. Cook, 2015.

Perry, Cindy. "Bhai-Tika and 'Tij Braka': A Case Study in the Contextualization of Two Nepali Festivals." *Missiology: An International Review* 18, no. 2 (1990): 177-83.

Pew-Templeton Global Religious Futures Project. n.d. "Data Explorer." Accessed May 1, 2020. globalreligiousfutures.org/explorer#.

Philips, Abu Ameenah Bilaal. *The Fundamentals of Tawḥeed: Islamic Monotheism*. Birmingham, UK: Al-Hidaayah Publishing and Distribution, 1982.

———. *The True Religion*. Riyadh, SA: Cooperative Office for Call and Guidance, 1995.

Pinnock, Clark H. *Flame of Love: A Theology of the Holy Spirit*. Downers Grove, IL: IVP Academic, 1996.

Plantinga, Alvin. *Warrant and Proper Function*. New York: Oxford University Press, 1993.

Platvoet, Jan, and Henk J. van Rinsum. "Is Africa Incurably Religious? Confessing and Contesting an Invention." *Exchange* 32, no. 2 (2003): 123-53.

Polanyi, Michael. *Personal Knowledge: Towards a Post-Critical Philosophy*. Corrected edition. Chicago: University of Chicago Press, 1962.

Polkinghorne, J. C. *Rochester Roundabout: The Story of High Energy Physics*. New York: W.H. Freeman, 1989.

Qureshi, Nabeel. *Seeking Allah, Finding Jesus: A Devout Muslim Encounters Christianity*. Grand Rapids, MI: Zondervan, 2014.

Qutb, Sayyid. "That Hideous Schizophrenia." In *Christianity through Non-Christian Eyes*, edited by Paul J. Griffiths, 73-81. Maryknoll, NY: Orbis Books, 2004.

Rahner, Karl. *The Trinity*. Translated by Joseph Donceel. Milestones in Catholic Theology. New York: Crossroad Publishing, 2005.

Ramachandra, Vinoth. *Faiths in Conflict? Christian Integrity in a Multicultural World*. Leicester, UK: Inter-Varsity Press, 2000.

———. *Gods That Fail: Modern Idolatry and Christian Mission*. Downers Grove, IL: Inter-Varsity Press, 1996.

———. *The Recovery of Mission: Beyond the Pluralist Paradigm*. Grand Rapids, MI: Eerdmans, 1997.

———. *Subverting Global Myths*. London: SPCK, 2008.

Reichelt, Karl Ludvig. "Buddhism in China at the Present Time and the New Challenge to the Christian Church." *International Review of Mission* 26, no. 2 (1937): 153-66.

Richard, H. L. *Following Jesus in the Hindu Context: The Intriguing Implications of N.V. Tilak's Life and Thought*. Pasadena, CA: William Carey Library, 1998.

Richardson, Don. *Eternity in Their Hearts*. Ventura, CA: Regal Books, 1981.

Rietkerk, Wim. *If Only I Could Believe*. Carlisle, UK: Solway, 1997.

Robbins, Joel. "Can There Be Conversion Without Cultural Change?" *Mission Studies* 34, no. 1 (2017): 29-52.

Rogers, Matthew D. "Paganism/Neopaganism." In *The Brill Dictionary of Religion*, edited by Kocku von Stuckrad, translated by Robert R. Barr, Vol. III, M-R: 1393-96. Leiden: Brill, 2006.

Rommen, Edward. *Come and See: An Eastern Orthodox Perspective on Contextualization*. Pasadena, CA: William Carey Library, 2013.

Rosner, Brian S. *Greed as Idolatry: The Origin and Meaning of a Pauline Metaphor*. Grand Rapids, MI: Eerdmans, 2007.

Rothermundt, Gottfried. "Apologetic Tendencies in Modern Buddhism." *Bangalore Theological Forum* 11, no. 2 (1979): 109-21.

Sahoo, Sarbeswar. *Pentecostalism and Politics of Conversion in India*. Cambridge: Cambridge University Press, 2018.

Saliba, John A. *Christian Responses to the New Age Movement: A Critical Assessment*. London: Geoffrey Chapman, 1999.

Samartha, Stanley J. "The Cross and the Rainbow: Christ in a Multireligious Culture." In *The Myth of Christian Uniqueness*, edited by John Hick and Paul F Knitter, 69-88. London: SCM Press, 1988.

Sanneh, Lamin O. *Translating the Message: The Missionary Impact on Culture*. Maryknoll, NY: Orbis Books, 1989.

Satyavrata, Ivan. *God Has Not Left Himself without Witness.* Oxford: Regnum Books International, 2011.

Schleiermacher, Friedrich Daniel Ernst. *On Religion: Speeches to Its Cultured Despisers.* Edited and translated by Richard Crouter, Cambridge: Cambridge University Press, 1996 [1799].

Schmidt-Leukel, Perry. "'Light and Darkness' or 'Looking through a Dim Mirror'? A Reply to Paul Williams from a Christian Perspective." In *Converging Ways? Conversion and Belonging in Buddhism and Christianity,* edited by John D'Arcy May, 67-88. St. Ottilien, Edinburgh: Eos Klosterverlag, 2007.

Scorgie, Glenn G. "Confrontational Apologetics versus Grace-Filled Persuasion." *Perichoresis* 10, no. 1 (2012): 23-39.

Scott, Ridley. *Gladiator.* Universal Pictures Germany GmbH, 2000.

Shehadeh, Imad N. "The Predicament of Islamic Monotheism." *Bibliotheca Sacra* 161, no. 642 (2004): 142-62.

Shourie, Arun. *Missionaries in India: Continuities, Changes, Dilemmas.* New Delhi: ASA Publications, 1994.

Sims, John A. "Postmodernism: The Apologetic Imperative." In *The Challenge of Postmodernism: An Evangelical Engagement,* edited by David S. Dockery, 324-43. Grand Rapids, MI: Baker Books, 1995.

Singgih, Emanuel Gerrit. "A Postcolonial Biography of Sadrach: The Tragic Story of an Indigenous Missionary." *Al-Jami'ah: Journal of Islamic Studies* 53, no. 2 (2015): 367-86.

Singh, David Emmanuel. "Sunder Singh and N. V. Tilak: Lessons for Missiology from 20th Century India?" *Dharma Deepika* (December 2010): 3-16.

Singh, Sundar. *Reality and Religion: Meditations on God, Man and Nature.* London: MacMillan and Co., 1924.

———. *The Search After Reality: Thoughts on Hinduism, Buddhism, Muhammadanism and Christianity.* London: MacMillan and Co., 1925.

———. *With and Without Christ: Incidents Taken from the Lives of Christians and Non-Christians Which Illustrate the Difference in Lives Lived with Christ and without Christ.* New York: Harper and Brothers Publishers, 1929.

Sire, James W. *The Universe Next Door: A Basic Worldview Catalog.* 5th ed. Downers Grove, IL: IVP Academic, 2009.

Slade, Emma. *Set Free: A Life-Changing Journey from Banking to Buddhism in Bhutan.* London: Summersdale, 2017.

Sleasman, Michael J. "Swords, Sandals, and Saviors: Visions of Hope in Ridley Scott's Gladiator." In *Everyday Theology: How to Read Cultural Texts and Interpret Trends,* edited by Kevin J. Vanhoozer, Charles A. Anderson, and Michael J. Sleasman, 132-251. Grand Rapids, MI: Baker Academic, 2007.

Smart, Ninian. *The World's Religions: Old Traditions and Modern Transformations.* Cambridge: Cambridge University Press, 1989.

Smith, Alex G. "The Christian Response to Buddhism." In *Christian Witness in Pluralistic Contexts in the 21st Century*, edited by Enoch Yee-nock Wan, 135-68. Evangelical Missiological Society Series 11. Pasadena, CA: William Carey Library, 2004.

Smith, C. Fred. "Apologetic Approaches to Hinduism." *UBS Journal* 6, no. 2 (2009): 116-31.

Smith, Gordon T. *Evangelical, Sacramental, and Pentecostal: Why the Church Should Be All Three*. Downers Grove, IL: IVP Academic, 2017.

Smith, James K. A. *You Are What You Love: The Spiritual Power of Habit*. Grand Rapids, MI: Brazos Press, 2016.

Sosa, Ernest. "The Raft and the Pyramid: Coherence versus Foundations in the Theory of Knowledge." *Midwest Studies in Philosophy* 5, no. 1 (1980):3-25.

Stackhouse, John G. *Humble Apologetics: Defending the Faith Today*. Oxford: Oxford University Press, 2002.

Stanley, Brian. *The Bible and the Flag: Protestant Missions and British Imperialism in the Nineteenth and Twentieth Centuries*. Leicester, UK: Apollos, 1990.

Stein, Robert H. *An Introduction to the Parables of Jesus*. Philadelphia, PA: Westminster Press, 1981.

Stinton, Diane B. *Jesus of Africa: Voices of Contemporary African Christology*. Maryknoll, NY: Orbis Books, 2004.

Stott, John R. W. *I Believe in Preaching*. London: Hodder & Stoughton, 1982.

———. *The Contemporary Christian: An Urgent Plea for Double Listening*. Leicester, UK: Inter-Varsity Press, 1992.

———. *The Message of Acts: To the Ends of the Earth*. 2nd ed. Bible Speaks Today. Leicester, UK: Inter-Varsity Press, 1991.

Strange, D. "For Their Rock Is Not as Our Rock: The Gospel as the 'Subversive Fulfillment' of the Religious Other." *Journal of the Evangelical Theological Society* 56, no. 2 (2013): 379-95.

Streeter, Burnett Hillman, and Aiyadurai Jesudasan Appasamy. *The Sadhu: A Study in Mysticism and Practical Religion*. London: Macmillan, 1921.

Sundkler, Bengt, and Christopher Steed. *A History of the Christian Church in Africa*. Cambridge, England: Cambridge University Press, 2000.

Talman, Harley. *Understanding Insider Movements: Disciples of Jesus within Diverse Religious Communities*. Pasadena, CA: William Carey Library, 2015.

Tan, Kang-San. "Dual Belonging: A Missiological Critique and Appreciation from an Asian Evangelical Perspective." *Mission Studies* 27, no. 1 (2010): 24-38.

———. "Elements of a Biblical and Genuine Missionary Encounter with Diaspora Chinese Buddhists in South-East Asia." In *Sharing Jesus in the Buddhist World*, edited by David S. Lim and Steve Spaulding, 19-30. Pasadena, CA: William Carey Library, 2003.

———. "Genesis 1–11 and Buddhist Scripture: How the Gospel Can Transform Buddhist Worldviews." In *Communicating Christ in the Buddhist World*, edited by Paul H. De Neui and David S. Lim, 25-46. Pasadena, CA: William Carey Library Publishers, 2006.

——. "The Inter-Religious Frontier: A 'Buddhist-Christian' Contribution." *Mission Studies* 31, no. 2 (2014): 139-56. doi.org/10.1163/15733831-12341330.

Tanner, Kathryn. *Theories of Culture: A New Agenda for Theology*. Minneapolis, MN: Fortress Press, 1997.

Taylor, Charles. *A Secular Age*. Cambridge, MA: Belknap Press, 2007.

Taylor, John V. *The Primal Vision: Christian Presence amid African Religion*. London: SCM Press, 1963.

Tilak, Pradeep. "A Christian Worldview Apologetic Engagement with Advaita Vedanta Hinduism." PhD Thesis, Louisville, KY: Southern Baptist Theological Seminary, 2013.

Tillich, Paul. *Systematic Theology*. Vol. 1, Reason and Revelation, Being and God. Chicago, IL: The University of Chicago Press, 1951.

——. *Systematic Theology*. Vol. 2, Existence and the Christ. Chicago, IL: The University of Chicago Press, 1957.

Torrance, Thomas F. *Ground and Grammar of Theology: Consonance Between Theology and Science*. Edinburgh: T&T Clark, 2005.

——. "Theological Persuasion." In *God and Rationality*, by Thomas F Torrance, 195-206. London: Oxford University Press, 1971.

——. *Theological Science*. London; New York: Oxford University Press, 1969.

Turnau, Theodore A., III, "Popular Culture, Apologetics, and the Discourse of Desire." *Cultural Encounters* 8, no. 2 (2012): 25-46.

Turner, Harold W. "The Primal Religions of the World and Their Study." In *Australian Essays in World Religions*, edited by Victor Hayes, 27-37. Bedford Park: Australian Association for World Religions, 1977.

Turner, Max. *The Holy Spirit and Spiritual Gifts: Then and Now*. Carlisle, UK: Paternoster, 1996.

Urban, Hugh B. *Zorba the Buddha: Sex, Spirituality, and Capitalism in the Global Osho Movement*. Oakland, CA: University of California Press, 2015.

Valea, Ernest M. *Buddhist-Christian Dialogue as Theological Exchange: An Orthodox Contribution to Comparative Theology*. Eugene, OR: Wipf and Stock, 2015.

van den Toren, Benno. "African Neo-Pentecostalism in the Face of Secularization: Problems and Possibilities." *Cairo Journal of Theology* 2 (2015): 103-20.

——. *Christian Apologetics as Cross-Cultural Dialogue*. London: T&T Clark, 2011.

——. "Christianity as 'True Religion' According to Karl Barth's Theologia Religionum: An Intercultural Conversation with Selected Asian Christian Theologians." *Asia Journal Theology* 35 (2021): 155-70.

——. "Discerning the Spirit in World Religions: The Search for Criteria." In *The Spirit Is Moving: New Pathways in Pneumatology: Studies Presented to Professor Cornelis van Der Kooi on the Occasion of His Retirement*, edited by Gijsbert van de Brink, Eveline van Staalduine-Sulman, and Maarten Wisse, 215-31. Studies in Reformed Theology. Leiden; Boston: Brill, 2019.

———. *La doctrine chrétienne dans un monde multiculturel. Introduction à la tâche théologique.* Carlisle, UK: Langham Global Library, 2014.

———. "Growing Disciples in the Rainforest: A Contextualized Confession for Pygmy Christians." *Evangelical Review of Theology* 33, no. 4 (2009): 306-15.

———. "Human Evolution and a Cultural Understanding of Original Sin." *Perspectives on Science and Christian Faith* 68, no. 1 (2016): 12-21.

———. "Intercultural Theology as a Three-Way Conversation: Beyond the Western Dominance of Intercultural Theology." *Exchange* 44 (2015): 123-43.

———. "Kwame Bediako's Christology in Its African Evangelical Context." *Exchange* 26, no. 3 (1997): 218-32.

———. *A Pocket Guide to Christian Belief.* Oxford: Lion Hudson, 2009.

———. *Reasons for My Hope: Responding to Non-Christian Friends.* Oxford: Monarch Books, 2010.

———. "The Relationship between Christ and the Spirit in a Christian Theology of Religions." *Missiology: An International Review* 40, no. 3 (2012): 263-80.

———. "Religion." In *Evangelical Dictionary of Theology*, edited by Daniel J. Treier and Walter A. Elwell, 736-37. 3rd ed. Grand Rapids, MI: Baker Academic, 2017.

———. "The Significance of Postcolonial Thinking for Mission Theology." *Interkulturelle Theologie. Zeitschrift Für Missionswissenschaft* 45, nos. 2–3 (2019): 210-28.

van den Toren, Benno, J. Bosco Bangura, and Dick Seed, eds. *Is Africa Incurably Religious? Secularization and Discipleship in Africa.* Regnum Studies in Mission. Oxford: Regnum, 2020.

van der Lugt, A. S. "Gereformeerde christenen ontmoeten Surinaams-Hindostaanse hindoes in het Rijnmondgebied: een analyse van de ontmoeting vanuit de verschillen in cultuur en religie." PhD Thesis, Kamoen, NL: Theological University Kampen, 2016.

Van der Walt, B. J. *Afrocentric or Eurocentric? Our Task in a Multicultural South Africa.* Potchefstroom, ZA: Potchefstroomse Universiteit vir Christelike Hoër Onderwys, 1997.

van Klaveren, Joram. *Apostate: From Christianity to Islam in Times of Secularisation and Terror.* The Hague: 't Kennishuys, 2019.

Van Til, Cornelius. *The Defense of the Faith.* 3rd ed. Phillipsburg, NJ: Presbyterian and Reformed Publishing Co., 1967.

Vanhoozer, Kevin J. "'One Rule to Rule Them All?' Theological Method in an Era of World Christianity." In *Globalizing Theology: Belief and Practice in an Era of World Christianity*, edited by Craig Ott and Harold A. Netland, 85-126. Grand Rapids, MI: Baker Academic, 2007.

———. "The Trials of Truth: Mission, Martyrdom and the Epistemology of the Cross." In *To Stake a Claim: Mission and the Western Crisis of Knowledge*, edited by J. Andrew Kirk and Kevin J. Vanhoozer, 120-56. Maryknoll, NY: Orbis, 1999.

———. "What Is Everyday Theology? How and Why Christians Should Read Culture." In *Everyday Theology: How to Read Cultural Texts and Interpret Trends*, edited by Kevin J. Vanhoozer, Charles A. Anderson, and Michael J. Sleasman, 15-60. Grand Rapids, MI: Baker Academic, 2007.

Varghese, Allan. "Social Action as Christian Social Apologetics: Through the Lives of Pandita Ramabai and Amy Carmichael." In *Advancing Models of Mission: Evaluating the Past and Looking to the Future*, edited by Kenneth Nehrbass, Aminta Arrington, and Narry Fajardo Santos, 153-68. Evangelical Missiological Society Series 29. Littleton, CO: William Carey Library, 2021.

Virtue, Doreen. "About Doreen's Conversion to Christianity." *DoreenVirtue.Com* (blog). March 12, 2018. www.angeltherapy.com/2018/03/12/about-doreens-conversion -to-christianity/.

Vokes, Richard. "Rethinking the Anthropology of Religious Change: New Perspectives on Revitalization and Conversion Movements." *Reviews in Anthropology* 36, no. 4 (2007): 311-33.

Volf, Miroslav, and Matthew Croasmun. *For the Life of the World: Theology That Makes a Difference*. Grand Rapids, MI: Brazos Press, 2019.

Vroom, Hendrik M. *No Other Gods: Christian Belief in Dialogue with Buddhism, Hinduism, and Islam*. Grand Rapids, MI: Eerdmans, 1996.

Wallace, Anthony FC. "Revitalization Movements." *American Anthropologist* 58, no. 2 (1956): 264-81.

Walls, Andrew F. "Ephesian Moment: At a Crossroads in Christian History." In *The Cross-Cultural Process in Christian History: Studies in the Transmission and Appropriation of Faith.*, 72-81. Maryknoll, NY: Orbis, 2002.

———. "The Gospel as Prisoner and Liberator of Culture." In *The Missionary Movement in Christian History: Studies in the Transmission of Faith*, 3-15. Edinburgh: T&T Clark, 1996.

———. "Introduction." In *The Missionary Movement in Christian History: Studies in the Transmission of Faith*, xiii-xix. Edinburgh: T&T Clark, 1996.

———. "Primal Religious Traditions in Today's World." In *Religion in Today's World: The Religious Situation of the World from 1945 to the Present Day*, 250-78. Edinburgh: T&T Clark, 1987.

———. "The Translation Principle in Christian History." In *The Missionary Movement in Christian History: Studies in the Transmission of Faith*, 26-42. Edinburgh: T&T Clark, 1996.

Ward, Keith. *Religion and Revelation: A Theology of Revelation in the World's Religions*. Oxford: Clarendon Press, 1994.

Wells, Samuel. *Speaking the Truth: Preaching in a Diverse Culture*. Norwich, UK: Canterbury Press, 2018.

Westerlund, David. "Ahmad Deedat's Theology of Religion: Apologetics through Polemics." *Journal of Religion in Africa* 33, no. 3 (2003): 263-78.

Westermann, Claus. *Genesis 1-11: A Continental Commentary*. Minneapolis, MN: Fortress Press, 1994.

Wielenberg, Erik J. *God and the Reach of Reason: C. S. Lewis, David Hume, and Bertrand Russell*. Cambridge: Cambridge University Press, 2008.

Wilkinson, Loren. "Circles and the Cross: Reflections on Neo-Paganism." *Evangelical Review of Theology* 22 (1998): 28-47.

Willard, Dallas. *The Allure of Gentleness: Defending the Faith in the Manner of Jesus*. New York: HarperOne, 2015.

Williams, Paul. "Buddhism, God, Aquinas and Morality: An Only Partially Repentant Reply to Perry Schmidt-Leukel and José Cabezón." In *Converging Ways? Conversion and Belonging in Buddhism and Christianity*, edited by John D'Arcy May, 117-54. Edinburgh: T&T Clark, 2007.

——. *The Unexpected Way: On Converting from Buddhism to Catholicism*. Edinburgh: T&T Clark, 2002.

Williams, Stephen N. *Revelation and Reconciliation: A Window on Modernity*. Cambridge: Cambridge University Press, 1995.

Wittgenstein, Ludwig. *Philosophical Investigations: The German Text with a Revised English Translation*. Translated by G. E. M. Anscombe. 3rd edition. Malden, MA: Blackwell Publishers, 2001.

Wolff, Hans Walter. *Anthropology of the Old Testament*. London: SCM Press, 1974.

Wright, Christopher J. H. *The Mission of God: Unlocking the Bible's Grand Narrative*. Downers Grove, IL: IVP Academic, 2006.

Wright, N. T. *The Resurrection of the Son of God*. Christian Origins and the Question of God 3. Minneapolis, MN: Fortress Press, 2003.

Wu, Jackson. *Saving God's Face: A Chinese Contextualization of Salvation through Honor and Shame*. Pasadena, CA: William Carey International University Press, 2012.

Yadav, Bibhuti S. "Vaisnavism on Hans Küng: A Hindu Theology of Religious Pluralism." *Religion and Society* 27, no. 2 (1980): 32-64.

Yamauchi, Edwin M. *Africa and the Bible*. Grand Rapids, MI: Baker Academic, 2006.

Yandell, Keith E., and Harold A. Netland. *Buddhism: A Christian Exploration and Appraisal*. Downers Grove, IL: IVP Academic, 2009.

Yoder, Jason J. "The Trinity and Christian Witness to Muslims." *Missiology* 22, no. 3 (1994): 339-46.

Yong, Amos. *Beyond the Impasse: Toward a Pneumatological Theology of Religions*. Carlisle, UK: Paternoster Press, 2003.

——. "The Turn to Pneumatology in Christian Theology of Religions: Conduit or Detour?" *Journal of Ecumenical Studies* 35, nos. 3–4 (1998): 437-54.

Young, Frances M. *The Making of the Creeds*. London: Trinity Press International, 1991.

Zagzebski, Linda Trinkaus. "Religious Knowledge and the Virtues of the Mind." In *Rational Faith: Catholic Responses to Reformed Epistemology*, edited by Linda Trinkaus Zagzebski, 199-225. Vol 10. Library of Religious Philosophy. Notre Dame, IN: University of Notre Dame Press, 1993.

Zurlo, G. A., T. M. Johnson, and P. F. Crossing. "World Christianity and Mission 2020: Ongoing Shift to the Global South." *International Bulletin of Mission Research* 44, no. 1 (2020): 8-19.

GENERAL INDEX

Abe, Masao, 188
Abū Qurrah, Thāwdhūrus, 66
Adamo, David Tuesday, 146
Adeney, Miriam, 191
Advaita Hinduism, 58, 73, 156-58
African contextual theology, 14
African Instituted Churches, 138
African Pentecostal Churches, 138
African Traditional Religion(s), 51, 60, 110-11, 133-51, 209
  characteristics of, 135-37
Aka-Pygmies, 141-42
Akhtar, Shabbir, 198
al-Faruqi, Isma'il Raji, 199
anattā, 177, 182, 185-87
ancestor veneration, 4, 32, 88, 135, 137, 139, 150
  Chinese, 32
Anderson, Bernhard, 44
anicca, 177
anomaly, 108-9
anthropocentrism, 137-38
anthropology, cultural, 47
anthropology, theological, 42-45, 60
  sin, 46, 81, 108-9, 120-21, 126, 144, 176, 203, 238
anomaly, 48, 108
apatheia, 119
apologetics
  battering ram, 104
  Christian, 2, 16, 17, 26, 35, 42, 80, 85-86, 96
  contextual, 5, 8
  definition of, 26-27
  as dialogue, 3 (*see also* dialogue)
  embodied, 28-40
  external, 26
  holistic, 3, 5, 28, 96-98, 114-20, 226-27
  interfaith, 2, 5, 21, 26, 97, 241
  internal, 26
  narrative, 114, 121-23

  as persuasion, 3, 40, 96-99, 115, 117, 124, 151
  western Christian, 1, 14-15, 19, 39, 41, 63-64, 78, 234
  as witness, 3-5, 20, 26, 28, 35, 78-94, 98, 120-21, 184
Appasamy, Aiyadurai Jesudasan, 159
Aquinas, Thomas, 203
argumentation patterns, 39-40
Ariarajah, S. Wesley, 74
Aristotle, 124
Asian cultures, 39
atman, 156
Auffarth, Christoph, 59
Augustine of Hippo, 160, 188, 219-20
avatar, 65, 157, 167, 170
Avis, D. L., 210
Baagø, Kaj, 167
Babel, tower of, 44
Baker-Hytch, Max, 80
Bambrough, Renford, 55, 118
Banerjea, Krishan Mohan, 159, 169
Bangura, J. Bosco, 148, 209
Barth, Karl, 17, 43, 57, 60, 63-64, 67, 78, 82, 104, 120, 163, 189, 196-97, 203, 205, 231
Bauckham, Richard, 60, 126, 201
Bauman, Chad M., 140
Beale, G. K., 219
Bediako, Kwame, 79, 133-37, 140, 145, 147-48, 150-51
Berger, Peter L., 15, 31, 143, 186, 223
Berkhof, H., 231
Berkouwer, Gerrit C., 63
Berlo, David K., 115
Besançon, Alain, 193
Besant, Annie, 225.
Bevans, Stephen B., 145, 221
Bhagwan Shree Rajneesh. *See* Osho.
Bhai Tika (also Bhai Dhooj, Bhai Ponta, Bhaubeej), 152, 154, 171

SCRIPTURE INDEX